Foundation Accounting

Fifth Edition

A. H. Millichamp B.A., M.Soc.Sc., F.C.A., F.C.C.A., A.T.I.I.

Alan Millichamp is a former lecturer in accounting at
the University of Wolverhampton

Letts Educational
Aldine House, Aldine Place
142/144 Uxbridge Road
London W12 8AW

1997

Acknowledgements

The author wishes to thank the Royal Society of Arts Examination Board for permission to reproduce some past examination questions.

ISBN 1 85805 312 9

Typeset by KAI Typesetting, Nottingham

Printed in Great Britain by Ashford Colour Press, Gosport

Preface

Aim

1. This book provides a thorough understanding of the theory and practice of accounting at Foundation level. It presents all the information necessary for students to approach with confidence the foundation examinations of the professional and other bodies. It offers a complete first course in accounting.

The fifth edition

2. The fifth edition has been radically changed with a new format. I hope that it will prove even more user friendly. New features include:

   (a) Restructuring the chapters.

   (b) More on management accounting.

   (c) More on the not-for-profit sectors.

   (d) More exercises and assignments.

   (e) More exercises suitable for computerised accounting packages.

   (f) More assignments in Appendix C.

NVQs and SVQs

3. Accounting syllabuses have been adapted to reflect the Standards of Competence as the author well knows, being a member of the Lead Body for Accounting (Levels 2-4). This book is suitable for use on these syllabuses as it covers all the relevant accounting topics including the knowledge and understanding requirements as well as the practical competences.

GNVQs

4. The GNVQ in Business contains a number of accounting units and this book covers these requirements. Specifically coverage is at all levels but has been aimed at the Advanced level. Specific units covered are Units 6 and 7.

Approach

5. The approach adopted is:
   (a) There are 34 chapters.
   (b) In each chapter, there is text and examples which explain the background and theory connected with each subject as well as teaching the practice of accounting.
   (c) At the end of each chapter there is:
      (i) A summary of the points made in the section.
      (ii) Points to note. These cover difficulties, exceptions and points that need emphasising.

(iii) Comprehensive self-testing questions. These are useful in ensuring that the student has fully grasped the points made and are essential in revision.

(iv) Graded exercises.

(v) An assignment.

6. Accounting standards and accounting conventions are introduced and explained when they are first encountered and are summarised in Chapter 34.

Appendices

7. There are four appendices:

(a) Appendix A gives the answers to selected exercises.

(b) Appendix B is a set of six case studies. They are designed to enable students to integrate material from several chapters and to give scope for imagination. They could also be used as assignments. Outline answers to these are given in the lecturers supplement which is available from the publishers.

(c) Appendix C contains six new assignments.

(d) Appendix D is a glossary of accounting terms.

Lecturers' supplement

8. A lecturers' supplement is available, free of charge, to those lecturers who adopt the book as a main course text. It is in the form of a disk and is made up of three elements:

(a) Outline answers to the end of section questions, the assignments and the case studies.

(b) Some additional exercises and assignments with answers.

(c) Many of the exercises set up on spreadsheets in Excel. These are easily exportable to other spreadsheet packages, and can be copied for students if desired.

Suggestions and criticisms

9. In the preparation of this new edition I have drawn on my own long experience of teaching and examining and have also received many helpful suggestions from colleagues. I would welcome many more.

Alan Millichamp
April 1997

Contents

Contents

1 The accounting scene

Bookkeeping and accounting form a large body of knowledge with an amazing amount of detail. You are about to start to study these fascinating subjects. But before you do it is a good idea to see how bookkeeping and accounting fit into the world of business and not-for-profit enterprise. This chapter explains what accounting is and introduces some of the important business documents. Then it shows you how business is carried on and who own and manage businesses. Finally we look at how accounting fits in with related activities like computing and auditing.

What is accounting?

Introduction

1. Accounting is an essential part of business activity. However accounting is not confined to business which we may define as the activity carried on by people and organisations hoping to make a **profit**. It is also an important activity in **non-profit** organisations. These include central government, local government, the health service, schools, colleges and universities and also charities, clubs and societies. In this part we will look at some definitions of accounting and then explore the sub-divisions of accounting which these definitions imply.

Definitions

2. Here are two definitions of accounting:
    (a) Accounting is the art of recording, classifying and summarising in a significant manner and in terms of money, transactions and events which are, in part at least, of a financial character, and interpreting the results thereof.
    (b) Accounting is the process of identifying, measuring, and communicating economic information to permit informed judgements and decisions by the users of the information.

3. These definitions do not make easy reading but I suggest you may like to re-read them when you have absorbed the rest of this part of the chapter. However they do suggest that accounting has three strands or sub-divisions:
    (a) Recording and classifying transactions. You are doing this yourself when you make a note of the payee on the counterfoil of a cheque and perhaps recalculate the balance on your account. Businesses do this in a more complete and precise way and all their transactions are recorded in appropriate recording media such as account books or in a computer system. Transactions mean business activities such as sales of goods, purchases of goods, payment and receipt of money, the incurring of an expense etc. The process of classifying and recording transactions is known as **bookkeeping**.
    (b) Summarising the overall effect of a large number of transactions in documents called **financial statements** (for example profit and loss accounts). Financial statements can then be presented to interested parties (for example the owners of the business) who may then use them to assess the performance of the busi-

ness and perhaps assess its future prospects. This production and use of financial statements is called **financial accounting**.

(c) Using the records of transactions, together with information about future possibilities, costs of alternative courses of action to make business decisions. This branch of accounting activity is known as **management accounting**. You may be engaging in management accounting when you gather and compare the prices charged by different suppliers for a new TV set, or compare the costs of different types of central heating systems, or budget your expenditure for the next month or year.

Bookkeeping

4. Bookkeeping is the making of records of business transactions. The need to record business transactions is as old as civilisation itself and the great majority of writings excavated from the Middle East are business records. One 4,000-year-old writing listing expenditure on sheep and cattle is notable as containing an error of calculation.

5. Modern bookkeeping was developed in Italy in the period 1300–1500 AD. Merchants of the time would join together to organise expeditions to the east to trade Italian products for the spices and silks of the east. Careful recording of all the goods bought and sold and the expenses incurred had to be made. A merchant would make the recording on any scrap of paper, but would then run the risk of losing it! He would do better to record all transactions in a formal, logical way. Until recently the recording of transactions or bookkeeping as it is called was done by hand in leather bound volumes. This is still done today to some extent but modern bookkeepers generally use computers. The system of bookkeeping which has been in common use since at least the fifteenth century is called **double entry bookkeeping**. When you have worked right through this manual you should be proficient in the art of double entry. Note that computerised bookkeeping systems (e.g. Sagesoft, Pegasus etc) all use double entry.

Profit or loss and capital measurement and reporting

6. Consider two situations:

(a) John buys a house with ten acres of ground on 1 April 19x2. In the year to 31 March 19x3 he buys 30 goats and grazes them on the land. The goats breed and ten kids are born. The goats produce milk, some of which he sells, and some of which he turns into cheese and then sells the cheese.

Six goats and four kids are sold. Two goats are killed for meat and eaten by John and his family.

Various expenses are incurred including some (e.g. goat food and vet's fees) which relate solely to goat-keeping, and some (e.g. local rates) which relate to the house and the pasture land.

After 31 March 19x3 John wonders whether it was all worthwhile financially. The Tax Inspector sees that John has a business and thinks John should pay tax on the profit arising from it. His bank has lent him money and wants to know if the goat business is sufficiently profitable to enable John to repay the loan.

The way the **profit** is measured has to be done in a way which is acceptable to both John and the Tax Inspector and the bank manager.

Accounting is about measuring the *profit* or *loss* made by a *business* over a period of time. This is not a simple matter as you will have gathered from the example. When you have studied all of this book, you should know how accountants might measure the profit or loss made by John's business.

(b) Enoch, a poor but energetic music teacher, dreams of opening a music shop in the centre of his home town. £20,000 is needed to start the venture off and although he has no money of his own, he is able to persuade three of his friends to buy shares in the business. After the shop has been open for one year, his backers want to know what has happened to the money (= **capital**) they have invested in the business. They expect Enoch to tell them in the form of a **financial statement**.

7. Bookkeeping is about making a record in a formal manner, of each business transaction. It is necessary for day-to-day business control as a businessman will need to be continuously aware of, for example, who owes him money and how much; or who he owes money to and how much. These records also form the raw data from which the *summary* statements of profit and loss and capital can be extracted. These reports can then be used by owners and investors (backers) alike to judge how the business has progressed.

Management accounting

8. The definition of management accounting is the application of professional knowledge and skill in the preparation and presentation of accounting information in such a way as to assist management in the formation of policies in the planning and control of the undertaking.

Thus management accounting (and its subsidiary subject – costing) is concerned with information which is used by *management* in planning and controlling the business and in making decisions. Management accounting is covered in depth in a companion volume.

However this manual includes the basic ideas of management accounting in sufficient detail for most first courses in accounting.

Types of business activity

9. Different types of businesses and organisations have different accounting requirements. It is always necessary to bear in mind the *type* of business when preparing financial statements.

10. For accounting purposes we can divide businesses into the following different types:

(a) **Retailing.** This is the most familiar. The retailer is a *trader*, that is, he buys goods at one price and sells the goods unchanged at a higher price.

(b) **Wholesaling.** The wholesaler is also a trader. He buys goods from others (e.g. manufacturers and importers) and sells the goods to retailers. The goods are essentially unchanged but an important role of the wholesaler is the breaking of bulk.

3

Wholesaling and retailing involve the activities of marketing of products, the breaking of bulk and the holding of stock.

(c) **Manufacturing.** The manufacturer makes *things* (products) from materials and components and sells them to the public, retailers, wholesalers, exporters, etc.

(d) **Service industries.** Service enterprises supply not a product but a service to their customers. Such enterprises include professional people (e.g. accountants, doctors), transport undertakings (e.g. bus companies, hauliers), banks, insurance companies, teaching institutions etc.

(e) **Non-profit making organisations.** Not all undertakings exist to make profits. Some exist to supply services with no intention of making a profit, although income is generally required to match expenditure. Examples of non-profit making organisations include central government and its agencies, local government, hospitals, schools, colleges, universities, clubs, societies, trade unions and professional bodies.

Modes of ownership

11. Ownership of business enterprises can be in any of a number of different modes. Again, the accounting requirements of a business will vary with the mode of ownership and it is important to understand how the Financial Statements of businesses are designed to reflect the differing modes of ownership.

12. We will look briefly at some of these modes:

(a) **Sole trader.** This is the simplest form of ownership. It means that the business has just one *proprietor* who both owns and manages the business personally. The business and its owner are one and the same.

(b) **Partnership.** The business is *owned* and *managed* by two or more people who are called partners. In general the law restricts the number of partners to twenty.

(c) **Limited company.** The business is owned by shareholders. The number of shareholders can be as few as two (for example, a man and his wife) or as many as required. Large companies can have over 100,000 shareholders. With a company its owners (shareholders) *may* be different from its management (directors). Clearly all 100,000 shareholders of a company cannot concern themselves with day-to-day management. Small companies tend to be called, for example, Joe's Cafe Limited and larger ones, for example, Tarmac PLC (short for Public Limited Company).

(d) **Associations.** These are clubs, societies and groups of people who join together for sporting, educational, social or charitable purposes. Some clubs trade, for example, by having a bar.

(e) **Public ownership.** The nationalised industries, local and central government. The accounting requirements of public sector enterprises are outside the scope of this book, although the financial statements of nationalised industries are prepared on similar lines to the accounts you will learn to prepare.

(f) **Semi-autonomous public ownership.** Many organisations are now still in the public sector but have a large degree of independence including, at least in theory, the right to go bust. Examples include colleges and the hospital trusts.

13. There are a few other modes of ownership such as trusts, or incorporation by Royal Charter or special Act of Parliament but we need not concern ourselves with these.

Trading on credit

14. Before studying the measurement of business profit, we have to understand the basic notions of how business is done. If I want to buy a magazine, I walk into the local newsagents and buy it. Simple, but in fact a number of things have occurred:

    (a) The *possession* and *ownership* of the magazine has passed from the newsagent to me.

    (b) I have paid by passing *cash* to the newsagent.

    The sale and the payment are *simultaneous*. This is called a *cash sale*.

    It may be that I have forgotten my wallet but remembered my cheque book, so that instead of paying cash I give the newsagent a cheque. This is still called a cash sale because sale and payment are **simultaneous**.

    If I like the magazine, I may arrange for future editions to be delivered together with my morning newspaper. I then pay for it at the end of each month, for the obvious reason that it would be inconvenient for all concerned for the newsboy to collect payment every morning.

    In this case, the *sale* and the *payment* are not simultaneous. The sale comes first and the payment comes later. This is called *trading on credit*. In practice, most retail sales are cash sales and most sales by manufacturers and wholesalers are on credit. You will appreciate that selling on credit means the seller parting with ownership and possession of the goods without any certainty about when, if at all, payment will be made.

Credit cards

15. In addition to cash sales and credit sales, another form of trading is now very common. That is the use of credit cards – Access, Visa, American Express etc.

    The procedures that are applied are:

    (a) Members of the public have a small plastic credit card.

    (b) This is used to pay for goods. The retailer fills in a form with details of the goods and uses the embossed nature of the credit card to print the data on the customer on the form. The customer retains a copy of the form.

    (c) Each day the retailer sums the amounts on the forms and pays them into the bank. The amounts are credited to his account and debited in the bank account of the credit card company.

    (d) Each month the credit card company charges the retailer with commission on the deals and extracts it from the retailer's bank account by direct debit. The rate of commission varies between 1% and 4%.

    (e) The credit card company sends a monthly account to its card holders who pay or, if they do not pay, suffer an interest charge until they do.

    Modern technology has now updated the procedures and many retailers now have equipment which allows the card to be passed through (swiped through) a reader and the documentation to be printed automatically.

From the point of view of the retailer, credit card selling is equivalent to cash sales except that there is a cost – a monthly commission charge.

Methods of payment

16. There are now several other ways by which money can be paid by one person or business to another. We have already considered cash, cheques and credit cards. Others include:

(a) **EFTPOS** – Electronic funds transfer at point of sale. You may have a 'switch' card which will be passed through and read by the equipment and there will then be an automatic transfer of funds from your bank account into the bank account of the retailer.

(b) **Direct debits** – I use electricity in my home. Instead of receiving a bill once a quarter and sending off a cheque, I have arranged to pay by direct debit. I have given a general authorisation to the Electricity Board to collect the money due, directly from my bank account. Clearly there have to be safeguards with this method. For example, there is a maximum amount, which I can specify, and the Electricity Board tell me a few days in advance that the bill is £x and they will collect it on a particular date.

(c) **Direct credits** – I own a few shares in a number of companies and these companies pay me dividends from time to time. Instead of sending me cheques I have authorised them to pay the dividends directly into my bank account. Effectively this means that funds are transferred directly between bank accounts without the trouble of dealing with cash or cheques. The companies still send me notification of the dividend through the post so we have not yet achieved a paperless society. In a similar way, many employers now pay the wages and salaries of employees directly by transfer between bank accounts. Businesses can also transfer sums owing directly from their bank accounts into the bank accounts of their suppliers through BACS – bankers automated credit system. Some of my readers may have an account with a bank such as First Direct. Such banks allow customers to make payments by transfer from their accounts on telephoned instructions.

(d) **Standing orders** – I have agreed to pay a sum on the first day of each month to my local church. I do this by standing order rather than pay over cash or a cheque. Again, this is an authorisation by me so that funds are transferred directly from my bank account to the Church's bank account.

(e) **Smartcards** – At the time of writing these are in the experimental stage only. The experiment is in the town of Swindon but their use may become universal in time. Instead of drawing cash from the bank or cashpoint, bank customers can transfer (download) money equivalent onto a plastic card. To pay at the supermarket or pub or anywhere, the card is swiped through a reader and the amount payable deducted from the smartcard and recorded on it. When all the money on the card has gone it is necessary to download more from the bank or cashpoint. This method does mean a genuinely paperless society as there is nothing to sign. The card is used just as notes and coins are used now.

Documents

17. There are a large number of common business documents. Examples are invoices, clock cards showing the number of hours worked by a worker, personnel records and stock record cards. Try to examine any business document you come across!

At this stage we need to consider three only of the main documents.

(a) **The invoice** (See Fig. 1.1).

The purpose of the invoice is to evidence a sale by the seller (vendor) to the buyer (purchaser). It is sent by the seller to the buyer. Try to think of the purpose of each field (= item of information). Note that the *terms of trade*, in this case net 30 days, means that the seller hopes that the buyer will pay within 30 days. In practice, few keep to the terms!

INVOICE		No. 11747			**N**H**L**

INVOICE   No. 11747

To: Smith Hardware
      187 The Croft
      Northtown NO6 8JQ

Nutcase Hardware Limited
Unit 8, Foley Industrial Estate
Tettenhall
Wolverhampton WV6 8LL
Telephone 758095
VAT No. 900 27734 321

Your order number	Despatch date	Delivery note no.	Invoice date	Remarks
432689A	24.6.–6	B76543	25.6.–6	

Product description	Quantity	Price	Per	VAT rate	Amount
Small Widget sets	36	£2.40	each	15	86.40
Nylon collars	500	£18.98	100	15	94.90

Terms and conditions: Nett thirty days	Total goods	181.30
	Total VAT	27.19
	Amount Due	£208.49

Nutcase Hardware Ltd: Company number 2786542   Directors: J. Jones, D. Jones.

Fig. 1.1

(b) **The credit note** (See Fig. 1.2).

CREDIT NOTE

No. 345

NHL

To: Smith Hardware
      187 The Croft
      Northtown NO6 8JQ

VAT No. 900 27734 321

Nutcase Hardware Limited
Unit 8, Foley Industrial Estate
Tettenhall
Wolverhampton WV6 8LL
Telephone 758095

Your debit number	Our invoice number	Date of receipt	Credit note date
43	11747	n/a	29.6.-6

Product description	VAT rate	Amount
Incorrect price – 36 small widgets charged at £2.40 – should be at £2.30	15	3.60
Nylon collars short delivery by ten items		1.90
	Total goods	5.50
	Total VAT	0.82
	Total credit	£6.32

Fig. 1.2

The functions of a credit note are:

(i) To evidence the acceptance of the return of goods by the seller from the buyer. Usual reasons for the return of goods are that they were faulty or otherwise unsatisfactory or they were damaged.

(ii) To evidence to a buyer that he need not pay for goods invoiced to him because the goods have been lost in transit.

(iii) To correct errors on invoices. Such errors may be overpricing or inclusion of goods not actually sent.

(c) **The statement of account** (See Fig. 1.3)

This document is sent by the seller to a customer who is buying goods on credit. Usually it is sent monthly. It summarises the transactions between the seller and the buyer since the previous statement. Note that brief details of the invoice and credit note illustrated earlier appear on this statement.

```
STATEMENT    Date: 30/6/-6
                                       No. 345                    NHL

To:    Smith Hardware                Nutcase Hardware Limited
       187 The Croft                 Unit 8, Foley Industrial Estate
       Northtown NO6 8JQ             Tettenhall
                                     Wolverhampton WV6 8LL
VAT No. 900 27734 321                Telephone 758095
```

Date	Reference	Descripton	Value
16.4.-6	9032	Invoice	240.68
27.4.-6	9039	Invoice	387.95
18.5.-6	10054	Invoice	132.99
25.6.-6	11747	Invoice	208.49
29.6.-6	345	Credit note	6.32
		Statement total	£963.79

Accounts overdue for payment

3 months and over	2 months	1 month	current month
nil	628.63	132.99	202.17

Fig. 1.3

(d) **Delivery and advice notes**

In addition to the main documents you may also find two more called the advice note and the delivery note.

When goods are despatched to a customer many firms send an *advice note* (sometimes called the despatch note). This is just a document informing the customer that the order has been received and the goods have been sent. A similar document is a *delivery note*. Its purpose is to go with the goods (but sometimes it is sent separately) to enable the buyer to check the goods delivered against what the delivery note says is being sent. Sometimes the delivery note is in duplicate to enable the buyer to check the goods and, if found correct, to acknowledge acceptance on the duplicate which is then returned by the carrier to the seller.

Business contact groups

18. The main contact groups for a business are:

(a) **Owners.** Owners of businesses may be sole proprietors, partners, or shareholders of limited companies. Sole proprietors, partners and shareholders who are also directors of their companies, will also manage the business. Shareholders who are not also directors of their companies, will not normally have day-to-day contact with the business. It is not always clear who are the owners of non-profit organisations. Who are the owners of the Barsetshire Hospital Trust, the Child Support Agency, the Sheinton Magna Tennis Club?

Legally the ownership may vest in a company which is of a particular kind called an unlimited company or perhaps with a legal entity called a trust. You may care to explore the ownership of some organisation that you familiar with, for example, your college.

(b) **Managers.** Managers of businesses may also be the owners (sole proprietors, directors, shareholders) but may be salaried directors or simply employees. In non-profit organisations, the general direction may be in the hands of a Board of Directors or trustees or a committee of management (e.g. the Governors of a school). These people are often unpaid and part time. The day to day management may be in the hands of full-time professional managers (e.g. the Headteacher).

(c) **Lenders to the business.** Businesses often borrow money from individuals or more commonly from their bankers.

(d) **Customers.** People or firms who buy goods or services from the enterprise. In non-profit organisations, these may be specific members of the public, for example, patients of a hospital or pupils of a school.

(e) **Suppliers.** Firms or organisations who sell goods or services to the organisation.

(f) **Employees.**

(g) **The Government.** Businesses today are subject to a wide range of government regulations (for example, on health and safety at work, planning, pollution, redundancy). The principal government office with contact with a business is the Inland Revenue who are concerned to extract taxation from the business. It is difficult to answer the contention that with Corporation Tax at 33% of taxable profits, the Government has nearly as great an interest in a company as its shareholders.

Information needs

19. Each of the contact groups we have noted requires information about the business in order that they can take rational decisions in their dealings with the business. It is not possible to summarise all the information that each group might want but we will consider some of their more important information needs and how accounting meets their requirements.

(a) **Managers and owners who also manage.** Managers of enterprises need day-to-day information on all aspects of the business and of the outside world in which the business operates. They will also need an understanding of the probable outcome of present uncompleted matters and of the future generally. Accounting cannot possibly provide for more than a fraction of management's information needs. However it does provide information on:

(i) Up-to-date information on how much and to whom money is owed; how much and by whom money is owed to the business; and the cash balance at bank and in hand.

(ii) A summary of how much profit or loss the business has made in each year (or more frequently) and the capital employed in the business.

(b) **Owners who are not concerned with day-to-day management.** Owners are concerned to receive information about the progress of their business and the competence of those who manage it. The financial statements go some way towards meeting this need.

(c) **Lenders.** Bankers and others who lend money to a business are primarily concerned with the ability of the business to make payments of interest and repayments of capital in the future and of the possibility and the consequences of a default. Bankers regard the financial statements as meeting a small part of their information needs.

(d) **Customers.** Customers also have information requirements (e.g. about products, prices, quality, reliability, delivery dates) about the business which are not met by accounting. Customers may also like to know whether a business is financially sound so that they know that guarantees are worthwhile, or spare parts etc. may be obtained in the future.

(e) **Suppliers.** The primary information needed by suppliers of goods on credit to a business is whether or not the business is able to pay for the goods and the probability of delay in payment. Financial statements can be of assistance to suppliers in assessing the credit worthiness of potential customers but in practice the financial statements are not always available to them.

(f) **Employees.** Employees clearly have need of information about their employer's business in connection with their personal dealings with the company (e.g. work requirements, hours, pay, holidays). They do not, in general, have an interest in the profitability or capital employed in their employer's business. However, many people are now worried that their employer may go out of business and so employees are becoming more interested in the fortunes of their employer.

(g) **The Government.** Government agencies have a wide range of information needs about a business including statistical data about employment and production. These needs are frequently met from the data found in bookkeeping records. More directly, the financial statements provide data from which taxes (e.g. VAT, national insurance, PAYE, income tax, corporation tax) can be assessed and collected.

Information needs and accounting

20. Contact groups have widely different information needs about a business. Accounting provides information of a very limited kind. Accounting information has two particular characteristics which limit its usefulness:

(a) It is *historical*. Accounting is concerned to record events as they happen or within a short time of occurrence but always after the event. Financial statements summarise profit or loss and capital employed in the recent past. Historical information is useful in predicting the future but accounting is not concerned with the systematic collection of probable future happenings.

(b) It is in terms of *money*. Accounting provides information on events and transactions that are of a financial nature or can be expressed in financial terms. It does not give information in quantity or size terms or in qualitative matters like usefulness.

Professional bodies

21. Many accountants are members of professional bodies. The six major bodies in the UK and the Republic of Ireland are the Institute of Chartered Accountants in England and Wales (which is by far the largest body), the Institute of Chartered Accountants of Scotland, the Institute of Chartered Accountants in Ireland, the Chartered Institute of Management Accountants, the Chartered Association of Certified Accounts and the Chartered Institute of Public Finance & Accountancy. The Certified Accountants and Management Accountants have a large overseas membership especially in the Far East. In addition there is a fast growing body for accounting technicians – the Association of Accounting Technicians and the Certified Accountants are about to introduce a new accounting technician qualification.

Auditing

22. Accounting is about the preparation of financial statements which can take many forms. The best known are the profit and loss accounts and balance sheets of businesses and the income and expenditure saccounts of not-for-profit undertakings. In the specific case of limited companies, financial statements are produced annually and take the form of an 'Annual Report and Accounts' which include a profit and loss account and balance sheet. The annual reports of companies are produced by directors of companies (the work is usually delegated to accountants) who send them to the shareholders. The difficulty which arises is that the annual report may be misleading, fraudulent, or full of errors. To prevent financial statements from showing other than a true and fair view, the law provides for an *audit*. An audit is a detailed examination of the financial statements with a search for *evidence* to *substantiate* all the figures in the statements and of the records from which they were prepared. The audit is followed by an expression of opinion by the auditor who says whether or not the statements give a true and fair view.

Audits can be carried out on any set of financial statements not only those of limited companies. Audits are carried out by professional accounting firms whose reputation for independence, integrity and competence give the financial statements credibility.

Taxation

23. The amount of income tax paid by private businesses and firms and corporation tax paid by limited companies is dependent on the amount of profit made. As accountants are concerned with the preparation and audit of financial statements it follows that they should also be concerned with the computation of tax payable. This work is usually carried out for their clients by professional accounting firms. The work involves agreement of the amount of profit assessable and of the amount of tax payable, with HM Inspectors of Taxes. In practice accountants also have ex-

pertise in other taxes and they also give advice to clients on how to arrange their affairs to minimise the tax payable.

Insolvency

24. Not all businesses are successful and failure is followed by legal consequences. The law is concerned to ensure that the business assets are realised (turned into cash) and the resulting cash is properly distributed to those entitled. The consequences of failure by individuals and partnerships may include bankruptcy when the Court appoints a trustee to look after the affairs of the bankrupt. The consequences of failure by a limited company may be the appointment of a receiver or of a liquidator or both. Persons appointed as trustees in bankruptcy and as receivers or liquidators of companies are usually accountants, specially licensed for these duties.

Computing

25. Bookkeeping is a tedious process involving entry into the books of large numbers of similar transactions. In consequence, bookkeeping is an ideal subject for computerisation and the rapid development of cheap computer systems has led to many businesses maintaining their books by computer. The one-off nature of the preparation of financial statements has meant that these are still manually produced in most cases.

The development of computerised bookkeeping has deeply involved most accountants in computing and many accountants have become recognised as experts in this field.

Summary

❑ Accounting is the art of recording and classifying business transactions, summarising the records into financial statements showing profit or loss and capital and reporting these summary facts to interested parties so that they can make informed business decisions.

❑ Three sub-divisions of accounting are:
   (i) Bookkeeping.
   (ii) The production of financial statements.
   (iii) Management accounting.

❑ Business activities are of several different types. They can be listed as:
   (i) Retailing.
   (ii) Wholesaling.
   (iii) Manufacturing.
   (iv) Service Industries.
   (v) Non-profit activities.

❑ Ownership of businesses can be one of several different modes: sole trading, partnership, limited companies, unincorporated associations and public ownership. In some, ownership and management can be by different persons.

❏ Trading or the sale of goods and services can be for cash or on credit.

❏ Payment can be by cash or cheque but there are many other methods now in use. These include credit cards, direct debits, EFTPOS, BACS, direct credits and cash-cards.

❏ Invoices, credit notes and Statements of Account are important business documents.

❏ Contact groups who are interested in a business include:
  (i)   Owners.
  (ii)   Managers.
  (iii) Lenders.
  (iv)   Customers.
  (v)   Suppliers.
  (vi)   Employees.
  (vii) Government.

❏ Each contact group has particular needs for information about the business to enable it to make rational decisions.

❏ Accounting provides a very limited range of information.

❏ The principal limitations of accounting information are that accounting information is:
  – historical
  – of a financial nature.

❏ Accounting is carried out by accountants who combine into professional bodies. There are six major accounting bodies in the UK and one fast growing body of accounting technicians. Accountants in practice also engage in related activities including auditing, taxation, insolvency and computer work.

Points to note

❏ Bookkeeping serves two purposes:
  (i) A record of business transactions is useful in itself – most people keep a note of the amount in their bank accounts by notes in the cheque book. Businesses need to know, for example, how much is owed by each customer and how much the business owes to each supplier.
  (ii) It forms the information from which the formal financial statements of profit or loss and capital can be extracted.

❏ The 'books' and the formal accounting summary statements are themselves useful to the management. However, management have information needs which are not satisfied from the traditional bookkeeping records and management accounting has developed to meet these needs.

❏ Accounting is always in terms of money. This does not mean that accountants think of nothing else but money! It means that money forms a common standard with which business activity can be measured. Note that money has several uses. It is a **store of value** – it can form your savings. It is a **means of exchange** – you can buy things with it. But is also a measure of value. Accountants primarily use money as a **measure of value** and you must be careful not to confuse something measured or valued in money terms with actual money.

❏ Accounting is concerned to record and summarise transactions and events which have already occurred. It is largely a historical process. However accountants are also interested in the future and the accounting record of recent past events is very useful in considering future activities.

❏ Accounting is an *art* rather than a science. This manual will instruct you in numerous formal rules but the business world is so diverse and so complex that formal rules often have to be bent or modified to fit special situations and to make accounting information useful and meaningful.

❏ We have talked about the business. Accountants distinguish the business from the owner. A businessman may have more than one business; for example, he may have an engineering business, a farm and a supermarket. Each year the profit made by each activity is separately measured.

❏ It is also important to realise that the ownership and management of a business may be by different persons. For example, a large Public Limited Company (PLC) may have 70,000 shareholders who own it but it is managed by a Board of Directors of eight people, some of whom do not own shares in the company.

❏ Try to realise that selling involves two separate but related activities. The sale with transfer of ownership and possession of the goods, and the payment. There may be a time lag between the two happenings.

❏ We have distinguished different types of business. Some businesses are mixed. For example, the local pharmacist supplies both goods and a service, and many manufacturers also import finished goods and wholesale them.

❏ In considering contact groups, those currently dealing with the business have information needs but those who are considering contact also have information needs. For example, potential suppliers may need information to help them decide whether or not to supply goods on credit.

❏ The historical nature of accounting is fundamental to accounting. However management accounting is largely concerned with forecasting the future.

❏ Accountants have in recent years come to hold important positions in industry and commerce, frequently as chairmen or managing directors or chief executives of companies. This has led to some criticism that in executive decision making, too much weight is given to financial considerations.

❏ The different information needs of contact groups has led to the legend that businesses keep three sets of books. By this means the annual profit can be measured as:
  (i) High – so that the bank manager will regard the business as one to which he will wish to lend money.

(ii) Accurate – to enable the proprietor to make rational decisions.

(iii) Low – so as to pay little tax.

Businesses do not really do this!

❐ Accountants regard accounting as a profession. It is not easy to define the word profession. However the following attributes characterise most professions including accounting:

(i)   A recognisable, discrete body of knowledge.

(ii)   An educational process.

(iii) A system of examinations.

(iv) A system for licensing practitioners.

(v)   A professional association.

(vi) A sense of responsibility to society.

(vii) A code of ethics.

(viii) A set of technical standards.

❐ In addition the professional bodies now have in place a system of supervision of practising members and firms and an enforceable disciplinary code.

Self-testing questions

1. Give two definitions of accounting.
2. Give three sub-divisions of accounting.
3. How do bookkeeping and profit reporting relate?
4. When was modern bookkeeping developed?
5. Why is it desirable to measure the profit made by a business?
6. In what way does accounting use money?
7. In what way is accounting a historiographical process?
8. In what way is accounting an art?
9. List the different types of business activity.
10. List the different modes of ownership.
11. Distinguish cash sales from credit sales.
12. Design an invoice for a limited company engaged in manufacturing.
13. Outline the procedures involved in credit card trading. Who are the parties involved and to what extent are they taking or receiving credit and at what cost?
14. What fields would be different on an invoice compared with a credit note? (a 'field' is an item of information on a document).
15. What is the purpose of a statement of account? How does it differ from an invoice?
16. What is a trader?
17. Summarise the methods of payment available today.
18. Summarise the groups who have contact with a company.
19. What are the main limitations of accounting as a source of information about business?
20. List the professional accounting bodies in the UK.
21. What services are provided by professional accounting firms?
22. What are the characteristics of a profession?

Exercises

1. Penny is in business as a builder. She erects garages and other small extensions to the houses of customers. She also effects domestic building repairs. She has a small yard at the back of her house to store materials and her van and pick up truck. She employs three people and also uses sub-contractors.

    Required:

    (a) In what way will accounting as an art affect Penny and her business?

    (b) Will accounting affect Penny in her private life?

2. You read in the paper that Rich left £2,624,000 when he died. What do you understand by this piece of information?

3. Keep a record of your receipts and payments in cash and of your transactions with the bank for a period of one week. Consider how the record relates to the three main branches of accounting.

4. Obtain the annual accounts of some social, sporting or charitable organisation with which you are connected. See how much of the information given in them is understandable to you.

5. Dave and Marge intend to set up a business as dealers in light fittings. They intend to import goods from the Far East and also to buy from British firms. Some goods will come as components and they will assemble and pack them. They intend to sell the goods to retailers around the country and also to the public in their own shop in North Bromwich. They also intend to use their knowledge of import documentation to advise other importers.

    Required:

    (a) What types of business activity will Dave and Marge be carrying on?

    (b) What mode of ownership will be used?

    (c) In what ways will their sales of goods and resulting cash inflows differ in time?

    (d) What trading documents will they receive? and send out?

6. Obtain an invoice, a credit note and a statement of account. How do they differ from the examples given in this chapter?

7. Consider the following businesses:

    (a) William Nutcase Limited who buy chocolates from specialist manufacturers on the continent and sell them to retailers in the UK.

    (b) Hogwash, Rott & Co, Certified Accountants.

    (c) Tring who repairs motor bicycles for motor cyclists and local garages.

    (d) The Tettenhall Sporting Club which supplies squash and tennis facilities to its members.

    What type of business activity do they carry on?

    What mode of ownership is concerned?

    Will they sell for cash or on credit?

8. What are the purposes of a credit note? Draw up a series of credit notes to illustrate each purpose.

9. Visit a large supermarket. What methods of payment are available to the customers?

10. Chump Garages PLC is a public company whose shares are traded on the Stock Exchange. The company has 3,500 shareholders, none of whom own more than 5% of the share capital. The company is managed by its board of directors – seven people, none of whom own more than a tiny fraction of the share capital. The principal business of the company is operation of a chain of garages selling new and second hand cars and trucks, petrol and diesel oil and spares and accessories. They also do repairs. The company has in recent years moved into property development as a consequence of developing some of its own properties and is heavily indebted to the bank.

    Required:

    What actual or potential contact groups will have need of information about the company?

11. 'The profits made by my business and the capital I have employed in it is no concern of anybody but myself' – a quotation by Jim, an insurance broker. How true is this statement?

12. Ted trades as Ted Limited, suppliers of widgets to local manufacturers. What groups would have contact with the business?

13. Find some advertisements from accountants operating in your area. What services do they offer?

14. (a) Distinguish between accounting and auditing.
    (b) Consider the suggestion that computers have made accountants obsolete.
    (c) Consider the statement that the sole objective of an accountant is to save tax for his clients.

15. Ivor Jones has a business selling widgets on credit. Each sale has a consecutive number. His terms of trade are nett one month. His VAT number is 900 27734 322 and VAT is added at 17.5%. Three of his sales are:

    No. 234: Sold 240 widgets at £30 each to J. Oldroyd at 1 High Street, Newcastle on 5 April 19x4 as a result of order number x429. The goods were delivered with a delivery note number C1800.

    No. 235: Sold 100 widgets at £30 each and 24 Thingies at £12.50 a dozen to R.Plum Ltd at 24 Bridge Street, Oldcastle on 12 April 19x4 as a result of order number 886. The goods were delivered with a delivery note number C1801.

    No. 236: Sold 28 Gummles at £43 each to J. Oldroyd at 1 High Street, Newcastle on 6 April 19x4 as a result of order number 879. The goods were delivered with a delivery note number C1802.

    Sale number 234 was sent out with only 239 widgets as the despatcher miscounted. Rather than send another, Jones agreed to send a credit note. Sale number 236 was mispriced and the Gummles should have been priced at £41.50. Jones agreed to send a credit note for this also.

    Required:

    Design an invoice and a credit note and input the details above.

16. Jones (see exercise 15) sells on credit to Ivor Ltd of 12 Market Street, Newtown. At the end of March 19x6, Ivor owes for goods sold in January £320.56 and in February £240.98. In addition Ivor Ltd owe for invoices in March: No. 254 (5 March) £128.32 and No. 298 (13 March) £314.67. There was also a credit note number 76 for £12.71 on 28 March.

    Design and complete a Statement of Account to send to Ivor Ltd.

Assignment

❑ *Gordon Ltd is a wholesaling company in High Street, Carlisle with two directors John and Jean Gordon. Jean is also the company secretary. The company sells motor parts on credit, requiring payment by the end of the month following the invoice date. They have recently expanded and have a large loan from the Cumbrian Bank PLC.*

Required:

(a) *Design an invoice for them and enter details of a sale of 12 Foden Silencers at £210 each + VAT at 17.5% to Sheinton Garages Ltd of Shrewsbury. Two silencers were slightly damaged in transit and Gordons later allowed a 10% reduction in the price on these. Design a credit note.*

(b) *Tick & Co, Certified Accountants are the auditors of the company. Describe the work they could do for the company, using information from the advertisements of accountants.*

19

2 Receipts and payments and the cash book

We begin our study of accounting and bookkeeping with an area which is very important and yet easy to understand – cash. Every business and indeed every person receives cash and makes payments and all businesses and many people make a careful record of all receipts and payments. The matter is complicated because although cash is still used sometimes, most business receipts and payments are made through the banking system. We will see how businesses deal with receipts and make payments and record them a book called the cash book.

Introduction

1. Receipts and payments are recorded in a book of account called the *cash book*.

   From the beginnings of the double entry bookkeeping, businesses have found that a very large number of transactions consisted of receiving and paying sums of money. In earliest times these transactions involved actual payment and receipt of *cash*. Hence the cash of cash book. It was also found that the transactions were so numerous that a separate book had to be devoted to these transactions. So we have the phrase – cash book.

   In later times, while cash was still used, payments and receipts came to be made by cheque through a bank account. Cash is still the pattern in many countries but in the UK business transactions are almost wholly settled by cheque or some other bank *instrument* such as a *direct debit*. Such small and few cash transactions as do happen are recorded in the petty cash book. Thus a cash book is now used to record bank transactions but it is still called the cash book.

   Retail transactions by, for example, shops are still carried out using cash, or more correctly a mixture of cash, switch, cheques and credit cards. These can still be regarded as bank transactions as at the end of each day the retailer will count the takings (cash, cheques etc) and pay the lot into the bank or find that it is already in the bank by electronic transfer.

Columnar cash books

2. A typical design for the cash book is:

Dr			RECEIPTS			PAYMENTS		Cr
Date	Source	Discount	Amount	Banking	Date	Payee	Discount	Amount
1.8.x3	Balance b/f			1,231.64	2.8.x3	Oxford	31.30	968.20
3.8.x3	Wellington	24.31	839.20		2.8.x3	Keele		131.00
3.8.x3	Stowe	4.60	182.20		2.8.x3	Cash – Wages		1,240.00
3.8.x3	Westminster		313.00	1,334.40	2.8.x3	Gas Board		61.30
4.8.x3	Loan – XY Ltd		1,000.00		3.8.x3	AHM PLC	21.20	761.40
4.8.x3	Eton	21.30	763.00	1,763.00	4.8.x3	Brown		313.20
4.8.x3	Cash sales			500.00	4.8.x3	Balance c/d		1,353.94
		50.21		4,829.04			52.50	4,829.04
4.8.x3	Balance b/d			1,353.94				

(a) You will note that the receipts are on the left hand side and payments are on the right hand side. This is a universal convention.

(b) On the extreme top left appears the sign Dr. This is an abbreviation for the word Debit (or more correctly, but not now used, Debitor). In double entry accounts, each account has two sides as has the cash book. The left hand side is always called the debit side. Commit this to memory!

(c) On the extreme top right appears the sign Cr. This is an abbreviation for the word Credit (or more correctly but not now used, Creditor). In double entry accounts the right hand side is always called the credit side. Commit this to memory also.

(d) On the left side of the debit and of the credit side is the date of each transaction. The cash book is ongoing and may last for years so this is very important.

(e) In the second column is the source of each receipt. These can be from several possible sources:

(i) Cash and cheques received from sales over the counter.

(ii) Cheques received through the post.

(iii) Switch card receipts (if the firm has set up systems for the use of switch cards).

(iv) Credit card receipts (if the firm has set up systems for VISA, ACCESS etc).

(v) Receipts through the BACS (Bank Automated Credit System) whereby customers make payments by direct transfer between bank accounts.

(vii) Receipts from direct debits if the firm has set up arrangements to collect from customers this way.

(viii) Receipts for standing orders from customers if the firm has set up arrangements in this way.

In the example I have not shown the *means* of payment. I have shown the *person* or firm making the payment (eg Wellington). In the case of *cash sales*, the total paid into the bank each time a banking is made is shown. So, on 4 August, a payment-in of £500 was made. It is not necessary to give the names of customers who pay in this way. Indeed this information would be either voluminous or not known at all.

(f) The debit side has three columns. The middle one is labelled amount and records the actual individual cheques (or other means of payment) received from customers (or a lender, in the case of XY Ltd). The column labelled Banking gives the actual payments in to the bank. When a banking is made, several cheques are usually paid in at once. For example, on 3 August three cheques were received and these were all paid into the bank on that day. Check that the sum of £839.20 + £182.20 + £313.00 = £1,334.40. We need to know the actual amounts of individual cheques – so we have the amount column. But we also need to compare the bankings with the bank statement when we receive it. Hence the banking column. The cash sales do not need to go into both columns but would do so if they were paid in with cheques in a banking of several items.

(g) The discount column records discounts given to customers for prompt payment. Some firms offer their customers a small deduction or discount if they pay by a specific (early) date. The discount is normally a percentage – for example $2\frac{1}{2}\%$ – for payment within say 7 days. The discount is called a cash discount or a settlement discount.

(h) The credit side has four columns. The first gives the date of payment. The second records the name of the person (usually a supplier) who has been paid or, in some cases records the type of payment. What name or description is recorded depends on the ultimate use of the information and to see that we need to know more double entry. We do that in later chapters.

(i) The third is a discount column and it is to record discounts given by suppliers for prompt payment.

(j) The fourth gives the amount actually paid.

(k) At the beginning of August, the balance in the bank was £1,231.64 and this appears on the debit side. During the month bankings were £1,334.40 + £1,763.00+ £500.00. The total in the bank would thus be £4,829.04 if there had been no payments out. In fact there were payments out of £968.20 +..........+ £313.20. Total payments out are £3,475.10. You can now see that the balance left is £4,829.04 – £3,475.10 = £1,353.94. The custom is to enter this on the credit side with a description: Balance c/d (carried down). The effect is to have both debit and credit with totals of £4,829.04. The process of finding and entering the balance at the end is called balancing the account.

(l) Finally, the closing balance forms the opening balance of the next period and it is entered in the new period on the debit.

3. We will now look at the evidence or documents from which the debit side of the cash book is written up. The primary evidence is usually the paying in book. Here is an example but you may have one of your own to compare it with. Most cheque books have a few forms at the bank for paying in – look at yours.

Front

| Date _____ | Date _____ | BANK GIRO CREDIT | 401–74–59 |

Credit _____

£50		
£20		
£10		
£5		
50p		
Silver		
Bronze		
Total		
Cheques		
£		

Quarry Bank plc

1 High Street
Cloghampton CL0 1AA

Cash

Cheques

£

Credit _*Financial Chicanery Ltd*_

⑈000⑈⑈6⑈⑈ 401⑈74591: 610145791⑈ 84

↑
─────── *counterfoil*

Back counterfoil

Cheques etc £			£50			Cheques etc
			£20			
			£10			
			£5			
			50p			
			Silver			
			Bronze			
			Total			
			Cheques			
Total cheques carry over			Total Cash Carry over			£
						carry over

Notes:

(a) The paying in slip has a front and a back. It also has the part retained by the bank, and the counterfoil which is retained by the bank's customer – the person paying in the money and cheques.

(b) The procedure for many firms is:

    (i)   Gather together cheques and cash as they are received through the post.

    (ii) Enter the details in the paying in book.

    (iii) Go to the bank and make the paying in.

    (iv) Enter the details in the cash book.

Evidence for other means of money transfer is information sent by the payer or by the bank. Many firms pay by BACS. The system is for the paying firm to notify the bank who is to be paid and what amounts. This information is given to the bank by computer link, telephone, fax or other electronic means. The bank then takes money from the paying firm and this money is transferred to the bank accounts of the firms that are being paid. The paying firm normally sends information about the payment to the recipients in the form of a **remittance advice.** Here is an example:

WISTERIA LTD REMITTANCE ADVICE		24 August 19x8
To: Periwinkle Ltd Sheinton		Your account No. P132
Date	Description	Amount due
7 July 19x8	Invoice	212.87
9 July 19x8	Invoice	34.90
14 July 19x8	Invoice	56.23
	Cheque enclosed	£304.00
Settled by BACS		

23

4. Many payments are made by cheque. Here is an example:

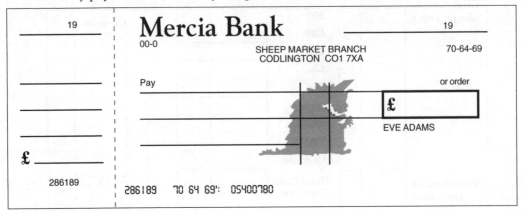

Note:

The payer has to insert the date (the 19 is part of the date), the payee, the amount in both words and figures and sign it under his printed name.

The cheque book normally has a counterfoil which the payer should fill in with the payee, the amount and the date. This counterfoil, sometimes called the cheque book stub, is the documentary evidence for the credit side of the cash book. In the case of payment by other means, evidence may be the remittance advices prepared for payments by BACS or information received from the recipient or the bank. As an example, the Electricity Board send me a note to the effect that it will extract £x from my account by direct debit on 7 March for my quarterly electricity bill. Another example is a monthly mortgage payment by standing order. The firm knows it is going but does not always remember. It is reminded when the bank statement, received from the bank, is compared with the cash book.

Three column cash books

5. In the past (and in some countries still) a *three column* cash book was used. This has columns as:

Dr   **Cr**
Date Source Discount Cash Bank Date Payee Discount Cash Bank

The cash columns are used for actual cash receipts and payments and there is an assumption that an actual cash balance is kept as well as a bank account.

The cash book and double entry bookkeeping

6. The cash book is part of the double entry bookkeeping system. In double entry the system consists of a series of accounts each with a debit side and a credit side. The cash book is one such account and you will meet many more, beginning in Chapter 6.

Writing up a cash book

7. Let us see how the entries are made in a cash book and how it is balanced at the end of a period. On 1 April 19x3 Mandy's cash book showed balances of £168.04 in the

bank and £76.98 in cash. She maintains a balance of cash in her office and this is used to make some payments but at intervals some of the cash is paid into the bank. This is unusual in the UK but is still common in many countries. We will illustrate a cash book with cash and bank columns because it is common in many countries and because many examiners expect it.

Mandy received the following amounts:

By cheque			In cash		
Date	Payer	Amount in £	Date	Payer	Amount in £
2	John	27.00	2	Jean	25.87
3	Paul	186.54	5	Sean	220.00
4	George	38.20	7	Penny	168.00
6	Richard	373.01	8	Wilfred	400.00
8	Henry	34.76	12	Albert	23.99
12	Guy	28.00			
13	Alphonse	103.29			
By BACS			**By credit card**		
8	Lenny	65.65	12	Dover	185.00
13	Joseph	234.00	13	Gordon	123.11

Mandy made the following payments:

By cheque	Payee	Amount in £	In cash	Payee	Amount in £
3	Jenny	125.87	7	Walter	298.66
6	Exton	243.56	9	Patel	102.00
9	Julie	101.00	13	Delroy	50.00
12	Levi	354.20			
By BACS			**By direct debit**		
12	MEB	213.20	4	Gas	176.00
12	Peter	103.00	7	Parsley	54.20
By standing order					
8	Alliance	100.00			

Mandy paid in to the bank the first four cheques received (John to Richard) on 6 April. The other cheques received were paid in individually on the dates received.

Mandy paid into the bank £200 of the cash balance with the first four cheques. The cash consisted of £10 notes.

Write up the paying slip for the banking on 6 April.

Enter up the cash book for the period to 14 April and bring down the balance:

Here is the paying in slip:

Date 6.4.19x3 **BANK GIRO CREDIT** 401–74–59

Quarry Bank plc

1 High Street
Cloghampton CL0 1AA

Cash	200.00
Cheques	624.75
£	824.75

Credit Mandy

⑈000116⑈ 401⑉7459⑆ 61014579⑈ 84

I have omitted the counterfoil and the reverse side of the paying in slip where the details of the four cheques and the make up of the cash (£10 notes) would be entered. Notice the MICR numbers (000116 401 7459 etc). This number can be read by a computer and ensures that the payment in is credited to the right account in the bank - the account of Mandy.

The cash book might look like this:

DEBIT					**CREDIT**			
Date	**Details**	**Cash**	**Bank detail**	**Bank**	**Date**	**Detail**	**Cash**	**Bank**
1	Balance b/f	76.98		168.04	3	Jenny		125.87
2	John		27.00		4	Gas		176.00
2	Jean	25.87			6	Exton		243.56
3	Paul		186.54		6	Bank	200.00	
4	George		38.20		7	Walter	298.66	
5	Sean	220.00			7	Parsley		54.20
6	Richard		373.01		8	Alliance		100.00
6	Cash		200.00	824.75	9	Julie		101.00
7	Penny	168.00			9	Patel	102.00	
8	Wilfred	400.00			12	Levi		354.20
8	Henry			34.76	12	MEB		213.20
8	Lenny			65.65	12	Peter		103.00
12	Albert	23.99			13	Delroy	50.00	
12	Guy			28.00	13	Balance c/d	264.18	192.28
12	Dover			185.00				
13	Joseph			234.00				
13	Gordon			123.11				
		914.84		1663.31			914.84	1663.31
14	Bal b/d	264.18		192.28				

Notes:

(a) The cash book begins a new period (1 to 13 April 19x3) with the opening balances entered on the debit side.

(b) Mandy has received various sums - by cheque, in cash, by BACS and by credit card. The amounts have been entered on the debit side in date order. The means by which payments were made are not relevant in entering a cash book. What matters is the date, the payer and the amount. It is of course important that cash receipts are entered in the cash column and bank receipts in the bank column.

(c) The bank detail column is used where several items are paid into the bank together. You will see later that the bank statement will just have a single entry £824.75.

(d) Mandy has made many payments - by cheque, in cash, by BACS, by direct debit and by standing order. All of these are entered in date order.

(e) Finally the columns are added up and the totals found. The cash debit total is £914.84 and the cash credit total is £650.66. This means that there is £264.18 (£914.84 - £650.66) left and the balance is entered on the credit side so that now the total of the credit side is also £914.84. The balance is entered on the debit side of the new period as balance brought down (b/d). Hopefully the actual cash in the office is the same as the book figure! The bank balance is found in the same way and should agree with the balance shown by the bank statement. In practice it will not but we will deal with bank reconciliation statements in a later chapter.

(f) We have used three money columns on the debit and two on the credit. You will sometimes find alternatives:

Debit side:	**Date**	**Received from**	**Discount**	**Cash**	**Bank**
Credit side:	**Date**	**Paid to**	**Discount**	**Cash**	**Bank**

(i) In the UK people do not keep cash in the office except petty cash which we will meet in a later chapter. All cash received is usually paid straight into the bank so that it becomes in effect a bank transaction. This means that cash columns are normally unnecessary.

(ii) Some bookkeepers dispense with the bank detail column on the debit. This has the disadvantage that it is difficult to reconcile the cash book entries with the bank statements.

(iii) Some companies give and/or take discounts for quick payment. Where this occurs additional columns are usually found for discounts. We will deal with discounts in a later chapter.

Summary

❒ The cash book is a book in which receipts and payments through the bank accounts are entered. It is still called the cash book despite being now used only for transactions through the bank.

❒ The cash book is also a double entry account.

❒ The cash book also provides a book of prime entry for settlement discounts given for early or prompt payment of sums due.

- ❏ Actual cash (notes and coins) transactions are now recorded in a petty cash book.

- ❏ Retail receipts consist of notes, coin, cheques, credit card vouchers and other instruments. These are regarded as bank transactions as the total takings are normally totalled and paid intact into the bank.

- ❏ Primary evidence from which cash book entries are made includes paying-in books, cheque books, remittance advices, direct debit advices, information from payers and payees, and the bank statement.

Points to note

- ❏ The traditional three column format, which is now rare in the UK, should really have four columns on the debit:

  Discount   **Cash**   **Bank detail**   **Actual banking**

- ❏ Note that receipts (money etc into the bank) go on the debit and payments (cheques etc) go on the credit.

- ❏ Usually, the payer of a cheque who is taking settlement discount notes this fact on the remittance advice copy or on the cheque stub. This enables the bookkeeper, who makes the entries in the cash book, to enter also the discount. For example, suppose AB owes CD £80 and CD have offered AB 3% off if payment is made by 5 March. On 4 March AB draws a cheque for £77.60 and sends it to CD. He notes on the cheque counterfoil Cheque £77.60 and Discount £2.40 and the bookkeeper enters this information in the cash book. Firms receiving money note from the remittance advice that discount has been taken.

Self-testing questions

1. Why is a cash book so called?
2. Draw up an appropriate ruling for a retailer's cash book.
3. On which side are receipts and payments entered in a cash book?
4. List some modern payment methods.
5. Show precisely with an example how a cash book (or any double entry account) is balanced.
6. Design a paying in book and make some entries.
7. Design a remittance advice.
8. What evidence is used to write up the credit side of a cash book?
9. Explain the procedure for entering discounts in a cash book.

Exercises

1. Draw up a cash book and enter the following transactions:

Receipts				Payments			
		Discount	Cheque			Discount	Cheque
January 2	Richard	23.34	267.90	January 5	Gray	2.34	100.45
January 4	David	10.87	254.45	January 6	Dove		45.32
January 5	Hugh		68.65	January 6	Gas board		189.09
				January 7	Wages		432.95

The above were paid into the bank on January 6.

January 6	Cash sales	674.76
January 9	Access vouchers	234.76

The above two items were paid in on January 8 and 10 respectively.

The cash book balance at 1 January was £1,643.

2. Enter the following transactions in a properly ruled cash book:
(Note that all amounts are after deducting discount, if any)
Paid Joan £237.21 (discount £2.56), received cheque from Dan £345.00, paid Lionel £200, received cheque from Henry £459.00 (discount £12.08), paid in cheques received so far, paid Ken £298.77 (discount £3.90), received and banked cash sales £570.00.
The opening balance at 1.1.x8 was £39.00 overdrawn and the above transactions happen on successive days.

3. David owns and manages a seaside cafe. All sales are for cash and a till with till rolls is maintained. Half his expenditure is also made by cash for such items as drawings, wages, eggs, vegetables etc, to local farmers. These payments are made from cash takings before he banks the takings daily. He is able to take settlement discounts from a number of his suppliers. Design a suitable cash book.

Assignment

❑ *Paul is in business as a trader. At the beginning of October 19x5 he had £1,290.00 in the bank and £140.00 in cash in his office.*

Paul received the following amounts in October:

By cheque			In cash		
Date	Payer	Amount in £	Date	Payer	Amount in £
2	Rebecca	12.00	2	Thomas	32.76
5	Lauren	140.76	13	James	600.00
7	Jessica	238.90	16	Jack	43.12
12	Charlotte	170.34	18	Daniel	50.76
18	Hannah	50.00	27	Matthew	30.00
18	Sophie	980.00			
21	Amy	6.23			

By BACS			By credit card		
8	Emily	100.00	12	Ryan	234.12
13	Laura	762.31	13	Joshua	111.11

Paul made the following payments in October:

By cheque			In cash		
7	Barbara	235.00	11	Abdul	100.00
13	Mary	68.90	13	Robert	20.00
18	Elizabeth	190.43	25	Mehmet	34.12
21	Christine	23.11			

By BACS			By direct debit		
15	SEB	270.44	5	Water Co.	65.77
19	Tracey	23.97	23	Amar	321.00

By standing order			By the bank		
14	Allied	60.00	28	Charges	23.44

Paul paid in to the bank the first three cheques received (Rebecca to Jessica) on 7 October. The other cheques received were paid in individually on the dates received.

Paul paid into the bank £700 of the cash balance with the cheque from Elizabeth on 18 October. The cash consisted of £600 in £5 notes and the balance in £1 coins.

Required:

(a) Write up the paying-in slip for the banking on 18 October.

(b) Enter up the cash book for the month of October and bring down the balance.

3 The measurement of profit

In the last chapter we looked at cash and learned how the management of cash is essential to all enterprises. In this chapter we look at the measurement of profit. Businesses have, as a primary aim, the earning of a profit. Some businesses make a loss and, in the short term, can survive. However, in the long term, every business must be profitable to survive. Some enterprises do not have the objective of earning a profit. They include local and central government, the health service, state schools and charities. While they do not earn profits, it is essential for their long-term survival that income should exceed expenditure. Consequently measurement is made of their annual surpluses or deficits. The methods of measuring surpluses and deficits are much the same as the methods of measuring profits in businesses.

In this chapter we study the trading account and the profit and loss account. We will leave non-profit enterprises and also limited companies to a later chapter.

The trading account

1. This chapter begins a study of *profit* measurement by introducing the trading account. The way the trading account is constructed and *gross profit* measured is not obvious or intuitive but is done in a similar way everywhere using *accounting conventions*. In this section we will introduce the *realisation convention* and the *matching convention*. Finally we will look at some *ratios* – the gross profit percentage and the average mark-up.

The format of the trading account

2. The format of the trading account is a matter of personal taste. A common format is this.

		£	£	Line
Henry – his business				1
Trading account for the year ending 30 June 19x8				2
		£	£	3
Sales			100,000	4
Less Cost of goods sold:				5
	Opening stock	24,000		6
	Purchases	71,000		7
	Available for sale	95,000		8
	Less Closing stock	27,000		9
			68,000	10
Gross profit			32,000	11

3. We will deal with each line in turn.

    Line 1

    It is essential to identify the *business entity*. Remember that it is the business profit that is being measured. Henry's other interests are excluded.

Line 2

A precise title to the financial statement is required. The heading must also identify exactly the time period concerned.

Line 3

It may seem obvious that financial statements give information in terms of pounds sterling (or other currency). However, good practice requires an indication of the standard of measure used.

Line 4

Sales is a technical term. It means:

(a) Sales of goods dealt in. For example, a greengrocer sells fruit and vegetables, a garage sells cars and petrol. Businesses may occasionally sell other things, for example redundant fixed assets such as Plant and Machinery or other equipment used in the business. Such items are not 'sales' in the technical sense and should not be included in the 'sales' figure in the trading account.

(b) Sales made in the period. This means the inclusion of goods sold in the period for which the cash was received in the period and also for which cash was received in the preceding period or the next period. It excludes sales made in other periods even if the cash was received in *this* period.

Note that this is not what the layman would imagine.

Line 5

Sales represents the sum of all the individual sales made in the period. Cost of goods sold represents the sum of all the cost prices of the items sold in the year. In practice this is difficult to measure. For example, a shopkeeper always records a sale (e.g. of an orange) but does not usually record at the same time what that orange cost him.

Instead, lines 6 to 10 are used to calculate the input cost of all the goods sold in the period.

Line 6

Opening stock is the value of the items in stock at the beginning of the year. The value was obtained by:

(a) Identifying each category of stock.
(b) Counting, weighing or measuring the quantity of each category of stock.
(c) Determining the cost (not the selling price) of each category.
(d) Valuing each category by multiplying quantity x cost price.
(e) Summing the values of the individual categories to find the total cost of stock owned.

Line 7

'Purchases' is also a technical term. It means:

(a) All purchases of *goods dealt in* (bicycles for bicycle shop, widgets for a widget wholesaler). Only goods intended for resale in the normal course of business should be included.

Exclude:
  (i) Purchases of fixed assets.
  (ii) Purchases of goods which are intended for use but not for resale (e.g. cleaning materials or office stationery).
(b) *All* purchases made in the period even if payment was made in preceding or following periods.

Note again that this is not what is intuitively expected.

Line 8

We now have all the goods that could be sold, namely:

(a) What was in stock at the beginning of the year.

(b) What was bought during the year.

Line 9

Closing stocks represents the cost price of all the stock owned at the end of the period. If the cost price of all the goods available for sale in the period was £95,000 and the cost price of the goods unsold at the end was £27,000, then the cost price of the goods sold in the period must have been £68,000.

Line 10

Cost of goods sold. Note that this is at the cost to the enterprise.

Line 11

Gross profit. If a good is sold for £1.00 and it had cost the business 68p, then a profit of 32p is made. The gross profit of the period is the sum of the profits made on all the goods sold in the period.

The gross (= large or fat) profit is thus the difference between the selling price and the cost price of all the goods sold in the period.

All businesses incur overhead expenses (rent, rates, wages etc), and the net (= after necessary deductions) profit is the gross profit less the overhead expenses. This is dealt with in the next section.

Theory and criticism

4. **The realisation convention**

   This convention means accountants only recognise a profit when the good is sold.

   Consider the following sequence of events in Henry's business:

Jan 10	Ordered a widget from Joe.
Mar 4	The widget is delivered to Henry invoiced at £100 and placed in stock by Henry.
May 11	Henry paid Joe.
June 4	Order received by Henry for the widget from Keith.
June 7	The widget is delivered to Keith and invoiced at £140.
Aug 14	Keith pays.

   At what date has Henry earned a profit?

   There are several possibilities, but the use of the realisation convention means that 7 June is the date selected.

Henry – Trading Account for year ending 30 June, 19x8

Inclusion of the widget deal

	£	£	£	£	
Sales		100,000		140	(June 7)
Less Cost of goods sold:					
Opening stock	24,000		–		
Purchases	71,000		100		(March 4)
Available for sale	95,000		100		
Closing stock	27,000	68,000	–	100	
Gross profit		32,000		40	

5. **Criticism of the realisation convention**

   The realisation convention has been criticised for the following reasons:

   (a) It is unduly pessimistic and conservative. Profit in a period is *restricted* to those gains which have been realised through a transaction which gives legal rights to receive an agreed sum of money.

   (b) It is unduly optimistic as sales made in a period where the customer has not paid by the period end may not result in cash being received. In practice, the majority of sales on credit do result in cash.

   (c) It distorts the process of measuring income in successive time periods. Accounting purports to measure profit by comparing 'wealth' at the end of the period with wealth at the beginning and yet increases in value which have not been realised (turned into cash or a legally enforceable debt) are excluded from this wealth.

   (d) It is inappropriate in businesses with a long trading cycle such as ship builders, civil engineers and building contractors. In practice, modifications to the convention are applied in such cases.

6. **The matching convention**

   This is a more general convention than the realisation convention but is closely related. It implies that revenue (= income, especially from making a sale) should be matched with associated costs and expenses and both dealt with in the same period.

   In a trading account, which measures the profit from the sale of goods, the matching convention is clearly demonstrated in that sales are matched with the cost of the goods sold.

   In businesses, other than retail and wholesale, the matching convention is much more difficult to apply and we will deal with this more in a later chapter.

7. **Problems in implementation**

   Cut off

   The matching convention is strictly applied in practice but a problem called *cut off* causes more errors in accounting than any other.

Consider the following sequence of events:

June 27   Alf despatches goods by rail to Henry and invoices them at £108.

June 30   Henry counts the stock in his warehouse.

July 3   The goods are delivered to Henry.

The trading account in Henry's books should include for this event:

	£	
Sales		–
Opening stock		–
Purchases	108	
Available for sale	108	
Less closing stock	108	
		–
Gross profit		–

Because the goods were despatched to and invoiced to Henry in the year to 30 June, they should be included in purchases of that year and as they were owned by Henry at 30 June, they were part of this stock. However, as they were in *transit* at the year end, they were not counted at the stocktake and unless great care is taken to identify such matters, stock will be understated.

Any failure to apply cut off precisely will mean that the matching convention is not properly applied.

Returns

8. Sales are made and evidenced by invoices. However:

   (a) The invoice may have an error, resulting in overcharging.

   (b) The goods may be returned by the customer as damaged, unsuitable or not as ordered.

   (c) The goods may be lost in transit.

   In such cases, the business will issue a credit note.

   The effect of (a) to (c) is that the amount of the sale evidenced by the invoice is over-stated. The true sales figure must be the sum of invoices less the sum of credit notes.

9. Purchases evidenced by suppliers' invoices may also be returned and evidenced by credit notes. Treatment in the trading account is similar to the treatment of sales returns.

Carriage

10. Suppliers may include the cost of transporting the goods from their premises to the buyer in the invoice price. They may also pay for an external carrier and bear the cost. Alternatively, they may not, in which case the buyer will need to arrange for and pay for such transport.

    In the second case, the cost of transport is part of the cost of the goods supplied and 'purchases' in the trading account should include such costs. Treatment will usually be:

	£	£
Purchases	46,000	
Carriage Inwards	1,800	47,800
or simply:		
Purchases		47,800

Finding sales and purchases

11. The procedures for finding the total sales and total purchases in an accounting period are dealt with in a later chapter, but in outline they are:

Sales are found by:

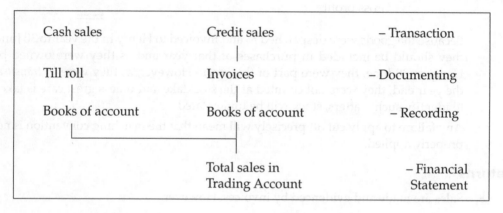

Purchases are found by:

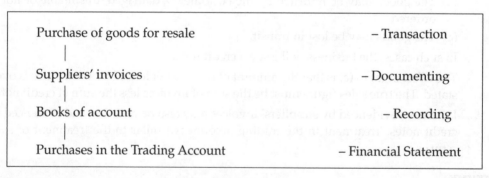

Cost of goods lost otherwise than by sale

12. In the explanation to line 9, I said that:

Line 8 gave the total goods available for sale in the year and that line 9 gave the goods still in stock at the year end, and therefore, line 8 minus line 9 gave the cost of goods which left the business in the year. The presumption was that these goods had been sold. However, in practice goods are also lost by other means, for example:

(a) Theft.

(b) Breakages.

(c) With liquids; evaporation.

(d) With perishables; natural deteriorations.

(e) With some foodstuffs; eaten by mice.

It is not normally possible to measure the cost of losses occasioned by these causes and no mention of them is made in the trading account. You should note that gross profit is actually:

(a) The sum of gross profit of all sales made in the period.

   less

(b) The cost of all goods lost in the period through theft, breakages, etc.

Gross profit ratio

13. The trading account can be reduced to three elements:

	£	
Sales	20,000	(a)
Cost of goods sold	15,000	(b)
Gross profit	5,000	(c)

Item (c) can be expressed as a percentage of (a) or (b).

If (c) is expressed as a percentage of (a), the ratio is called:

Gross Profit as a percentage of sales

   or gross profit percentage

   or gross profit margin

In this case the calculation is $\dfrac{5,000}{20,000} \times 100 = 25\%$

The information conveyed by this ratio is that for every £1 of sales, the average cost of the goods sold was 75p and the profit element 25p.

If (c) is expressed as a percentage of (b), the ratio is called:

Average mark up

In this case the calculation is $\dfrac{5,000}{15,000} \times 100 = 33\%$

The information conveyed by this ratio is that the business adds an average 33% onto the cost to fix the selling price of its goods. If a good costs the business £6, it will on average sell for £6 + £2 = £8.

14. In practice, it is important to *specify* which ratio (gross profit percentage or average mark up) is being discussed. Each ratio can be derived from the other.

The formula is GP ratio = $\dfrac{\text{COGS}}{\text{Sales}} \times$ Average mark up

15. Traders calculate and derive much information from using these ratios.

Information derived can include:

(a) A check on the accuracy of the trading account.

(b) A check that *all* sales have been included. It would be possible for a shop manager to steal and not record some cash sales.

(c) A comparison of price levels, or profitability with those achieved in previous years; forecasts and other businesses.

As an example, consider a retailer of fruit and vegetables whose policy is to add 50% on to cost to fix his selling price.

If the trading account showed:

	£
Sales	120,000
Cost of sales	85,000
Gross profit	35,000

Then his achieved mark up is only 41%. Possible causes will be considered:

(i)   Not all goods were priced at cost + 50%.

(ii)   Losses caused by natural deterioration.

(iii)   Inaccurate weighing.

(iv)   Omission of sales.

(v)   Theft.

(vi)   Unsold goods having to be thrown away.

(vii) Errors in stocktaking.

(viii) Failing to record goods taken by the proprietor for his own use.

(ix)   Cut-off errors.

(x)   Accounting errors, e.g. inclusion of non-purchases in purchases.

The profit and loss account

16. The modern format of a profit and loss account is:

Henry

Profit and Loss account for the year ending 30 June 19x8

		£	
			a
			b
			c
Gross profit		32,000	d
Less Expenses:			e
Wages and Salaries	8,300		
Rent	1,000		
Rates	1,300		
Insurance	425		
Heating and lighting	861		
Repairs	380		
Telephone	514		
Motor expenses	2,320		
Printing and stationery	1,100		
Advertising	500		
Loan interest	300		
Accountant's fee	500		
Sundries	1,103	18,603	f
Net profit		13,397	g

(a) The name of the business must be given.

(b) The period must be precisely stated. In this account, we are measuring the profit earned in the year ending on 30 June 19x8.

(c) The unit of account must be indicated.

(d) The account starts with the gross profit derived from the trading account.

(e) The expenses are listed under suitable categories. The precise categorisation of expenses depends on the type of business and the type of expense incurred.

(f) The individual expenses accounts are shown in an inset column and the total thrown out so that the total is below the figure of gross profit.

(g) The net profit is then calculated.

Expenses

17. An inspection of the list of expense headings will give you some idea of the meaning of the term expense. Expenses are the costs of goods and services consumed by the enterprise in the year.

Certain items are *excluded*. These include:

(a) **Capital expenditure**. Capital expenditure is the *acquisition* of an item which will give benefit to the business for more than one year. Examples are the acquisition of *fixed assets*. If Henry's business buys a delivery van, this is the acquisition of a fixed asset which will appear on the balance sheet. The van will give benefit to the business over several years. The *cost of acquisition* is *not* an expense of the year and is, therefore, excluded from the expenses in the profit and loss account.

Clearly the van wears out over the years and a *portion* of its acquisition cost can be regarded as an expense of each year that it is used. This portion is determined by the depreciation process which is described in the chapter on depreciation.

Trivial items of capital expenditure (e.g. a ruler for use in the office which may be in use for several years) are treated as expenses.

(b) **Purchases**. These are dealt with in the trading account.

(c) **Drawings**. Profit is earned so that drawings can be made. Profit is measured so that the proprietor can determine how much he can safely draw out of the business.

(d) **Loan repayments**.

Accruals

18. Expenses are the costs of goods and services consumed by the enterprise in the year.

Consider the cycle:

(a) Business commences 1 Jan 19x8 and electricity supply is connected.

(b) Electricity is consumed continually during the year 19x8.

(c) The meter is read on 3.3.x8; 25.5.x8; 4.9.x8; 29.11.x8.

(d) Invoices are received from the electricity board following the meter readings. These invoices are dated 7.3.x8; 2.6.x8; 7.9.x8 and 3.12.x8. The amounts are £164; £132; £162 and £191 respectively.

(e) Payment is made, following reminders by the electricity board, on 3.4.x8; 3.7.x8; 8.10.x8 and 4.1.x9.

How much do we include as an expense in the profit and loss account under the heading electricity?

Date of Reading	Date of Invoice	Date of Payment	Amount £
3.3.x8	7.3.x8	3.4.x8	164
25.5.x8	2.6.x8	3.7.x8	131
4.9.x8	7.9.x8	8.10.x8	162
29.11.x8	3.12.x8	4.1.x9	191
			648

Clearly the answer is the amount *consumed*. The cost of this up to 29.11.x8 is £164 + £131 + £162 + £191 = £648. But this excludes the amount consumed from 30.11.x8 to 31.12.x8. This must be determined or estimated from:

(a) Reading the meter and calculating the cost from the tariff charged by the electricity board.

(b) Apportioning the bill received in February 19x9.

(c) Guessing intelligently.

Suppose the amount was £75, then the expense for the year in the profit and loss account would be £648 + £75 = £723. Thus £723 is the cost of electricity consumed in the whole year going right up to the end.

The £75 is described as an *accrual*.

Prepayments

19. Expenses are the costs of goods and services *consumed* by the enterprise in the year. Accruals are required because invoicing and payment for an expense consumed in the year often occurs *after* the year end. Sometimes invoices are received and/or payments made *in the year* for expenses items which will give *benefit* (= be consumed) in the following year. These are called *prepayments*.

Motor and other insurances are normally paid in advance. Thus if a business has its year end on 31 December 19x8 and an insurance premium of £240 is paid in July 19x8 for insurance cover for the year ending on 31 July 19x9, then the amount to be included in the profit and loss account for 19x8 would be $\frac{5}{12} \times £240 = £100$. The remainder £140 will be an expense in 19x9.

The accruals convention

20. The accruals convention can be stated as requiring that costs and expenses are recognised and included in the profit and loss account as they are incurred and not as money is paid. This, like the cost convention and the realisation convention, is contrary to the expectations of those untutored in accounting.

21. The accruals convention means that the cost of the resource consumed is included for each year. This means that comparisons of expenditure under each heading can be made from year to year. The alternatives to accrual accounting are:

    (a) Including expenses only when invoiced in the year. This has the drawback that invoices may be sent at random intervals. For example, electricity bills are sent when the meter is read and this is not done at precisely regular intervals. In addition, some expenses, e.g. discounts, are not evidenced by incoming invoices.

    (b) Including expenses in accordance with cash payments. This suffers the drawback that payments are made randomly and no comparisons can be made. For example, three payments of quarterly rent might be made in 19x4 and five payments in 19x5. This may occur because it is almost a chance event whether the December 19x4 quarter is paid at the end of 19x4 or the beginning of 19x5.

Problems of implementation

22. The consumption of resources under most expense headings is relatively easy to find. There are certain expenses which are made for specific periods of time, e.g. rent, rates, insurance premiums, vehicle licences.

23. Some expense headings are more difficult:

    (a) **Heat and light**. Precise measurement of the cost of consumption up to date of the balance sheet is difficult as meter readings are not usually taken at year ends. In the case of coal or oil, it is necessary to take stock of any fuel in stock at the year end.

    (b) **Repairs**. Strictly speaking, the cost of property or equipment repairs should not fall in the period when the repairs took place but in the periods when the deterioration, that the repairs are making good, took place. In practice, however, repairs are usually, but not always, allowed to fall into the period when the repairs took place.

    (c) **Advertising**. It is sometimes argued that the benefits of advertising are long term (especially with the launch of a new product) and that the cost of advertising should fall into the periods when the benefit is felt. However, in practice, the date of appearance of the advert is taken as the determining date.

    (d) **Accountant's fee**. The work of preparing (and/or auditing) the financial statements for the year ending 30 June 19x4 will mostly be done in the following year and the accountants' fee will be invoiced and paid in the year ending 30 June 19x5. None the less, the fee for preparing the Accounts to 30 June 19x4 is put back into the Accounts for that year.

    (e) **Depreciation, discounts, bad debts**. These items are discussed in separate chapters.

    (f) **Losses on stocks; sales and purchase returns**. These items appear in the trading account and are not profit and loss account items. However, if a measurable uninsured loss of stock due to fire or theft occurs, it may appear in the profit and loss account with a corresponding reduction in the figure of purchases.

(g) **Carriage of goods**. Carriage of goods from suppliers to the business's shop, factory or warehouse (carriage in) is considered part of the cost of the goods and appears in the trading account. Carriage of goods to customers (carriage out) is a profit and loss account expense.

Revenues

24. Some businesses also have additional *revenues* such as rents received and interest received from investments and financial deposits. These can be shown in the profit and loss in one of two places as:

		£	£'000
Gross profit			643
Add	Interest receivable	61	
	Rents receivable	19	80
			723
Less	Expenses:		
or			
Net profit on trading			160
Add	Interest receivable	61	
	Rents receivable	19	80
Net profit for the year			240

Revenues are subject to the accruals convention in the same way as expenses.

Summary

❐ Businesses which trade by buying goods and reselling them, measure their profit from buying and selling in the form of a trading account with the format:

Sales	X
Less cost of goods sold	X
Gross profit	X

'Cost of goods sold' is derived from

Opening stock	X
Plus Purchases	X
Goods available for sale	X
Less Closing stock	X
Cost of goods sold	X

❐ 'Sales' and 'purchases' are technical terms and include only sales and purchases of goods dealt in.

❐ The realisation convention implies that the accountant recognises a profit at the moment when a good is sold. The practical consequences in a trading account are that sales and purchases include all items sold and bought in the period irrespective of cash receipts and payments.

❒ The matching convention implies that revenues (e.g. from sales) should be matched with associated costs and expenses and dealt with in the same period. The consequences for the trading account are:

    (i) That sales and the cost of the goods sold should be precisely matched. Cut-off is a technical term for the practical difficulties in doing so.

    (ii) Losses (e.g. from theft) should appear in the trading account in the accounting period when they occur.

❒ Sales and purchases should be net of returns.

❒ Purchases should include associated costs such as carriage-in and import duties.

❒ The trading account includes 'cost of goods sold'. In practice this term includes also the cost of goods stolen or otherwise lost and destroyed. This fact is not usually stated as the cost of such losses is not measured.

    (i) The gross profit percentage is $\dfrac{\text{Gross profit}}{\text{Sales}} \times 100\%$

    (ii) The average mark up is $\dfrac{\text{Gross profit}}{\text{Cost of goods sold}} \times 100\%$

❒ The net profit for an accounting period (usually one year) is calculated and demonstrated by showing gross profit, taken from the trading account, and deducting the itemised expenses.

❒ Expenses are categorised according to custom or convenience to inform readers of the type of expense incurred.

❒ The amount of an expense is not the amount invoiced or the amount paid but the cost of the resource consumed in the period.

❒ The effect of taking precise consumption as the amounts of expenses in the profit and loss account is that at the year ends there are accruals and prepayments. Accruals are the cost of resources consumed by the year end but not invoiced or paid. Prepayments are the costs of resources paid for in the year but not consumed until the following year.

Points to note

❒ Remember that sales and purchases are sales and purchases made in the period and not cash received and paid.

❒ It is normally too expensive to have a recording system such that would measure directly the cost of goods sold. Instead a global figure of *cost of goods sold* is obtained from:

$$\text{Opening stock} + \text{purchases} - \text{closing stock}$$

❒ This item includes the cost of goods lost otherwise from sales but measurement of the cost of such losses is not normally obtained.

❒ The trading account heading must always indicate the precise period covered. Avoid:

Trading account for the period ending .... as the length of the period is not speci-fied.

❏ Do not include in sales and purchases any sales and purchases of goods such as fixed assets which are not the goods dealt in.

❏ *Sales* is sometimes referred to as *turnover*.

❏ In this chapter, I have assumed stock is valued at cost (not selling price). In practice, some stock can be valued at *below* cost and this is dealt with in a later chapter.

❏ Be careful to deduct items when *less* occurs in the trading account. Arithmetic errors are very easy to make. After the preparation of a trading account, always calculate the gross profit percentage and ask yourself if it appears to be reasonable.

❏ The realisation convention and the matching convention may appear similar. Remember that the realisation convention is concerned with the timing of profit recognition and that the matching convention is concerned with the relation of revenues with associated costs and expenses

❏ In practice a trading account and a separate profit and loss account are not usually produced. Instead they are combined as per Fig. 3.1.

❏ The word 'accrual' stems from a Latin root meaning 'to grow'. Thus interest due on a loan accrues or grows with the passage of time.

Humphrey

Trading and Profit and Loss Account for the year ending 31 December 19x8

	£'000
Sales	163
Less Cost of goods sold:	99
Gross profit	64
Less Expenses:	52
Net profit	12

Fig. 3.1

❏ In preparing a profit and loss account for presentation to the owners or managers of a business (or to examiners!), the calculation of the amounts to be included under an expense heading should be done in *workings* which are *not* part of the profit and loss account. Thus:

Workings:	£
Rent and rates – paid	2,000
Add accrued rent	400
	2,400
Less rates in advance	520
Expense of the year	1,880

The profit and loss account entry would simply be:

Rent and rates	£1,880

❏ The precise placing of an expense into the correct years is not always done in practice. For example, the expense, motor running expenses, would include the cost of petrol consumed. Strictly to place the cost in a particular year, the stock of petrol in the tanks of vans and cars should be determined. But as the difference made to the expense measurement of the year would be small and the organisational problems considerable, this would not be done. However, if the difference made was large (**material** is the accountant's word), then the stock would be taken. This might occur in shipping companies where the stock of fuel oil can be very significant and differ from year to year.

❏ The order in which expense headings are listed is not important. However, the largest amounts are often placed at the top of the list. Depreciation is usually placed at the bottom.

❏ If the number of expense headings is very large, then sub-divisions can be used. For example:

	£'000	£'000
Occupancy costs		
Rent	400	
Rates	280	
Fire insurance	36	
Repairs	143	859
Selling costs		
Salesmen's salaries	361	
Motor expenses	110	
Advertising	292	763

Self-testing questions

1. Draft a trading account.
2. What is included in sales?
3. What is included in purchases?
4. What is meant by gross profit?
5. How does the gross profit relate to the net profit?
6. What is the realisation convention?
7. List the criticisms of the realisation convention.
8. What is the matching convention?
9. Define cut-off.
10. How are 'returns' treated?
11. How is 'carriage in' treated?
12. Why are goods lost other than by sale? How are these accounted for in a trading account?
13. How is the gross profit ratio calculated? What information can be derived from it?
14. Distinguish the gross profit to sales ratio from the average mark-up.
15. List causes of unexpected gross profit ratios.

16. What is the function of the trading account?
17. What is the function of the profit and loss account?
18. Draft a profit and loss account.
19. Explain the word 'expense'.
20. What items must be excluded from expenses?
21. What are accruals?
22. What are the alternatives to the accruals convention?
23. What treatments are possible for revenues in a profit and loss account?
24. How should the workings used to calculate the amount to be included under an expense heading be shown in a profit and loss account?
25. When is sub-categorisation of expenses appropriate?

Exercises

1. From the following separate sets of data, draw up trading accounts:

	£	£	£	£
	a	b	c	d
Sales	6,500	14,000	3,600	2,390
Purchases	3,200	4,200	1,970	2,000
Opening stock	1,400	2,790	680	620
Closing stock	1,100	2,930	715	734

Calculate (a) average markup on cost and (b) the gross profit to sales percentage in each case.

2. From the following separate sets of data, draw up trading accounts:

	£	£	£	£
	a	b	c	d
Purchases on credit	8,000	13,000	6,000	15,000
Cash purchases	3,000	–	8,000	800
Opening stock	700	800	3,700	1,200
Closing stock	850	1,250	4,800	900
Sales on credit	12,200	14,900	17,200	–
Cash sales	1,200	3,000	2,000	18,000

Calculate (a) the average mark up on cost, and (b) the gross profit to sales percentage in each case.

3. Should the following items be included in the 'purchases' of (a) a motor car dealer and (b) a hardware shop and (c) a business equipment dealer?

   (i)   A motor car.
   (ii) A lawnmower.
   (iii) A typewriter.
   (iv) A jar of coffee.
   (v)   A mousetrap.
   (vi) A car alarm system.

4. Discuss why the 'cost of goods sold' cannot usually be measured directly (think of a newsagent's business).

5. Why does determining a date when profit is considered to have been earned matter to an accountant?

George is a retailer of car accessories. The good (a special steering wheel) involved in one of his transactions was dealt with like this:

October 4	Ordered the good from Wilson at a price of £35
November 2	The good arrived and was invoiced to George
November 27	Flash Harry Ltd ordered the good from George
December 6	The good was sold and invoiced on credit to Flash Harry Ltd for £77
January 9	Flash Harry paid
February 1	George paid Wilson

Required:

When was the profit on this transaction made? What was the gross profit margin on this deal?

6. Insert the missing figures in the following trading accounts:

	£	£	£	£	£	£
Sales		1,400		2,700		?
less cost of goods sold:						
Opening stock	250		300		490	
Purchases	1,200		?		2,670	
Available for sale		1,450		1,760		3,160
Closing stock	?	1,000	800	960	?	2,900
Gross profit		?		1,740		1,100

7. Should the following be included in 'sales' for the year ending 31.12.x8 of a fishmonger?

(a) Sales of fish for cash in the year.

(b) Sale of a car no longer used by the business.

(c) Sales of fish on credit to Hugh on 23.12.x8 (payment received on 2.1.x9).

(d) Sales of fish on credit to Evan on 30.12.x7 (payment received on 3.2.x8).

(e) Returns of fish which were off – refund given 5.6.x8.

(f) Credit notes given to Martin on 30.12.x8 for fish short delivered.

8. Mary is in business selling hand made jewellery. Her year end is 31 March. In the year 19x8 the following transaction occurred:

1 January Mary ordered a special jewel from Alphonse; 3 February the jewel arrived with invoice for £120; 5 March sold the jewel to Lady D on credit and invoiced it at £232; 7 April paid Alphonse; 8 May Lady D paid.

(a) When is the profit made by Mary on this transaction?

(b) In which financial year is this profit made?

(c) What accounting convention is involved?

   (d) Mary produces MONTHLY trading accounts. Show the entries for this transaction in each of her monthly trading accounts for January, February, March, April, May and June.

9.   Samantha has a bookshop. She expects to make a gross profit on sales price of 30%. In fact her trading account showed a gross profit to sales ratio of only 28%. List all the possible causes of the difference.

10.   Ludwig sells music and records. His trading account includes a figure of £36,782 as cost of goods sold. His accountant explains that that figure is not only the cost of the goods actually sold to customers. What else is included in it?

11.   Assemble the following information about three separate businesses for the year ending on 31 December 19x4 into trading and profit and loss accounts

	Alfred	Brian	Colin
Purchases of goods for resale	23,500	26,500	56,000
Sales	44,300	39,700	69,870
Stock 1 Jan 19x4	2,560	3,690	17,100
Stock 31 Dec 19x4	3,400	2,600	18,600
Wages	6,800	1,100	8,500
Rent	960	–	2,200
Insurance	640	280	546
Motor expenses	1,200	580	1,200
Depreciation	1,480	430	1,100

12.   Consider the figures in Question 11. Further investigations reveal:

   For Alfred's business:

   (a) Rent does not include the rent for the final quarter ending on 31 December 19x4 £320.

   (b) Insurance includes a fire policy (annual premium £200) which was for the year ending 30 June 19x5.

   (c) Motor expenses do not include a bill for repairs which is expected to be about £100.

   For Brian's business:

   (a) Rent includes £300 for the quarter to 31 January 19x5.

   (b) Insurance includes £30 for a fire policy for the year ending 30 April 19x5.

   (c) Motor expenses include motor tax for the year ending 31 May 19x5 £120.

   For Colin's business:

   (a) Wages do not include a bonus to Joe payable in respect of his good work in 19x4 but payable in January 19x5 £100.

   (b) Insurance includes an E.L. premium for the year ending 31 March 19x5 £60.

   (c) Rent does not include the month of December 19x4. Rent is £2,400 a year.

   (d) Purchases do not take account of some goods delivered in November 19x4. These were still in stock at 31 December but were not counted as the cost was disputed. In January the price of the goods to Colin was settled at £600 and he then paid for them.

Required:

(a) In each business, recast the trading and profit and loss account to reflect any necessary adjustments.

(b) For each business, calculate the average markup on cost and the gross profit to sales ratio. Why do you think these ratios are different for each business?

13. Karl commenced business on 1 June 19x4 and makes up his accounts to 31 May in each year. His payments included:

Insurance		£
3. 6.x4	Fire insurance year to 31.5.x5	135
10. 8.x4	Employer's liability – provisional premium (a) year to 31.7.x5	530
31.10.x4	Consequential loss (b) year to 31.10.x5	625
30.11.x4	Public liability – year to 30.11.x5	430
15. 8.x5	Adjustment to E.L. (a) premium year to 31.7.x5	68

Notes:

(a) Employer's liability insurance is compulsory for employers and insures against the risk of having to pay damages to employees who are injured at work. The premium is based on the wages paid in the year and if this is not known at the time of payment of the premium, an adjustment is required later.

(b) If a fire occurs, the loss of property is recovered under the fire policy but the loss of profits due to disruption of the fire is recovered under a consequential loss policy.

Telephone		£
13. 6.x4	Installation charge	190
	Rent – quarter to 31.8.x4	80
18.10.x4	Calls – quarter to 31.8.x4	101
	Rent – quarter to 30.11.x4	80
19. 1.x5	Calls – quarter to 30.11.x4	124
	Rent – quarter to 28.2.x5	80
1. 5.x5	Calls – quarter to 28.2.x5	130
	Rent – quarter to 31.5.x5	80
2. 8.x5	Calls – quarter to 31.5.x5	146
	Rent – quarter to 31.8.x5	100

Printing and stationery		
3. 8.x4	Letterheads and sundries invoiced 2.6.x4	440
3.11.x4	Sundry stationery invoiced 1.10.x4	260
14. 6.x5	Letterheads delivered and invoiced 25.5.x5	300

Interest		
30.11.x4	Interest on loan of £40,000 bearing interest at 10% per annum for the half year to 30.11.x4	2,000
	Repayment of part of the loan	2,000

Calculate the accruals and the amounts to be included in his profit and loss account under each expense heading for the year 31 May 19x5.

14. The following figures relate to (A) Paul's bicycle business (B) Clare's boutique and (C) Wayne's car spares business for the year ending 31 December 19x7.

	A	B	C
Purchases	36,000	58,000	36,000
Sales	59,000	93,000	57,000
Stock 1.1.x7	10,800	9,820	4,700
Stock 31.12.x7	12,467	12,300	6,400
Sales returns	760		800
Purchase returns		1,500	1,300
Carriage inwards	254	318	210
Wages	6,877	8,933	7,540
Drawings	5,700	4,770	3,600
Interest receivable		1,232	
Rent	2,800	2,590	2,400
Rates	1,600	1,820	1,800
Repairs		1,622	2,600
New van	2,677		
Extension to shop		4,500	
New racking system			3,500
Electricity	1,790	1,200	970
Accountant's fee	400	800	500
Carriage outwards	300	321	320
Van expenses	980	2,310	2,400
Stationery	543	780	590
Advertising	200	1,654	1,650

Notes:

(a) For A: Rent includes rent for the quarter ending 28.2.x8 £600; electricity accrued is £432; the stock at 31.12.x7 did not include £300 from Black which was for goods in transit at 31.12.x7 which were invoiced in 19x7 and included in purchases.

(b) For B: Rates includes rates for the half year ending 31.3.x8 £750; van expenses does not include a repair carried out in December 19x7 but not yet invoiced. It is expected to cost £258; stationery stocks at 31.12.x6 were £105 and at 31.12.x7 £143.

(c) For C: Rent includes rent for the half year to 30.4.x8 £900; advertising includes a prepaid advertisement which will appear on 23.1.x8 £270; repairs includes £1,000 for a new shopfront.

Required:

(a) In each case, prepare trading and profit and loss account for the year.

(b) In each case, explain your treatment of drawings, carriage inwards, capital expenditure, carriage outwards and all accruals and prepayments.

Assignment

❏ Boffin is a retail pharmacist. He derives his income from retail sales and from prescription charges made to the local health service authority and to customers. Data for his business for the years to 31 December 19x7 and 19x8 were:

	19x7	19x8
Sales and prescription charges to customers	196,500	210,400
Prescription charges to Health Service	48,200	66,200
Purchases	170,100	180,600
Opening stock	21,720	30,490
Closing stock		25,300
Wages	25,800	27,300
Drawings	20,500	19,700
Rent and rates	9,400	13,200
Insurance	1,380	1,620
Motor expenses	2,200	2,410
New car		16,300
Loan received from Bank for car		12,000
Other overheads	14,900	15,300

Notes:

(a) Rent is payable in advance. The 19x7 rent includes £2,400 for the half year to 31 March 19x8 and the 19x8 includes £3,600 for the half year to 31 March 19x9.

(b) Other overheads for 19x7 do not include the electricity bill for the final quarter of 19x7 £430 (it is included in the 19x8 figures). The corresponding figure for 19x8 is £510.

(c) Ignore depreciation.

Required:

(a) Prepare the trading and profit and loss accounts for the two years (show workings).

(b) Calculate the gross profit to sales margin and suggest reasons for any difference between the two years.

(c) Explain the use in this example of the realisation, matching and accruals conventions. Discuss whether the matching convention is fully complied with in this case.

(d) Discuss, as well as you can with limited information, the performance of the business.

4 The balance sheet

A balance sheet is a financial statement which lists:

(a) The assets of the enterprise.

(b) The liabilities of the enterprise.

(c) How the enterprise is financed – its capital.

and gives values to each item.

All enterprises produce a balance sheet at least once a year.

Firstly we look at the balance sheet of the sole trader and we consider some more accounting conventions – periodicity, money measurement, entity, cost and the going concern. Finally we explore the effects of transactions on balance sheets.

The balance sheet of a sole trader

1. In this chapter we describe the balance sheet of a sole trader. Balance sheets of other organisations are much the same and differ primarily in the financing section. We will meet a lot of balance sheets of all types of enterprises later in this book. You should try to see as many actual balance sheets as you can. You may find them in the accounts of students' unions, building societies (just take one off the counter), charities etc.

Format

2. At Fig. 4.1 is the general format of the balance sheet of a sole trader.

			line
James Brown			a
Balance sheet as at 31 December 19x8			b
Fixed assets		£	c
Premises		20,000	d
Plant and equipment		11,500	e
Vehicles		16,200	f
		47,700	g
Current assets	£		h
Stock	65,200		i
Debtors	31,000		j
Prepayments	400		k
Cash in hand	800		l
		97,400	m
		145,100	n
Current liabilities			o
Creditors	27,000		p
Accruals	1,000		q
Bank overdraft	34,000		r
		62,000	s
		83,100	t
Capital		83,100	u

Fig. 4.1. Balance Sheet Vertical Format

3. I will discuss each line separately.

    (a) The **name of the business** is given first. The objective is to identify the business. In many cases, as here, just the name of the proprietor is given. The name of the business (e.g. The Foley Fish Company) may also be given.

    (b) **Balance sheet** – it is clearly necessary to identify the document as a balance sheet.

    As at 31 December 19x8. A balance sheet describes the situation at a particular specified moment in time; in this case as at 31 December 19x8.

    (c) **Fixed assets** – assets are things which the business owns or possesses and which have value to the business. Fixed assets are those assets which were acquired for continuous use in the business and which have useful lives extending over a number of years.

    (d) **Premises** – or land and buildings. All the items in a balance sheet are shown as having monetary values. The values quoted are often not the values that a layman would expect. Accounting is very much about deriving appropriate methods of valuation for balance sheets. In most sole trader balance sheets, premises will be valued at what they cost the business when they were acquired.

    (e) **Plant and equipment and vehicles**. The valuation of these fixed assets is more complicated and is dealt with under the heading of depreciation. At this stage, it is enough to know that they are valued by reference to the original cost of acquisition.

    (g) **The balance sheet is divided into sections** – fixed assets, current assets, current liabilities, capital – and it is necessary to show the total value of each section.

    (h) **Current assets** consist of goods which were acquired for the purpose of sale (stock), sums due to the business by others (debtors), benefits of paid expenditure which are still be come, e.g. rent paid in advance (prepayments), and cash at bank and in hand. The distinguishing characteristic of current assets is that they exist for a short time only before being converted into assets of other kinds. For example, stock is sold on credit and thus converted into debtors. Debtors pay and thus the sum due is converted into cash.

    (i) **Stock** (sometimes known as inventory)

    Consists of:

    (i) Goods held for resale.

    (ii) Raw materials held for conversion into a saleable product.

    (iii) Work in progress – partly finished goods which on completion will be held for sale.

    (iv) Stock may also include consumable stores (heating oil, cleaning materials, lubricants, stationery etc) and spare parts for machinery.

    (v) Counting and valuing stock is the most difficult and time consuming part of preparing the data for inclusion in a balance sheet.

    (j) **Amounts due by debtors**. Debtors are people or firms who have bought goods before the balance sheet date (in our case 19x8) but who had not paid by that date but will pay after the balance sheet date (in our case in 19x9).

(k) **Prepayments** – they arise out of payments which were made before the balance sheet date but which will give the business benefits after the balance sheet date. Examples are rent, rates or insurance paid in advance.

(l) This business has no cash at bank (it has an overdraft) but many businesses will have cash at the bank as well as cash in hand.

(m) As in line g, the total of each section must be shown.

(n) The total value of all the assets is shown.

(o) **Current liabilities** – liabilities are amounts owing by the business. Current liabilities are usually defined as amounts falling due within one year. In this case, the current liabilities are payable by 31 December 19x9. In practice most of them will be paid early in 19x9.

(p) **Creditors** – this item includes mainly sums due for goods which were supplied to the business in 19x8 but which had not been paid for in 19x8. Clearly, most goods bought in 19x8 are paid for in 19x8 but as Brown buys on credit, some goods bought in 19x8 will be paid for in 19x9.

(q) **Accruals** – this will be an unfamiliar word to you. In this context it means sums due for those services supplied in 19x8 which had not been paid for by the end of 19x8. Examples are electricity used but not paid for, or interest on loans which has become due by the passage of time but which has not been paid.

(r) **Overdraft** – many businesses have money in the bank but many others, like James Brown's, have with the bank's approval drawn more from the bank than they have put in. The excess is known as an overdraft and is a liability of the business. It is a current liability because it is technically repayable on demand.

(s) Similar to g and m.

(t) It is useful to measure and show the total value of the assets employed in the business less the liabilities to other people.

(u) **Capital** – so far the idea of listing and valuing the assets and liabilities of the business is one which is not difficult to grasp. The financing section of the balance sheet is slightly more difficult to understand. In this case, the financing section consists of one item only – capital. It means:

  (i) That all the resources needed to acquire the net assets (assets minus liabilities) came from the proprietor, James Brown.

  (ii) The value of the resources invested by James Brown in the business amounts to £83,100.

  (iii) The business can be said to owe £83,100 to its proprietor, James Brown.

Methods and procedures

4. The best approach to the preparation of a balance sheet is:

   (a) *Memorise* the format and write down the words.

   (b) Complete the balance sheet by filling in the appropriate amounts. In examinations, the required data is often given in the form of a *trial balance* and notes or in the form of notes only.

   Once the format has been memorised, the preparation is usually relatively simple as all balance sheets are basically similar in content.

Theory and criticism

5. The form and content of balance sheets were not originally given to mankind in the way that the law was given by God to Moses and Moses to the people. Instead the present form and content developed over the centuries by the experiment and experience of businessmen by trial and error methods. In recent times academic accountants have developed a body of theory to describe the actual *practice* of accountants in producing balance sheets.

6. The theory consist of a series of ideas variously known as postulates, principles, concepts, conventions or other words. In this work, I shall use the word *convention* but you will find other words meaning the same thing.

7. In this chapter, we will look at four conventions: periodicity, business entity, money measurement and historical cost.

8. **Periodicity.** Balance sheets can be prepared as often as is desired but there is some considerable labour involved and in consequence, the convention has grown up by preparing them at yearly intervals. The life of a business is divided into individual accounting years. Each business proprietor needs to determine at the business commencement what date his accounting year will end on. There are *no rules* on this but many businesses choose from:
   (a) The month end nearest the anniversary of commencement.
   (b) The calendar year end, i.e. 31 December.
   (c) The Government's year end, i.e. 31 March.
   (d) A month end when business is usually slack so that the year end things can receive reasonable attention.
   (e) The end of a business cycle. For example some new Universities have adopted 31 July as their year end because this is the end of the academic year.

9. **Business entity**. In drawing up his balance sheet, a business proprietor is concerned only with the assets and liabilities of the *business*. He excludes other assets and liabilities which are private or domestic or are assets of another, completely separate, business. The convention has therefore developed of looking upon the business as a separate entity from its proprietor. By so doing, it is possible to see the business entity as *owing* the amount of its capital to the proprietor. The business entity convention is a fiction (the assets and liabilities of the business are still legally the assets and liabilities of the proprietor) but a convenient one.

10. In practice, it is not always easy to decide if some assets are private assets or business assets. For example a car may be used for business *and* private purposes. Where duality of purpose or use is found, the asset is commonly regarded as a business asset.

11. **Money measurement**. If I have three oranges and buy four more, I have seven in total. Similarly if I have a home, a car and six tins of soup, I have eight things altogether. But the number eight here, is hardly useful information. The problem is to find some common unit in which to convert assets and liabilities so that the total number of units becomes meaningful. The convention in accounting is to use pounds sterling (or in Nigeria, Naira; in India, Rupees; etc).

Money has several uses including:

(a) It is a store of value.

(b) It is a means of exchange.

(c) It is a *measure* of value.

This use by accountants of money as a measure of value has two difficulties:

(a) Accountants have acquired a reputation (undeserved) of being obsessed with money to the exclusion of other, more human factors.

(b) Those unversed in accounting may confuse the uses of money with money itself. For example 'capital' measures the total value of assets less liabilities, it is not itself money.

12. **Historical cost**. In a balance sheet, assets such as premises have values placed upon them. There are several possible ways of finding a basis for valuing business premises (imagine a shop). Here are three:

(a) What the shop could be sold for, if sold as a shop.

(b) What the shop could be sold for, if sold for some other use.

(c) What the business originally paid for it when the business acquired it.

Methods (a) and (b) seem useful at first sight but the figure can only be obtained by forming opinions, making an estimate or simply guessing. Such methods are *subjective* and accountants prefer to be *objective*, and so prefer method (c).

It is possible to argue that showing the shop on the balance sheet at historical cost £20,000 because it cost that amount twenty years ago, gives information of no possible relevance. This argument is in fact accepted and company balance sheets usually have the estimated resale value shown also, as a note.

13. In times of high inflation, the historical cost convention used by accountants has been much criticised and the profession has developed a methods of adjusting accounts to reflect the effects of inflation without abandoning the basic preference for cost as a measure of value. At the time of writing inflation is at a low level. As a result there is not a great deal of interest in inflation-adjusted accounting at present.

Alternative formats

14. The format shown at Fig 4.1 is a common one. It is known as the vertical format. Other formats are acceptable and include the horizontal format. We will stick to the vertical format as it is now almost universal in the UK.

The horizontal format is the more traditional one and the vertical format is considered to be more modern. Horizontal balance sheets can have assets on the left and the capital and liabilities put on the right. This is a matter of taste.

Students are often confused by differences in format. Think of a balance sheet as having sections (fixed assets, current assets, current liabilities, capital) which can be arranged in different ways. A slight rearrangement of the vertical format is often found as:

		£
Fixed Assets		47,700
Current Assets	97,400	
less Current liabilities	62,000	35,400
		83,100
Capital		83,100

This changes the effect on a reader produced by the balance sheet, in that emphasis is placed on the relative totals of current assets and current liabilities (this net total is called the *working capital*).

Categories

15. You will have realised that a balance sheet is not a long list of individual assets. (Adam owes us £60, Alfred owes us £75 …). Such lists may be useful but the aim of a balance sheet is to show the overall position. Assets and liabilities are summarised into categories. The categories selected are a matter of choice on appropriateness and convenience. Fixed assets in a shop business may be best categorised as:

    (a) Fixtures and fittings (to include shelving, counters, display cabinets, etc).

    (b) Equipment (to include cash registers, cold cabinets, etc).

    Other types of businesses may use different categories.

Common errors

16. Here is a list of errors made by students in preparing balance sheets which you should try to avoid:

    (a) Failure to state the name of the proprietor and/or the business.

    (b) Incorrect heading. 'Balance Sheet as at …' is always correct.

    (c) Failure to use the general headings: fixed assets, current assets, current liabilities etc.

    (d) Untidiness; for example, failing to write down words and figures directly underneath each other.

    (e) Failure to show sub-totals of the general categories; fixed assets, current assets, etc.

    (f) Writing down the current assets in the wrong order. This may seem a petty sin but in practice, the order shown is always used.

    (g) Failing to use more than one column.

    (h) Putting the lines ___ or ── in the wrong places. Note where I have put them.

    (i) Abbreviating – do not be impatient.

    (j) Failure to realise that other people will have to make sense of your work.

    (k) Errors in addition.

Transactions and their effect on the balance sheet

17. A balance sheet is a classified summary of the assets and liabilities of a business at a specific moment in time. It has been likened to a snapshot or a 'still' from a moving picture. If successive balance sheets were prepared with only a short time interval between them, each succeeding balance sheet would show small differences in the assets and liabilities.

    The events which cause changes in the constituent parts of a balance sheet are known as *transactions*. In this chapter we will look at a range of possible transactions and examine their effect on successive balance sheets.

    In practice, balance sheets are not prepared after each transaction, but in preparing balance sheets at intervals of a year the accountant is summarising for the *proprietor* (or other user) the *cumulative* effect of all the transactions in that year.

Transactions

18. At Fig. 4.2 is the balance sheet of Alfred Harbridge at 31 July followed by a table of some possible transactions (Fig. 4.3) with their effect on the constituent parts of the balance sheet.

Alfred Harbridge ... costume jewellery wholesaler
Balance sheet as at 31 July, 19x8

	£	£
Fixed assets		
Fixtures and Fittings		15,200
Vehicles		17,100
		32,300
Current assets		
Stock	18,920	
Debtors	21,300	
Cash at Bank	1,250	
Cash in hand	85	41,555
		73,855
Less **Current liabilities**		
Creditors		16,800
		57,055
Capital		57,055

Remember that capital simply measures the total amount of assets less liabilities.

Fig. 4.2

Table of transactions

	Category	Amount £	Assets	Effect on: Liabilities	Capital
a)	Purchase of new storage rack on credit	800	Fixtures +	+	0
b)	Purchase of stock for resale, on credit	1,050	Stock +	+	0
c)	Purchase of second-hand van by cheque	500	Vehicles + Cash at bank –	0	0
d)	Debtor pays by cheque	720	Debtors – Cash at bank +	0	0
e)	Payment of a creditor in cash	40	Cash in hand –	–	0
f)	Purchase of stock by cheque	200	Stock + Cash at bank –	0	0

Key: + = increase in an asset or liability – = decrease in asset or liability 0 = no effect

Fig. 4.3

You should make sure that you can follow the effect of each transaction on the balance sheet items.

Notes:

(a) Each transaction changed two of the items composing the balance sheet. This is known as the *dual aspect principle*.

(b) None of these transactions changed the net sum of assets and liabilities; that is, none of them changed the capital. While the detailed components of the balance sheet changed, the total remained the same.

The cumulative effect of the transactions is summarised in a balance sheet after the transactions have been effected (Fig. 4.4).

Alfred Harbridge
Balance sheet at conclusion of transactions a-f

	£	£
Fixed assets		
Fixtures and Fittings		16,000
Vehicles		17,600
		33,600
Current assets		
Stock	20,170	
Debtors	20,580	
Cash at Bank	1,270	
Cash in hand	45	42,065
		75,665
Less **Current liabilities**		
Creditors		18,610
		57,055
Capital		57,055

Note that the capital has remained unchanged after all these transactions.

Fig. 4.4

19. **Transactions which change the assets and capital of a sole trader.** Fig. 4.5 is a table of some categories of transactions which change individual assets and also the capital.

Category	Amount £	Assets	Effect on: Liabilities	Capital
g) Cash taken by proprietor for his own private use (drawings)	20	Cash in hand	−20 0	−20
h) Sale on credit of stock which had cost £30	55	Debtors Stock	+55 0 −30	+25
i) Sale for cash of stock which had cost £7	9	Cash in hand Stock	+9 0 −7	+2
j) Proprietor took a brooch from stock to give to his daughter (= drawings). Brooch had cost £15.	15	Stock	−15 0	−15
k) Proprietor won a lottery prize and paid the cheque into his business account.	1,000	Cash at bank	+1,000 0	+1,000
l) Proprietor inherited a bicycle valued at £50 which he put into the business.	50	Vehicles	+50	+50
m) Paid by cheque rent for the quarter year to 31 Oct.	270	Prepayment Cash at bank	+270 0 −270	0

Fig.4.5

20. These transactions are more difficult to follow, so we will examine them in detail.

Item (g) The *entity* convention points out that we regard the assets and liabilities in the business as the subject of the balance sheet and disregard all private assets of the proprietor. Consequently when a business asset (part of the cash in hand) ceases to be a business asset and becomes a private asset, the balance sheet must reflect the smaller quantity of cash held as a business asset. Cash or other assets taken from the business by the proprietor are known as drawings.

The effect on Capital may be seen in two possible ways:

(a) The net total of *assets less liabilities* (which = capital) has been reduced by £20.

(b) The capital can be seen as a liability of the business to the proprietor. By paying £20 to the proprietor, this liability has been reduced.

Note that the purpose to which the £20 is put is irrelevant to our purposes as we are concerned only with the business.

Item (h) As we have seen, assets are usually recorded in the balance sheet at their cost of acquisition. Thus when stock which had cost £30 leaves the business, the asset stock must be reduced by this amount in order to *leave* the rest of the stock at its cost. However, the sale is at a selling price of £55 and the debtors (sums due by customers for goods supplied but not paid for) must go up by £55 as this is the amount due. The effect on the *net total* of *assets less liabilities* is an increase of £25 and hence capital is increased by £25.

You may have noticed that three items in the balance sheet have been affected despite the dual aspect principle. We could say that the sale is really two transactions viz:

(a) The transfer of stock to the customer.

(b) The taking of a *profit* of £25.

Each of these transactions has a dual aspect.

Item (i) This is similar to (h).

Item (j) This transaction is similar to (g) but stock is reduced instead of cash. Drawings of this type are called *drawings in kind*.

Again, the ultimate use of the brooch is irrelevant to our purposes.

Item (k) This transaction is called *capital introduced*. A *private* asset has been introduced into the business, thus increasing the business asset Cash at bank. From the *capital* point of view this can be viewed in two possible ways:

An increase in assets less liabilities (net assets) which equals capital by definition.

An increase in the amount owed by the business to the proprietor.

Item (l) This is similar to (k).

Item (m) You have already met this type of transaction when considering the expenses in the profit and loss account. Clearly the asset Cash at bank has been reduced by £270, and if we assume that all these transactions occurred very shortly after 31 July 19x8 then the benefit of the rent (the right to occupy the premises) is a future benefit. Hence we regard the payment as bringing into existence an asset 'prepayment'.

As time goes on the prepayment will cease to be an asset and become an expense.

21. The effect of all these transactions on the business can be summarised as:

Alfred Harbridge
Balance sheet at conclusion of transactions a–m

	£	£
Fixed assets		
Fixtures and Fittings		16,000
Vehicles		17,650
		33,650
Current assets		
Stock	20,118	
Debtors	20,635	
Prepayment	270	
Cash at Bank	2,000	
Cash in hand	34	43,057
		76,707
Less **Current liabilities**		
Creditors		18,610
		58,097
Capital		
as at conclusion of transactions a – f		57,055
Add net profit from transactions g – m		27
assets introduced to business		1,050
		58,132
Less **Drawings**		
as at date of balance sheet		35
		58,097

You should follow the transactions to see that this balance sheet is correct.

22. You will notice that the Capital section of the balance sheet is an expansion of the previous simple statement of capital £57,055. What we are showing is:

(a) The capital as it was at the date of the previous balance sheet.

(b) Changes in the capital since the last balance sheet. These are usually:

(i) Introductions of capital.

(ii) Profit.

(iii) Drawings.

and are shown *in this order* with a sub-total £58,132.

This expansion is normally given in balance sheets of sole traders.

Theory

23. The dual aspect principle means that:

(a) Every transaction will affect two items in a balance sheet.

(b) Each item will be affected by the same amount.

(c) The balance sheet will always balance (because capital = assets – liabilities.)

(d) Total assets will always equal total liabilities plus capital.

The points to grasp are:

(a) The balance sheet must always balance because capital is the difference between assets and liabilities. It is helpful to view the balance sheet as firstly, a list of assets and secondly, as a list of claims against those assets. The creditors have the first claims against the assets and the proprietor has *residual* claim against all the rest of the assets.

(b) By thinking clearly about the effect of a transaction and recognising that two balance sheet items change (two assets, two liabilities, or an asset and a liability), it should be possible to ensure that the balance sheet always balances.

(c) The capital will only be changed by:

(i) Profit, for example, stock at cost being changed into debtors at selling price.

(ii) The proprietor putting private assets (e.g. goods or cash) into the business – capital introduced.

(iii) The proprietor taking assets out of the business (goods or cash) for private use – drawings.

Problems in implementation

24. So far, we have included as liabilities only *current liabilities*. Current liabilities are defined as liabilities which are due and payable within one year of the balance sheet date. In practice most current liabilities are paid within a short time of the balance sheet date. For example, if Leo, a trader pays his suppliers three months after he receives the goods and his balance sheet date is 31 December, 19x8, then the creditors figure at 31 December 19x8 will be the total of goods supplied in October, November and December 19x8. Payment will be made in January, February and March 19x9 respectively.

25. One particular current liability which is not obviously payable within one year is 'bank overdraft'. The reason is that the normal agreement with the bank is for the overdraft to be repayable on demand. In practice, banks do not usually demand repayment, and overdraft *facilities* are renewed on a regular basis, sometimes for many years.

Long-term liabilities

26. Some liabilities are payable more than one year after the balance sheet date. These liabilities are called long-term liabilities. Examples are loans.

The position for *long-term liabilities* in a balance sheet is as in the following example (Fig. 4.6).

David Watkins – Computer retailer
Balance sheet as at 29 February 19x8

Fixed assets		62,842
Current assets	49,044	
Less Current liabilities	33,266	15,778
		78,620
Financed by:		
Capital as at 28 February 19x7	46,589	
Net Profit for the Year	23,541	
	70,130	
Less Drawings	19,150	50,980
Long term liabilities		
Bank loan repayable 19x1	17,640	
Loan, Aunt Mary at 10% repayable 19x2	10,000	27,640
		78,620

Fig. 4.6

The business has assets and current liabilities which come to £78,620. The finance to acquire this quantity of net assets came from:

the proprietor	£50,980
long term lenders	£27,640

Summary

❐ A balance sheet is a view of the assets, liabilities and capital of a business at a single instant of time.

❐ A business will engage in *transactions* which will affect the individual assets and liabilities in a balance sheet.

❐ The *dual aspect* principle describes the fact that each transaction affects *two* items in a balance sheet.

❐ Some transactions affect the net total of assets less liabilities. Since capital is defined as assets less liabilities, such transactions affect the capital.

❐ The capital in a balance sheet usually shows the *balance* as in the previous balance sheet, a summary of changes and the *balance* at the balance sheet date.

   These changes are:
   (i) Introductions of assets into the business by the proprietor.
   (ii) Withdrawals of assets (drawings) from the business by the proprietor profits.

❐ Long-term liabilities appear below the capital in the balance sheet of a sole trader (see Fig. 4.6).

❐ The balance sheet of a business is a classified list with values of the assets employed in, and the liabilities of, the business at a particular date.

❏ Capital is defined as assets less liabilities.

❏ The vertical format for a sole trader balance sheet should be memorised.

❏ The periodicity convention recognises the fact that businessmen can draw up balance sheets for their businesses at intervals, usually of one year. Any date can be selected but is usually adhered to in successive years.

❏ The business entity convention requires a focus of attention on the business as a separate entity from its proprietor.

❏ Balance sheets are drawn up with values in terms of money. Money is used as a measure of value.

❏ Accountants value assets by reference to historical cost.

Points to note

❏ A balance sheet shows the assets and liabilities and capital at a particular moment in time. It is a static snapshot picture of what in reality is an ever changing thing. Students initially tend to confuse movements or flows of assets and liabilities with assets and liabilities at a particular moment. There are other financial statements to measure movements and flows over time.

❏ The words assets and liabilities are difficult to define with precision because of the diversity of assets and liabilities which can be found in the complex business world. Students should familiarise themselves with what is meant by a business asset or liability which should appear on a balance sheet by constant observation of actual balance sheets.

Liabilities must in general involve:

(i) A sum of money owing by the business at the balance sheet date.

(ii) For some goods supplied or services supplied or other happening before the balance sheet date.

❏ The balance sheet is a summary. In practice:

Fixed assets	£6,432,000

is too much of a summary and some breakdown into sub-categories is usually made. Perhaps as:

Fixed assets	£
Land	1,000,000
Buildings	2,342,000
Plant and machinery	1,190,000
Motor vehicles	1,900,000
	6,432,000

It is difficult to generalise as to how much sub-categorisation is appropriate. You should try to see as many balance sheets as you can. Clubs, societies, students' unions and public companies all publish their balance sheets.

❏ Businesses can have many different types of assets and liabilities but all balance sheets are basically similar. Once you have learned the basic form and content, you will find that more complex balance sheets (for example, those of partnerships, limited companies and groups of companies, charities) still follow the basic design and only the detail has to be understood and learned.

❏ Note carefully that assets and liabilities and capital are *measured* in money terms, they are not themselves money.

❏ The idea of a fixed asset is that it is some asset which has cost more than some trivial amount and will last and give *future benefits* over several years. Thus buildings and machinery are both expensive and long lasting and are thus fixed assets.

❏ Current assets are also things of value which will give future benefits. But they are of a transitory nature such that the benefits will be received entirely in the *near* future.

❏ The four categories of current asset are the common ones and you should commit them to memory. They are always found in the same order and you should design your balance sheets that way also.

❏ The capital of the business is simply equal to the total of assets minus the total of the liabilities. Commonly, the word capital is used but other words can be found including:
  – proprietorship
  – net worth
  – owner's equity

James Brown owns his business. The business is not an abstract idea, it is composed of a set of specific assets and it also has liabilities. It is useful to determine the net amount of the assets less liabilities because:

(i) It tells the owner/proprietor what resources he has tied up in his business. If he sold the assets and paid off the liabilities he would have money which he could use in other ways.

(ii) Any change in the capital since the previous balance sheet was drawn up needs to be explained.

❏ The notion that Capital = Assets – Liabilities is often known as the Accounting Equation. The equation can be manipulated so that, for example, Assets = Capital + Liabilities.

❏ Be careful to distinguish the capital of the proprietor from the long term liabilities.

❏ Interest is usually payable on loans at a percentage rate. Interest accrues (grows) on a time basis. Thus a loan of £10,000 at 20% made on 1 July 19x4 would begin to earn interest from that date at £2,000 a year. In the balance sheet of the borrower at 31 December 19x4, the loan would appear in long term liabilities at £10,000. If the interest had been paid for the half year to 31 December, no liability would appear for interest. However, if the interest for the half year had not been paid, then the interest outstanding £1,000 would appear in accruals in current liabilities.

Self-testing questions

1. Explain the following words:
   (a) transactions
   (b) capital
   (c) dual aspect principle
   (d) drawings
   (e) in kind
   (f) prepayment
   (g) long term liabilities

2. Why are bank overdrafts included in current liabilities? What is an overdraft facility?

3. Sara's business has had a loan from The Extortive Loan Co. Ltd. of £10,000. The loan was taken up on 1 January 19x5 and the terms are for interest at 12% per annum, payable quarterly on 31 March, 30 June, 30 September and 31 December. Repayments begin on 31 March 19x7. How would the loan and interest appear in the Balance Sheet at 31 December 19x5 if (a) the interest was paid on the due dates or (b) the interest for the December quarter was overdue at 31 December 19x5?

4. (a) Draft a balance sheet for a sole trader:
      (i)   Showing the assets total (vertical format).
      (ii)   Showing working capital (vertical format).
   (b) Explain:
      (i)   Fixed assets.
      (ii)   Current assets.
      (iii)   Stock.
      (iv)   Debtors.
      (v)   Current liabilities.
      (vi)   Accruals.
      (vii)   Capital.
   (c) What is the periodicity convention?
   (d) What is the entity convention?
   (e) What is the money measurement convention?
   (f) What is the historical cost convention?
   (g) What are the uses for money in an economy?
   (h) What formats are possible for a balance sheet and why might the format be changed?
   (i) Why are assets grouped into categories and only the total of each category shown?
   (j) List the common errors in balance sheets made by students.
   (k) What exactly is Capital?
   (l) What is the Accounting Equation?

Exercises

1. (a) Draw up balance sheets for the following businesses as at 31 December 19x3:

	John	Edith	Thomas
Premises	50,000	42,000	
Stock	16,440	780	23,000
Trade creditors	13,920	5,870	18,320
Vehicles	11,600	17,700	5,300
Furniture and fittings	5,300	3,700	4,050
Accrued rent	200		
Prepaid rent			460
Prepaid insurance	361	249	502
Cash at bank	320		2,980
Bank overdraft		2,100	
Prepaid rates	890	340	380
Cash in hand	35	150	320
Trade debtors	12,610		1,300
14% Loan repayable 4.3.x4 from James	1,000		
Accrued interest on the loan	70		

Note: John's business is wholesaling widgets, Edith is a fishmonger and Thomas is a retail pharmacist.

(b) Can you see any connection between the balance sheets and knowing the type of business?

2. Which of the following would appear in the balance sheet as at 30.6.x9 of William, a greengrocer with a lock-up shop. In each case say whether the item is (a) a fixed asset, (b) a current asset, (c) a current liability, and, if none of these, state why.

(a) A contract for two years to 19x0 to supply a local restaurant.

(b) A caravan at Brighton for holidays.

(c) A pair of scales.

(d) A life assurance policy paid in advance.

(e) Overdue rent on the shop.

(f) A bank loan.

(g) Amounts owing to wholesalers.

(h) An Austin estate car.

(i) A fur coat for Mrs William paid for from the shop bank account.

(j) Stock of tinned goods.

(k) Costs of redecorating the shop.

(l) A cash register bought in June 19x9.

(m) The amount owing for the cash register. This was paid in August 19x9.

(n) A contract signed in June 19x9 for the erection of a chill room in the shop for £2,000, work to commence in July 19x9. This will enable William to sell fish.

(o) A lease of the shop for seven years signed on 31.12.x6 at an annual rent of £1,500.

(p) A personal computer which William uses for business and which William Jr. is using for his studies at the local college.

      (q)   A refrigerator in the shop owned by AHM Icecream Ltd.

3.   'My capital appears on the liabilities side of the balance sheet. I thought that the capital of the business was my main asset.' Explain.

4.   A local newspaper reports that Mr John Rich, an accountant aged 45, had died of over-work leaving £260,000. Do you think this means £260,000 in the bank? If not, what might it mean?

5.   Draw up balance sheets for the following businesses.

	Alan	Betty	Ceri	Donald
	£	£	£	£
Creditors	7,430	23,260	7,200	31,400
Vehicles	8,300	40,100	31,000	–
Prepayments	1,420	2,300	1,640	2,300
Accruals	860	1,700	800	900
Capitals	?	89,100	?	150
Bank balance (overdraft)	(2,460)	?	1,240	?
Premises	10,000	25,000	–	15,000
Plant	7,240	1,200	12,600	12,600
Stock	16,300	34,295	15,200	2,000
Debtors	11,200	16,800	9,600	–
Cash in hand	830	–	400	–

Identify the mistakes you have made using the list of common errors in paragraph 16 of the chapter.

6.   Lou owns a grocery and general goods shop in the high street of a small town and he and his family live in rooms at the back of the shop. What accounting conventions would be applied to the balance sheets of his business? What specific problems would exist in applying these conventions?

7.   Consider the following matters in connection with Gail's restaurant business:

    (a) She sold her van for £2,000 in December 19x7 and paid the cheque into the bank on 16 December 19x7.

    (b) She negotiated an overdraft facility with her bank for £10,000. At 31 December 19x7, the actual overdraft was £2,760.

    (c) She paid the rates for the restaurant on 14 November 19x7 for the half year to 31 March 19x8 £2,100.

    (d) She ordered a consignment of frozen foods on 18 December 19x7 costing £4,200. These were delivered and invoiced to her on 4 January 19x8.

State precisely how these items would appear (if they do) in the business balance sheet at 31 December 19x7.

8.   Ken dies on 1 January 19x8 leaving his car sales business to his cousin Griselda. The accountant provided a balance sheet at 31 December 19x7 for the business showing a capital of £31,200. Griselda's husband Graham was sorry about Ken's death but could not help thinking about how he would spend the £31,000.

Explain Graham's misconception.

9.   The accruals of Sid's business at 31 August 19x7 are Rent £200, Rates £521, Electricity £240, Wages £240.

Explain how these items would appear in the balance sheet at 31 August 19x7. Also explain why they appear in the way you have suggested.

10. George started in business as a retailer of office machinery on 1 January 19x7 by transferring £1,000 to his business bank account. On 1 January he completed the following transactions:

(a) Regarded his car, valued at £3,000, as a business asset.

(b) Purchased on credit from Bill, office machinery for resale – £1,000.

(c) Paid the insurance premium for the car for the year ending 31 December 19x7, £220, by cheque.

(d) Sold an office machine for £300. He was paid immediately by cheque. The machine had cost £210.

(e) Drew £10 from the bank for a petty cash float.

(f) Borrowed, interest free, £3,000 by cheque from his aunt with repayment due by half-yearly instalments of £500 beginning on 30 September 19x8.

(g) Took £3 from the petty cash to buy himself a theatre ticket.

(h) A cheque for £620 was received for redundancy money from his previous employment. He paid this into the business bank account.

(i) Sold an office machine which had cost £85 to Ted for £105 on credit.

(j) He decided to use a typewriter, which had cost £100, as his office typewriter. It had been included in trading stock.

Draw up a table to show the effect of these transactions on the assets, liabilities and capital of the business and prepare a balance sheet at the conclusion of the transactions.

11. Phil's balance sheet as at 31 July 19x8 was:

	£		£	£
Capital	29,800	**Fixed assets**		
		Premises at cost		10,000
		Vehicles at cost		6,000
				16,000
Current liabilities		**Current assets**		
Creditors	6,000	Stock at cost	15,000	
		Debtors	4,000	
		Prepayment	–	
		Cash at bank	800	19,800
	35,800			35,800

Shortly afterwards, the position had become:

	£		£	£
Capital	36,000	**Fixed assets**		
		Premises at cost		15,000
		Vehicles at cost		9,000
				24,000

	£			£	£
Current Liabilities			**Current Assets**		
Creditors	6,600		Stock at cost	14,900	
Overdraft	1,550	8,150	Debtors	4,900	
			Prepayment	350	20,150
		44,150			44,150

Given that there were no drawings, explain the transactions that had probably occurred.

Assignment

❒ The balance sheet of Gill at 31 December 19x7 showed:

	£		£
Capital	2,095	Fixed Assets	500
Creditors	429	Stock	760
Accruals – rent	80	Debtors	1,020
		Bank	324
	2,604		2,604

During January 19x8, the following transactions occurred.
(a) Gill introduced her car valued at £2,000 into the business.
(b) Rent paid for the three months ending 28 February 19x8 – £240.
(c) A debtor paid £200.
(d) Paid a creditor £129.
(e) Gill withdrew £100 for her own use.
(f) Bought goods on credit for £700.
(g) Sold on credit goods that had cost £205 for £348.
(h) Borrowed £100 interest free from Dan, the sum is repayable in August 19x8.
(i) Bought by cheque a red van for £1,500.
(j) Drew a cheque for cash £20 for a petty cash float.
(k) Bought goods for £150 paying by cheque.

Required:
(a) Draw up a table showing the effect of each transaction on individual assets and liabilities and on capital.
(b) Draw up a balance sheet in good form as at 31 January 19x8.
(c) Draw up a trading and profit and loss account for January.
(d) Write up a cash book for the month.
(e) Write a commentary on your financial statements about the accounting conventions used.

5 Depreciation

This chapter is concerned with depreciation of fixed assets and is divided into six topics.

(a) What depreciation is.
(b) Depreciation methods.
(c) Particular fixed assets.
(d) Disposals of fixed assets.
(e) Entries in financial statements.
(f) Problems of implementation.

What depreciation is

1. Before describing depreciation, the definitions of fixed assets and capital and revenue expenditure must be considered.

Fixed assets are long lived resources which are used in the production of goods or services; examples are land, buildings, plant and machinery, office equipment, vehicles.

Capital expenditure is expenditure incurred in the *acquisition* of a fixed asset. *Revenue expenditure* is expenditure on a good or service which is consumed either immediately or within the space of the current or next accounting period.

It is the nature of a fixed asset that it gives benefit to the business for more than one accounting year. As an example, consider the purchase for £5,000 of a motor van to be used in the business for delivering goods to customers. The van will be used in the business for several years until it wears out or is otherwise disposed of.

The van will have a limited life, and if we assume that it will be used for five years and then be sold for scrap for £100 then it will give benefit to the business for five years and the net cost of that benefit is expected to be £4,900.

Profit for any given year is computed by summing the revenues of that year and deducting all the expenses incurred in earning those revenues. The van will be used in five separate accounting years and, therefore, its cost (or part of it) will be an expense of each of the years. The depreciation process is required to determine how much of the net cost of the van should be *allocated* to each year it was in use.

Causes of an asset having limited life

2. Causes include:
    (a) **Wear and tear**. Physical assets inevitably decline with use, the effects of weather and other physical causes.
    (b) **Obsolescence**. Assets which are operationally effective may cease to be economically effective due to the effect of technological change or changes of fashion.
    (c) **Effluxion of time**. Some assets have intrinsically limited lives. For example, leasehold property and patent rights.

Depreciation methods

3. There are numerous *methods* of depreciating fixed assets. Three are considered here, two common methods: the straight line method and the reducing balance method and a third, which is rarely used: the sum of digits method.

In addition to the cost of acquisition of the fixed asset, there are two estimates required:

(a) The *estimated* useful life.

(b) The *estimated* residual, disposal or salvage value.

4. **The Straight Line method**

    This is the simplest and most common method. It *assumes* that the fixed asset net cost should be allocated in equal amounts to the years in which it is used.

    Example:

    > Cost £5,000 on 1 Jan 19x3
    >
    > Estimated useful life five years.
    >
    > Estimated salvage value £100.
    >
    > Assume the accounting year ends on 31 December.
    >
    > Depreciation will be: = £980 a year.

    Thus profit will not be reduced by £5,000 in 19x3, but by £980 in each of the years 19x3 to 19x7.

5. **The Reducing Balance method**

    This method is used where it is assumed that more of the net cost of a fixed asset should be allocated to the earlier years of use than later years.

    The computation takes place using the following stages:

    (a) Determine cost (c) and estimate useful life (n) and salvage value (s).

    (b) Insert in the formula:

    $$r = 100 \left(1 - n\sqrt{\frac{s}{c}} \right) \text{ to find } r, \text{ a percentage}$$

    In our example: $r = 100 \left(1 - 5\sqrt{\frac{100}{5,000}} \right) = 54.27\%$

    (c) Allocate as:

		£
	Cost	5,000
19x3	54.27% of 5,000	2,713
		(i) 2,287
19x4	54.27% of 2,287 (i)	1,241
		1,046
19x5	54.27% of 1,046	568
		478
19x6	54.27% of 478	259
		219
19x7	54.27% of 219	119
		100

    (i) The £2,287 is described as the reducing or diminishing balance.

Thus profit will be reduced not by £5,000 in 19x3 but by different amounts in each of the five years of use, with the first year having the largest allocation (£2,713) and each succeeding year having a reducing or diminishing amount.

6. **The Sum of Digits method**

This method also assumes that more of the net cost of the fixed asset should be allocated in the earlier years, but it avoids extremes (£2,713 in 19x3 and only £119 in 19x7 in the reducing balance method).

The method is:

(a) Determine cost and estimate useful life and salvage value.

(b) Count down from number of years of useful life as follows:

$$
\begin{array}{r}
5 \\
4 \\
3 \\
2 \\
\underline{1} \\
\text{and sum:} \quad 15
\end{array}
$$

(c) Apply:

		£
19x3	5/15 of £4,900	1,633
19x4	4/15 of £4,900	1,307
19x5	3/15 of £4,900	980
19x6	2/15 of £4,900	653
19x7	1/15 of £4,900	327
		£4,900

7. **The methods compared**

A table showing the effects on profit of each method is:

	Straight Line £	Reducing Balance £	Sum of Digits £
19x3	980	2,713	1,633
19x4	980	1,241	1,307
19x5	980	568	980
19x6	980	259	653
19x7	980	119	327
	4,900	4,900	4,900

The overall effect on profits for the whole five year period is the same but the distribution or allocation to each year within the five year period is different.

The profit shown by the business will be the same for the whole five year period, *but the profits of the individual years will differ according to which depreciation method is chosen.*

Which depreciation method should be used?

8. This is a matter of *policy* on the part of the management of the business. However, consistency must be applied. This means:

   (a) All similar assets should be depreciated by the same method.

   (b) The same method should be used in successive years.

   Consistency is an accounting convention of great importance. Where choice is available as it is in depreciation, it is possible to change to another policy. However this is generally frowned upon and the regulations require any change to be fully disclosed, the reasons given and the money effects fully spelt out.

9. Factors to be taken into account include:

   (a) Ease of calculation. Clearly, the reducing balance method, in theory, means applying the formula to possibly thousands of separate items of plant. In practice, this is overcome by adopting a blanket rate, say 25%, and ignoring the estimated lives and salvage values.

   (b) A view that the *benefit to the business* of a new fixed asset is greater than an older fixed asset. As depreciation is in effect a charge against profit for using an asset, depreciation should be greater in the earlier years of life.

   (c) Repairs and maintenance increase through the life of an asset and thus depreciation should reduce. This is a specious argument but is often quoted.

   (d) Whether the wearing out of the asset is a function of time (e.g. a patent right) or usage (e.g. a van).

Particular fixed assets

10. The method (Straight line etc) and the expected lives of fixed assets vary according to the type of fixed asset. For example:

    (a) **Land**. Land can be said to have an infinite life and, therefore, is not depreciated.

    (b) **Buildings**. Buildings do have a limited life. Depreciation should be applied to buildings on the straight line basis over the estimated useful life. Useful life is often taken as 40 or 50 years.

    (c) **Plant, machinery, equipment** etc. Practice varies widely and both methods of depreciation are found. Estimated lives vary from three to twenty years. It is notable that estimated lives of plant and machinery are falling with the rapid advance of technological change and the onset of early obsolescence.

    (d) **Leasehold property**. This asset should be amortised (amortisation is the word used for this asset. It means the same as depreciation), on the straight line method over the period of the lease. Leasehold property, where the lease has more than 50 years to run, is often not amortised.

    (e) **Wasting assets**. Wasting assets is a term that can be applied to all assets with a limited life but it is commonly applied to assets such as mines or quarries. If a mine is acquired at cost of say £1 million, it will have a useful life until no more minerals can be extracted economically. Clearly none of the depreciation methods so far explained are appropriate and the usual method is to estimate total extractable quantities, say, 200,000 tonnes and to measure the output each year.

Thus, if 25,000 tonnes were extracted, then $\dfrac{25,000}{200,000} \times £1,000,000 = £125,000$ – this is the depreciation.

This method is known as the *depletion* method.

Disposals of fixed assets

11. The methods described work well if in fact the van does last five years and is sold for £100, but in the majority of cases this does not happen.

Example:

Alf commences in business on 1 January 19x4.

On that day he bought a van for £4,000. He estimated its useful life to be four years and its salvage value as £400. The depreciation policy chosen was the straight line method. Profit will, therefore, be reduced by including depreciation on the van as follows:

	£
Cost	4,000
Depreciation in 19x4	900
Net book value 31.12.x4	3,100
Depreciation in 19x5	900
Net book value 31.12.x5	2,200
Depreciation in 19x6	900
Net book value 31.12.x6	1,300
Depreciation in 19x7	900
Estimated salvage value at 31.12.x7	400

In fact, Alf sold the van at the end of 19x6 for £1,900. Thus the actual loss on the van was £4,000 – £1,900 = £2,100. The usage of the van was in the three years 19x4, 19x5 and 19x6. By the time the vehicle was sold, the accounts for 19x4 and 19x5 had been prepared with depreciation of £900 in each and these accounts cannot be altered. Consequently, profit has been reduced by £1,800 and the remainder of the loss (£300) will be regarded as depreciation in 19x6. Thus the depreciation will be allocated to account years as:

	£
Cost	4,000
Depreciation	900
Net book value 31.12.x4	3,100
Depreciation in 19x5	900
Net book value 31.12.x5	2,200
Depreciation in 19x6	300
Actual salvage value	1,900

Had the proceeds of sale been £2,350, then the depreciation in 19x6 would have been a negative figure of £150. That is, it would have been a revenue and not an expense.

The depreciation in the year of sale is thus the net book value at the beginning of the year less the proceeds of sale. Depreciation is based on estimates but in the year of sale, estimates are not required as the actual loss is known.

Depreciation in the year of sale is sometimes known as depreciation adjustment and sometimes as profit on sale (or loss on sale).

Entries in financial statements

12. (a) **Profit and loss account**

Depreciation is an expense and appears in the list of expenses, usually at the end of the list.

Depreciation can appear as a single figure, e.g.

	£
Depreciation	42,620

or it may be itemised, e.g.

Depreciation:		£
Buildings	10,200	
Plant	19,320	
Vehicles	13,100	42,620

(b) **Balance sheet**

Fixed assets usually appear as:

	Cost	Accumulated depreciation	Net book value
	£	£	£
Land	100,000	–	100,000
Buildings	231,000	40,700	190,300
Plant	168,904	72,308	96,596
	499,904	113,008	386,896

The accumulated depreciation is all the depreciation that has been debited to profit and loss account up to the date of the balance sheet. For example, if a machine was depreciated on the reducing balance method at 30% as:

	£
Cost in 19x4	1,000
Depreciation 19x4	300
Net book value 31.12.x4	700
Depreciation 19x5	210
Net book value 31.12.x5	490
Depreciation 19x6	147
Net book value 31.12.x6	343

It would be included in successive balance sheets as:

	Cost	Accumulated depreciation	Net book value
	£	£	£
31.12.x4	1,000	300	700
31.12.x5	1,000	510	490
31.12.x6	1,000	657	343

Net book value is that part of the original cost which has not yet been included in the profit and loss account. It is thus the unused part of the original cost. It is not the amount that would be realised if the asset were sold. This is counter to the expectations of those unversed in accounting. Note it well.

Theory and criticism

13. When a fixed asset is acquired (say for £10,000), it is presumed to be capable of giving the business £10,000 of use. If part of this is recoverable at the end of its useful life (the salvage value, say £2,000), then the *use* over its life is presumed to be worth £8,000. As this use value is applied over several accounting periods, a means has to be found of spreading the use over the relevant accounting periods. The depreciation process is this means.

The depreciation process is a consequence of the *matching* convention whereby revenue and profit dealt with in the profit and loss account are matched with associated costs and expenses by including in the same account the costs incurred in earning them.

Part of the cost of earning the sales of the year will be the use of the representatives' cars. The depreciation process provides part of the original cost of the cars as an expense associated with those sales.

The depreciation process is also related to the *going concern* convention. The value of a fixed asset on a balance sheet is not the potential selling price of the asset. You may wonder why. The reason is that it is assumed that the business will continue in operational existence for the foreseeable future. Therefore, there is no *intention* or *necessity* to sell the fixed assets. The likely proceeds of sale if the assets were sold is, therefore, an irrelevant piece of information. It is, in any case, subjective and accountants like to be objective.

Students wonder why the resale value cannot be used to determine net book value when the resale value can be fairly estimated as it can be with, for example, cars. The answer is that the net book value is not the realisable value (= the value to an outsider who might buy it) but its *value to the business*. The value to the business is considered to be that part of the original cost which has not yet been exhausted.

The managers of a business have a choice of:
(a) Straight line.
(b) Reducing balance.
(c) Sum of digits.
(d) Several other methods we have not discussed.

Each method will give a different measure of profit and value to fixed assets. This means that the management can, within limits, select the profit they desire.

In addition, estimates of:

(a) Useful life.

(b) Salvage value.

will vary according to the subjective views of the persons making the estimates. Consequently, profits and asset values will also vary for this reason.

For both the above reasons, comparisons of profit and capital employed can only be made between businesses with knowledge of the depreciation methods and estimates used. *Disclosure* in notes attached to the accounts is required. Here is an example:

> 'the cost of leasehold property is amortised on a straight line basis over the period of the lease. Other fixed assets are depreciated at 25% a year on cost.'

Statement of Standard Accounting Practice No 2 requires disclosure of all material accounting policies (see chapter on Accounting Conventions).

Problems of implementation

14. **Depreciation in year of purchase**

If the year end is 31 December 19x4 and a fixed asset was acquired on 1 January 19x4, then in the 19x4 accounts, a full year's depreciation will be taken. If the fixed asset was acquired on 20 March, should a full year's depreciation or only a proportion of a year's depreciation be taken? The proportion being 286/365 where 286 is the number of days use in 19x4.

Practice varies. Some companies apportion depreciation in the year of purchase; others take a full year. Each company is said to have an *accounting policy* on the matter. In examinations, instructions are given or if they are not, take a full year's depreciation and state that you have done so.

Depreciation in the year of sale

Common practice is to regard depreciation in the year of sale as the net book value at the beginning of the year less the proceeds of sale. Some accountants (and examiners) continue to depreciate up to the date of disposal and then make a depreciation adjustment of the net book value at that date less the disposal proceeds.

Use of fully depreciated assets

If it is estimated that a fixed asset will last four years and have a nil salvage value and the policy is to use straight line depreciation, then at the end of the fourth year, the asset will be fully depreciated and have a net book value of nil. However, it may be that the asset is not then disposed of, but continues in use. In that case, no depreciation of that fixed asset will appear in the profit computations of later years.

Statement of Standard Accounting Practice No 12 – Accounting for Depreciation

15. SSAP 12 gives the current view and requirements of the UK accounting profession on the subject of depreciation. This chapter accords with it. It is worth noting some of its definitions and requirements:

(a) Fixed assets are those assets which are intended for use on a continuing basis in the enterprise's activities. Virtually all fixed assets have finite useful economic lives.

(b) Depreciation is a measure of the wearing out, consumption or other reduction in the useful economic life of a fixed asset, whether arising out of use, effluxion of time or obsolescence through technological or market changes. Depreciation should be allocated so as to charge a fair proportion of cost or valuation of the asset to each accounting period expected to benefit from its use.

(c) The useful economic lives should be reviewed regularly and, when necessary, revised. If at any time there is a permanent diminution in the value of an asset and the net book amount is not considered recoverable in full, the net book amount should be reduced to the estimated recoverable amount.

(d) There is a range of acceptable depreciation methods. Management should select the method regarded as most appropriate to the type of asset and its use in the business.

(e) A change from one method to another is permissible only on the grounds that the new method will give a fairer presentation of the results (profit and loss account) and financial position (balance sheet). Any change must be fully disclosed.

(f) The following should be disclosed in the financial statements for each major class of depreciable asset: the depreciation methods used, the useful economic lives or the depreciation rates used, the total depreciation charge for the period, and, the gross amount of depreciable assets and the related accumulated depreciation.

Summary

❏ Capital expenditure is expenditure on items which will give benefit over more than one year – fixed assets.

❏ If such assets have a limited life, then their cost is an expense of each year in which they are used.

❏ Life limitation is caused by use, wear and tear, obsolescence or the effluxion of time.

❏ There are numerous methods of allocating the expenditure to specific time periods – the depreciation process. Methods include straight line and diminishing balance.

❏ Estimates are required of life and salvage value.

❏ A balance sheet shows the cost less accumulated depreciation which gives that part of the cost which has not yet been expensed to the profit and loss account.

❏ Disposals of fixed assets give rise to a depreciation charge (or credit) which is the difference between the net book value at the beginning of the year and the disposal proceeds.

❏ The depreciation process is a consequence of the *matching* convention.

❏ The showing of fixed assets in a balance sheet at unamortised cost is possible because of the going concern convention. It is assumed that the business is not going to be closed down and that therefore the fixed assets are not going to be sold. Thus there is no purpose to showing the amount they could be sold for. It is better to show

❏ The amount of value-in-use still to be enjoyed. Value-in-use is a proportion of the original cost.

❏ The method of depreciation used and the estimation of life used should be disclosed in notes to the Accounts.

❏ Choice of depreciation policy gives some flexibility to management in measuring the profit but consistency of method over fixed assets and years is required.

❏ Accounting for depreciation is governed by SSAP 12.

Points to note

❏ The expression 'net book value' is often replaced by the expression 'written down value'. Other expressions include 'carrying value', 'undepreciated cost' and 'unamortised cost'.

❏ The taking of part of the cost of a fixed asset and including it in the profit and loss account is often called 'providing' for depreciation and the accumulated amount of depreciation is called the provision for depreciation.

❏ The inclusion of an amount in the profit and loss account is sometimes called writing off. If an asset has a net book value of £100 and is scrapped with no salvage recovered, then the asset is said to be written off to profit and loss account.

❏ The meaning of capital expenditure should be particularly remembered.

❏ The formula for computing the rate for reducing balance depreciation is not known by all accountants of the older generation. In practice, many accountants use reducing balance but take an arbitrary percentage, such as 25%.

❏ The depreciation in the year of sale or disposal is often called a depreciation adjustment or a profit or loss on sale.

❏ We have seen that it is possible to manipulate the profit measurement by selecting a particular depreciation policy. However:
  (i) The method, once chosen, must be used consistently.
  (ii) The estimates made must be reasonable. They have to be acceptable to *auditors*.

❏ I cannot emphasise enough that net book value is not an estimate of saleable value.

❏ Property (land and buildings) generally does not depreciate in value, although the limited life of buildings requires that the buildings part should be subject to depreciation. Some businesses revalue their property at intervals and change the net book value to the new (usually higher) valuation. This is permissible although full disclosure must be made. The new higher building value is then depreciated. The effect of this is that the assets are increased in value and profits are then diminished (because depreciation is based on a higher figure). The lower inflation rates, currently obtaining in the UK, may mean that revaluation will be less frequently encountered and may even be downward.

❑ If there is a revision of the estimated useful life of an asset, the unamortised cost should be charged over the revised remaining useful life.

❑ An item in a balance sheet:

	Cost	Accumulated depreciation	Net book value
Vehicles	200,000	74,000	126,000

includes numerous vehicles bought at different times. The depreciation is the sum of the depreciations on each vehicle. Some vehicles will have one year's depreciation, some several.

❑ Some enterprises use other valuation methods for fixed assets – particularly land and buildings. These methods include depreciated replacement cost. We will consider these in the chapter on not-for-profit organisations.

❑ The **consistency convention** in accounting is particularly relevant to fixed assets and depreciation. It is possible to change a depreciation policy - say from straight line to reducing balance – but this is frowned upon and the change must be fully disclosed.

Self-testing questions

1. What is a fixed asset? Give examples.
2. What is capital expenditure? Give examples from your own household.
3. What are the causes of an asset having a limited life?
4. State three depreciation methods and illustrate them.
5. What is the formula for computing 'r' in the reducing balance method?
6. How is the depreciation of a fixed asset calculated in the year of disposal?
7. How do fixed assets appear in a balance sheet?
8. Define net book value.
9. What is the connection between (a) the matching convention and (b) the going concern convention, and the depreciation process?
10. What does SSAP 12 say about: the definition of fixed assets, the definition of depreciation, changes in economic lives of fixed assets, depreciation methods and changes therein, disclosure?

Exercises

1. Compute the annual depreciation for each year of life and the year end net book value for the following vehicles:

	Cost £	Estimated life years	Estimated salvage value £
1.	8,000	5	200
2.	16,000	4	5,000
3.	7,500	3	0
4.	14,300	5	2,800

under the:

(a) Straight line method.

(b) Reducing balance method.

(c) Sum of digits method.

Show the entries to be made in the Annual Accounts. (Assume all were acquired in 19x4 and the year end is 31 December.)

2. A machine was purchased on 1.7.x4 for £10,000. Depreciation policy is 20% on cost (assuming a nil salvage value).

Calculate the depreciation provisions in all years to 31 December 19x1 on the basis of:

(a) A full year's charge in 19x4.

(b) A half year's charge in 19x4.

and assuming (independently)

(a) The machine was sold on 31.5.x7 for £4,500.

(b) The machine was sold on 31.5.x7 for £2,600.

(c) The machine was sold on 31.12.x1 for £500.

(d) The machine was scrapped (no salvage) in 19x7.

3. Yucky Products Ltd acquires the following assets in 19x8:

(a) A piece of land next to its factory for £10,800.

(b) A factory extension built on the land. The extension is estimated to have a useful life of 30 years. The original factory has already been depreciated for 12 years of this estimated life. The cost of the extension was £70,000 plus architects' fees of £3,500.

(c) A leasehold warehouse in Darlaston with six years left on the lease. The cost of the lease was £4,000 plus legal fees £340. The annual rent is £400.

(d) A machine costing £16,000. The machine was purchased in July 19x8 and first used in October 19x8. Its estimated life is 10 years with a residual value of £2,000.

(e) A quarry in Shifnal for £62,000. The quarry contains about 600 tons of the rare mineral hedonite. In 19x8 the amount extracted was 30 tons. It is estimated that without the minerals the quarry would have cost only £2,000.

Yucky's year end is 31 December.

Required:

(a) Suggest suitable depreciation methods for each asset and calculate the 19x8 charge.

(b) What is an alternative phrase for 'acquires the following assets'?

4. What are the causes of limited life in the following assets:

A fork lift truck, a lease of a shop, a copper mine in Zambia, a freehold factory, a machine for making electronic devices, machinery in a gold mine in South Africa, a wind turbine in Northern Scotland, a patent to make an unusual kitchen appliance, the copyright in a celebrated textbook.

5. Complete the annual depreciation for each year and the year end carrying value for the following vehicles:

		Cost	Estimated life	Estimated salvage value
		£	years	£
1.		23,200	5	4,000
2.		6,000	3	1,200

...continued

	Cost	Estimated life	Estimated salvage value
	£	years	£
3.	7,200	9	50
4.	7,600	4	nil

under the:

(a)   Straight line method.

(b)   Reducing balance method.

(c)   Sum of digits method.

Show the entries in the accounts for 19x6, 19x7 and 19x8, assuming all were purchased in 19x6 and the year end is 31 December.

6.   Alf purchased two lorries:

	A.	June 30 19x9	17,100
	B.	Sept 23 19x9	16,300

He sold them:

	A.	on July 16 19x2 for	3,000
	B.	on Aug 24 19x3 for	8,400

Calculate depreciation and profit/loss on sale on the following separate assumptions:

(a)   Straight line depreciation over six years is used with nil salvage value and depreciation is calculated from the date of purchase and to the date of sale.

(b)   Reducing balance depreciation is used at 25% a year with a full year's charge in the year of purchase and no charge in the year of disposal. Year end is 31 December.

7.   Note that this question covers material from all the chapters up to here in the book.

From the following data relating to the businesses of Hogg, Pigg, and Bore, prepare trading and profit and loss accounts and balance sheets for the year ending 31 December 19x6:

	Hogg	Pigg	Bore
	£	£	£
Land at cost	20,000	30,000	16,000
Buildings at cost	39,000	67,000	50,000
Buildings depreciation to 31.12.x5	3,900	17,400	12,300
Equipment at cost	41,000	102,000	37,000
Equipment depreciation to 31.12.x5	12,700	32,900	22,000
Sales 112,500	243,000	190,000	
Equipment sold – proceeds of sale		1,700	7,000
Purchases	64,900	128,000	86,000
Stock 31.12.x5	12,430	12,900	14,900
Stock 31.12.x6	13,980	18,570	13,100
Wages	17,500	61,600	22,000
Trade debtors	23,100	32,000	38,000
Trade creditors	11,650	28,000	15,800
Rates and insurances	3,570	12,370	6,100
Other overheads	12,200	15,800	11,100
Loan from Hamm at 12%		10,000	
Interest paid		600	

	Hogg	Pigg	Bore
	£	£	£
Drawings	7,300	17,800	9,010
Capital at 31.12.x5	103,170	123,950	36,878
Cash introduced		8,000	
Rent received			2,400
Cash at bank	2,800		
Cash in hand	120	300	128
Bank overdraft		15,420	3,860

Notes:

For Hogg:

(a) Buildings are being depreciated over 30 years with no residual value.

(b) Equipment is depreciated on the reducing instalment method at 25% a year.

(c) Rates paid for the half year ending 31.3.x7 £1,100 were not included above and were paid on 5.1.x7.

(d) Fire insurance premium of £600 (included above) was for the year ending 30.4.x7.

(e) Other overheads do not include electricity for the period to 31.12.x6 (estimated at £1,430).

For Pigg:

(a) Buildings are being depreciated at 2% on cost, straight line.

(b) Equipment is depreciated at 20% on the reducing instalment method.

(c) Sales and debtors do not take into account the return of goods which were invoiced to Hugh at £900. The goods were not included in the above stock valuation and were worth only £100 at the year end.

(d) The equipment sold had cost £4,000 on 1 January 19x2. It is included (at 31.12.x5 figures) in the above figures for equipment and depreciation.

(e) There is a bonus due to the staff of £1,900 not included in the wages figure above.

(f) Insurances include the EL premium £1,600 which relates to the year ending 31.3.x7.

(g) The interest on the loan for the half year to 31.12.x6 had not been paid at year end.

(h) The drawings did not include a withdrawal of stock (held for resale) for private purposes in November 19x6. This stock had cost £1,300 and is included in purchases above.

For Bore:

(a) Buildings are being depreciated at 4% a year straight line.

(b) The Equipment is being depreciated at 25% reducing balance.

(c) The Equipment sold had cost £12,000 on 1 January 19x3. It is included in the Equipment and depreciation above as at 31.12.x5.

(d) The above figures do not include a purchase of equipment for £16,000, made in December 19x6 and paid for in February 19x7. It should receive a full year's depreciation in 19x6.

(e) There is a bonus due to the manager of 10% of the net profit (before charging the bonus) and a bonus of 5% of the gross profit due to the sales representative.

(f) Rates include rates for the half year ending 31.3.x7 £1,400.

(g) Rent received is for the rent of a spare piece of land.

(h) Overheads do not include the accountants fee for preparing the 19x6 Accounts £600.

Assignment

☐ Davina started in business on 1 January 19x7 as a wholesaler of frozen foods. She buys on credit from a few manufacturers and sells, also on credit, to retailers, hotels etc. She requested overdraft facilities from the Border Bank and, for them, produced the following cash flow and profit forecast:

Cash flow forecast:

Quarter	March	June	September	December
Inflows:				
From customers	10,000	25,000	25,000	25,000
Capital introduced	15,000			
Total	25,000	25,000	25,000	25,000
Outflows:				
Van	10,000			
Equipment	8,500		4,000	
Furniture etc	2,600			
Rent	1,400	1,400	1,400	1,400
Rates and insurances	2,700	1,500		1,500
Wages	1,000	1,000	1,000	1,000
Other overheads	2,500	3,000	2,600	2,600
Drawings	900	900	900	900
Suppliers	15,000	15,000	15,000	15,000
Total	44,600	22,800	24,900	22,400
Balance b/f	–	(19,600)	(17,400)	(17,300)
Balance c/f	(19,600)	(17,400)	(17,300)	(14,700)

The Profit Forecast was:

Sales		106,000
Purchases	65,000	
Closing stock	12,000	53,000
Gross Profit		53,000
Rent	5,600	
Rates	3,000	
Insurances	2,700	
Wages	4,000	
Other overheads	10,700	
Depreciation	5,000	31,000
Net Profit		22,000

The Bank was impressed and granted facilities to overdraw up to £25,000.

At the end of the first year, the figures collected were:

Sales	101,000	Wages	6,000
Purchases	73,000	Other overheads	9,400
Closing stock	17,000	Drawings	6,800
Van	11,500	Debtors	22,000
Equipment	13,000	Trade creditors	15,700
Furniture	2,400	Bank overdraft	24,450
Rent	5,600	Rates	3,400
Insurances	3,050	Capital introduced	15,000

Some further information is necessary to prepare the financial statements and this is:

(a) Rates includes £1,400 which is the business rate for the half year up to 31 March 19x8.

(b) In December 19x7, goods were invoiced at £850 to the Hotel Splendide. This invoice was included in the sales and debtors above. These proved to be bad and Davina agreed to issue a credit note for half the amount and to supply free replacement goods costing her £300. Both these things were done in January 19x8.

(c) Electricity accrued due at 31 December 19x7 was estimated at £204.

(d) The estimated economic lives and salvage values of the fixed assets are:

   (i) Van : three years and £3,000.

   (ii) Equipment: five years and £1,000.

   (iii)Furniture: ten years and £1,000.

Required:

(a) Prepare trading and profit and loss account for the year ending 31 December 19x7 and balance sheet as at that date. You should prepare this in good form showing all workings on separate schedules. You should select suitable depreciation policies and state the policies chosen. (40%).

(b) Write a short report on the accounting conventions used, how they are manifested in your financial statements and what alternatives might exist to the conventions and how these would affect your financial statements. (20%).

(c) Write a report on the year's activities. This should include commentaries on the actual events compared with the forecasts. (40%).

6 Bookkeeping

This chapter introduces the subject of bookkeeping. All the transactions of a business are recorded using a bookkeeping system. They are summarised into financial statements at least annually. The process is as follows:

(a) Transactions take place (e.g. sales, purchases, receipts, payments).

(b) Documents evidencing the transactions are created (invoices, cheque stubs, etc).

(c) Entries are made in the books of account.

(d) Year end adjustments are made.

(e) Production of financial statements.

The process of entering the details of transactions in the books of account is known as book-keeping. Bookkeeping is done in a formal manner using the method known as double entry book-keeping. We start with the objectives and go on to the entries for sales and purchases. Next we deal with the entries for expenses. And finally, we look at bookkeeping and accounting using computerised methods.

Objectives of double entry bookkeeping

1. The method of bookkeeping known as double entry bookkeeping is practised worldwide and has a long history. This chapter outlines the purposes served by bookkeeping, explores its origins, begins your study of how it is done and concludes with a note on the involvement of computers in bookkeeping.

Bookkeeping fulfils needs

2. The following are the objectives of keeping books of accounts:

(a) A permanent record is made of all transactions.

(b) Management have a continuous record of debtors (who owe the business money) and creditors (who the business owes money to).

(c) Management can control and safeguard the business assets (fixed assets, cash at bank, etc).

(d) Managers have *information*, without which management would be impossible.

(e) The law requires certain records – PAYE, VAT, Statutory Sick Pay – for all businesses. Companies are required to maintain certain specified records.

(f) Failure to maintain records can be an offence in bankruptcy or liquidation.

(g) Records are essential for the production of financial statements.

Luca Pacioli and the Italian method

3. Double entry bookkeeping developed gradually in Italy in the years after about 1200 AD. By the end of the fifteenth century the method was well established and in 1494 an Italian monk and mathematician Fra Luca Pacioli published a great work on mathematics. One of the sections of this book was a treatise on double entry bookkeeping which is the oldest surviving text book on accounting. It is available in English translation in several versions and I commend it to you. There have been developments since 1494 but in essence the method is still used today.

4. Pacioli is especially good at disciplining his readers in making entries so that they can avoid errors. He includes a chapter summarising the rules. Among them are:

    (a) All entries must be double, that is if you make one creditor you must make one debtor.

    (b) Each entry in the debit or in the credit must contain three things; viz. the day of the payment, the amount of the payment and the reason for the entry.

    These are examples of his very simple instructions. Bookkeepers have failed to keep them for five centuries.

Debit and credit

5. The essence of the double entry method is:

    (a) The keeping of a book or a series of books called the books of account or simply 'the books'.

    (b) The division of each book into separate 'accounts'. Account is another word for *story*. A separate account is required for each subject on which a record is to be kept.

    (c) Each account is divided into two halves, a left-hand side called the debit (abbreviated to Dr) and a right-hand side called the credit (Cr). It is advisable to memorise, now, which side is which.

    (d) All transactions are entered on *two* accounts (hence double entry); on the debit side of one account and the credit side of another.

Computerised records

6. Bookkeeping has traditionally been carried out by bookkeepers in bound books of good quality paper. However, bookkeeping is a tedious process and the costs of the skilled labour required for a complete set of records has become very high. Various devices were developed to mechanise the process including accounting machines and punched card machines.

7. The invention of the computer and especially the cheap micro computer has brought automated bookkeeping within the financial means of almost all businesses. It has been suggested that the existence of cheap hardware (the actual machines) and software packages (the computer programs) will make the accountant and the bookkeeper redundant. This is unlikely to be so because:

    (a) The computer has not changed the fundamentals of bookkeeping, only the method of processing and the media on which the information is stored. A ledger account recorded on a hard disk is still a ledger account.

    (b) Using and interpreting the information recorded in the 'books' requires a technical knowledge of the processes and organisation of bookkeeping information. This knowledge is not usually held by computer people.

    (c) Bookkeeping is not an end in itself but a means to an end (or several ends). The bookkeeper and accountant use the information in their work. For example, the chasing of slow payers is still required whatever medium is used for bookkeeping.

8. Bookkeeping is usually done using proprietary software such as Sagesoft or Pegasus. Many colleges have Sagesoft in their computer laboratories and many of the exercises in this book can be carried out using Sagesoft software. They can usually be carried out on other accounting software so not having Sagesoft specifically should not preclude you from trying out computerised bookkeeping.

Bookkeeping for sales and purchases

9. In a double entry bookkeeping system it is not feasible to maintain an account called 'stock' in which all inputs and outputs of stock are entered with a balance which shows the total stock on hand at cost. This is because the account would need to record outputs (sales) at cost price and too much labour would be required to determine this for each sale.

If it is necessary to record stock quantities for each category of stock this is done *outside* the bookkeeping system. This is known as *continuous* or *perpetual* inventory.

In order to prepare the trading account a total of sales is required and this is accumulated in an account called 'sales account'.

Debits and credits

10. Sales, both cash *and* credit, are entered on the *credit* side of the sales account.

For every entry on the credit (right hand) side of the sales account, there has to be an equal and opposite entry on the debit (left hand) side of another (or in some cases the same) account. So, for each sale entered on the Cr of Sales Account there must be a Dr on another Account. Usually this will be:

Sales for cash or other immediate payment   – Dr the Cash Book (see Chapter 2)
Sales on Credit   – Dr the Account of the Customer

The easiest way to appreciate these entries is to see an example. Fundamentally, the only way to learn bookkeeping is endless practice. I found it very hard to learn but one day, after a lot of practice, the penny dropped and I understood the whole thing. Once learned, it is probably never forgotten!

Here are some transactions of Fringe Ltd, dealers in widgets:

Jan 1 Sold Widgets on credit to Alma	£278
Jan 2 Sold Widgets on credit to Brown	£598
Jan 3 Sold Widgets on credit to Crown	£190

All sales are subject to Value Added Tax (VAT) at standard rate. This means that the Invoice is sent to Alma showing the sum due as £278.00 + VAT at 17.5% £48.65. This is a total due from Alma of £326.65. When Alma pays the £326.65 to Fringe Ltd, then £278.00 belongs to Fringe but £48.65 belongs to Customs and Excise (a government tax collecting department). Fringe will pay the whole cheque into their bank account but will later pay over the sum due to the Customs and Excise. Double entries are:

	Alma			Sales	
Dr		Cr	Dr		Cr
Jan 1 Invoice 326.65		*	*	Jan 1 Alma 278.00	
				Jan 2 Brown 598.00	
				Jan 3 Crown 190.00	

* There are no entries yet on the Cr. of Alma or on the Dr. of Sales

	Brown			Crown	
Dr		Cr	Dr		Cr
Jan 2 Invoice 702.65				Jan 3 Invoice 223.25	

	Customs & excise	
Dr		Cr
		Jan 1 Invoice 48.65
		Jan 2 Invoice 104.65
		Jan 3 Invoice 33.25

Note: Each entry has a description or narration e.g. invoice or Alma. Many bookkeepers use the words 'goods' or 'invoice' instead of 'sales' or 'purchases'. The important thing is that the nature of the transaction should be clear.

11. Follow the entries for each transaction and note:

   (a) For each debit there is a credit and vice versa.

   (b) The debit of each transaction is entered in a customer account.

   (c) The credit is split between the Sales Account (for the net amount of the sale) and Customs and Excise Account (for the VAT added).

Meaning of each account

12. (a) The accounts of the customers (Alma etc) have entries on the debit side of sales made. It is now possible to look at each of these accounts and see the amounts owing – Alma owes £326.65 etc. It is clearly desirable for Fringe Ltd to know who owes money and how much. These accounts fulfil that need. Also the total owing by all debtors is information needed to draw up a balance sheet. you will remember that current assets has a slot for debtors. You may have already connected the fact that customer balances are on the debit with the description – debtors.

   (b) The account 'Sales' has three entries all on the credit. We can now see that the total of this account (£1,066.00) represents the total of sales made in the period. This represents useful information, Managers like to know the amount of sales as they can compare the figure with previous periods and reassure themselves that all is well (or know that all is not well and special measures are necessary). You will also remember that the trading account has an entry for sales. The sales account collects the information for this entry.

   (c) The account Customs and Excise shows the amount owing to the Customs and Excise for VAT as a result of the sales. Operationally, managers need to know how much is owing to Customs and Excise to complete the periodic **VAT Return** (sent to Customs and Excise) and to make payment. The item is also a creditor (a sum owing) which is included in creditors on the balance sheet.

Payment and returns

13. Brown paid the amount owing on 9 January. Payment was in the form of a cheque which Fringe Ltd paid into its bank account. Suppose that the goods sold to Alma were unsatisfactory. Fringe Ltd accepted them back and sent, on 8 January, a credit note to Alma for £326.65.

    Entries for these transaction will be:

Alma			**Sales**		
Dr	Cr	Dr			Cr
Jan 1 Invoice 326.65	Jan 8 Credit 326.65 note	Jan 8 Alma 278.00	Jan 3 Total 1,066.00		

Brown			**Cash Book**		
Dr	Cr	Dr			Cr
Jan 2 Invoice 702.65	Jan 9 Cheque 702.65	Jan 9 Brown 702.65			

We can now inspect the accounts and see that the debits and credits on Alma's account are now equal. This indicates correctly that Alma now owes nothing (because the goods were returned to Fringe). Similarly with Brown (because Brown has paid). Sales now has £278.00 on the debit and £1,066 on the credit. We say that the balance of the account is £788.00. This is correct as the actual sales which have 'stuck' are those to Alma (who has now paid) and to Crown (who will pay soon). The debit in the cash book is the entry of a receipt (among many) on the debit side – see Chapter 2. The VAT on the credit note is debited on the Customs and Excise Account.

Purchases

14. Entries of purchases on credit from suppliers are on the opposite sides from those of sales:

    Purchase on Credit from Davis: Debit – Purchases Account with Net Purchase
                    – Customs and Excise with VAT portion
                Credit – Davis Account with Net Purchase + VAT

    Payment to Davis: Debit – Davis Account
                 Credit – Cash Book

    The amounts of VAT suffered on purchase invoices is recoverable from Customs and Excise.

Sales and purchases not on credit

15. Not all sales and purchases are made on credit. In such cases the whole transaction would be recorded in one go as:

    Sale to Edwin who pays immediately:

              Debit – Cash Book with payment (Net + VAT)
               Credit – Sales Account (net amount of sale)
                – Customs and Excise (with the VAT)

    Purchase of goods with payment by cheque immediately:

Debit – Purchase Account (Net amount of purchase)

– Customs and Excise (VAT)

Credit – Cash Book (payment, being Net + VAT)

Balancing accounts

16. Suppose that Fringe Ltd continues to sell goods on credit to Alma and several hundred invoices are sent in the year. There will also be some credit notes and many payments by Alma. At any time the balance owing can be calculated by adding up both sides and finding the difference. However this can be cumbersome so generally balances are taken at intervals like this:

Dr			Alma			Cr
Feb 1	Invoice	235.90		Feb 16	Credit note	101.00
Feb 8	Invoice	145.78		Feb 29	Balance c/d	747.88
Feb 10	Invoice	467.20				
		848.88				848.88
Mar 1	Balance b/d	747.88		Mar 14	Cheque	381.68
Mar 13	Invoice	327.87				
Mar 19	Invoice	222.43		Mar 31	Balance c/d	916.50
		1,298.18				1,298.18
Apr 1	Balance b/d	916.50				

VAT

17. You have now learned that there is an account for Customs and Excise which shows the amount due (VAT on sales) to Customs and Excise and the amount due from them (VAT suffered on purchases). On the credit side there is the amount due to Customs and Excise and on the debit side, amounts due from Customs and Excise. It would be possible to make a cheque out to Customs for the sum payable and to receive a cheque from Customs for the sum receivable. In practice the two totals are netted off and a cheque for the difference is passed.

Daybooks and journals

18. In modern bookkeeping systems all accounts are kept on hard disks (or perhaps floppies). However, some systems are still manual. Manual systems have a quantity problem – too many entries for one book. This problem is solved by having separate books as:

Cash Book: there are numerous receipts and payments so they require a separate book

Sales Ledger: in here are entered all the accounts of customers

Purchase Ledger: in here are entered all the accounts of suppliers

Nominal Ledger: in here are kept all other accounts (including the Sales Account, the Purchases Account and the Customs and Excise Account).

This partially solves the problem. However the entries on the sales, purchases, and Customs and Excise accounts are also numerous and would take too many pages. The solution to this problem is to enter the sales and purchases in separate books called daybooks or journals like this:

Sales daybook

Date	Invoice number	Customer name	Folio	Net	VAT	Gross
May 4	100	Wilkes Ltd	W14	126.89	22.20	149.09
May 10	101	Hafeez	H12	239.34	41.88	281.22
May 21	102	Penny Bros	P06	670.00	117.25	787.25
Total for May				1,036.23	181.33	1217.56

These books are seen as memorandum and are not part of the double entry. The actual double entry is effected by entering £1,036.23 on the credit of sales account, £181.33 on the credit of Customs and Excise account and £126.89 on the debit of Wilkes Ltd's account in the sales ledger, £239.34 on the debit of Hafeez's account and similar for Penny Bros. Of course, there may be many more invoices than the three shown in the example. You will see that the sales daybook becomes a detailed record of sales made with lots of entries. Each sale has an entry on a customer's account in the sales ledger. The actual entries in the sales account, purchases account and Customs and Excise account are relatively few since they are totals only. Thus they do not fill up the nominal ledger with unnecessary detail. The detail is however available, if required, in the daybooks.

The rulings for a purchase daybook are exactly the same as the sales daybook and the double entries are:

Debit: Purchases Account: with total of net purchases column
       Customs and Excise Account: with total of VAT column
Credit: Individual supplier Accounts: amount (net + VAT) of individual purchases

Returns

19. When sales are made, invoices are made out and sent to the customers. Sometimes the goods are faulty and are then returned by the customer. The practice is not to cancel the invoice, but to issue a credit note. Credit notes are entered in a journal or daybook called the sales returns daybook with rulings much as the sales daybook. Entries in the double entry system are the reverse (= on the opposite side) of those for sales. Reasons for credit notes can be: return of goods, adjustment of prices or quantities, non-arrival of the goods etc. Purchases returns are treated in the same way with a separate book and with double entries which are the reverse of purchases.

Trading and profit and loss account

20. We have seen that the objective of having sales and purchases accounts is to gather the information on total sales and purchases for the purposes of preparing the trading and profit and loss account.

At the end of the financial year of Wenlock Ltd, the sales account looked like this:

Sales

Dr   Cr

Dec 31 Invoices	364,800
Dec 31 Cash sales	132,300

The system is that Wenlock Ltd keeps a sales daybook and enters all credit sales invoice details in it. The total of these is added up at the end of the year and an entry made in the sales account. Cash sales are entered in the cash book as a daily total and the total for the year is entered in the sales account as one figure. Note that these figures are net of VAT.

Now that the trading and profit and loss account is being prepared the total is transferred into the trading account like this:

Sales

Dr			Cr
Dec 31 Trading account	497,100	Dec 31 Invoices	364,800
		Dec 31 Cash sales	132,300
	497,100		497,100

The consequences of this entry is:

(a) The completion of the double entry for £497,100 is an entry in the trading account **which is a double entry account**.

(b) The sales account now has a nil balance – it is empty. It is now available for accumulation of the sales of next year.

The entries for purchases account are similar but opposite.

Bookkeeping for expenses

21. So far in this chapter, you have learned how to make entries for sales and purchases on credit and for cash. Now we can look at expenses.

The profit and loss account categorises the expenses into suitable and informative headings. For example: Wages, Rent, Rates, Insurances, Motor expenses, Electricity, Stationery, Advertising. The actual headings used vary from firm to firm. Some might have separate headings for Rent and for Rates. Some might combine them as Rent and Rates. The classification adopted is a matter of taste or policy but should be informative and useful in the circumstances.

The data for the profit and loss account comes from the double entry system. The system must have individual accounts in the nominal ledger for each expense heading. For example there may be an account for Wages, an account for Rent, an account for Interest etc.

Bookkeeping procedures – expenses

22. Procedures are:

(a) Determine what expense headings (rent, sales, heat and light etc) are to be used.

(b) Open accounts in the ledger under each expense heading in the form:

Dr			Repairs to equipment		Cr
Date	Details	£	Date	Details	£

(c) Enter details of incoming invoices for supplies and services into the appropriate account, e.g.

Dr		Printing and Stationery	Cr
19x5		£	
Jan 15	Philip – Letterheads	200	
Apr 19	Quintin – Posters	152	
July 24	Roger – Envelopes	181	
Nov 8	Steve – Sundry	63	
Dec 4	Cash*	102	
		698	

Notes:

(i) Entries on expense accounts are made on the debit side.

(ii) The double entry is completed by crediting the accounts of the suppliers (Philip, Quintin etc), or if the supply was not on credit, the cash book (as item starred).

(iii) The total expenditure in the year is determinable by totalling the account.

Bookkeeping procedures – revenues

23. Procedures are:

(a) Determine what revenue headings are required. There are unlikely to be many – perhaps:

(i) Rent receivable.

(ii) Interest receivable.

(iii) Dividends from investments.

(b) Open accounts for each in the same manner as for expenses.

(c) Enter details of revenues as they accrue or are received in the appropriate accounts as:

Dr		Rent Receivable		Cr
		19x5		£
		Jan 19	Rent due from Tom	80
		Mar 14	Cash	20
		June 30	Rent due from Una	104
		Nov 8	Rent due from Tom	80
				284

Notes:

(i) Revenues are entered on the credit side.

(ii) Double entry is completed by debiting the cash book (e.g. the 14 March item) or the account of Tom or Una.

(iii) The total revenue in the year is determinable by totalling the account.

Year-end procedures

24. During the year 19x5, the following expenditures have occurred:

Dr		Insurance	Cr
19x5		£	
Jan 15	Fire – year to 31.12.x5	620	
Mar 18	Burglary – year to 31.3.x6	428	
May 24	E.L. to 31.5x6	710	
July 19	P.L. to 31.7.x6	464	
		2,222	

Note:

E.L. = Employer's liability.

P.L. = Public liability (insuring against risk of paying damages for injury caused to a member of the public).

25. Procedures are:

(a) Review the expenditures to see if any relate to 19x6.
The following do so:

Burglary	1.1.-6 – 31.3.x6	$\frac{3}{12} \times 428 =$	107
E.L.	1.1.-6 – 31.5.x6	$\frac{5}{12} \times 710 =$	296
P.L.	1.1.-6 – 31.7.x6	$\frac{7}{12} \times 464 =$	271
			674

This total is a prepayment and must be taken out of the account. This is accomplished by *crediting* as prepayment c/d and debiting the account in the next period as prepayment b/d.

(b) Consider if there are any unpaid insurances. Suppose that a special short period insurance cover for an explosion risk was negotiated for the Christmas 19x5 period. This was paid for in January 19x6 and cost £30. This is an *accrual* and should be *added* to the other expenditures by debiting the account as an accrual c/d. This is entered on the *credit* of the account in the next period – 19x6.

(c) The balance of the account now represents the total cost of insurance cover for the 12 months ending 31 December 19x5. Double entry is:

> **Credit:** Insurance Account
> **Debit:** Profit and Loss Account

	£
The total is: Fire	620
Burglary $\frac{9}{12} \times 428$	321
E.L. $\frac{7}{12} \times 710$	414

... continued

	£
P.L. $\frac{5}{12} \times 464$	193
Explosion	30
	1,578

(d) The account will appear as:

		£			£
	Balance as above (para 6)	2,222	31.12.x5	Prepayment c/d	674
31.12.x5	Accrual c/d	30	31.12.x5	Profit and loss account	1,578
		2,252			2,252
1.1.x6	Prepayment b/d	674	1.1.x6	Accrual b/d	30

Note:

The prepayment and the accrual will appear in the balance sheet at 31.12.x5 in current assets, and current liabilities respectively.

Book of prime entry

26. The nominal ledger will contain many expense accounts. The actual number depends on how many classifications of overheads are needed for the profit and loss account. Probably the number will be somewhere between 8 and 20. In some accounts, the number of entries would be very large if every invoice was entered individually. In order to keep the number of entries down to a few a year in each account a book of prime entry called the expense journal or expense daybook is used. A typical ruling might be:

Expense Daybook

Date	Supplier	Invoice number	Gross	VAT	Heat & Light	Motor expenses	Rent & Rates
Jan 2	AB Estates	100	500.00				500.00
Jan 4	Electricity Board	101	234.56	34.93	199.63		
Jan 5	CD Garages	102	429.00	63.89		365.11	
Jan 12	Wem Council	103	700.00				700.00
Jan 18	Duff Petrol	104	361.37	53.82		307.55	
			2,224.93	152.64	199.63	672.66	1,200.00

Notes:

(a) The expense daybook is a book of prime entry. Entries in it are not part of the double entry.

(b) The double entry is achieved by:

Debit: Expense accounts in the nominal ledger with column totals (£199.63 to £1,200.00).

Customs and Excise with VAT column total.

Credit: Individual supplier accounts (AB Estates etc) in the purchase ledger with amounts payable (£500 etc).

(c) You will see that some of the invoices do not include VAT. This is because some products and services are not subject to VAT. Some supplies are exempt – insurance, education, health services etc, and some are zero rated – food, books, children's clothing etc.

(d) I have shown five invoices. In practice there will be many more.

(e) The invoice numbers are not those put on by the supplier. The numbers need to be put on by the bookkeeper. They are necessary for reference purposes – to look up the actual invoice if it has been filed away.

(f) Some daybooks will have a column for the net amount of the invoice. Then the Net + VAT column totals will equal (hopefully) the Gross column total. The expense column totals will sum to the Net column total. It is important to check that the column totals cross-cast to the Total column.

Combined purchase and expense daybooks

27. You may have realised that the expense daybook is very like the purchase daybook that you met in the last section. The expense daybook just has more columns. It is possible to buy very wide books with numerous columns from stationers. Many bookkeeping systems do not have separate expense and purchase daybooks but combine them in one. Possible column headings might be:

Date   Supplier   Number   Gross   VAT   Net   Purchases   Motor expenses   Insurance

+ as many expense columns as are needed!

Computerised accounting

28. Bookkeeping has been done in books of account for centuries. It still is for many small businesses. I am treasurer of a small charity and keep the books (actually, just one book – a cash book) using a biro. I have tried using a computerised system (Money Manager) but found it took longer to make the entries on the computer than to write up a book manually. The computer system had the advantage of automatic production of reports and accounts but I can do these by hand quickly if there are only a few entries. However, if the number of entries were greater, the balance of advantage begins to lie with the computer.

In the last few decades, mechanical systems were used and then punched card systems. These worked well but the computer is now the universal method once the volume/contents have made manual methods too slow and cumbersome.

There are many systems on the market and it is possible to design bespoke systems for particular businesses. Most systems follow the normal rules of double entry and it must be emphasised that computerised accounting is just double entry bookkeeping and financial accounting done by computer. To be an effective bookkeeper or accountant using computer software needs just as much knowledge as doing it by hand.

Computerised systems

29. Most systems offer the following:
    (a) Details of products sold with prices so that a price list can be automatically produced.
    (b) Facilities for storing details of credit customers and producing lists thereof.
    (c) Facilities for creating and printing invoices using details of quantities of products sold and customer details.
    (d) Facilities for creating and printing credit notes.
    (e) Facilities for entering sales invoices and credit notes in customers' accounts.
    (f) Facilities for printing statements of account.
    (g) Details of suppliers on credit.
    (h) Facilities for entering suppliers' invoices and credit notes and automatic entry of these on suppliers' accounts.
    (i) Facilities for recording bank accounts.
    (j) Facilities for entering credit customer payments and payments to credit suppliers, all with discounts, where given or taken.
    (k) Nominal accounts (fixed assets, loans, capital, profit and loss accounts etc).
    (l) Facilities for entering non-credit receipts (e.g. cash sales, loans etc) and non-credit payments (wages, salaries, repayment of loans etc).
    (m) Automatic calculation of VAT at various rates and production of the VAT return.
    (n) Production of the financial statements after journalising closing entries.
    (o) Production of all manner of lists, returns and reports such as aged lists of debtors and creditors.
    (p) Customising stationery such as letters to customers, statements and invoices.
    (q) Facilities for reconciling the cash book with the bank statements.

    Some systems also offer stock control with information on stock levels and reports on movements, order processing, and management accounting reports. Payroll and job costing can also be included.

Learning how to use computerised systems

30. The easiest way to learn computerised bookkeeping is:
    (a) Master double entry for use in manual systems
    (b) Explore the computer system by reading the manual and making trial entries. Modern systems are very user friendly and the use of prompts makes it all very easy. All entries can be set up and altered until they are right and then be saved. Entries can be abandoned at any stage and can also be deleted.

    Many people try to learn computerised bookkeeping without knowing double entry. This is possible but difficult. Double entry bookkeeping is a simple but profound and subtle method. It cannot be learned easily but only by careful and systematic study and much practice.

31. In the exercises to this section is an exercise suited to computerised accounting and I have included some instructions. The methods vary from system to system and

the best way is to explore the system in a hands-on manner. Computer buffs enjoy exploring new programmes and most are so complex that new discoveries can be made for a very long time. The exercise is continued in Chapter 9. The other exercises in this chapter can also be executed on a computer system.

Summary

❏ Bookkeeping fulfils several business needs. It is also a statutory requirement in many cases.

❏ Double entry bookkeeping developed in Renaissance Italy. The earliest surviving text book is that of Luca Pacioli published in 1494.

❏ The essence of bookkeeping is the entering of the details of transactions in separate accounts. Each account is in effect a story about some relevant subject – an asset, a liability, an expense, a revenue etc.

❏ Accounts have two sides – a debit on the left and credit on the right.

❏ 'Books' are now frequently kept by computers with the information stored on magnetic disks. This changes the processes and storage media but has left bookkeeping unchanged in its essence.

❏ Double entry bookkeeping records sales and purchases on credit.

	Debit	Credit	With
Sales	Customers		Gross
		Sales A/c	Net
		Customs	VAT
Purchases	Purchases A/c		Net
		Customs	VAT
		Suppliers	Gross

❏ Sales and Purchases can be made for immediate settlement. Most retail sales are like this. The double entry then is simply:

Debit:	Cash Book	with	Gross amount
Credit:	Sales A/c	with	Net amount
	Customs	with	VAT

Purchases are similar but on the opposite sides.

❏ Accounts can be balanced off at intervals. In such cases the balance is entered on one side in the old period and on the opposite side in the new period. The totals of both sides should be equal once the balance has been entered.

❏ The Customs and Excise account shows the amounts due to and from this tax collecting department. It is normally settled quarterly by a single cheque either way.

❏ In manual systems, the bookkeeping system double entry accounts are not kept in a single book but the accounts are divided up into: cash book, sales ledger for customers' accounts, purchase ledger for suppliers' accounts, nominal ledger for all other accounts. Sales and purchase invoice details are usually entered first in special books called daybooks or journals. These are called books of **Prime entry**. Entries are made in the system proper from the daybooks.

❏ Credit notes are treated by entries on the opposite sides to the original invoices.

❏ At year ends, balances on sales and purchases accounts are transferred to the trading account, which is a double entry account.

❏ Expense accounts in a double entry system are used to collect the data required of total analysed expenses for entry in the annual profit and loss account.

❏ Entries are made on the debit with double entry completed in the credits of accounts of suppliers or by a credit in the cash book.

❏ Revenue accounts are similar but are entered on the credit side.

❏ At the year end, accruals are added on the debit and prepayments are deducted by entry on the credit. The double entry is completed by entries in the same account in the next period.

❏ At the financial year (or perhaps shorter intervals) end the expense accounts are balanced off and a transfer made to profit and loss account of the expense of the year.

❏ Expense invoices are normally collected together, given a consecutive number and entered in an expense daybook.

❏ In practice the expense daybook and the purchase daybook are combined. This is often simply called the purchase daybook.

❏ Computerised bookkeeping and accounting is now cheap enough for virtually all firms. Some systems have so few entries that manual methods may remain the best option.

❏ The best way to learn computerised systems is to master manual systems first.

Points to note

❏ A book in which double entry accounts are kept is called a ledger. The accounts themselves are sometimes called ledger accounts.

❏ If double entry accounts are maintained on a computer, the expressions accounts, ledgers, books are still used.

❏ The only way to learn double entry bookkeeping is practice.

❏ Short cuts and slightly different approaches are common in practice.

❏ Terminology varies. Some people make entries. Some people make **postings**. The nominal ledger is sometimes called the general ledger or the private ledger. The purchase ledger and daybook are sometimes styled the bought ledger and daybook.

❏ When an account has a balance, it must have some meaning. Make sure you can see what the meaning is.

❏ Every account has some connection with the balance sheet or profit and loss account. For example the sales account balance is the total needed for the trading account. The cash book balance is entered in the current assets section of the balance sheet and the total of suppliers' accounts is entered as creditors in the current liabilities section of the balance sheet.

❏ Entries need some form (usually very short e.g. one word) of **narration**. Practice varies but the name of the account with the double entry completion may be given and is usually satisfactory.

❏ VAT on sales is commonly called output tax. VAT on purchases is commonly called input tax.

❏ An account is filled up, say with the rent and rates, of 19x4. It must then be emptied so that the account is free to accept 19x5 items. If this was not done, then the total rent and rates would accumulate for ever. The emptying is done by crediting the account with 'profit and loss account £x' and completing the double entry in the profit and loss account.

❏ The purchase and expense daybook is only used for incoming supplies of goods or services **on credit**. The double entry is Dr: purchases account or an expense account, Cr: the Account of the supplier. Some services and goods are supplied against immediate payment. Examples are wages and bank interest. The double entry for these is simply Cr: Cash Book and Dr : Expense Account – Wages or Interest etc.

❏ A VAT column has been included in the daybook in this section as VAT is a reality for all but the smallest businesses. Note that the net cost of the good or service is entered in the purchases or an expense account and the VAT is debited to the Customs and Excise account. The gross amount (net + VAT) is entered in the supplier account because that is what is payable to the supplier.

❏ Students find bookkeeping for expenses difficult. Practice is the only way to learn it!

❏ The whole purpose of having expense accounts in the system is to gather together the information required for entries in the profit and loss account. Note that the profit and loss account is itself a double entry account.

❏ Hands-on exploration with constant reference to the manual is the best way to learn computerised bookkeeping. This is true of all computer software.

Self-testing questions

1. List the objectives of bookkeeping.
2. What may be the effect of computers on bookkeepers and accountants?
3. What is:
   (i) An account?
   (ii) A ledger?
   (iii) The debit side?
4. Why will computerisation not make accountants obsolete?
5. What are the 'books'?
6. Why are sales and purchases of stock not recorded in a stock account?

7.   What information is conveyed by the balances on sales and purchases accounts? How are these balances used in preparing the trading and profit and loss account?

8.   Give the entries for cash sales.

9.   Give the entries for sales on credit.

10. What is the meaning of balances on a sales account, a customer's account, a supplier's account, purchases account, Customs and Excise account, cash book?

11. Give the entries for the payment of a supplier's account and a customer's account.

12. Give the entries for purchases on credit.

13. Show how an account can be balanced off.

14. How is the amount due to or from Customs and Excise settled?

15. State how a manual bookkeeping system is divided up into separate ledgers.

16. What is the function of daybooks? Draw up a ruling and make some entries.

17. How are credit notes entered into books of prime entry and the double entry system proper?

18. Show how sales and purchases accounts are closed off at the year end.

19. On which side of an expense account are the expenses incurred entered?

20. What is the function of an expense account?

21. Summarise the year end procedure re an expense account.

22. What is the purpose of the entry 'transfer to profit and loss account' in an expense account?

23. What revenue accounts may be required?

24. State the relationship between an daybook and the actual double entry accounts.

25. Give column headings for a combined purchase and expense daybook.

Exercises

1.   Ognir Ltd trades as a music publisher. The company buys from printers and other suppliers on credit and sells to retailers also on credit. Payment of royalties is made to each composer on a quarterly basis based on sales of that composer's music in that quarter. The company trades on an overdraft and needs to monitor the amount closely. The company is registered for VAT and employs five staff. The company monitors the sales of each composer's work and has continuously to make decisions on whether or not to reprint or to publish new and existing composers.

The books are kept by a part-qualified trainee certified accountant. The directors are considering making him redundant, buying a computer and appointing a computer operator with no knowledge of bookkeeping or accounting to maintain the computerised records.

Why is it necessary for the company to maintain good double entry records? How can the current bookkeeper argue to keep his job if a computer is installed?

2.   Dave is setting up a business wholesaling widgets. He will employ five workers and have a bank overdraft facility of £5,000.

Explain to Dave why he will need comprehensive double entry records.

3.   Phil, a manufacturer, is considering using a computer with some accounting packages to do his bookkeeping. He reckons that by using a computer, he can use a person who

has only office skills and some moderate typing ability and thus not employ a more expensive person with a knowledge of bookkeeping and accounting. Is he right?

4. Locate a copy of Luca Pacioli's great work and read some or all of it.

5. Frank is in business as a supplier of proprietary software selling and buying on credit with occasional cash sales and purchases. He is registered for VAT.

At the beginning of 19x5, he had the following balances (among others) in his books:

Customers:	Alf Jones	£236.87
	Tom Williams	£348.90
	Ted Evans	£1,703.32
Suppliers:	Hugh Fraser	£12.90
	Neil McLeod	£2,700.32
	Ian Scott	£324.00
Cash in Mercian Bank		£560.61
Due to Customs and Excise		£3,900.20

In January 19x5, he had the following transactions:

Sales:	Jan 12	Alf Jones	£640.00 + VAT
	Jan 20	Tom Williams	£230.00 + VAT
	Jan 23	Ted Evans	£600.00 + VAT
	Jan 27	Alf Jones	£210.00 + VAT
Purchases:	Jan 4	Hugh Fraser	£270.00 (inc VAT)
	Jan 7	Ian Scott	£700.00 (inc VAT)
	Jan 24	Hugh Fraser	£600.00 (inc VAT)
Returns:	Jan 13	A credit note was issued to Alf Jones for £32 + VAT	
	Jan 19	A credit note was received from Ian Scott for £105.00 + VAT	
Receipts:	Jan 18	Alf Jones	£236.87
	Jan 20	Cash Sales	£107.00 (including VAT)
	Jan 30	Tom Williams	£100.00
Payments:	Jan 9	VAT	£3,900.20
	Jan 10	Ian Scott	£324.00
	Jan 17	Cash Purchases	£100.00 (including VAT)

Required:

(a) Set up ledger accounts (including the cash book) and enter the opening balances.

(b) Enter the details in books of prime entry – cash book, sales daybook, purchases daybook.

(c) Enter (post) the details into the ledger accounts (customers, suppliers, customs and excise, sales, purchases).

VAT will have to be calculated. It is at the rate of 17.5%. To calculate VAT from VAT inclusive items use the formula: VAT = Gross × 17.5/117.5. For example, the £107.00 item above: VAT = £107 × 17.5/117.5 = £15.94 so that the cash sales were actually £91.06 + VAT at 17.5% £15.94 = £107.00. Check it!

(d) Balance off each account and bring down a balance as at the end of January. What is the meaning of each balance? Where will it appear in the trading and profit and loss account and balance sheet?

6. Clare is in business as a veterinary surgeon. At 1 February, she has the following balances:

Customers:		Suppliers:		Other:	
Mrs Edwards	£104.00	Vet drugs Ltd	£204.00	Country Bank	£870.12
Larkins	£50.00	Dog suppliers	£50.70	Customs & Excise	£1,290.00
Miss Marple	£78.00	Medicines Ltd	£190.00		
Holmes	£140.36				

In February she has the following transactions (any date in February will do):

Sales:		Purchases:		Receipts	
Larkins	£200.00	Vet drugs Ltd	£106.50	Mrs Edwards	£104.00
Holmes	£78.00	Dog suppliers	£201.00	Miss Marple	£288.00
Miss Marple	£210.00	Medicines Ltd	£76.32	Holmes	£100.00
Holmes	£400.00	Vet drugs Ltd	£32.91	Cash sales	£320.00
Todd	£120.00	Chews Co.	£120.43		

Sales Credit Notes:		Purchases Credit Notes:		Payments:	
Larkins	£23.56	Dog suppliers	£23.12	Vet drugs Ltd	£204.00
Todd	£5.67	Medicines Ltd	£10.00	Dog suppliers	£27.58
				Medicines Ltd	£50.00
				Cash purchases	£120.00

Notes:

(a) For all credit sales add VAT at 17.5%. Todd is a new customer.

(b) All credit purchases are inclusive of VAT. Chews Co is a new supplier.

(c) Cash sales and cash purchases are both inclusive of VAT.

Required:

(a) Open ledger accounts (including cash book) and enter opening balances.

(b) Enter all items in books of prime entry.

(c) Post all items to ledger accounts.

(d) Draw up separate lists of debit balances and credit balances at the end of the month. Note that debit balances are accounts with more monetary amount on the debit than the credit. Credit balances are the reverse. State the meaning of each balance and how each balance will end up in the financial statements.

7. From the following data, write up the account:

'Heating Oil' in Adam's ledger for 19x5:

		£
1. 1.x5	Stock of heating oil at cost	420
4. 3.x5	Invoice received from Evan for oil	586
3. 7.x5	Invoice received from Frank for oil	269
5.10.x5	Cash paid to local church for surplus heating oil	100
28.12.x5	Invoice received from Evan for oil	1,390
31.12.x5	Stock of oil at cost	1,240

You should complete the account and show the transfer to profit and loss account and bring down any balance into the new period.

8. Jeff started in business on 6 April 19x4. He took on one employee, Marvin, and paid him monthly at an annual rate of £4,800. Each monthly cheque was £314:

being	gross		400
less	PAYE	50	
	national insurance	36	86
			314

Eleven cheques were paid. The cheque for the month ending 5.4.x5 was paid to Marvin on 10.4.x5. Ten cheques were sent to the Collector of Taxes being the PAYE,national insurance deducted from Marvin and the employer's contribution to national insurance up to 5.2.x5.

Each cheque was:

PAYE		50
national insurance:	employee	36
	employer	42
		128

Write up the 'salary' expense account for the year ending 5 April 19x5.

9. Data concerning weekly salaries of Bert's business for 19x5 was:

	£
Cheques paid to salaried employees during the year	87,643
Cheques paid to the Collector of Taxes in the year	
for PAYE and national insurance	24,310

At the year end, the following were outstanding:

Salary cheques for December 19x5	8,200
PAYE and national insurance	2,919

Write up the account. Make the transfer to profit and loss account at the year end, bring down the balances.

10. Graham is a printer, but he also publishes a monthly newspaper which he started in October 19x4. Advertising revenues invoiced for the newspaper for the year ending 31 December 19x4 were:

		£
Invoiced in October:	for October issue	2,105
	for November issue	684
	for insertion in all issues October 19x4 to March 19x5	
		540
Invoiced in November:	for November issue	3,680
	for December issue	2,086
	for insertion in all Issues November 19x4 to February19x5	1,080
Invoiced in December:	for December issue	5,200
	for January issue	2,335

January 19x5 invoices included £400 for the December 19x4 issue.

Credit notes were issued in November 19x4 for £10 and in December 19x4 for £180 for cancelled advertisements.

Write up the advertising revenue account for the year ending 31 December 19x4, showing the transfer to profit and loss account and bringing down the year ending balances.

11. Enter the following transactions into the books of Walter, a trader, and balance the accounts. (Hint – you will need separate accounts for P.M. Supplies Ltd and Packing Materials Expense.)

		£
at 30 June 19x3	Owing to P.M. Supplies Ltd	380
	Stock of packing materials	260
in 19x3/x4	Invoices from P.M. Supplies Ltd for packing materials	1,390
	Credit notes from P.M. Supplies Ltd	102
	Cash paid to P.M. Supplies Ltd	1,161
	Packing materials transferred by Walter to his private use (for moving home)	120
	Damaged and scrapped packing materials (estimated cost)	100
at 30 June 19x4	Stock of packing materials	290

12. Draw up an appropriate ruling for a sales day book and enter the following amounts, adding 17.5% VAT in each case:

19x4		£
August		
12	A.J.M. Ltd	260.40
14	PMM PLC	100.00
16	Defoe & Co	1,420.66
20	Lucas Eng Ltd	49.00

Sum up the columns and state in which accounts the double entries would be made.

13. Draw up an appropriate ruling for a purchase and expense day book for Alan Widgets Ltd, widget wholesalers, with suitable analysis headings, and enter the following invoices received:

August 19x4		£	Type of goods/service
1	Albert & Victoria	138.00	Widgets
1	Edward Ltd	4,600.00	Delivery van
	George & Co	59.80	Heating oil
7	Charles Publishing	37.40	Books
9	William & Partners	883.20	Widgets
12	Electricity Board	431.00	Electricity
14	Daily Gazette	200.00	Advertising

All items include VAT at 17.5% except the books which are zero rated.

Sum the columns and state in which double entry account the items should be posted.

14. Draw up an appropriate ruling for a purchase and expense day book for Sheila Ltd, motor cycle retailers, with suitable analysis headings and enter the following invoices received:

Sept	19x4	£	Type of goods/service
1	Eden	6,246	Motor cycles
3	Fredric	134	Posters
9	Gas Board	431	Gas
11	Georgina Ltd	1,984	Motor cycle
15	J.J. Builders	1,046	Repairs to premises
19	Daily News	500	Advertising
24	Kim Fuels Ltd	624	Heating oil

All items include VAT at 17.5%

Sum the columns, test the cross cast and state in which double entry accounts the items should be posted.

Exercise – computerised accounting

15. This exercise is in a number of stages; however it is all for the month of your choosing.

Stage I   Load the software.

Stage II   Set up the system defaults and details about your own 'firm'. Choose Defaults from the menu bar and explore the menu. Initially, you will need to select your company preferences and the financial year end date. Select save when you have entered the relevant data. You may explore the other options later. Moving through fields can be done with the mouse or with the tab key.

Stage III   Set up some products that you will sell. Choose Products and then Record. Follow the instructions. You may care to set up the following products:

Code	Description	Price
A100	Widget Mk 1 (Std)	6.50
A200	Widget Mk 1 (Large)	8.90
A300	Widget Mk 2	14.30
A400	Widget Mk 3	28.70

or choose your own. You will need to select a (VAT) tax rate – 17.5% – and a nominal code for sales.

When you have saved the details, choose Price List and preview. You will see a list on the screen. You can explore the appearance of the price list using layout, header etc. When you have the price list to your satisfaction, print it on the printer. Note that you can exit any screen by using abandon, cancel, close, or control + x.

Stage IV   Set up some customers. Select Customers and Record. Fill in the details. Initially name and account number will suffice but you can explore the other details which can be entered. You can also design the invoices.

You may care to set up the following customers:

Account No	Name	Account No	Name
G1	A. Green	B1	B. Brown
C1	C. Crimson	P1	D. Pink

When you have saved the customers, choose Report + Customer List + Preview. When this is to your satisfaction, print it on the printer.

Stage V   Create some invoices to send to your customers. You may care to set up the following invoices:

Name	Products
A. Green	10 × A100 and 20 × A300
B. Brown	4 × A200 and 3 × A300
C. Crimson	2 × A100 and 4 × A400
D. Pink	15 × A400

The procedures are:

– Invoicing + Invoice. Enter customer account number (e.g. G1), product code (e.g. A100) and number of items (e.g. 10). When details of an invoice are complete, press save. When all the invoices are in press close. Then select Print +Preview. Set up the invoices and then print them out. Remember you can move through the fields of the documents using the mouse or tab.

Stage VI   Create some credit notes to send to your customers. you may care to enter the following:

Customer	Products
A. Green	1 × A100
B. Brown	1 × A200
C. Crimson	1 × A100 and 1 × A400

Choose Invoicing + Credit Notes and proceed as for invoices. You can then print these.

At this point, you should choose Customers when you will see that the amounts due now appear against the list of customers. Choose Reports and explore these and print some out.

Stage VII Create some suppliers. Choose Suppliers + Record and fill in fields: Account number, name and nominal code.

You may care to enter these suppliers: (Enter the amounts in the next stage)

A/c number	Name	Nominal Account	Amounts (net)
PT1	Tulip	Material purchases	201.14
PB1	Buttercup	Material purchases	68.39
PD1	Daisy	Material purchases	352.20
PR1	Rose	Material purchases	36.00
PG1	Gas Supply Co	Gas	120.00
PP1	Primrose garage	Repairs and servicing	64.00

Stage VIII Enter some purchase invoices. Select Suppliers + Invoices and enter fields for account number, amount and nominal code. Description should be goods for material purchases, gas for gas, and repairs for repairs and servicing.

Note that you can enter the amounts in the net column and the program will automatically calculate the VAT and the gross amount of the invoice.

Stage IX   Enter some purchase credit notes. Choose Suppliers + Credit notes.

You may care to enter these:

Supplier	Amount (net)
Tulip	4.00
Buttercup	7.00
Rose	8.00
Primrose	9.00

Stage X   Enter some cash receipts and payments. Firstly set up bank account details. Choose Bank + Record and enter nominal code (select the coding offered for a bank account), details of the bank account and a nil balance. Then enter some receipts. You may care to enter these:

From customers:	Name	Amount
	A. Green	404.79
	D. Pink	60.00

You enter these by entering account number, and moving to paid column. Then, using the mouse, press Pay-in-full or enter the amount (if not paid-in-full). This will update both bank account and the customer account – thus completing a double entry.

Other receipts:	Nominal code	Description	Amount	VAT Rate
	Share capital	Shares issued	2,000.00	Zero
	Sales	Cash sales	350.00 +VAT	Standard

These are entered by Bank + Payments. Enter nominal code, name, description, amount and VAT rate.

Stage XI   Enter some payments. You may care to enter the following:

Name	Amount
Gas Supply Co.	£141.00
Rose	£32.90
Tulip	£100.00
Wages	£284.00

The first three are entered from Bank + Suppliers, entering name, amount, and, if settling specific part of sum owing, then cursor in paid column and press Pay-in-full or Settlement. The last item is entered from Bank + Payments. Enter nominal code (for wages), description, amount and VAT code (zero).

Stage XII   (Optional) You have now entered many of the routine items of any commercial bookkeeping system. You can now explore some of the other features. These may include:

– Suppliers : activity and reports
– Nominal : activity and reports
– Financials: Trial Balance, P and L and Balance Sheet.

You can then explore possible content and formats of reports and lists and make some print outs.

Assignment

❏ Note that this exercise can also be used as an exercise in computer accounting.

Doreen is in business as a caterer, supplying vegetarian meals for business lunches and functions.

Her year end is 31 December and on 31 December 19x8 the balances in her books were:

Customers:		Suppliers:		Other:	
Bacon	235.87	Gibbs	104.47	Cash at bank	456.78
Cox	131.20	Hagen	300.23	Customs	
Darby	700.21	Jones	76.34	& Excise (Cr)	258.91
Evans	108.62	King	237.58	Stock	239.21
		Wills	200.00		

Transactions in January were:

Sales:		Purchases:		Receipts:	
Bacon	234.11	Lloyd	30.00	Bacon	235.87
Darby	400.23	Gibbs	543.10	Darby	700.21
Adcote	799.00	Mylne	100.34	Adcote	300.00
Evans	329.00	King	290.00	Cash Sales	240.00
Darby	500.00				

Payments:		Sales returns:		Purchases returns:	
Gibbs	104.47	Bacon	65.00	Lloyd	12.54
Jones	76.34	Adcote	46.00	Mylne	45.00
King	200.00				
Second hand van	800.00				
Cash purchases:	150.00	Expenses on credit:			
Wages	245.00	Morris	101.00	(van repair)	
Rent	90.00	Austin	54.00	(petrol)	
Stationery	140.00	Wills	100.00	(advertising)	
Wages	200.00	Popeye	30.00	(Paraffin)	
Drawings	100.00				
Wills	50.00				

Notes:

(a) VAT should be added to all sales (and sales returns) at 17.5%.

(b) All purchase and expense invoices and returns include VAT at 17.5%.

(c) Cash sales and purchases include VAT at 17.5%.

(d) There is no VAT attachable to the Van, wages or rent but stationery does include VAT at 17.5%.

At the end of January, relevant data includes:

(a) Stock was valued at £189.22.

(b) The rent paid (£90) is for the three months to March 31.

(c) A reading of the electricity meter indicates that January consumption cost £98.00 + VAT.

(d) A reading of the gas meter indicates that January consumption cost £54.00 + VAT.

(e) Stationery was for letterheads and invoices. About 10% of these were used in January.

(f) The wages paid are up to 27 January. The remaining four days will cost £60.00. Deductions of £152.50 have been made from the wages for tax and insurance and the figures above are net payments. The tax and insurance deducted are due to the Collector of Taxes.

(g) Doreen catered for a party for Adcote on 28 January. She has not yet invoiced the client, but the bill is expected to be £210.00 + VAT.

(h) The van is to be treated as a fixed asset. Ignore depreciation.

Required:

(a) Open double entry accounts for the opening balances.

(b) Enter sales, sales returns, purchases and expense invoices and returns in appropriate books of prime entry.

(c) Enter receipts and payments in the cash book.

(d) Post all entries to appropriate ledger accounts indicating which ledger the accounts would be in.

(e) Balance off all accounts including the adjustments (ignore the stock account – we deal with that later in the book).

(f) Prepare a profit and loss account for the month of January.

(g) Calculate the capital at 31 December and then prepare a balance sheet as at 31 January.

(h) Write a commentary on the profit and loss account and balance sheet explaining to a non-accountant what the financial statements mean and the meanings of each entry in them. You should include a commentary on the accounting conventions used.

7 Bookkeeping for fixed assets and depreciation

This chapter continues the study of double entry bookkeeping. We begin with the entries required for fixed assets, which are very simple. We continue with the entries for depreciation, which are a trifle more complicated.

Introduction

1. Bookkeeping for fixed assets is relatively simple: all purchases are entered on the debit side.

Procedures

2. Procedures are:

   (a) **Select and open appropriate accounts**. These are usually just the major classifications: Land, Buildings, Plant and Machinery, Motor Vehicles, Office Furniture and Equipment. They may be more specialised. For example a plant hire firm might have Hire Plant as its major account. A farmer might have: Farmhouse, Agricultural Land, Agricultural Buildings, Farm Equipment. An insurance broker might have: Motor Cars, Office Equipment. A quarry company may have: The Quarry, Fixed Quarrying Equipment, Moveable Quarrying Equipment and Vehicles, Lorries, Motor Cars. A dairy might have Dairying Equipment, Electric Milk Floats, Diesel Milk Delivery Vehicles, Milk Collection Lorries. It is possible to have a separate account for each individual fixed asset. This would mean lots of accounts and it is more usual to have only accounts in the major classifications to collect all the fixed assets together.

   (b) Enter acquisitions on the Debit side. Thus the bookkeeping for acquisitions is:

   Dr Fixed Asset A/c with net cost   Cr Supplier A/c with cost + VAT
   Customs and Excise with VAT   (or cash book if item is not on credit)

   Most fixed assets are subject to VAT. Exceptions are land, which is an exempt supply, and the construction of buildings for residential or charitable use, which is zero-rated.

   A fixed asset account might look like this:

Dr		Motor Vehicles	Cr
21.3.x6	Ford van	2,379.00	
14.7.x6	Sherpa van	7,900.87	
12.9.x6	Vauxhall Corsa	7,100.00	
		17,379.87	
4.5.x7	Toyota Carina	12,750.00	
		30,129.87	

Notes:

(a) Strictly speaking, the account should be balanced off at the end of each year (31 December here) but the approach used above has the same effect with less fuss.

(b) The cost of a fixed asset is sometimes not entirely straightforward. For example the cost of acquisition of land and buildings will include conveyance and survey costs. The cost of construction of buildings will include architects' and quantity surveyors' charges. The cost of a van may include the cost of sign-writing. Care must be taken in entering motor vehicle invoices as they usually include tax and some petrol. These are not part of the cost of the vehicle but motor expenses to be debited to the motor expenses account. The balance of the motor expenses account ends up in the profit and loss account.

(c) Consider what the 'story' of this account is. It shows that the business acquired three vehicles in 19x6 with a total cost of £17,379.87. In 19x7 a further vehicle was acquired. The total cost of all vehicles owned at the end of 19x7 was £30,129.87.

(d) Fixed asset accounts are always debit balances.

Depreciation

3. There are two methods of recording depreciation of fixed assets.
4. **Method I** is:

Morris Van

		£			£
1.1.x5	Cost (i)	5,600	31.12.x5	Depreciation (ii)	1,250
			"	Balance c/d (iii)	4,350
		5,600			5,600
1.12.x6	Balance b/d	4,350	31.12.x6	Depreciation (ii)	1,250
			"	Balance c/d (iii)	3,100
		4,350			4,350
1. 1.x7	Balance b/d	3,100	31.12.x7	Depreciation (ii)	1,250
			"	Balance c/d (iii)	1,850
		3,100			3,100
1. 1.x8	Balance b/d	1,850	31.12.x8	Depreciation (ii)	1,250
			"	Balance c/d (iii)	600
		1,850			1,850
1. 1.x9	Balance b/d	600			

Notes:

(a) Depreciation is over four years on the straight line method with an estimated salvage value of £600.

(b) The double entry is completed by:
   (i) A credit to the supplier's account.
   (ii) A debit to the profit and loss account.

(c) The original cost is entered on the debit side. As the van's original cost value (£5,600) is used up, a part of the cost (£1,250) is taken away by an entry on the credit side and placed on the debit side of the profit and loss account where it is an expense.

(d) The remaining, undepreciated part of the cost (iii) is the balance on the account and is the net book value of the asset.

5. **Method II** is slightly more difficult to follow but is much more common in practice. The procedure is:

(a) Maintain the asset at COST:

Morris Van at Cost

£

1.1.x5   Cost   5,600

This will be the only entry in the account until the van is disposed of.

(b) When the first depreciation entries are required, open a new account as:

Provision for Depreciation of Morris Van

£

31.12.x5   Profit and loss a/c   1,250

The double entry is completed by a debit in the profit and loss account.

If the two accounts (van and provision for depreciation) are looked at as if they were one account, then the bookkeeping is the same as in method I.

(c) At each subsequent accounting date:

Provision for Depreciation of Morris Van

£

31.12.x5	Profit and loss a/c	1,250
31.12.x6	Profit and loss a/c	1,250
		2,500
31.12.x7	Profit and loss a/c	1,250
		3,750
31.12.x8	Profit and loss a/c	1,250
		5,000

Note:

(i) The net book value at any accounting date is found by (for example at 31.12.x7):

Morris van at cost	5,600	
Less accumulated depreciation	3,750	1,850

(ii) The cost and also the accumulated depreciation are immediately available using method II.

Disposals – single assets

6. The treatment of disposals depends on the method of recording depreciation. We will assume that the van was sold on 31.7.x7 for £2,630.

   (a) **Method I**

   Morris Van Account

	£			£
1. 1.x7 Balance b/d	3,100	31. 7.x7	Proceeds of sale (i)	2,630
		31.12.x7	Profit and loss a/c (ii)	470
	3,100			3,100

   Notes:

   (i) The double entry is completed by a debit to the person who bought the van or to the cash book.

   (ii) This is the depreciation for the year and is debited to profit and loss account. This entry is sometimes called the depreciation adjustment or profit (or loss) on sale.

   (b) **Method II**

   Morris Van Account

	£			£
1. 1.x5 Cost	5,600	31. 7.x7	Disposal a/c (i)	5,600

   Provision for Depreciation on Van Account

	£			£
31. 7.x7 Transfer to Disposal	2,500	1. 1.x7	Balance b/f	2,500

   Disposal of Van Account

	£			£
31. 7.x7 Cost (i)	5,600	31. 7.x7	Accumulated depreciation (ii)	2,500
		31. 7.x7	Proceeds of sale (iii)	2,630
		31.12.x7	Profit and loss a/c (iv)	470
	5,600			5,600

   Note: The double entry is (i) and (ii) which removes the vehicle from its own account and the accumulated depreciation from the provision account and enters both on a disposal account. The disposal account now has a balance of (£5,600 – £2,500) which is £3,100 and the net book value. The proceeds of sale (iii) are then entered and the depreciation (or loss on sale) for the year (iv) is found.

Disposals – grouped assets

7. The treatment of disposals in the last section is simple and may seem cumbersome for such small needs, but it becomes more complex when several or numerous fixed

assets are grouped into one fixed asset account for a particular type of fixed asset, e.g. vehicles or plant and machinery.

8. The method for dealing with the sale of a fixed asset is as follows. We shall consider a farmer who maintains a farm equipment account at cost and a provision for depreciation of farm equipment. We follow the sale of a tractor:

   (a) Open a disposal of tractor account.

   (b) Dr disposal account and Cr farm equipment account with the cost of the tractor.

   (c) Dr depreciation account and Cr depreciation account with the accumulated depreciation.

   (d) Dr cash (or customer) and Cr disposal account with the proceeds of sale.

   (e) Dr profit and loss account and Cr disposal account with the balance of the disposal account if there is a debit balance (this is the loss on sale) or Dr disposal account, if it is a credit balance, and Cr profit and loss account (this is a profit on sale).

   (f) The disposal account has now been closed, the tractor at cost has been removed from the farm equipment at cost account and the accumulated depreciation on the tractor has been removed from the provision account.

Fixed asset registers

9. Fixed assets are usually recorded in financial accounting accounts in a fairly simple way as you have learned in Chapter 5. Many firms keep more detailed and complex records for each asset. These records are kept in a fixed asset register, usually today on a computer. The layout of such a register is a matter of taste or convenience. The fields used may be:

Description	Estimated life
Location	Estimated residual value
Supplier	Estimate costs to make good after scrapping
Manufacturer	Insured value
Serial number	Depreciation policy
Identifying number	Depreciation applied
Cost of purchase	Major repairs (details costs + dates)
Cost of installation	Capital allowances claimed (for tax)
Date of purchase	Function in the firm
Date of first use	Cost centre application
Guarantee warranty expiry	Machine hour rate applicable
Grant received (if any)	Responsible officer
Manufacturer's invoice number	Internal audit inspection dates
Internally generated invoice number	Health and safety inspection dates
Statutory inspection dates/reports/certificates	Major breakdowns
	Expected replacement date
Record reviewed dates	

You may think of other fields which may be appropriate.

It is important that the data recorded is up to date and accurate. To ensure that this occurs, there should be regular reviews of the records by senior officials and a systematic comparison of the records with the actual assets. Both reviews and comparisons should be recorded and reports made.

The advantage of having fixed asset registers on computerised databases is that searches can easily be made and lists printed out. For example, schedules of maintenance, schedules of required inspections, schedules of major repairs etc can be prepared.

Summary

☐ Fixed asset accounts are debit balances.

☐ There are two methods of recording depreciation. Method I is to put the depreciation on the asset account so that the balance on the account is the net book value (= written down value). Method II is to open a separate provision for depreciation account, with the asset account remaining at cost. By looking at both accounts – asset at cost and provision for depreciation – the net book value can be found.

☐ Fixed asset accounts can be for single fixed assets (e.g. a particular motor car) or for a class of fixed assets (e.g. motor cars).

☐ Disposals are usually dealt with by removing the cost and accumulated depreciation of the asset from the asset and depreciation accounts and entering them in a disposal account. You then have the net book value of the asset on the disposal account. By entering the proceeds of sale, the depreciation adjustment (= profit or loss on sale) can be found and entered in the profit and loss account.

☐ Ideally a fixed asset register should be used.

Points to note

☐ In practice, the grouped fixed asset account (e.g. motor vehicles) is more commonly found than individual accounts for each asset and this seems to cause difficulty to students. Remember that the grouped account is really only a collection of individual assets.

☐ If there are several classes of fixed asset or the fixed assets have individual accounts, then the depreciation may be assembled in a 'depreciation for year account' as:

Depreciation for Vans for Year

19x5		£	19x5		£
Dec 31	Morris van	826	Dec 31	Profit and loss a/c	2,076
	Ford van	520			
	Renault van	730			
		2,076			2,076

Self-testing questions

1. What are the two methods of dealing with depreciation in a double entry system?
2. How are disposals dealt with?
3. What is the purpose of transferring the accumulated depreciation on an asset to a disposal account on disposal of that asset?
4. Distinguish between a provision for depreciation account and a depreciation expense account.

Exercises

1. Dill acquired the following machines for his factory:

19x5	Jan 19	Lathe	£2,100.00	July 4	Press	£246.00
19x6	Feb 24	Mill	£3,600.00	Oct 19	Stamper	£540.00

   His year end is 31 December and his policy is to depreciate machines on the straight line basis over five years assuming a nil salvage value and giving a full year's depreciation in the year of purchase.

   Required:

   Write up the asset account (machines) and depreciation for the years 19x5 to 19x0 using either Method I or Method II (or do both!).

2. Pepper acquired the following trucks for his transport business:

19x1	Feb 23	Iveco	£12,000.00	Sept 29	Skoda	£24,900.00
19x2	Mar 1	Renault	£17,800.00	Dec 23	Toyota	£40,900.00

   His year end is 31 December.

   Required:

   Write up the trucks account and depreciation for the years ending 19x1 to 19x4 assuming:

   (a) Depreciation policy is straight line over four years with nil salvage value.

   (b) Depreciation policy is reducing balance at 30% a year.

   (c) Depreciation policy is sum of digits over four years.

   In each case give a full year's depreciation to new acquisitions.

   Consider the complications involved in using orthodox depreciation methods, namely finding a salvage value and an expected life for each lorry. How might computers assist in this?

3. Consider again question 1. Suppose the lathe was sold on 24 July 19x7 for £500. Write up the machines account with depreciation and disposal account for 19x7 and the asset account and depreciation for 19x8.

4. Consider again question 2. Suppose that the Skoda was sold on 12 March 19x4 for £8,000.00. Write up all relevant accounts for the years 19x4 and 19x5. Give the entries for those years in the profit and loss account and balance sheet.

5. Graham has motor vehicles in his balance sheet as at 31 December 19x4 as:

	£
Motor vehicles at cost	684,936
Less accumulated depreciation	413,726
Net book value	271,210

In 19x5, the following occurred:

Acquisitions

Renault	7,100
Audi	8,620

Disposals

Fiat (original cost in 19x2 £6,000)	1,500
Peugeot (original cost in 19x0 £4,300)	500

Depreciation policy is straight line with estimated life four years and nil salvage value. A full year's depreciation is charged in the year of acquisition.

Show:

(a) The vehicles (at cost) account for 19x5.

(b) The provision for depreciation on vehicles account for 19x5.

(c) The disposals account in 19x5.

(d) The profit and loss account and balance sheet entries in 19x5.

6. Gordon is in business as a house remover and furniture storer. He received the following invoice in March 19x9:

From : Wellington Vans PLC Date 2 March:

One removal van	22,000.00
Tank of diesel fuel	51.20
Delivery and number plates	651.00
One year's vehicle tax	455.00
Signwriting	450.20
	23,607.40
VAT at 17.5%	4,051.67
	27,659.07

Enter this invoice in double entry accounts.

7. Lesley acquired a van for her business on 7 July 19x4 at a cost of £12,760. Her year end is 31 December. She is not sure how to depreciate it as she has not had a vehicle before. Explore possible depreciation calculations and show how the van and van depreciation would be shown in successive profit and loss accounts and balance sheets. She feels that a four or five year life is reasonable and that the salvage value would be some-where from £3,000 to £4,000.

Note that this exercise could be set up on a spreadsheet to explore the various options.

8. The newly appointed head of the Berrington College discovered that it was not known what fixed assets the college possessed and was disturbed to discover a tape recorder in the home of a lecturer with a label 'Property of the Berrington College'.

Required:

(a) What fixed assets might the college own?

(b) Design a suitable fixed asset register for the college.

(c) Suggest procedures for ensuring the register was correct and up to date.

(d) List possible uses for the register.

Assignment

☐ Lennie started in business as a plumber on 1 January 19x4 and bought a van. The invoice showed:

Secondhand Ford van	5,820.00
Road fund licence for 12 months	240.00
Signwriting 'Lennie's Plumbing is best'	180.00
Full tank of diesel fuel	26.00
	£6,266.00

Required:

(a) Show how the purchase of the van will be entered in the books assuming that Lennie pays the full amount by cheque on the invoice date of 1 January.

He is not sure whether to depreciate the van on the straight line basis or the reducing balance basis.

(b) Explain these two methods and calculate the depreciation for the years 19x4 through 19x7 on the assumption that the van will last four years and have a salvage value of £1,900.

(c) Show how the van and the depreciation will appear in the profit and loss accounts and balance sheets for these years.

On 30 June 19x6, he sold the van for £2,500. Enter the sale in the books and explain how the van and depreciation will appear in the financial statements for 19x6 and 19x7.

(d) Use this example to demonstrate that profit is not measurable with certainty and is not a sum of cash.

8 Trial balances

A trial balance is simply a listing, divided into debit and credit columns, of the balances on all the accounts in a double entry system. Its objective is to determine or prove the accuracy of the bookkeeping. The trial balance has come also to be used in the preparation of final accounts and this is also discussed in this chapter.

A difference is often encountered on extraction of a trial balance and a suspense account opened for the difference. Correction of these differences and the errors which cause them is discussed and we continue with the use of the journal.

Trial balance uses

1. The following uses are made of trial balances:
   (a) Testing the accuracy of some aspects of the double entry. However not all errors are revealed by a difference on a trial balance.
   (b) The preparation of the financial statements.

2. The basic principle of double entry requires that the total of debit entries must equal the total of credit entries. Many entries consist of a debit entry and a credit entry, both of the same amount. For example if a customer pays her account then the cash book is debited and the customer credited. It is not essential that an individual debit has a credit of an equal amount. For example cash sales of £235 will require a debit entry of £235 in the cash book but credit entries of £200 in the sales account and £35 in the VAT account. However the important thing is that the total of debit entries must equal the total of credit entries. If they do not then the trial balance will not balance. This will alert the bookkeeper to the fact that an error or errors have occurred. The following types of error can occur:

   (a) **Errors of omission**. This means the complete omission of a transaction from the bookkeeping system. Suppose a sales invoice was completely omitted. This is an error as the sales account and the customer account should receive entries. However its omission does not affect the agreement of the trial balance.

   (b) **Errors of principle**. This is where the double entry occurs but where one side of the entry is in the wrong class of account. For example the purchase of a computer may be debited in the stationery (expense) account instead of the office equipment (fixed asset) account. Errors of principle do not affect the agreement of the trial balance either.

   (c) **Errors of commission**. This is similar but occurs when the entry is on the wrong person's account, for example the account of A. Singh instead of B. Singh.

   (d) **Compensating errors**. These should not be common but occur when two errors cancel each other out. An example might be if the total of the sales account was overadded by £100 and the total of the stationery expense account was also overadded by £100.

   (e) **Errors of original entry**. This occurs when the original figure is incorrect but entries are otherwise correct. For example a bad debt of £120 may be wrongly entered as £210 both in the customer's account and the bad debt expense account.

(f) *Complete reversal of entry*. This occurs when the correct accounts are used but the entries are put on the wrong sides. For example a bad debt caused by the failure of Duff Ltd requires a debit of £50 in bad debts account and a credit of £50 in Duff Ltd's account. In fact the £50 was entered on the credit side of bad debts and the debit side of Duff.

All of the above are errors but none of them affects the balancing of the trial balance. You will appreciate that the fact that the trial balance balances does not necessarily mean that there are no errors!

3. Some errors do affect the balancing of the trial balance. Some examples :

(a) *One-legged entries*. These occur when the double entry is not completed. For example a wages payment is entered in the cash book but is not entered in the wages account.

(b) *Transposition of figures*. These occur when say £58 is entered in the cash book and £85 is entered in the wages account. This will cause a difference of £27 (£85 - £58) in the trial balance. Note that transposition of amount errors always cause a difference in the trial balance which is divisible by 9 and leaves no remainder.

(c) *Errors of addition*. These can occur in the trial balance (do not look for a difference before you are sure you have one!) and in individual accounts. Also an account can be balanced wrongly. The additions may be correct at say £80 debit and £25 credit but the account balance carried down as £65.

(d) *Non extraction of balances*. A trial balance is made by listing the balances on the individual accounts in the double entry system. It is always possible to omit one or more account balances when extracting the trial balance.

Error correction

4. All errors should be corrected by using the journal and we shall look at the journal a little later in this chapter.

Errors and profit calculations

5. Some errors affect profit calculations. As an example if the stationery account was debited with £560 instead of the office equipment account, then the profit should be more by £560 (as stationery expense is more than it should be) and less by perhaps £112 (because the office equipment is depreciated by 20%). Some examiners make this type of error into a problem. Here is an example:

Prone's trial balance has showed a debit total of £286,630 and a credit total of £286,319 and a suspense account was opened for the difference. While search was made for errors the profit and loss account was extracted and showed a profit of £45,876.

The errors found were:

(a) The purchases account was over added by £100.

(b) A debit to interest account £589 was in fact interest of £89 and £500 off the loan.

(c) A payment of wages of £630 had been posted to wages as £360.

(d) A receipt from Hobbes, a customer, of £481 had not been posted to Hobbes' account.

Show that the trial balance now balances and calculate the correct profit.

Trial balance:

	Debit	Credit
Previous totals	286,630	286,319
Error a. Purchases a/c	- 100	
Error c. Wages a/c	+ 270	
Error d. Hobbes, a debtor		+ 481
New totals	286,800	286,800

Statement of corrected profit

Net profit per the accounts:	45,876
Error a. (purchases were overstated)	+100
Error b. (£500 erroneously included in interest)	+500
Error c. (wages increased by £270)	- 270
Corrected profit	46,206

The extended trial balance

Following business practice, many examination questions consist of a trial balance, a list of notes on adjustments to be made, and a requirement to prepare final accounts.

Example

Trial balance of H. Flashman, bicycle dealer, at 31.12.x9.

	Dr £000	Cr £000
Capital 31.12.x8		68
Stock 31.12.x8	46	
Purchases	234	
Sales		288
Expenses	37	
Drawings	8	
Debtors	48	
Creditors		40
Bank		51
Fixed assets at cost	132	
Depreciation to 31.12.x8		58
	505	505

Notes:

(a) Stock at 31.12.x9 was valued at £58,000.

(b) Depreciation is 15% straight line.

(c) Expenses include prepayments at 31.12.x9 of £12,000 and omit accruals of £23,000.

Required:

Prepare trading and profit and loss account for the year ending 31 December 19x9 and balance sheet at that date.

Answer

There are many ways of tackling this type of question. One way which many people find simple is to use a matrix as follows:

H. Flashman

	Trial Balance Dr £000	Trial Balance Cr £000	Adjustments Dr £000	Adjustments Cr £000	Trading & P&L a/c Dr £000	Trading & P&L a/c Cr £000	Balance Sheet Assets £000	Balance Sheet Liabilities £000
Capital		68	8					60
Stock	46		58	46	46	58	58	
Purchases	234				234			
Sales		288				288		
Expenses	37		23	12	48		12	23
Drawings	8			8				
Debtors	48						48	
Creditors		40						40
Bank		51						51
Fixed Assets	132						132	
Depreciation		58		20	20			78
	505	505	89	86	348	346	250	252

The resulting trading and profit and loss account will be:

	£000	£000
Sales		288
Less Cost of sales		
– opening stock	46	
– purchases	234	
	280	
– closing stock	58	222
Gross profit		66
Expenses	48	
Depreciation	20	68
Net loss		2

and **Balance sheet as at 31 December 19x9**

	£000	£000
Fixed assets at cost		132
Less accumulated depreciation		78
		54

Current assets		
Stock	58	
Debtors	48	
Prepayments	12	118
		172
Less **Current liabilities**		
Creditors	40	
Accruals	23	
Bank overdraft	51	114
		58
Capital at 1.1.x9		68
Net loss for year		2
		66
Drawings		8
		58

Trial balance differences and the suspense account

7. Suppose a trial balance is extracted from the books of I. Legge, a wholesale fruiterer, at 31.12.x9 as:

	£	£
Capital 1.1.x9		41,200
Sales		132,380
Purchases	66,410	
Stock 1.1.x9	4,300	
Overheads	19,204	
Debtors	8,760	
Creditors		12,244
Fixed assets at cost	30,000	
Depreciation		11,000
Drawings	9,100	
Bank	63,240	
	201,014	196,824

Clearly the trial balance does not balance and there is a difference of £4,190. To make it balance an account can be opened called a 'suspense account' thus:

Suspense Account

		£
31.12.x9	TB difference	4,190

Inserted in the trial balance, the trial balance now balances.

8. The difference was caused by errors, and on investigation the following errors were found:

(a) An invoice to Lemon of £264 was entered in the books as £246.

(b) A purchase from Pear of £320 was entered on Pear's account but omitted from purchases account.

(c) A receipt from Apple of £3,000 being a loan received was entered in the cash book but not credited to any account.

(d) A drawing of £200 was debited to drawings account as £2,000.

(e) An invoice to Nutt of £136 was omitted from the books altogether.

(f) An invoice for £290 from G. Plum was credited in error to both G. Plum and H. Plum.

Correcting these errors will require bookkeeping entries as:

Dr			Cr	Dr		Cr
Sales				**Lemon**		
	Lemon		18	Sales	18	
	Nutt		136			
Suspense				**Purchases**		
Loan	3,000	b/f	4,190	Suspense	320	
Drawings	1,800	Purchases	320			
		H. Plum	290			
	4,800		4,800			
Loan Account				**Drawings**		
	Suspense		3,000		Suspense	1,800
Nutt				**H. Plum**		
Sales	136			Suspense	290	

Notes:

(a) I have omitted all entries on the above accounts except those arising out of the correction of errors.

(b) The suspense account has now been eliminated.

(c) An entry on the suspense account was only required when the error involved a non correspondence of debit and credit entry – items (b), (c), (d) and (f).

(d) The trial balance now balances:

	£	£
Capital		41,200
Sales		132,534
Purchases	66,730	
Stock	4,300	
Overheads	19,204	
Debtors	8,914	
Creditors		11,954
Fixed assets and depreciation	30,000	11,000
Drawings	7,300	
Loan		3,000

	£	£
Bank	63,240	
	199,688	199,688

The journal

9. The majority of transactions are first entered in one of the following books of prime entry:

(a) Sales daybook.

(b) Sales return daybook.

(c) Purchases and expenses daybook.

(d) Purchases and expenses returns daybook.

(e) Cash book (and discount columns).

(f) Petty cash book.

We will study the petty cash book in detail in the next chapter. For now, note that it is used for the small payments in notes and coin.

Some transactions, especially those of a non-routine nature, are not appropriate for the above books of prime entry. For them, a special book of prime entry is maintained called the journal.

Example

Carl, a dealer in antiques, acquired the assets of a rival business owned by Robin for £20,000. The deal was financed by Carl paying cash £10,000 and leaving the remainder on loan from Robin at 15%. The assets acquired were valued as: leasehold premises £3,000; delivery van £2,500; fixtures and fittings £1,500; rent and rates prepaid £500 and stock £7,650.

This transaction has to be entered in Carl's double entry system but first transactions are entered in the journal as:

			£	£
1.	Dr	Leasehold premises	3,000	
		Delivery van	2,500	
		Fixtures & fittings	1,500	
		Rent and rates	500	
		Stock	7,650	
		Goodwill (see (g) below)	4,850	
	Cr	Purchase of Robin's business a/c		20,000

Being the assets acquired on the acquisition of Robin's business per agreement dated ....

2.	Dr	Purchase of Robin's business a/c	20,000	
	Cr	Cash		10,000
		Loan a/c Robin		10,000

Being consideration given for the purchase of Robin's business.

Notes:

(a) Each journal entry is numbered.

(b) The debit entries to be entered in the ledger are given first and then the credit.

(c) One to one correspondence of double entry is not required but the total debits and credits for any journal entry must be the same.

(d) Each entry is accompanied by a narrative which explains the entry.

(e) Each entry is ruled off.

(f) Cash entries appear in the book of prime entry, the cash book, but it is customary to include them in the journal to complete a series of entries such as those on the purchase of a business.

(g) Goodwill is the extra paid for the business over the physical assets. It is treated as a fixed asset.

Summary

❑ The trial balance is used to test the accuracy of bookkeeping and also as the starting point in the preparation of final accounts.

❑ Final accounts can be prepared from a trial balance using a matrix approach.

❑ The difference on a trial balance is often entered in a suspense account. The discovery and correction of the errors leads to the progressive closing of the suspense account.

❑ The journal is a 'catch all' book of prime entry used for entries which do not go through the routine books of prime entry.

Points to note

❑ Students find correction of errors and the suspense account difficult. The secret of success is:

(i) Visualise the correct entry.

(ii) Consider how the actual entry differs.

(iii) Correct the difference.

(iv) Where one-legged entries are concerned (i.e. where total Dr and Cr do not correspond) include an entry in the suspense account.

In recent times the journal has tended to fall out of use. However, the advent of computerised bookkeeping has brought a revival. Computer systems usually contain routines for: credit sales and returns, credit purchases and returns, credit expenses and returns, cash and cheque receipts, cash and cheque payments and wages. All other transactions go through a journal.

Self-testing questions

1. What is a trial balance?
2. What are the uses of a trial balance?
3. What does a credit balance on a suspense account indicate?
4. What is the journal used for?

5.   List possible errors and their effect on the trial balance.

Exercises

1.   The trial balances of three separate businesses (those of King, Leeanne and Mary) showed the following balances at 31.12.x7:

	King £	Leeanne £	Mary £
Capital at 31.12.x6	58,646	42,189	104,009
Drawings	12,500	8,500	7,400
Debtors	45,900	13,900	31,000
Creditors	22,640	8,545	21,754
Stock 31.12.x6	15,300	2,510	11,090
Sales	222,000	76,500	178,000
Purchases	136,000	21,000	114,950
Rent		10,200	
Rates	12,300	8,700	7,680
Wages	43,431	23,700	11,800
General overheads	16,900	13,371	15,879
Interest payable	4,500		1,000
Loan from Usury Co Ltd at 20%	30,000		10,000
Land at cost	10,000		20,000
Buildings at cost	38,900		64,000
Plant and equipment at cost	12,655	23,090	28,000
Vehicles at cost	32,180	12,760	63,829
Depreciation on Buildings to 31.12.x6	6,300		21,000
Depreciation on Plant to 31.12.x6	3,580	6,400	13,900
Depreciation on Vehicles to 31.12.x6	13,700	5,697	19,765
Rent receivable			3,500
Balance in Bank		2,600	
Bank overdraft	23,700		2,700
Proceeds of sale of Nissan car		3,000	
Proceeds of sale of plant			2,000

Notes:

For King:

(a) Stock at 31.12.x7 was valued at £33,431.

(b) Rates includes £3,600 being rates for the six months to 31.3.x8.

(c) General overheads does not include an electricity bill for the quarter ending 31.12.x7 of £1,900 or an accountant's fee of £400.

(d) The loan was taken out on 1 January 19x7.

(e) Depreciation policies are: Buildings – straight line over 25 years with nil salvage value; Plant – reducing balance at 25%; Vehicles – straight line over five years with nil salvage value (none of the vehicles are over four years old).

For Leeanne:

(a) Stock at 31.12.x7 was valued at £2,981.

(b) Sales do not reflect the return of some goods by Hope, a customer, in December 19x7. A credit note was issued in January for £568. The returned goods were damaged and have no value.

(c) Rent does not include rent for the month of December £960.

(d) General overheads include telephone rental for the quarter to 31 January 19x8 of £360 but do not include an Advertising bill for £990 for three monthly insertions in a trade magazine beginning with the December 19x7 issue.

(e) Depreciation policy on the plant is 20% a year reducing balance.

(f) Depreciation policy on the vehicles is 25% a year reducing balance. The Nissan car was purchased on 1 January 19x4 for £6,400.

(g) On 28 December 19x7, a replacement was obtained. The invoice for this car (a Honda) was dated 28.12.x7 and paid for in January 19x8. The amount £9,200 is not included in the trial balance figures. The Honda should be depreciated in 19x7.

For Mary:

(a) Stock at 31.12.x7 was valued at £12,200.

(b) Drawings do not include goods valued at £2,000 withdrawn by Mary for her private use in June 19x7.

(c) Rates include £3,100 being rates for the half year ending 31.3.x8.

(d) Wages do not include a bonus to the manager of 5% of the net profit for the year.

(e) General overheads include an insurance premium of £2,400 for the year ending 30.4.x8.

(f) The loan was taken out on 1 April 19x7.

(g) Depreciation policies are: Buildings – 4% straight line; Plant – straight line over five years with nil salvage value; Vehicles: 30% reducing balance. The plant, sold for £2,000 had been purchased on 1.1.x3. for £5,600. The plant at cost includes one item, costing £1,200 which was bought before 19x3.

Required:

For each business:

(a) Prepare a trial balance to show that it balances.

(b) Prepare a profit and loss account and balance sheet.

2.   The trial balances of Dick and Doris at 31.12.x8 showed:

	Dick		Doris	
	Dr	Cr	Dr	Cr
Capital 1.1.x8		12,608		23,876
Stock 1.1.x8	2,567		3,510	
Purchases and sales	15,908	28,981	40,700	70,432
Expenses		6,200	17,500	
Drawings	5,700		10,322	
Debtors and creditors	3,400	2,300	15,680	5,600
Fixed assets at cost	12,700		10,438	
Depreciation to 31.12.x7		6,230		3,428
Bank	4,006		4,810	

For Dick, the following errors were found:

(a) Drawings of £200 were debited in error to expenses.

(b) Purchases from Fred, a supplier, £36 were debited to his account.

(c) The sum due from Alf was omitted from the trial balance – £80.

(d) Fixed asset purchases of £380 were entered as £830 in the fixed asset account.

(e) Drawings by Dick of stock valued at £45 were made in June 19x8 and not recorded in the books.

(f) A payment of casual wages £80 was entered in the cash book but the double entry was not completed.

For Doris, the following errors were found:

(a) The account of Joshua, a customer, was extracted in error as £354 instead of £454.

(b) A payment for advertising £190 was credited in the expenses account.

(c) An invoice for goods purchased for resale from Wally £278 was omitted from the books altogether.

(d) The sales invoice to Hodge was correctly entered in the sales day book as £560 but entered in Hodge's account as £650.

(e) The payment of an advertising account to Noos Ltd £50 was debited in the expenses account and also in Noos Ltd account. The original invoice was correctly entered in Noos Ltd's account.

(f) The balance of Geoff's account was entered as £320 Dr. In fact the two sides of his account totalled:

Dr £890   Cr £534

Required: (for each business)

(a) Compute the difference on the trial balance.

(b) Identify which errors cause the difference.

(d) Produce an amended trial balance and show that it now balances.

Assignment

❑ A difference on the trial balance of Singh at 31.12.x8 was resolved by opening a suspense account. The profit and loss account was then prepared and showed a profit of £12,600. The suspense account was included in the balance sheet to make it balance. Subsequent investigation disclosed:

(a) A page of the sales day book totalling £576 had not been posted to the sales account.

(b) An accrual of rates £371 had not been taken account of.

(c) A repayment of part of the loan from Patel £300 had been entered on the loan interest account.

(d) The petty cash balance had been included as £57 instead of £75.

(e) A credit note £120 had been entered in the customer's account but not in the sales account.

(f) Drawings £200 had been entered in the sundry expenses account.

(g) An invoice for car repairs £380 had been entered in the wages account.

(h) The rent received account balance £600 had been entered on the wrong side of the trial balance and the profit and loss account.

(i) *Advertising account with a balance of £2,759 had been omitted altogether.*

(j) *Closing stock had omitted some items valued at cost at £2,000.*

Required:

(a) *Frame the journal entries to clear the suspense account (narratives not required). Prepare a statement showing the corrected amount of the profit.*

(b) *Explain why each error did or did not cause a difference in the trial balance and in the profit.*

9 The asset of stock

The asset of stock is not recorded continuously and this chapter tells you how stock is dealt with in the bookkeeping system and in the trading account.

Bookkeeping for stock

1. You will have noticed that purchases are recorded in a purchases account and that sales are recorded in a sales account. Both purchases and sales are movements or changes in the asset 'stock'. Note well that changes in the asset stock are not recorded continuously. Why is this?

   In order to record the asset stock on a continuous basis common pricing must be used. Thus purchases are recorded at cost but also sales would have to be recorded at cost. However input cost is not known for each sale. Imagine a newspaper shop owner trying to record his stock continuously and having to determine the cost to him of each newspaper he sells.

   For the preparation of the profit and loss account and balance sheet it is sufficient to record total sales and purchases. Of course opening and closing stocks must be known and these values are obtained by counting and valuing the stock at period ends. The only time the value of the asset stock is known then is at the period end when it is counted.

2. The actual bookkeeping entries for stock are:
   (a) At the first period end:
       Dr Stock Account   Cr Trading Account
       With the stock at that date.
   (b) At each subsequent period end:
       Dr Trading Account   Cr Stock Account
       With the stock as it was at the previous period end
       and
       Dr Stock Account   Cr Trading Account
       With the stock at the period end

Example

Georgina commenced in business on 1.1.x7. At 31.12.x7 her stock was valued at £2,300. At 31.12.x7 bookkeeping entries were:

Stock Account

31.12.x7 Trading account	£2,300	

Trading Account

		31.12.x7 Stock account	£2,300

At 31.12.x8 her stock was valued at £3,780 and entries were:

Stock Account

31.12.x7 Balance b/f	£2,300	31.12.x8 Trading account	£2,300
31.12.x7 Trading account	£3,780		

Trading Account

| 31.12.x7 | Opening stock | £2,300 | 31.12.x8 | Closing stock | £3,780 |

The trading account *is* a double entry account and is part of the double entry system. In former times (in my youth!) it appeared like any other double entry account like this:

31.12.x7	Opening stock	2,300	31.12.x8	Sales	32,665
31.12.x8	Purchases	21,700	31.12.x8	Closing stock	3,780
31.12.x8	Gross profit c/f to profit and loss account	12,445			
		36,445			36,445

We now live in more presentation conscious times and trading accounts are now reformatted, for presentation to interested people, in the vertical form we have used in this book.

Note that the stock account contains a balance of £2,300 for the whole year 19x8. The balance is only changed once a year. Thus in trial balances you usually see the stock of the previous year. The value of the stock at the trial balance date is given, not in the trial balance, but in a note.

Summary

❑ There is an account for stock in most double entry systems but this is not continuously updated.

❑ The account for stock is updated once a year when stock is counted and valued. The double entries are to the trading account.

Points to note

❑ Most beginning students want to debit purchases and sales to a stock account. This is not correct and purchases and sales are entered in the purchases and sales accounts. Stock is updated only when a trading account is prepared.

Self-testing questions

1. What is the double entry for:
   (a) Sales of goods?
   (b) Purchases of goods?
2. What is the double entry for goods counted and valued at the end of a financial year?
3. At what date will the stock be in a trial balance?

Exercise

1. The following items appear in the trial balance of Foster as at 31 July 19x3. The previous trading account was prepared for the year ending 31 July 19x2:

	£	£
Stock at 31 July 19x2	23,005	
Purchases	145,800	
Sales		174,700
Purchase returns		1,745
Carriage inwards	6,700	

The stock was counted on 31 July 19x3 and valued at £25,987.

Required:

Show the stock account and prepare a trading account for the year to 31 July 19x3.

Note: Carriage costs on goods carried from supplier to customer are often paid by the seller. If they are paid, as here, by the buyer, they are treated as part of the cost of the goods sold.

Assignment

❑ *The books of Denzil, who operates a local bus service, show the following balances at his year end on 31 December 19x3:*

	£		£
Depot at cost	*105,000*	*Capital 31.12.x2*	*61,406*
Buses at cost	*264,800*	*Bank overdraft*	*43,700*
Stock of diesel 31.12.x2	*1,800*	*Fares*	*354,900*
Equipment at cost	*17,200*	*Loan from Scrooge PLC*	*90,000*
Diesel oil	*123,300*	*Proceeds of sale – bus*	*15,000*
Licences	*3,900*	*Creditors*	*31,500*
Insurances	*28,400*	*Depreciation of depot to 31.12.x2*	*11,000*
Wages	*89,470*	*Depreciation of buses*	*125,028*
General overheads	*29,544*	*Depreciation of equipment*	*6,210*
Rates	*6,410*		
Interest	*16,900*		
Repairs of buses	*31,700*		
Drawings	*22,000*		

The following facts are relevant.

(a) *The depot was considered to be Land £39,000 and Buildings £66,000. The Buildings are being depreciated over 30 years straight line with no salvage value.*

(b) *The buses are depreciated on the reducing balance method at a rate of 30% a year. A full year's depreciation is given in the year of purchase. There were four buses on 31.12.x2.*

    A Purchased in 19x0 for £64,000

    B Purchased in 19x1 for £80,000

    C Purchased in 19x1 for £40,800

    D Purchased in 19x2 for £80,000

    The bus sold in 19x3 was Bus A.

(c) *The equipment is being depreciated over five years straight line with nil salvage value. Of the equipment £4,100 at cost was purchased five years or more before 31.12.x3.*

(d) *The stock of diesel oil at 31.12.x3 was valued at £4,150.*

(e) *The licences include licences for the year ending 31.5.x4 of £1,800.*

(f) *The insurances include £800 in advance.*

(g) Rates do not include rates for the half year to 31.3.x4 £5,400

(h) The Loan carries interest at 15%. Interest is paid only up to 31.10.x3.

(i) The fares include season ticket sales to a group of commuters. These amounted to £26,000 and are for the four months to 31.3.x4.

(j) The trial balance does not balance. An investigation showed:

    (i) Fares £860 on one day were debited in the cash book but not entered in the fares account.

    (ii) Drawings of £1,200 were debited twice in error to drawings account.

    (iii) A cheque drawn for Telephone £190 was credited to General Overheads. It should have been debited.

Required:

(a) Prepare a profit and loss account for the year ending 31 December 19x3 and a balance sheet as at that date. Note that a trading account is not appropriate and the format should be:

Fares		x
Less: expenses:	x	
	x	x
	x	

(b) Describe the entries which are required to be made in the trial balance and show that it now balances.

(c) List the accounting conventions that have been applied to your financial statements and explain their application to them.

(d) Write a concise report to a prospective buyer of the business explaining what the financial statements show.

10 Petty cash

The majority of payments between commercial and industrial concerns and their customers are settled by cheque or other bank medium. The only significant cash (notes and coin) movement in business is in retail sales and even there, payment by cheque and credit card is increasingly important. Cash received from retail sales is usually banked intact and hence becomes in effect a bank transaction.

However, most businesses have a need to make small cash payments for such items as tips, bus fares, casual wages (e.g. cleaning), tea and coffee. These small payments are dealt with through a petty cash book (petty is from the French, small or little). The specific system commonly used is called the imprest system (from the Latin – to lend).

The imprest system

1. The system requires the following procedures:

    (a) The appointment of a person who is responsible for petty cash – the petty cashier.

    (b) The giving to the petty cashier by the cashier from the bank of a sum of cash called the imprest or the float – say £100.

    (c) The payment of petty cash expenses by the petty cashier against authorised and approved vouchers. It is necessary for the firm to specify who can authorise petty cash payments and documents should be designed to allow a space for the approval to be evidenced by signature or initials. An example might be:

PETTY CASH VOUCHER for what required:	Date: 24.2.x8 Amount
Bus Fares to college	£1.40
Lunch	£1.35
Total	£2.75
Signature: *A. Mills*	Approved by: J.Owen

    (d) The entry of all these transactions in the petty cash book which is both a book of prime entry and a part of the double entry system.

    (e) At intervals the cashier will examine the supporting evidence for the payments, take away and file this evidence and draw from the bank the total amount of payments. Thus if payments made totalled £64.25, then the cash remaining should total £35.75 and further cash will be given to the petty cashier of £64.25 making the float or imprest up to £100 again.

(f) At random intervals, a senior official should check the petty cash book, vouchers and balance. The petty cashier should always have a total of £100 in cash or in approved vouchers.

The petty cash book

2. A typical petty cash book ruling is shown in Fig. 10.1.

Dr		Total	Tips	Sundries	Station-ery	Travelling expenses	Cr Tools
		£	£	£	£	£	£
1.1.x4 Balance in hand 34.75	2.1.x4 Bus fares	4.13				4.13	
2.1.x4 Cash from bank 65.25	3.1.x4 Tips	2.00	2.00				
	4.1.x4 Tools	9.20					9.20
	6.1.x4 Petrol	11.50				11.50	
	7.1.x4 Tips	3.00	3.00				
	8.1.x4 Cleaning materials	4.60		4.60			
	9.1.x4 Tea/sugar	2.50		2.50			
	10.1.x4 Books	15.09			15.09		
	12.1.x4 Train fare	25.00				25.00	
		77.02	5.00	7.10	15.09	40.63	9.20
	12.1.x4 Balance c/d	22.98					
100.00		100.00					
12.1.x4 Balance in hand 22.98							
12.1.x4 Cash from bank 77.02							

Fig. 10.1

The petty cash book is a double entry account. The double entry of the credit side items will be completed by debit to:

Tips expense a/c	Tips	£5.00
Sundry expenses a/c	Sundries	£7.10
etc.		

Petty cash and VAT

3. Petty cash payments may be for goods or services to which VAT has been added. Businesses registered for VAT can recover any VAT included in such payments and so the petty cash system must allow for this. A possible ruling of the petty cash book credit side might be:

Payment	VAT	Net	Sundries	Tips	Stationery	Travelling expenses
(a)	(b)	(c)	(d)			

(a) This is the actual payment made.

(b) This is the VAT included in the payment. It is debited in the Customs and Excise account.

(c) This is the net amount excluding VAT. Columns (b) + (c) = (a).

(d) This is the first of the analysis columns. The total of all the analysis columns sums to column (c). The total of each analysis column is debited to the relevant expense account.

Summary

◻ Most cash movement today is through bank accounts.

◻ Small cash payments are dealt with through the petty cash system kept on an imprest system.

◻ Petty cash transactions are recorded in a petty cash book, which is part of the double entry system, as well as a book of prime entry.

Points to note

◻ Petty cash is vulnerable to fraud because the asset, cash, is obviously valuable, readily disposed of and easily portable. However sums involved are usually very small. It is important that petty cash is tightly controlled in order to avoid loss and good personnel management requires that employees should be protected from temptation.

◻ Petty cash is dealt with in Sage by treating petty cash as a bank account (*bank + choose petty cash*) and entries are made as for the bank account. Cash drawn from the bank for petty cash is dealt with by: *bank + bank transfer.*

Self-testing questions

1. Why are cash sales not dealt with in the petty cash book?
2. What payments are put through petty cash?
3. What is the imprest system?
4. How is VAT recorded in petty cash systems?

Exercises

1. Camp maintains a petty cash book with columns for travel, post, stationery, motor, sundries, credit accounts. At 19.1.x7 the balance was £16.44. The imprest is £100. In the week ending 24.1.x7 the following payments were made: tea bags £3.78; bus fares £2.33; milk £1.37; posters £4.11; petrol £5.00; taxi £2.44; envelopes £2.11; gift to nuns £5.00; oil filter £4.10; stamps £5.00; parcel £3.20; bus fare £1.50; petrol £6.00; settlement of credit account – Walters Ltd £12.00.

   On 20.1.x7 the imprest was made up resulting from the balance at 19.1.x7.

   Required:

   Show the petty cash book for the week and indicate the double entries required.

2. Clunk maintains his petty cash on the imprest system with an imprest of £80. At 16.1.x7 his balance in hand was £32.12.

   In the ensuing week the imprest was made up and the following payments made: paid credit account of Brown £5.90; invoice books £6.23; petrol £4.87; bus fares £1.20; train fare £2.00; loan to Clunk £5.00; sandwiches for auditor £3.80; petrol £7.63; advert £3.00; mileage payment to manager £12.00; leaflet printing £4.00; antifreeze £7.79.

   Required:

   Write up a suitably analysed petty cash book for the week indicating the double entries required.

141

3.   Charles Evans is a sole trader who keeps his petty cash on the Imprest system – the Imprest amount being £40. The petty cash transactions for the month of May 19x0 are as follows:

May	
1	Petty cash in hand £5.17.
1	Petty cash restored to imprest account.
6	Bought notepaper £3.28 inc. VAT.
7	Paid wages £9.14.
14	Bought postage stamps £3.75.
16	Paid to J. Thomas, a creditor, £5.36.
21	Paid wages £9.28.
23	Bought envelopes £4.37 inc. VAT.
27	Bought postage stamps £2.10.

Required:

Draw up the petty cash book for the month of May 19x0, recording the above transactions. You should also give the entry on 2 June 19x0, restoring the petty cash to the Imprest amount. Indicate how the double entry is completed.

Notes:

(a)   VAT is at 17.5%.

(b)   Your analysis columns should be for:

   (i)   Stationery.

   (ii)   Wages.

   (iii)   Postages.

4.   Revisit the exercise on computerised accounting in Chapter 6 and add the following entries:

(a)   Draw £150.00 by cheque from the bank on 6 October to form a petty cash float or imprest.

(b)   8 October spent from petty cash £25.74 + VAT on motor expenses.

(c)   18 October spent from petty cash £5 on tips.

(d)   19 October spent £4.50 on bus fares.

(e)   23 October spent £42.30 (inclusive of VAT) on stationery.

(f)   31 October drew a cheque for cash to replenish the imprest.

Assignment

☐ *Christine is in business as a hairdresser. At the beginning of week 14 she had £185.00 in the bank and £43.21 in petty cash. In the week she had the following transactions:*

   (a)   Restored petty cash to imprest of £100.00

   (b)   Paid cheque to Shampoo Ltd £54.00 less 5% cash discount

   (c)   Paid cleaner £10 in cash

   (d)   Banked £340.62 cash takings

   (e)   Paid electricity bill by direct debit (£120.76)

   (f)   Paid £13.98 cash for postage stamps

   (g)   Received cheque for £87.90 from customer and paid it into the bank

(h) Paid £20.00 tips to delivery people
(i) Paid cash £20.54 + VAT for equipment

Items (d) and (g) include VAT.

Required:

Enter all these items in a cash book or petty cash book as appropriate and explain how the double entry will be completed for each item. Bring down the balances at the end of the week.

11 Control accounts

Some double entry systems record many thousands of transactions, and errors detected by a difference on the trial balance may be difficult to find. In the days before computer systems I spent many happy (?) days checking and rechecking books searching for differences.

Breaking the system into sections will facilitate the discovery of errors.

In large systems, the bulk of the entries are in two areas:

(a) Credit sales.

(b) Purchases and expenses incurred on credit.

Therefore the sections kept separate from the rest of the system are these two. The sales system is explained first and then the purchases and expenses system.

Sales ledger

1. In a double entry system where there are a large number of accounts and in particular a large number of credit customers, the personal accounts of the credit customers are kept together in a book called the sales ledger. The sales ledger may be kept on media other than a book, a magnetic disk for example.

Sources of data in a sales system

Detail – to customer's accounts
Totals of sources (schedule of balances etc) – to control accounts

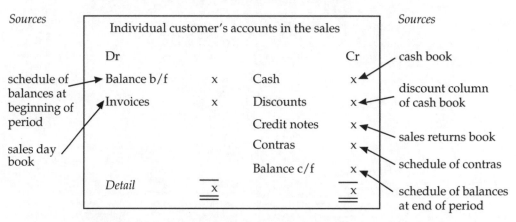

2. A typical sales ledger account may appear like this (in the books of AB, a trader):

CD Account

		£			£
1.4.x4	Balance b/f	282	5.4.x4	Cash	195
4.4.x4	Goods	341	5.4.x4	Discount	5
7.4.x4	Goods	262	14.4.x4	Credit note	28
19.4.x4	Goods	999	19.4.x4	Contra	49
			30.4.x4	Balance c/f	1,607
		1,884			1,884

The story told by this account is:

(a) At the beginning of April CD owed AB £282.

(b) In April, CD bought further goods totalling £1,602 (£341 etc).

(c) This means that CD had to pay or settle £1,884 in total.

(d) In April, he paid £195, was allowed discount £5 for paying the £195 promptly, returned goods value £28, settled £49 in contra – total £277.

(e) At the end of the month CD still owed £1,607.

Notes:

(a) Cash discount is considered in more detail in the next chapter. For the moment, note that some suppliers offer their customers a discount for payment within some specified date to hasten payment. For example, A Ltd might offer its customers 5% off for payment within five days of the invoice date.

(b) Contras (Latin = against) occur when a credit customer also sells on credit to a business. Instead of exchanging cheques the two indebtednesses are set against each other and one cheque only is sent. If A owes B £20 and B owes A £5, it is convenient for A to pay B £15. Since there are usually two accounts for this firm – as a customer in the sales ledger and as a supplier in the purchase ledger – there is a need for a transfer between the two accounts.

3. A system for entering the sales ledger accounts may be as follows:

(a) Sales invoices are entered in the sales daybook.

(b) Each sales invoice is entered on the debit of a customer account.

(c) The sales day book is totalled. If there are no errors this total is equal to the total amount entered on the individual customer account.

(d) Credit notes (in effect reverse invoices) are entered in a book of prime entry called the sales returns day book.

(e) Each credit note is entered on the credit of a customer's account.

(f) The sales returns day book is totalled and this total should equal the total credit notes entered on customers' accounts.

(g) The debit side of the cash book consists largely of receipts from credit customers which are credited to customers' accounts. The total of these receipts is obtained by an analysis of the debit of the cash book.

(h) The discounts given to customers are entered in a separate discount column in the cash book and credited to the customers' accounts. The total so credited can be obtained by summing the total of the discount column in the cash book.

(i) The contras are made individually. A list being kept to obtain the total.

An example

4. J.T. Ltd includes the following figures in its books:

		£
Sales ledger balances	1.1.x4	16,420
Sales day book total	19x4	82,761
Sales returns daybook total	19x4	1,210
Cash book debit (sales ledger items)	19x4	71,329

... continued

		£
Discount column total	19x4	1,785
Contras	19x4	2,410
Bad debts	19x4	560

Required:

Produce a memorandum account to show what the sales ledger balances should be at 31.12.x4.

Note: Bad debts will be explored more fully in the next chapter but for now realise that if a sum is owed by a customer and cannot be paid (e.g. if the customer is bankrupt) then the balance is removed from the account by a credit entry labelled bad debt. The double entry is on an account 'bad debt expense' which eventually goes as an expense to the profit and loss account).

Memo Sales Ledger Control Account y/e 31.12.x4

	£		£
Balance 31.12.x3	16,420	Sales returns DB	1,210
Sales daybook	82,761	Cash	71,329
		Discount	1,785
		Contras	2,410
		Bad debts	560
		*Balances 31.12.x4	21,887
	99,181		99,181

*obtained by balancing this account.

The next stage is to extract a list of the individual sales ledger accounts. Suppose this came to £21,981. Clearly some errors have occurred and an extensive search revealed:

(a) Two balance were omitted from the list: £136 and £240.

(b) The sales daybook was under cast (incorrectly added up) by £100.

(c) An invoice for £62 in the sales daybook was posted in error to two customers' accounts.

(d) An invoice for £46 correctly entered in the sales daybook, was posted to the customer's account as £64.

(e) A discount of £20 correctly entered in the customer's account was omitted from the discount column of the cash book.

(f) A contra of £100, included in the list had not been entered on the customer's account.

(g) A customer had overpaid by £100 and a cheque had been sent to reimburse him. This had been correctly entered in his account.

(h) A customer had paid his account and subsequently been given a credit note. His account was thus in credit by £55 and this had been wrongly put on the list as a debit balance.

There are two sorts of error here:

(a) Errors that affect the memorandum total account (errors in the books of prime entry).

(b) Errors that affect the individual ledger accounts and hence the list of balances.

Answer

The revised memorandum control account should show:

	£		£
Balances 1.1.x4	16,420	Sales return DB	1,210
Sales daybook total (b)	82,861	Cash	71,329
Credit balance 31.12.x4	55	Discount (e)	1,805
Cash (g)	100	Contras	2,410
		Bad debts	560
		Dr Balances 31.12.x4	22,122
	99,436		99,436

The list of balances total should be:

	£	£
Original list		21,981
Add (a)		376
		22,357
Less (c)	62	
Less (d)	18	
Less (f)	100	
Less (h)	110	290
		22,067

The total of £22,067 is composed of Dr balances £22,122 less Cr balances £55. Item (d) is an example of transposition of figures, a very common error. Note that the difference in transposition errors is always divisible by 9.

Purchase ledger

5. If you have understood the sectional balancing of the sales ledger, then the sectional balancing of the purchase ledger will present no difficulties as it is the mirror image of the sales ledger. Simply, the entries on the memorandum purchase ledger control account go on the opposite side to their counterparts on the sales ledger.

A common examination question which combines knowledge of both sales and purchase ledgers control accounts is:

Good Books Ltd includes the following items in its books for 19x5:

Balances 31.12.x4	£
Dr Sales ledger	16,220
Cr Sales ledger	141
Cr Purchase ledger	6,310
Sales daybook	101,005
Purchase daybook	52,666
Sales returns daybook	1,040

	£
Contras	1,551
Bad debts	2,150
Cash book debit:	
Sales ledger items	96,434
Purchase ledger items	152
Cash book credit:	
Purchase ledger items	49,200
Sales ledger items	1,400
Dr Side Discount column	1,920
Cr Side Discount column	867
Purchase ledger Dr balance 31.12.x5	65
Sales ledger Cr balance 31.12.x5	244

Required:

Prepare memorandum control accounts for the sales ledger and the purchase ledger.

Answer

Memorandum sales ledger control account y/e 31.12.x5

	£		£
Balances 31.12.x4	16,220	Balances 31.12.x4	141
Sales	101,005	Sales returns	1,040
Cash	1,400	Contras	1,551
Balance 31.12.x5	244	Bad debts	2,150
		Cash	96,434
		Discounts	1,920
		Balance 31.12.x5	15,633
	118,869		118,869

Memorandum purchase ledger control account y/e 31.12.x5

	£		£
Contras	1,551	Balance 31.12.x4	6,310
Cash	49,200	Purchases	52,666
Discount	867	Cash	152
Balances 31.12.x5	7,575	Balances 31.12.x5	65
	59,193		59,193

Summary

❏ Large bookkeeping systems need to be broken down into sections to facilitate the detection of errors.

❏ A common sectioning is the creation of a sales ledger sub-system and a purchase and expense ledger sub-system.

❏ The balance owing by customers or suppliers can be devised in two ways:
   (i) In total using the totals of the books of prime entry.
   (ii) In detail by extraction from the sales ledger and the purchase ledger.

Differences between these two totals should be investigated and the explanation found.

Points to note

❏ Students find this material very difficult to grasp in an academic way as it is really an extremely practical matter. Practice is needed to familiarise students with the ideas and the jargon. Bookkeepers and accountants spend a lot of time balancing the books and seeking differences. The coming of the computer which balances accounts automatically has largely eliminated the work (and the fascination) of error investigation but has introduced new sorts of errors.

❏ Some points to watch are:
   (i)   The total accounts (also known as control or summary accounts) are memorandum only. The real double entry is in the individual ledger accounts.
   (ii) The total entries in the control accounts go on the same side as the entries in the detail accounts.
   (iii) In the sales ledger, the debit entries set up the sums due by the customers and the credit side shows how these sums have been reduced or settled.
   (iv) The purchase ledger entries are on the opposite side to those of the sales ledger.
   (v)   Errors may be in the books of prime entry and thus affect the memo total account or in the individual accounts and thus affect the total extracted from the ledger.

❏ The purchase and expenses ledger may be called the *bought ledger*.

❏ Where separate bought and sales ledgers are kept, together with the cash book, all other accounts (real, nominal and some personal) are kept in a ledger called the nominal, private or impersonal general ledger.

❏ In Sage and other computerised systems, the double entry is automatic so control accounts as described in this section are unnecessary. However, this does not mean that errors cannot be made. It is possible to omit transactions or enter them twice or enter them on the wrong accounts and there are yet other possibilities.

Self-testing questions

1. What is the purpose of keeping a sales ledger?
2. What is a contra?
3. List the books of prime entry in which entries on a customer's account are first entered.
4. Write out a typical sales ledger control account.
5. What is a general ledger?

Exercises

1. From the following data prepare sales ledger and bought ledger control accounts for 19x5:

	Edward's business	Jane's business
	£	£
Debtors 1.1.19x5	23,678	116,745
Creditors 1.1.19x5	15,438	34,780
Purchase daybook	124,324	154,780
Sales daybook	98,710	763,243
Cash received	96,450	732,100
Payments to suppliers	123,789	149,980
Discounts received	1,670	1,453
Discounts allowed	880	21,579

Required:

(a) Balance the control accounts and bring down the balances.

(b) What would be the effect on the control account balances, of errors in the primary records from which the data was obtained?

2. Prepare control accounts from the following data for the year ending 19x2:

	Alice's business	Kewal's business
	£	£
Customers' Dr balances 1.1.x2	3,469	32,500
Customers' Cr balances 1.1.x2	34	1,453
Suppliers' Cr balances 1.1.x2	6,548	23,801
Suppliers' Dr balances 1.1.x2	45	678
Sales daybook	63,257	134,902
Sales returns daybook	3,780	1,439
Purchase daybook	82,456	278,030
Purchase returns daybook	1,272	2,453
Cash paid to suppliers	78,329	241,000
Cash paid to customers	780	1,547
Cash received from customers	58,340	110,456
Cash received from suppliers	1,459	86
Bad debts	872	249
Contras	1,322	756
Interest charged to customer	23	146
Discounts allowed	897	1,680
Discounts received	432	657
Customers' Cr balances 31.12.x2	54	435
Suppliers' Dr balances 31.12.x2	50	324

Balance the control accounts and bring down the balances. Explain the transactions – cash received from suppliers, contras, bad debts, interest charged to customer. How can a debit balance arise on a supplier's account?

3. Prepare the control account for the bought ledger for 19x4 from the following:

	Brenda's business	Simone's business
	£	£
Balances 1.1.x4	12,500	4,532
Purchase daybook	74,098	34,982
Cash to suppliers	71,567	33,450

For Brenda's business

The list of balances totalled £15,277 and the following errors were found:

(a) The purchase daybook was over added by £100.

(b) The cash to suppliers included, in error, a payment of wages £487.

(c) The list did not include the balance due to George of £231.

(d) The list included the balance due to Agnes at £540 instead of £450.

For Simone's business

The list of balances totalled £6,656 and the following errors were found:

(a) The list included June's balance £329 twice.

(b) The list was under added by £180.

(c) The total of a page in the daybook £278 was carried forward to the next page as £287.

(d) A refund from a supplier, who had been overpaid, of £452 should have been included in the control account.

For both businesses, amend the control account and the list of balances and show that the ledger now balances.

Assignment

❑ *Herbert has extracted a trial balance from his books and also a sales ledger control account. The trial balance balances after including the following the following*

	Debit	Credit
Suspense account	341.09	
Sales ledger balances	16,870.54	
Cash book balance	546.12	
Sales		197,765.34

The following errors were found later:

(a) A sale to Jones £700.00 had been entered in the sales daybook but not in Jones' account

(b) The list of sales ledger balances should total £100 less than the figure in the trial balance because of an addition error.

(c) Cash sales of £658.91 had been entered in the sales account but had been omitted from the cash book.

Required:

Make journal entries to correct the errors and show the how the balances would now appear in the trial balance. Explain how you would now look for the remaining difference.

12 Bank reconciliations

The cash book of an enterprise records the monies paid into the bank and the sums drawn from the bank through the media of cheques etc. The data for these entries comes from the paying-in book, the cheque book stubs and, for modern payment methods, various other documents.

The bank also records these items in its own books and issues its customer with a statement summarising the transactions between the bank and the customer.

To the business, the bank statement forms an external check on the accuracy of the cash book. However there are usually differences between the cash book and the bank statement and this chapter explores these differences and shows how extra entries should be made in the cash book and a bank reconciliation statement prepared.

Timing differences

1. Consider the following sequence of events:

1.1.x8	John draws a cheque in favour of Ted and an entry is made in the cash book
2.8.x8	Cheque is mailed to Ted
5.8.x8	Cheque received by Ted
6.8.x8	Ted pays the cheque into his bank account
8.8.x8	The bank deals with the matter through the clearing system and the transaction appears on John's bank statement.

    There is a timing difference of seven days between John's cash book entry and the corresponding entry on the bank statement.

2. Common timing differences include:

    (a) Cheques drawn (as illustrated above) – delays can be months if recipients of cheques fail to pay them in.

    (b) Payments into the bank – usually only a matter of a day or two.

    (c) Errors by the bank – banks can and do make mistakes and students do not always realise that these are in fact timing differences. George pays in a sum to his bank on 14 July and this is credited in error to Guy. The error is discovered and corrected on 7 August. In effect George's cash book has 14 July as the date and the bank statement will have 7 August.

Informational differences

3. Businessmen commonly write up their cash books from their paying-in books and their cheque book stubs. However, there are transactions which are not found from these sources. Examples are:

    (a) Dividends credited direct to the bank.

    (b) Payments by customers which are paid direct to the bank (e.g. traders' credits).

    (c) Bank charges and interest.

    (d) Cheques paid in by the business which have been dishonoured (colloquially 'bounced').

(e) Standing orders (an order made to the bank to make a regular payment – e.g. mortgage or hire purchase instalments).

(f) Cash point withdrawals.

(g) Direct debits – an arrangement whereby a person's account is debited with a sum at the direction of a supplier with, of course, the account holder's prior permission.

The business is usually informed of these transactions but tends to overlook them until a bank statement is received pointing them out. The entries should then be made in the cash book.

Bank reconciliation statements

4. Here is the cash book of Pip, a trader, for March 19x4:

19x4 March		£	19x4 March		£
8	Brown	164	1	Balance b/d	2,064
8	Jones	347	2	Walter	39
8	Robinson	163	4	Cash	610
8	Cash sales	20	7	Hughes	38
14	Hubert	830	9	Williams	915
14	Wilkes	910	14	Noll	37
21	Hinks	34	21	Graham	620
26	Lowe	1,013	28	Wem	99
26	Little	2	30	Xavier	12
30	Howe	137			
31	Balance c/d	814			
		4,434			4,434

The bank statement for the same month showed:

NORTHERN BANK PLC
Pip – Account Number 1342692

1.3.x4	Balance			2064 D
3.3.x4	106284	39		2103 D
5.3.x4	106285	610		2713 D
8.3.x4	Cash and cheques		694	2019 D
10.3.x4	Cash point	50		2069 D
11.3.x4	106287	915		2984 D
15.3.x4	SO UDT Ltd	67		3051 D
16.3.x4	Cheques		1740	1311 D
17.3.x4	106288	37		1348 D
20.3.x4	Dividend ICI PLC		24	1324 D
22.3.x4	Cheque		35	1289 D

... continued

23.3.x4	106289		620		1909 D
24.3.x4	251332		30		1939 D
27.3.x4	Cheques			1015	924 D
30.3.x4	Charges		36		960 D
	Interest		63		1023 D

NB D = Overdrawn

You will note that:

(a) The balance is given after each transaction.

(b) The entries are on the reverse side to the cash book.

(c) Payments in are not detailed.

(d) Cheques are distinguished by numbers only – information not often given in the cash book.

Procedures

5. (a) Compare the entries in the cash book with those in the bank statement by ticking them. You should find that unticked items are:

Place	Item		Reason and Action
Cash book	Hinks	34	Error in amount, presume bank is
Bank statement	Cheque	35	correct – alter cash book
Cash book	Howe	137	Timing difference
Cash book	Hughes	38	Timing difference
Cash book	Wem	99	Timing differences
Cash book	Xavier	12	Timing differences
Bank statement	Cash point	50	Enter in cash book
Bank statement	SO UDT Ltd	67	Enter in cash book
Bank statement	Dividend	24	Enter in cash book
Bank statement	251332	30	Error by bank – timing difference
Bank statement	Charges	36	Enter in cash book
Bank statement	Interest	63	Enter in cash book

(b) Complete the cash book

		£			£
20.3.x4	Dividend ICI PLC	24	31.3.x4	Balance b/d	814
21.3.x4	Hinks	1	10.3.x4	Cash point	50
31.3.x4	Correct		15.3.x4	SO UDT Ltd	67
	Balance c/d	1,005	31.3.x4	Bank charges	36
			31.3.x4	Bank interest	63
		1,030			1,030

(c) Reconcile the difference between the *adjusted* cash book balance and the bank statement balance as:

Bank Reconciliation Statement as at 31 March 19x4

	£	
Balance per cash book as *adjusted*	1,005	OD
Deduct error by bank – adjusted in April	30	
	1,035	OD
Deduct payments in credited after date	137	
	1,172	OD

		£	
Add Cheques presented after date			
Hughes	38		
Wem	99		
Xavier	12	149	
Balance per bank statement		1,023	

Theory

6. The adjusted balance of the cash book is the balance which is included in the balance sheet. Thus, the balance sheet item at 31 March 19x4 'Bank overdraft £1,005' is not the balance according to the bank (which is £1,023). This has the effect that all transactions effected with the bank by the year end are reflected in the bank balance, despite the fact that the bank may not have recognised them by that date.

   A second effect is that for example the cheque drawn in favour of Xavier £12 is reflected in the bank balance and therefore must be reflected in the account of Xavier to complete the double entry.

Practical difficulties

7. This subject does not present many difficulties to students, providing they have grasped the two stages:
   (a) Adjust the cash book.
   (b) Prepare the bank reconciliation statement.

   However, in some examination questions and nearly always in practice, the opening balance of the cash book differs from the opening balance of the bank statement. For example:

1.3.x4	Balance per cash book		£639

   Extract from bank statement:

		£	£
1.3.x4	Balance		1,146
2.3.x4	110311	460	686
3.3.x4	110313	38	648
3.3.x4	110312	47	601

   The technique is to tick off the £639 against 1,146 – 460 – 47 = 639, both the 460 and 47 being in the cash book in February and in the bank reconciliation at 29.2.x4.

8. When presented in the form I have used in this chapter, a student or a cashier can verify that he or she has the right answer because the two balances reconcile. To

155

avoid this facility, some examiners limit the data given and may, for example, omit the bank statement balance and ask the examinee to calculate it. The solution then is to write out the bank reconciliation statement and insert all known figures. The single unknown can then be found.

Summary

❒ The cash book balance can be proved by comparing it with the bank statement.

Two kinds of differences occur:
(i) Timing differences.
(ii) Transactions which need to be entered in the cash book.

❒ The three stages are therefore:
(i) Ticking over the cash book with the bank statement to identify differences.
(ii) Adjusting the cash book by making further entries.
(iii) Preparing a bank reconciliation statement to demonstrate that the two balances are the same, apart from timing differences.

Points to note

❒ Many people keep a note of the current balance of their own bank account on the cheque stubs, altering the balance after each transaction. No doubt my readers do. They will find also that the bank statement balance disagrees. Bank reconciliation statements prepared on the receipt of a bank statement will soon familiarise students with this simple technique.

❒ I still have momentary difficulty in knowing whether to add or subtract in the bank reconciliation statement. The trick is to remember that if there are, for example, unpresented cheques then the bank statement balance will be larger than the cash book balance.

❒ Some businessmen may wish their balance sheet to show a position which is different from that shown by a strict application of accounting principles.

For example, drawing a large number of cheques immediately before the year end (but not sending them to the creditors) will mean

(i) Reduced creditors – the businessman does not wish to show that the business owes a great deal of money.

(ii) Increased overdraft – a large apparent overdraft may indicate that the bank has confidence in the business.

This technique of showing a more attractive position than the proper one is known as *window dressing*. There are many such techniques – this is but one. Correctly, cheques should only be entered in the cash book if and when they are actually sent to the creditors.

❒ When using Sage or other computerised accounting systems, bank reconciliations still have to be done. However Sage offers some help. Choose *bank + reconcile*. Select each transaction on the bank statement, one after another and check it against the

Sage record. As you do so the Sage balance should agree with the statement. If transactions are not in the Sage record, then choose *adjustment* and make the necessary entry.

Self-testing questions

1. List some typical timing differences between the cash book and the bank statement.
2. List some typical informational differences between the cash book and the bank statement.
3. Draft the format for a bank statement.
4. What balance for 'cash at bank' should be included in a balance sheet?
5. Summarise the procedures for preparing a bank reconciliation statement.
6. Explain window dressing.

Exercises

1. The cash book of Juliet for January 19x7 showed

Dr				Cr	
		£			£
1.1.x7	Balance b/f	234	1.1.x7	Cray	320
2.1.x7	Harris	1,560	3.1.x7	Richardson	45
5.1.x7	Lowe	810	6.1.x7	Wages	1,800
14.1.x7	Gibbon	865	8.1.x7	Bowman	200
17.1.x7	Lizzie	2,340	10.1.x7	Aleric	1,567
21.1.x7	Xavier	54	15.1.x7	Visitis	311
27.1.x7	Younghusband	124	24.1.x7	Lewis	98
31.1.x7	Alice	1,566	28.1.x7	Guy	234
			31.1.x7	LEB	540
			31.1.x7	Balance c/d	2,438
		7,553			7,553

The bank statement showed for the same month:

Jan 1	Balance b/f			234	C
3	624		320	86	D
4	Sundries		1,560	1,474	C
6	625		45	1,429	C
6	626	1,800		371	D
7	Sundries		810	439	C
11	627	200		239	C
11	628	1,567		1,328	D
12	British Gas	100		1,428	D
15	Sundries		865	563	D
17	629	311		874	D
18	Sundries		2,340	1,466	C

... continued

22	Sundries		54	1,520	C
23	Wolvborough BC		1,000	2,520	C
27	630	98		2,422	C
31	Sundries		124	2,546	C

Required:

Tick over the two records and identify differences. Which differences are informational and which are timing? Complete the cash book and prepare a bank reconciliation statement as at 31.1.x7.

2. The cash book of Bowes for the month of July 19x7 showed:

4.7.x7	Hardwick	684	1.7.x7	b/f		39
8.7.x7	Benbow	72	4.7.x7	Ludwig	721	100
15.7.x7	Dwight	143	11.7.x7	Hart	722	84
15.7.x7	Grahame	93	1.7.x7	Gimlet	723	639
30.7.x7	Walters	116	20.7.x7	Dews	724	22
			24.7.x7	Cowes	725	58
			29.7.x7	Drain	SO	100
			31.7.x7	c/f		66
		1,108				1,108

The statement from the Priory Provincial Bank PLC for the same period showed

1.7.x7	Balance			103	C
2.7.x7	719	87		16	C
4.7.x7	Sundries		146	162	C
5.7.x7	Sundries		684	846	C
6.7.x7	721	100		746	C
7.7.x7	720	201		545	C
17.7.x7	Sundries		236	781	C
18.7.x7	722	84		697	C
19.7.x7	723	639		58	C
20.4.x7	Orchestral Society	60		2	D
22.7.x7	Dividends		439	437	C
26.7.x7	725	58		379	C
30.7.x7	Charges	71		308	C
31.7.x7	Drain	100		208	C

Note: £72 was credited to the deposit account by the bank in error.

Required:

Correct the cash book and prepare the bank reconciliation statement.

3. The accountant of Summerbee Ltd is attempting to reconcile the bank statements with the cash book as at 31.12.x7. The cash book shows a balance in hand of £578. After ticking over the two documents he finds:

(a) Cash paid into the bank of £489 has been entered in the cash book as £459.

(b) A transfer to the company's deposit account of £1,000 has not been entered in the cash book.

(c) A cheque drawn for £45 has been entered into the cash book as £54.

(d) Cheques for £390 and £231 in the cash book in December had not been presented by the year end.

(e) The cash book debit side page 24 £8,760 total had been carried to page 25 as £7,860.

(f) A standing order for £100 to the Association of Explorers had been omitted from the cash book.

(g) Bank charges of £412 had been omitted from the cash book.

(h) A credit to the bank from George had not been entered into the cash book – £250.

(i) Cheques paid in on 31.12.x7 in the amount of £4,988 has not been credited by the bank at 31.12.x7.

(j) In error the bank had charged the company £26 for a foreign transaction which had not taken place.

Required:

(a) An amended cash book.

(b) A bank reconciliation at 31.12.x7.

Note that you will have to calculate the bank statement balance.

4. Revisit the computer accounting exercise in Chapter 6. The bank statement was received from the bank and showed the following for the current month of October 19x1:

Balance		0.00	C
Cheque	404.79	404.79	C
001	150.00	254.79	C
BACS Pink		445.84	700.63	C
002	100.00	600.63	C
Cash and cheques		2,411.25	3,011.88	C
003	284.00	2,727.88	C
004	32.90	2,694.98	C

Required:

Use the 'reconcile' button in your accounting software to reconcile the cash book with the bank statement, make further entries if necessary and to print out a reconciliation statement.

Assignment

❏ *Keep a record of your cash and bank transactions over a period of one week. Enter them in a suitably ruled cash book and bring down the balances at the end of the week. Obtain a bank statement and reconcile it to your cash book and make out a bank reconciliation.*

13 Internal control

Frauds and errors easily occur in business and, sadly, also in non-profit organisations like the health service and charities. It is not easy to prevent or detect all errors and frauds. The newspapers tend to be full of them but rarely describe what actually happened or how the fraud was perpetrated in detail. Perhaps that is a good thing or copycat crimes might be committed! Happily there are some techniques which tend to help to prevent fraud and error and we will describe and review some of them here.

Definition

1. Internal control is defined as 'the whole system of controls, financial and otherwise, established by the management in order to carry on the business of the enterprise in an orderly and efficient manner, ensure adherence to management policies, safeguard the assets and secure as far as possible the completeness and accuracy of the records'. This is rather a lot to absorb in one go but it will make sense if you refer back to it as you continue this section.

Internal control techniques

Purchases, expenses and creditors

2. The objectives of internal control in this area is to ensure that goods and services are only ordered in the quantity, of the quality and at the best terms available after appropriate requisition and approval. In addition, goods should be inspected on arrival and only acceptable items accepted. All invoices should be checked against authorised orders and receipt of the subject matter in good condition. Also all invoices should be properly entered in the books.

Order forms might look like this:

JONES WIDGETS LTD Date: 31 March 19x7   OFFICIAL ORDER Number: 143

Supplier: Evans Supplies Ltd

Please supply : 200 Widgets Mark IV small   Approved: *J.Evans*

Notes:
(a) This is an outline only, there should also be addresses, delivery instructions, VAT No etc.
(b) Note the consecutive number – order forms cannot then be lost without discovery.

Before issuing the order a number of procedures need to be gone through. These include a requisition form (detailing need for the good or service) by a person authorised to make requisitions (managers etc), obtaining of competitive tenders or quotes, and approval and acknowledgement of the order by a senior official (here it is J.Evans, a director). Orders are usually in duplicate – one to supplier, one retained with, perhaps, a third to the manager requisitioning the supplies.

On arrival of the goods, they will probably be accompanied by a delivery note. Here is an outline example:

EVANS SUPPLIES LTD DELIVERY NOTE NUMBER 1,569   DATE 3 APRIL 19x7

To: Jones Widgets Ltd

Quantity: 200   Product: Widgets Mark IV small

Delivery: Supersonic Carriers PLC   Received by:

These can be used as a record of incoming goods but usually a new document is made out – a goods received note. Here is an example:

JONES WIDGETS LTD   Date : 4 April 19x7   GOODS RECEIVED NOTE No. 879

Supplier: Evans Supplies Ltd   Condition: *F.E.Brown*

                                 Quantity: *F.E.Brown*

Goods: 200 widgets Mk IV small. Agreement with Order   *J.Evans*

Note the consecutive number – by comparing incoming invoices with GRNs, it is possible to check if any invoices are outstanding. It is also possible to compare the GRNs with orders to see if any orders remain outstanding. Authorised persons are required to check condition and quantity and sign to say they have done so. Usually later, an authorised person checks the consignment against the order.

In due course, the invoice will arrive. This should be checked:

(a) Against the GRN and possibly the order.

(b) For arithmetical accuracy.

(c) For correct price.

(d) For correct VAT.

and a consecutive number applied. Also a coding should be put on so that the correct purchase or expense account is debited.

The checking should be acknowledged – many firms put a rubber stamp grid on the invoice for this purpose.

The invoice should be entered in the purchase and expense daybook. Consecutive numbering can ensure all invoices are entered. Accuracy of entry can be checked by prelisting. This means that the amounts of the invoices are added up on an adding machine to derive a total. When the invoices have been entered and totalled, the totals should be the same.

Subsequent controls and checks on purchases include the preparation of the purchase and expense ledger control account and the checking of the individual supplier account details with the Statement of Account sent by the supplier monthly.

We have talked about authorised persons. An important feature of internal control systems is that separate people should be responsible for each activity. If one person is responsible for the whole cycle, that is requisitioning, ordering, checking goods, checking invoices, entering invoices, preparing control accounts and checking accounts against the suppliers' Statements of Account, then frauds can be perpetrated.

Sales and debtors

3. The objectives of internal control in this area, is to ensure that all customers' orders are promptly executed, that goods are sold on credit only to good credit risks (people who can and will pay and reasonably promptly), that all goods sold are invoiced and at authorised prices with accurate arithmetic and VAT calculation. Also, all invoices must be entered in the books and every effort made to collect the money due from credit customers.

The usual procedure is to record all incoming orders on pre-numbered sales order forms. If the sale is on credit then appropriate credit control procedures should be applied. This means ensuring that the customer is on an authorised list or if he/she /it is not, then doing a creditworthiness investigation. How this might be done is considered in Chapter 14.

When the goods leave the firm, they should be accompanied by a prenumbered delivery note.

Sometimes these are in triplicate: one copy is retained and two are sent to the customer – the first is retained by the customer but the second is signed by the customer as an acknowledgement of receipt and retained by the issuing firm.

From the delivery notes, invoices should be made out and sent to the customer. The invoices should be prenumbered and, before sending to the customer, be checked independently for agreement with customer order, agreement with delivery note , correct pricing, calculations and VAT. All checking should be acknowledged with initials. At intervals a senior responsible official should check the consecutivity of numbers of the delivery notes to check that all goods sent out have been invoiced.

Invoices should be entered in the sales daybook. Consecutivity of numbers should be checked to ensure all have been entered. A prelisting of the invoice totals for comparison with the daybook total should be carried out.

Statements of account should be sent out monthly to all current credit customers. These should be prepared by personnel independent of the sales ledger staff and posting should be direct to avoid any interference with or destruction of Statements before they go to customers.

All accounts should be regularly reviewed by senior officials to ensure that customers' accounts are regularly settled and any unpaid accounts, accounts where payments do not match invoices, or accounts settled by round sums should be investigated.

Payments

4. The objective of internal control over cheque and other bank payments is to prevent unauthorised payments being made from bank accounts.

   A responsible official, unconnected with the rest of the bookkeeping system, should be responsible for the custody and use of cheque books. Before cheques are made out, the official should check the orders, the GRNs and the invoices and stamp these 'Paid by cheque No....' to prevent them being paid more than once.

   Cheques should be signed by two people out of small group of authorised personnel. No cheque should be signed without attached documentation.

   The bank reconciliation should be made by independent officials and anomalies investigated.

Receipts by post

5. The objective of control over receipts by post is to ensure that **all** cash and cheques received through the post are accounted for, paid into the bank and entered correctly into the books.

   There should be measures to ensure all post is not intercepted or interfered with before being opened by two senior officials. Details of cash and cheques should then be entered into a postlist of receipts, signed by both parties.

   All cash and cheques should then be entered into paying in slips, sent to the bank and entered into the cash book. At intervals an independent official should compare the post lists with the cash book entries and bank statements. The comparison should be in detail, checking names, amounts and dates.

Cash sales and collections

6. The object of internal control over cash sales (shops, pubs etc) and collections (bread, milk and other roundsmen etc) is to ensure that all cash which the firm is entitled to is received, accounted for, banked promptly and intact, and entered accurately in the books.

   The main problem is establishing a means of evidencing cash receipts. An example of a means is the use of prenumbered duplicate receipt forms. Another is the use of electronic cash registers which detail receipts and totals and which cannot be altered by the operators. Customers must be made aware that a receipt is required or that the sum payable must be correctly run up on the cash register which must be clearly visible to the customer. Cash registers must be checked and reset by responsible officials and 'overs' and 'shorts' investigated.

   Independent comparison should be made at intervals of till totals and receipt totals with cash book and bank statements paying attention to dates as well as amounts.

   Roundsmen should have a controlled issue of goods with a check, on their return, that they have cash or goods of the same amount.

Consequences of lack of security checks and internal controls

7. Fraud and theft are common occurrences. The consequences for the firm are loss of goods or cash and, for the criminal, perhaps the social and legal penalties. It is in the interest of the firm to try to avoid fraud and theft or, if it occurs, to detect it rapidly. It is in the interests of employees to have temptation taken away from them by strong systems. The consequences of unauthorised activity in a firm can be the collapse of the whole firm and even merchant banks can face failure as a consequence of unauthorised dealings.

Error can also cause problems and be disastrous. Simple mistakes can have serious consequences if they occur regularly. As an example, if the sales system is deficient and goods can leave the firm's premises and not be invoiced, then the loss of revenue can ruin the firm. Failure to invoice goods is a very grave matter but lesser problems can also be dangerous. I remember a firm which had a lax system for entering the sales ledger. As a consequence, invoices were entered on the wrong accounts or entered twice and the ledger got into a mess. Customers failed to pay, as the statements sent to them contained numerous errors. Ultimately this failure to pay led the firm to experience serious cash flow difficulties. Other consequences may include making wrong decisions as the information gathered is incorrect or producing incorrect financial statements. The latter may lead to investors and lenders taking actions which would be different if the financial statements had showed the correct results and position.

On a more mundane level, errors in calculating pay or dealing with PAYE Income Tax may have small effects on the firm but large repercussions to individual employees.

To summarise, the effects of errors and frauds can be:

(a) Errors in sales ledgers: failure to collect sums due, either at all or late.

(b) Errors in purchase ledgers: failure to pay correct amounts to suppliers leading to overpayments, possible loss of settlement discounts, supplier ill will.

(c) Errors in cash book: failure to realise that bank overdraft has exceeded facility and consequent possibility of cheques bouncing with loss of supplier and bank goodwill.

(d) Errors in financial statements (these can be deliberate or stem from errors in bookkeeping or in preparing the financial statements): users of the financial statements can be misled and take the wrong decisions. A PLC buy B Ltd on the strength of the financial statements of B Ltd. Later A PLC find the financial statements of B Ltd were incorrect and realise they would not have bought the company had the true position been known. Another consequence is that A PLC would probably sue the directors and auditors of B Ltd.

(e) Legal requirements are not met. There is much legislation on accounting records, PAYE, VAT, Companies Act etc. Failure to keep proper records can lead to penalties including fines and imprisonment.

(f) Incorrect monitoring of performance. Due to errors in bookkeeping, the Sheinton branch of Mega Stores PLC showed a loss. The manager was sacked, the staff lost their bonuses and some good staff left. Later it turned out that the branch actually made a good profit.

Summary

- ❏ Internal control systems can be developed to assist in the prevention and detection of frauds and errors.

- ❏ Internal control measures usually include separate personnel for each function, much documentation in multiple copies, checking of documents against other documents, consecutive numbering with checking for missing items, prelisting and other procedures.

Points to note

- ❏ This section is an outline only of the complexities of internal control. For a fuller treatment, I recommend my own book – *Auditing* – also published by Letts Educational Ltd.

- ❏ Some firms send out advice notes (which look much like delivery notes) to advise customers of impending deliveries. A delivery note will then follow with the actual goods. Today most firms only issue delivery notes.

- ❏ Firms also need procedures and documents for the returns of goods and the receipt and sending of credit notes.

- ❏ Internal control systems are often circumvented by staff who are under time pressure or who find the system irksome. This should be made difficult or impossible as internal control systems are not only designed for the purposes set out in the definition, but are also designed to take away temptation from staff who might succumb and then be subject to the law's and society's penalties.

- ❏ Cash sales are very difficult to control but modern electronic cash registers help considerably.

- ❏ Good systems require separation of responsibilities among several staff. Small businesses with few staff have difficulty in designing adequate controls.

- ❏ I find myself observing internal control systems in pubs, restaurants, supermarkets and other retail outlets. Try to do so yourself.

- ❏ Internal control systems are especially necessary in computerised accounting systems. The controls applied are much like the ones outlined in this section but some particular controls can be applied. We will look at these in a later chapter.

- ❏ We will look at wages systems in a later chapter.

Self-testing questions

1. Define internal control.
2. Enumerate the purposes of, and procedures for achieving internal control over purchases, expenses and creditors.
3. Enumerate the purposes of, and procedures for achieving internal control over sales and debtors.
4. Enumerate the purposes of, and procedures for achieving internal control over payments.

5. Enumerate the purposes of, and procedures for achieving internal control over receipts by post.

6. Enumerate the purposes of, and procedures for achieving internal control over cash sales.

7. What are the consequences of error and fraud?

Exercises

1. Speedicabs Ltd is a firm of taxicab operators. Take the definition of internal control. Draw up a list of things which could go wrong if there were no internal controls.

2. Cohen Noor Jewellery Ltd are large scale manufacturers of jewellery in gold, silver and precious stones. Design a system for the control of purchasing and for payments to suppliers. Detail the specific frauds and errors which the system is designed to prevent.

3. Classic Junk Ltd stock and sell parts and components for classic cars. These are despatched by the company's own van and by commercial carrier. Design a system for the control of sales and collection of debts. Detail the specific frauds and errors which the system is designed to prevent.

4. The Grand Theatre, Telford sells tickets for its productions by post, telephone (usually taking credit card payment) and at the Box Office. Design a system for the sales of tickets, the control of takings and the bank account. Detail the specific frauds and errors which the system is designed to prevent.

5. The honorary treasurer of St Mary's Church is in personal financial difficulties. He desperately needs money to pay off his gambling debtors. In his depression, he pays the cash received for John and Kay's wedding into his own account and he draws a cheque payable to himself for £500. He can do the latter because the Church Warden (who has to countersign cheques signed by the treasurer) has gone on holiday and has signed some blank cheques in advance.

   Do you think the auditor (who is a local maths teacher) would find these frauds? What internal control procedures might prevent these frauds?

Assignment

❑ *Caleb is the bookkeeper for Stoneage Ltd who are wholesalers of hand tools. He has become addicted to gambling and has lost large sums. He is in debt and is desperate to pay off his creditors. To obtain the necessary funds he determines to defraud his employers. He does this in a number of ways:*

   (a) *He creates a number of false petty cash vouchers and enters them in the petty cash book, taking the money. He also enters some genuine petty cash vouchers twice, taking the cash for himself on the second entries.*

   (b) *He takes some cheques payable to the firm by customers, alters the payee on the cheques and pays them into his own account. To cover up this fraud, he credits later payments by the customers against the invoices paid by the misappropriated cheques. For some customers, whose cheques he has stolen, he writes off the balance to bad debts account.*

   (c) *He presents false invoices from a non-existent supplier and makes out cheques to them. He then pays these cheques into an account he has opened in the name of the non-existent supplier. Later he draws all the money from this account.*

Required:
  (a) *Explain the possible consequences of these frauds for Caleb and his employer.*
  (b) *Explain in detail how good systems might prevent or detect these frauds.*

14 Discounts, bad debts and hire purchase

This chapter introduces some common business transactions – discounts, bad and doubtful debts, and hire purchase.

Discounts

1. There are two types of discounts of interest to accountants. These are:
   (a) Trade discounts which include bulk and quantity discounts.
   (b) Settlement or cash discounts.

Trade discounts

2. Trade discounts are literally *reductions of price*. A business may have a standard price for a product. The business may then give trade discounts to a particular customer or to particular classes of customer so that it sells to them at lower prices. The reasons for selling at lower prices to some customers are many and include bulk buying, regular buying, selling to wholesalers when sales are usually made retail, sales to staff or shareholders, sales to members of a particular group, etc.

   In some cases, trade discounts are given to all customers as in so-called discount stores!

Invoices

3. The effect of trade discounts on invoices is often:

	£
1 dozen Mark IV widgets at £20	240.00
Less trade discount at 20%	48.00
	£ 192.00

   Alternatively, as the price is effectively £16 a widget, the invoice may simply record:

	£
1 dozen Mark IV widgets at £16	192.00

   Where traders have a standard price and a specific range of trade discounts to particular types of customer and they wish each customer to be aware of the discounts given, the discount will probably be shown in the invoice. In other cases, realising that a trade discount actually means a different (lower) price, a trader will simply invoice as in the second example.

Cash discounts

4. A trader may sell his goods on credit, marking his invoices 'nett thirty days' or some other period. This means that he requires his customer to pay the amount of the invoice within 30 days of the invoice date. In practice, if the customer ignores this requirement and always pays three months after the invoice date, there is very

little that the trader can do. Legal action is expensive, takes time and upsets the customer who even if he takes a long time to pay is still giving profitable business. Refusing to sell further goods to the customer hurts the trader more than the customer.

A way of inducing customers to pay more quickly is to offer a settlement or cash discount to them. If a trader marks on his invoices 'cash discount 5% for payment within 10 days, otherwise net 30 days', then *some* customers will pay their invoices within the ten-day period but will deduct 5% from the sum due. Effectively, the cash discount is a cost to the trader but gives him the benefit of earlier receipt of money from his customers.

In practice, cash discount rates vary from 1% to 15% or more, and periods from five days to 'the end of the calendar month following the date of invoice'.

Financial statements

5. Trade discounts do not appear in the financial statements. The effect of a trade discount is to lower the price. The actual price of each invoice (which is net of trade discount) is entered into the system and is used in preparing the financial statements.

Cash discounts are either:

(a) Discounts received from suppliers (known as discounts received). These are incomes or gains and so appear in the profit and loss account as such under the heading 'discounts received'.

(b) Discounts granted to customers (known as discounts allowed). These are expenses and so appear in the profit and loss account as such under the heading 'discounts allowed'.

Notes:

(a) Discounts appear in the profit and loss account. The figures for sales and purchases appear in the trading account and these are before deducting discounts. Essentially the gross profit is the profit from buying and selling. The effect of giving and receiving settlement discounts is nothing to do with buying and selling. It is a financial matter. The giving of a cash discount is not to effect a sale but is to get the money in quickly.

(b) Cash discounts appear in the Profit and Loss Account in the period in which the payment is made, not in the period in which the sale or purchase is made if that is different.

6. In using Sage or other computerised accounting systems, enter the amount of discount in the discount column (in *bank + customers* or *suppliers*). This should be the amount of the discount, not the rate. Note that discount is taken on the net amount of the invoice. There is no discount on the VAT amount.

Bookkeeping for discounts

7. The entries for discounts allowed to customers are:
(a) Dr Expense a/c – Discounts allowed.
(b) Cr The customer's account on the sales ledger.

As there are usually numerous discounts allowed, it is customary to enter the discounts first in the cash book in a separate column (which is not, of course, part of the cash book). The ruling on the debit of the cash book might be:

Date	Customer	Discount	Detail	Bank
Jan 6	Hall & Co	23.00	387.62	
Jan 8	Howes Ltd	12.67	234.12	621.74

Notes:

(a) The bank column is the cash book proper and each entry will correspond with the bank statement.

(b) The detail column is the actual receipts from customers. These will be credited to the appropriate customer's account in the sales ledger (Hall & Co etc)

(c) The discount column is a prime entry. The entries will be summed at the end of each period and debited to the expense account – discounts allowed. The balance of that account will be transferred to the profit and loss account.

The entries for discounts received are simply the reverse of those for discounts allowed.

Bad and doubtful debts

8. It is common business practice to sell goods on credit. Ownership and possession of the goods is transferred at the time of sale and the vendor is left with a debt due from his customer. He hopes that this will be paid and within a reasonable period of time.

In practice, most credit sales do result in cash being received from the customer. However, some customers do not pay. Reasons for non-payment include:

(a) The customer disappears without trace – he is unwilling to pay.

(b) The customer becomes insolvent – he cannot pay.

If a debt is irrecoverable, it is said to be a bad debt.

At a year end, a business may have a large number of debtors. Most of these will be good, that is collectable, but some will prove to be bad. The prudence convention in accounting requires that debts which are *doubtful* should be valued at *net realisable value*. To this end, a deduction is made from debtors so that the debtors are shown at the amount that is expected to be received. This deduction is known as the *provision for doubtful debts*.

Notes:

(a) The prudence convention is an accounting convention which ignores profits or gains until they are realised but recognises expenses and losses as soon as they are known about. Realised means turned into cash or into a debt which is reasonably certain to be paid.

(b) Net realisable value is the amount an asset is expected to realise. In the case of a debt due by a customer, it is the amount he/she is expected to pay which may be nil if he is bankrupt or is a company in liquidation. Some assets may involve costs in realising them. Net realisable value is the amount expected after deducting these costs.

Financial statements

9. The bad debts recognised in a period are an expense and appear as such in the profit and loss account. At the end of the year, the debtors (totalling say £56,900) are reviewed and if some are thought be uncollectible in whole or in part, then the total uncollectible (say £1,230) is found and entries made in the financial statements as:

Profit and loss account:	Provisions for doubtful debts		1,230
Balance Sheet:	Debtors	56,900	
	Less: Provision for doubtful debts	1,230	55,670

In practice this is often shortened to: Debtors £55,670.

10. The provision for bad and doubtful debts is a charge to the profit and loss account. If the debts turn out to be actually bad, then in effect the same debt becomes an expense in the profit and loss account. To avoid charging it twice, the best approach is to see the charge for the provision in year 19x1 as an income in year 19x2. Then when the 19x2 debtors are reviewed, it is the provision for bad and doubtful debts at the end of that year (say £1,543) which is the 19x2 profit and loss account charge. In practice the two profit and loss account entries are netted off and you see:

Additional provision for bad and doubtful debts £313

If you find this tricky to understand, you are amongst the majority of students! Time and reflection may enable you to grasp it.

Credit control

11. Businesses who give credit to their customers, have to institute systems to ensure that bad debts are minimised. Such systems involve three stages:

   (a) **The decision to grant credit to prospective customers**

   Before granting credit to a new customers, the customer's *credit worthiness* must be established. Methods of determining this include:

   (i) Requesting references from:
   – the customer's bank
   – other suppliers who have given credit to the customer
   – trade associations (e.g. national association of widget manufacturers).

   (ii) Inspecting financial statements, which can be obtained by requesting the prospective customer to supply these, or in the case of a company, from Companies House.

   (iii) Impressions gained by representatives or agents who visit the prospective customer.

   Usually, a decision is made either to refuse credit or to grant credit facilities up to a maximum of £x.

   (b) **Continuous review of credit worthiness**

   Once credit has been granted to a customer, continuous review must be made of credit worthiness by:

(i)   Ensuring that each proposed sale does not take credit granted over the agreed limit.

(ii)   Watching that the credit *period* taken does not lengthen.

(iii) Receiving reports from trade associations and credit rating agencies.

(iv) Receiving financial statements if available.

(c) **Debt Collection**

Once a credit sale has been made, the vendor must have a system to ensure all that can be done is done, to collect the debt. Elements of such a system include:

(i)   Prompt preparation and submission of invoices.

(ii)   Prompt attention to customer queries to prevent non-payment due to disputes over the quality of the goods.

(iii) A system to ensure that the customer acknowledges receipt of the goods, e.g. by signing delivery notes.

(iv) Prompt preparation of monthly statements of account.

(v)   A system of polite but firm letters to slow payers.

(vi) Preparation of an aged analysis of debtors, i.e. one month in arrear, two months in arrear, etc. so that it is known who is in arrear.

(vii) A regular review of all accounts to ensure credit limits have not been exceeded.

(viii) A system for instigating legal action rapidly after other collection methods have failed.

Percentage provisions for doubtful debts

12. Some businesses have a large number of debtors and a review of each debt at the year end to determine which debts are doubtful may be economically impossible. However, it may be that from a statistical analysis of past experience, it appears that some percentage (say 5%) of the debts are likely to prove bad. In such cases, a provision may be made not for specific debts, but for debts in general.

13. Mary's business at 31.12.x4 has 1,400 debtors whose total indebtedness is £183,400. From previous experience she expects 3% to be bad:

(a) The profit and loss account will contain an expense:

	£
Provision for doubtful debts	5,502

(b) The balance sheet will include in current assets:

	£	£
Debtors	183,400	
Less Provision for doubtful debts	5,502	177,898

At the end of 19x5, the debtors totalled £171,900 and the books still contained the balance on the provision account at £5,502. If the estimate of 3% of doubtful debts is maintained, then the provision will need to be adjusted to £5,157:

(a) The profit and loss account will contain a credit (income) entry of:

Adjustment to provision for doubtful debts	£345

(b) The balance sheet will include:

	£	£
Debtors	171,900	
Less Provision for doubtful debts	5,157	166,743

(c) Any actual bad debts incurred in 19x5 will also appear in the profit and loss account as bad debts £x.

Bookkeeping for bad debts

14. If the sales ledger contains an account as:

Dr   **Herbert**   **Cr**

31.8.x4	Balance b/f	£800

and it has become clear that this debt is uncollectible, then entries should be made as:

Herbert Account

31.8.x4	Balance b/f	£800	1.9.x4	Bad Debt	£800

Bad Debts Account

1.9.x8	Herbert	£800

Essentially, the asset – Herbert owes £800 – is no longer of value and it is written off by a transfer to bad debts account, which is an expense account.

At the year end (31.12.x4), the bad debts account may contain more than one bad debt as:

Bad Debts Account

		£			£
1.9.x4	Herbert	800	31.12.x4	Profit and Loss a/c	2,550
15.10.x4	Denry	350			
30.11.x4	Andrew	1,400			
		£2,550			£2,550

The profit and loss account will include an expense: bad debts – £2,550. The balance sheet figure of debtors will not include the sums due from Herbert, Denry or Andrew.

Bookkeeping for doubtful debts

15. At each year end, the debtors' account should be reviewed and any that are *definitely bad*, should be written off to the bad debts account as explained in paragraph 14.

Some of the debtors may not be *definitely* bad, but may be *doubtful*. In such cases a provision for doubtful debts account should be opened:

The debtors' ledger of Frank at 31.12.x4 contains four accounts only whose balances are:

	£
Alan	6,320
Bertram	4,190
Carl	3,000
Davina	1,392
Total	14,902

At the year end, Frank reviews these accounts and forms the conclusion that Carl is in financial difficulties and it is probable that only half the £3,000 will be paid, and that the other half is unlikely to be received.

The bookkeeping entries are:

Dr	**Provision for doubtful debts**		**Cr**
			£
	31.12.x4	P&L a/c	1,500

The effect of this is:

(a) The profit and loss account will contain an expense.

(b) The balance on the provision account must be included in the balance sheet and is shown as a deduction from debtors:

	£	£
Debtors	14,902	
Less Provision for doubtful debts	1,500	13,402

(c) The full debt (£3,000) remains in the books as the system for chasing debtors will still be applied until the debt is *definitely* bad.

(d) The balance sheet entry is composed of the sums due from debtors less the credit balance on the provision account.

16. **At the following year end – 31 December 19x5**

(a) Debtors comprised:

	£
Hugh	4,891
Erica	1,340
Fiona	9,820
George	630
Total	£16,681

(b) During 19x5, Carl paid his £3,000 in full so that the 19x4 year end provision was unnecessary. However, the account remains at:

	Provision for doubtful debts		
			£
	31.12.x5	Balance b/f	1,500

(c) In reviewing his debtors at 31.12.x5, Frank forms a conclusion that the debt due from Hugh is doubtful, i.e. it will probably not be paid. The entry required is:

Provision for doubtful debts

			£
31.12.x5	Balance b/f		1,500
31.12.x5	P&L a/c		3,391
			£ 4,891

This entry can be seen in two ways:

(i) The entry in the profit and loss account was unnecessary and the profit in 19x4 was wrongly calculated. Therefore, an adjustment must be made to the 19x5 profit – a credit of £1,500. A charge must be made in the 19x5 profit and loss account of £4,891 to reflect the expected loss on the debt due from Hugh. The net effect is a charge of £3,391.

(ii) The provision must be topped up to £4,891 so that the balance sheet will include:

	£	£
Debtors	16,681	
Less Provision for doubtful debts	4,891	11,790

The adjustment to the provision will be a credit to the profit and loss account if the figure in year 2 is less than that in year 1.

Hire purchase

17. Hire purchase is a very common method of financing the purchase of commodities and services. The law relating to HP is very complicated and we shall not pursue it here. The accounting entries are included in many syllabuses.

Hire purchase transactions

18. In substance, hire purchase transactions proceed as:

(a) Antony, whose year end is 31 December, buys a car from Brenda on 15 July 19x4 for £3,000.

(b) Antony has only £1,000, so he borrows the balance from Car Finance Ltd, under an agreement as:

	£
Price of car	3,000
Deposit	1,000
Amount borrowed	2,000
Interest	400
Total amount due	£2,400

Payable in 24 monthly instalments of £100 each beginning on 15.8.x4.

(c) From Antony's point of view, he has bought a car for £3,000, paying £1,000 immediately and the balance plus interest over 24 months.

(d) From Brenda's point of view, she has sold the car and been paid immediately in full (£1,000 by Antony and £2,000 from Car Finance Ltd).

(e) From Car Finance Ltd's point of view, it has lent £2,000 and will be repaid plus interest over two years.

The entries in the financial statements are:

(a) The car is included in fixed assets in the balance sheet and depreciated.

(b) The loan is included in current liabilities as 'Hire Purchase Commitment'. The amount depends on the date. For example at 31 December 19x4 it will appear as £2,400 less five instalments of £100 and so will be £1,900.

(c) The interest is clearly an expense of the periods in which the loan is outstanding viz. 19x4, 19x5 and 19x6. The problem is to determine how much in each period. It should not be equal because the loan is steadily declining because part of each instalment is interest and part is a part repayment of the loan. The true interest rate is called the Annualised Percentage Rate or APR and the law requires it to be disclosed to borrowers. Strictly the APR should be used to calculate the division among the three years but in practice a method called sum of digits (or rule of 78) is used. This works like this:

First 5 instalments to 31.12.x4	24 + 23 + 22 + 21 + 20	=	110
Next 12 instalments to 31.12.x5	19 + 18 +...........8	=	162
Final 7 instalments to 31.12.x6	7 + 6 + ...1	=	28
			300

Finally the interest apportionment is calculated as:

year to 31.12.x4	110/300 × £400	=	£147
year to 31.12.x5	162/300 × £400	=	£216
year to 31.12.x6	28/300 × £400	=	£ 37
			£400

The entries in the profit and loss accounts for these years will be £147 etc under the heading 'Hire Purchase Interest' In the balance sheets there will be an entry under current assets of £253 (£216 + £37) as 'Hire Purchase Interest in advance.' in 19x4 and £37 in 19x5.

Alternatively the HP Commitment and the HP Interest in Advance can be netted off a one figure shown current assets – HP Commitment £1,647 (calculated as £1,900 – £253).

Bookkeeping for hire purchase

19. Continuing the example of Antony, we have in the books of Antony:

Motor Vehicles Account

		£			£
15.7.x4	Car Finance Ltd (i)	3,000			

Car Finance Ltd Account

		£			£
15. 7.x4	Cash (i)	1,000	15.7.x4	Car (i)	3,000
15. 8.x4	to				
15.12.x4	Five instalments (ii)	500	15.7.x4	Interest (iii)	400
31.12.x4	Balance c/d (iv)	1,900			
		£3,400			£3,400
			1. 1.x5	Balance b/d (iv)	1,900

Hire Purchase Interest Account

15.7.x4	Car Finance Ltd (iii)	400	31.12.x4	Profit and Loss a/c (v)	83
			31.12.x4	Balance c/d (vi)	317
		£400			£400
1.1.x5	Balance b/d (vi)	317			

Cash Book

15.7.x4	Deposit (i)	1,000
15.8.x4	–	
15.12.x4	Five instalments (ii)	500

Notes:

(a) The amount borrowed is £2,000 being £3,000 less the deposit £1,000.

(b) The instalments of £100 are paid monthly on 15 August, 15 September etc (probably by standing order with the bank).

(c) The interest should be added to the HP account in accordance with SSAP 21, that is by application of the strict interest rate. This is because the interest of £400 implies an interest rate (the APR). Each instalment includes both a capital repayment and interest on the amount outstanding. The amount outstanding is constantly reduced by the capital repayment and the interest is at the implied interest rate on the amount outstanding. These calculations are quite complicated and most firms, as we have in out example, use the rule of 78 method – so called because 12 + 11 + 10 + 9 + ... = 78. This is similar to the sum of digits method of depreciation.

Summary

❏ Trade discounts are reductions of price. An invoice may show trade discount but the effect for bookkeeping purposes is that the net amount of the invoice (after deducting the trade discount) is entered in the books.

❏ Cash or settlement discount is a deduction from the amount payable by a customer for paying promptly. It is entered in memorandum (not part of the double entry system) columns in the cash book. The totals are posted to the debit of discounts allowed account (for discount allowed to customers) or to the credit of discount received account (for discount received from suppliers). The individual discounts are entered on debit of the accounts of the suppliers and the credit of the accounts of customers.

❏ Bad debts occur when a debtor is unable to pay and the debt is recognised as uncollectable. The bookkeeping entries are to debit bad debts account and at the year end transfer the balance on that account to the profit and loss account and to credit the debtors account.

❏ When debts are considered as probably but not certainly bad then at each year a provision for bad debts is set up or adjusted to the appropriate amount on the credit side by a transfer to the profit and loss account.

❏ Businesses should have procedures in force under the general heading of credit control. These procedures are designed to prevent sales to potential customers who are not creditworthy and to collect debts promptly and with vigour.

❏ Hire purchase is a form of borrowing to enable people and firms to buy what they cannot immediately afford to pay for.

Points to note

❏ One method of selling on credit is to sell with reservation of title. This method of selling is named after the Romalpa case in 1976. Goods are invoiced and supplied in the normal way, but the title to the goods is expressed or agreed to pass only on payment. The benefit to the unpaid seller is that she can reclaim the goods if the buyer goes bust. However in practice it is difficult to establish the ownership of goods which may have been sold by the customer or incorporated into a product. The recommended bookkeeping is to treat a reservation of title sale as if it were an ordinary credit sale.

❏ Note that the profit on a sale may be taken to the profit and loss account in one year but the loss when the customer fails to pay may appear in the profit and loss account of a later year.

❏ The real loss on a bad debt is not the amount of the debt but the cost of the goods sold. Thus if Jayne sells goods (which cost her £600) to Keith for £900 and the debt proves bad, the actual loss is only £600. However the profit and loss account shows a bad debt of £900. The profit element of £300 is included in gross profit but is, of course, not shown separately. Note that the VAT element is recoverable on bad debts.

❏ After a debt has been written off as a bad debt, any subsequent receipt (perhaps a bankrupt debtor wins the lottery!) should be included in the profit and loss account as a bad debt recovered .

Self-testing questions

1. Why are trade discounts given?
2. Why are cash discounts given?
3. In what part of a trading and profit and loss account do settlement discounts appear?
4. Is it possible for the profit on a sale to appear in one year's financial statements and the associated cash discount to appear in the next?
5. Give the bookkeeping entries and the book of prime entry for cash discounts.
6. What is a bad debt?
7. How should doubtful debts be valued and appear on a Balance Sheet?
8 List the stages in credit control.
9. Summarise the year-end procedures for bad and doubtful debts, giving sample entries in the financial statements.
10. Give the bookkeeping entries for doubtful debts.
11. Explain the components of an hire purchase agreement.
12. Explain the bookkeeping entries for HP.

Exercises

1. Enter the following transactions in ledger accounts:
   (a) Sold 6 widgets to George on credit at £74 each less trade discount of 25%.
   (b) Sold goods to Joan on credit for £200.
   (c) Bought goods from Dindle on credit £700 less trade discount of 10%.
   (d) Received cheque from Joan for the goods bought on 2 January less settlement discount of 5%.
   (e) Paid for the goods bought from Dindle less 7% cash discount.

   Add VAT at 17.5% to items (a) and (b). Item (c) already includes VAT at 17.5%.

2. Gillian had the following transactions:

Jan 4	Sold on credit to Hugo goods for £600 less trade discount of 20%
Jan 6	Sold on credit to Janet goods for £560
Jan 8	Recorded and banked cash sales of £432.00
Jan 10	Purchased goods on credit from Maria at £890 including VAT
Jan 12	Received electricity bill for £278.00 + VAT
Jan 24	Received the sum due from Hugo
Jan 26	Received the sum due from Janet
Jan 28	Paid the sum due to Maria
Feb 8	Settlement was made with Customs and Excise

   Notes:
   (a) Gillian offers all her customers a settlement discount of 5% for payment within 30 days. Hugo and Janet both took the discount.
   (b) Gillian obtained a 3% cash discount when paying Maria.

   Enter all these transaction in appropriate books of prime entry and ledger accounts. State how any balances would appear in the financial statements drawn up on 31 January.

3. The trial balance of Alice at 31.12.x4 contained a debit balance: debtors £161,314. On reviewing the debts, Alice determined that the debts of Betty £3,104 and Carol £520 were bad and that the debt of Diane £610 and 60% of the debt of Elsie £830 were doubtful.

   Required:

   Give the bookkeeping entries and extracts from the financial statements which reflect these matters.

4. The trial balance of Fred at 31.12.x3 included:

	Dr	Cr
	£	£
Debtors	88,880	
Provision for doubtful debts at 31.12.x4		3,420
Bad debts	2,618	

   At the year end review, Fred determined that £1,240 of the debts were also bad and that £3,519 of the remaining debts were doubtful.

Required:

Give the bookkeeping entries and extracts for the financial statements to reflect these matters.

5. The trial balance of Gail at 30.6.x5 included:

	£
Debtors	431,920
Bad debts	6,380
Provision for doubtful debts at 30.6.x4	15,219

At the year end review, Gail decided that:

(a) A further £1,520 of the debtors were bad.

(b) A specific provision of £4,800 was required against three doubtful debts.

(c) A general provision of 3% was required against the remainder of the debts.

Required:

Show the bookkeeping entries and extracts from the financial statements to reflect these decisions.

6. Jane sold ten widgets to Paul at the retail price of £60 each + VAT but giving 20% off as a discount as Paul is a trade customer, with a settlement discount of 3% for payment by the end of the month following. The invoice was dated 28 December 19x6 and Paul paid on 27 January 19x7.

Required:

Give the entries and amounts in the financial statements of both Jane and Paul for 19x6 and 19x7. Both have 31 December as year end.

7. Lesley has a year end at 31 December 19x6. Her debtors at that date amounted to £640,000. On reviewing them, she reckons that £2,400 are positively bad, £12,200 are doubtful and, based on past experience, 4% of the remainder are also unlikely to pay. In 19x7, bad debts experienced and written off amounted to £31,080. At the end of 19x7 she felt that a further £1,600 were definitely bad, £15,900 were doubtful and the usual percentage provision should be made. The total debtors were £701,000.

Required:

(a) Give the entries in the financial statements for 19x6 and 19x7.

(b) Lesley feels that her bad debt losses are too high. How might she reduce them? How might she trade off lower turnover with fewer bad debts?

8. Chris bought a machine on HP in August 19x6. The agreement showed cost £12,000, deposit £2,000, interest £4,160, balance over 24 monthly instalments beginning on 15 September 19x6. Give the entries in the financial statements for all relevant years (year end is 31 December).

9. Douglas bought a car from Etty for £7,000 on 15.4.x8. He gave his old car (cost £7,000, accumulated depreciation £5,230) in part exchange at £2,000. The deal was financed by Claud who advanced £5,000 + interest £900 to be settled by 24 monthly instalments of £245.83 beginning 15.5.x8.

The instalments were met on time but on 14.2.x0 he paid off the amount owing with a settlement figure of £720.

Required:

(a) Enter all the items in double entry accounts in Douglas's books.

(b) Show how all these items would appear in the Financial Statements for all years ending 31 December.

(c) Why might Douglas wish to pay off the outstanding sum due early?

10. James, whose year end is 31 December, bought a car from Julia. The invoice dated 4th October 19x5 showed:

	£
Purchase price	7,000
One year's tax	85
Tankfull of petrol	22
	£ 7,107

James paid a deposit of £1,107. The balance was financed by Bernard. The agreement provided for interest of £600 and payment by 12 monthly instalments of £550, beginning on 4 November 19x5.

Required:

Record the transaction in the books of James for all relevant years, and show relevant extracts from the profit and loss accounts and balance sheets.

Assignment

❏ The following are the balances in the books of Wells who is in business as a wholesaler of maps at 31 December 19x5.

	£		£
Land at cost	26,900	Provision for depreciation Buildings	31,200
Buildings at cost	130,000	Provision for depreciation Equipment	7,200
Equipment at cost	15,400	Provision for depreciation Vehicles	15,900
Vehicles at cost	41,000	Sales	249,000
Stock 31.12.x4	31,000	Discount received	3,510
Debtors	28,791	Customs and Excise	5,300
Bad Debts	1,980	Provision for Doubtful debts 31.12.x4	1,320
Purchases	131,000	Proceeds of sale, Honda car	2,000
Wages	29,600	Bank Overdraft	5,300
Rates and insurances	12,719	Capital at 31.12.x4	140,225
Heat and light	6,342	Creditors	24,527
Other overheads	21,400	Loan from Binkey at 15%	12,000
Discount allowed	2,700	Rent received	6,200
Discounting charges	1,400		
Drawings	19,000		
Interest	2,370		
Petty cash balance	580		
Deposit on new car	1,000		
Instalments on new car	500		

Note:

(a) Stock at 31.12.x5 was valued at £34,000.

(b) Depreciation on buildings is over 25 years with nil salvage value.

(c) Depreciation on equipment is 25% on the reducing balance.

(d) Depreciation on the vehicles is 30% reducing balance. The Honda car sold had cost £8,400 in 19x1. The policy is to take a full year's depreciation in the year of purchase.

(e) A new Nisssan car has been purchased on hire purchase with Megafinance Ltd. The only entries made so far are the payment of the deposit and two instalments. The car cost £5,700. The arrangement is for a deposit of £1,000 and the interest charge is £1,300. Payment is by 24 instalments of £250 each.

(f) A review of the debtors indicates that £570 is definitely uncollectible. Past experience shows that some 5% of the remainder are likely to be bad.

(g) PAYE and NI £820 deducted from wages in December was not paid until January 19x6.

(h) Rates include those for the half year ending 31 March 19x6 of £4,300.

(i) Electricity accrued due at 31.12.x5 amounted to £720 + VAT.

(j) Interest on the loan from Binkey was paid up to 30 September 19x5 only.

(k) The rent received was for the rent of Wells' holiday flat which is nothing to do with the business. The business was short of money at the time the flat was let.

Required:

(a) Prepare financial statements for the year to 31 December 19x5.

(b) Wells is surprised that the business has an overdraft despite making a good profit. Write an explanation of the relationship between cash flow and profit, using Wells' profit and loss account as an example.

(c) Explain the accounting conventions used in this example, suggesting how the profit might have differed had different conventions been used.

15 Value Added Tax

This chapter is concerned with Value Added Tax (VAT). It appears in most accounting and book-keeping syllabuses and is very important in the UK and other parts of the European Community. VAT is an amazingly complex tax in practice but we will deal with the outlines only and they are fairly easy to understand.

An outline of Value Added Tax (VAT)

1. Any *person* (*person* = sole trader, partnerships, limited companies, clubs, associations, charities etc) who is carrying on a business which has a turnover greater than the limit currently in force (i.e. all but very small businesses) must *register* for VAT and be given a *VAT number*.

    VAT registered persons in making *taxable supplies* of goods or services (effectively all sales) must add VAT at the standard rate which at the time of writing is 17.5%.

    Example

    Jason, a trader in sheepskin coats, sells a dozen coats to Homer at £60. The taxable supply is $12 \times £60 = £720$, but the invoice must be for:

	£
12 sheepskin coats at £60	720
VAT at 17.5%	126
Total amount of invoice	846

    Notes:

    (a) Homer must pay £846.

    (b) Jason keeps the £720 (when and if Homer pays the £828 due).

    (c) The tax, £126, is payable by Jason to HM Customs and Excise.

    (d) VAT added to sales is known as output tax.

2. Jason also buys sheepskin coats and pays expenses. Many of these are invoiced in the form:

	£
6 Sheepskin coats at £40	240.00
VAT at 17.5%	42.00
Amount payable by Jason	282.00

    The VAT suffered by Jason on his purchases and expenses is called input tax. It is recoverable from HM Customs and Excise.

    Jason thus owes the Customs and Excise output tax and HM Customs and Excise owe Jason the input tax he has suffered. Clearly the correct way to deal with this is for Jason to send the Customs and Excise a cheque for the output tax less the input tax. Occasionally, input tax is greater than output tax and the Customs and Excise will send Jason a cheque for the difference.

3. The details of outputs, inputs, output tax and input tax are entered on a VAT return which is sent quarterly to the Customs and Excise office at Southend-on-Sea. Each taxable person has four accounting dates a year when a return is to be sent, for example, at the end of February, May, August, November. Some businesses account monthly and small businesses may account annually but make nine equal estimated payments and a final adjustment. It is possible to prepare the VAT return automatically if Sage or another computerised system is in use. Procedures are to go to *Financials + VAT*, specify the period and choose the calculate button.

Final consumers, e.g. the member of the public who buys a sheepskin coat, suffers VAT but cannot recover it.

4. Some businesses add output tax at a special rate, viz., zero, on some or all of their outputs. Zero rated outputs include:
   (a) Most foodstuffs (but not catering, e.g. meals, take away meals, drinks in public houses etc or non-essential foods, e.g. ice cream).
   (b) Books, newspapers, maps etc but not stationery.
   (c) Construction of buildings for residential or charitable use.
   (e) Transport but not taxis or hire cars.
   (f) Drugs and medicines on prescription.
   (g) Water and sewerage charges for domestic purposes.
   (h) Children's clothing and footwear.

   Persons who have zero rated outputs can nonetheless recover input tax suffered.

5. Some supplies are exempt supplies. Thus no VAT is added on selling them. Exempt supplies include:
   (a) Land.
   (b) Provision of insurance cover. Thus insurance premiums are an exempt supply.
   (c) Postal services.
   (d) Betting, gaming and lotteries, but not the takings from amusement machines.
   (e) Finance. Thus interest is an exempt supply.
   (f) The supply of medical services, e.g. by doctors, dentists, opticians.
   (g) Burial and cremation.
   (h) Education.

   Suppliers of exempt supplies cannot recover input tax suffered on inputs which relate to the exempt supplies.

   VAT started as a relatively simple tax. It has become immensely complicated with innumerable special schemes.

Bookkeeping for VAT

6. You have already seen examples of invoices and credit notes and you will have seen that VAT is usually included. Sales, purchase and expense daybooks need to have VAT entered separately. Here is an example of a sales daybook with VAT columns:

Date	Customer	Goods value	VAT	Gross
March 7	Beethoven	246.00	43.05	289.05
March 10	Bach	800.50	140.08	940.58
March 14	Bartok	167.92	29.38	197.30
March 23	Bart	700.00	122.50	822.50
		1914.42	335.01	2249.43

The ledger entries for these are:

(a) Invoice gross amounts are debited to the customers' individual accounts (£246.00 to Beethoven, £800.50 to Bach etc).

(b) Goods value total (£1,914.42) is credited to the sales account and the VAT total is credited to VAT account.

Thus the total debits are £2,249.43 and the total credits are also £2,249.43 being £335.01 + £1,914.42.

Here is an example of a combined purchase and expense daybook:

Date	Supplier	Gross	VAT	Net	Purchases	Motor Expenses	Rent & Rates
March 8	Goya	171.55	25.55	146.00	146.00		
March 13	Reynolds	213.85	31.85	182.00		182.00	
March 21	Etty	97.64	14.54	83.10	83.10		
March 26	Miro	230.78		230.78			230.78
		713.82	71.94	641.88	229.10	182.00	230.78

Notes:

(a) Some bookkeeping systems have separate purchase daybooks and expense daybooks.

(b) Some suppliers do not add VAT. These are from exempt suppliers or for zero rated supplies. The rent from Miro £230.78 is an example.

(c) The totals of Net + VAT columns should sum to the Gross column.

(d) The totals of the analysis columns (purchases, motor expenses etc) should sum to the Net column total.

(e) The bookkeeping is:

    (i) Debit the totals of the analysis columns to the appropriate expense account (e.g. purchases, rent and rates etc).

    (ii) Debit the VAT column to the VAT account.

    (iii) Credit the Gross items to the supplier accounts in the purchase ledger (e.g. £171.55 to Goya).

Input VAT can be suffered on invoices which do not go through the purchase and expense daybook. Some such payments may be made through the cash book. Many payments are to suppliers with accounts in the purchase ledger. Some payments are not. These include wages and salaries, repayments of loans, interest and dividends. These are outside the VAT system. These two categories (payments to suppliers with accounts in the purchase ledger and payments for items which are out of the VAT system) cover the vast majority of payments but there may be some which are in the VAT system and if this is so then a VAT column is required for the credit side of the cash book.

Most businesses also pay for goods and services through petty cash and some of these are subject to VAT. Consequently a VAT column is usually necessary in the petty cash book.

The VAT account

7. The VAT account should appear in the ledger like this :

Debit			Credit		
Date	Details	Amount	Date	Details	Amount
March 31	Purchase daybook	71.94	March 1	Balance b/d	670.76
March 31	Petty cash book	32.61	March 31	Sales daybook	335.01
March 31	Balance c/d	901.22			
		1005.77			1005.77

Notes:

(a) The balance b/d is the amount due to HM Customs and Excise at the beginning of the month. The output tax £335.01 adds to this but the input tax (£71.94 and £32.61) reduce it so that the amount due at the end of the month has become £901.22.

(b) If 31 March was the end of a quarterly *tax period* then £901.22 would have to be paid to HM Customs and Excise by 30 April together with the *VAT return*.

(c) The account is usually known as the VAT account but is really the personal account of HM Customs and Excise Department.

The VAT return

8. A return is sent to HM Customs and Excise at the end of each tax period. The format of a VAT return (known as VAT 100) shows:

VAT due in this period on **sales** and other outputs	1	23,860.00
VAT due in this period on **acquisitions** from other **EU Member States**	2	1,260.00
Total VAT due (**the sum of boxes 1 and 2**)	3	25,120.00
VAT reclaimed in this period on **purchases** and other inputs (including acquisitions from the EU)	4	13,673.95
Net VAT to be paid to Customs or reclaimed by you (**difference between boxes 3 and 4**)	5	11,446.05
Total value of sales and all other outputs excluding any VAT. **Include your box 8 figure**	6	143,122.00
Total value of **purchases** and all other inputs excluding any VAT. **Include your box 9 figure**	7	94,536.00
Total value of all **supplies** of goods and related services, excluding any VAT. to other **EU Member States**	8	6,780.00
Total value of all **acquisitions** of goods and related services excluding any VAT, from other **EU Member States**	9	1,240.87

Notes:

(a) Line 1 is obtained for the sales daybook VAT column.

(b) Line 2 is VAT at standard rate derived from goods and services imported from EU states. Invoices come in from EU states without VAT and effectively the VAT is paid in the UK by the importer.

(c) Line 3 is the sum of columns 1 and 2.

(d) Line 4 is the total of input taxes and includes line 2. Effectively the inclusion of line 2 in line 4 means that the amount in line 2 is put in and then taken out again so that no VAT is actually paid on imports from the EU.

(e) Line 5 is the tax actually payable. There are severe penalties for late payments!

(f) Lines 6 to 9 are statistical and help the Government know what is going on in the economy and in imports and exports to the EU.

(g) Line 7 includes purchases and expenses which are free of VAT because they are zero rated (e.g. children's clothing) or from non-registered suppliers (small businesses) or for exempt supplies (e.g. insurance premiums).

(h) Goods which pass from one EU country to another are not subject to VAT in the country of origin but in the country of final sale. Thus if goods are imported from France to the UK they arrive free of VAT. On arrival tax is payable (line 2, acquisitions = purchases) but is immediately recovered without actual payment being made (line 4). When the goods are sold on to a UK buyer VAT is added (line 1).

VAT and discounts

9. In selling their goods some firms give trade discounts, e.g. a sale of goods at £100 less 20% trade discount. Essentially the sale is goods £80 and it is on this amount that VAT is payable. Some firms give cash or settlement discounts. A Ltd might offer its customers 3% discount on the amount payable for payment within seven days of the invoice date. A Ltd sells £1000 of goods to B on 1st March. The VAT is calculated on the goods less the discount. So the VAT would be $0.175 \times £970$ (£1000 – £30) = £169.75. It would not matter if B paid after 8 March and did not take the discount.

Irrecoverable VAT

10. Some firms are outside the VAT system, for example small firms who are under the turnover limits and so do not have to register. They do not add VAT to their invoices and so their customers cannot recover input tax on their supplies. Firms outside the VAT system will however receive invoices with VAT added but this VAT is not recoverable and has to be seen as part of the cost of the goods. So Shah, a taxi driver who is not registered for VAT receives an invoice for repairs £100 + VAT £117.50 = £117.50. He would treat the invoice simply as Repairs £117.50.

VAT included in gross amount

11. In the case of the sale of small items, for example by retailers, it is easier to record the gross amount of each individual sale rather than the Net amount + VAT. So sales for the day might be £874. Such sales are really Net + VAT = £874 and in the

books it is essential to record the true total. To calculate the Net and VAT from the gross, the calculation is:

$$\text{Net} = \frac{\text{Gross}}{1 + \text{VAT rate}} \quad \text{or} \quad \frac{£874}{1.175} = \text{Net } £743.83 + \text{VAT } £130.17$$

The bookkeeping is:

(a)	Debit Cash Book	£874.00
(b)	Credit Sales	£743.83
(c)	Credit VAT Account	£130.17

VAT and financial statements

12. **Profit and loss account**

All items in the trading and profit and loss account are net of VAT. Thus in the case of Jason, sales would include just the £720 and purchases just the £240.

Balance sheet

The only item appearing in the balance sheet for VAT will be the sum due to or from HM Customs and Excise which will be entered under current liabilities or current assets.

Debtors and creditors will appear in the balance sheet gross of VAT since those are the amounts receivable or payable.

SSAP 5 – Accounting for value added tax requires that:

(a) turnover in the profit and loss account should exclude VAT;

(b) irrecoverable VAT allocable to fixed assets and to other items disclosed separately in published accounts should be included in their cost.

Examples of irrecoverable VAT is the VAT on cars and entertaining.

Summary

❒ Businesses add VAT at the standard rate or zero rate to their outputs (sales). This output tax is payable to HM Customs and Excise

❒ Businesses can recover VAT suffered on their inputs.

❒ Some supplies are exempt from VAT. Input related to such outputs is not recoverable.

❒ In the profit and loss account of a VAT registered enterprise, all items are net of VAT.

❒ In the balance sheet, the sum due to or from the Customs and Excise is shown as a creditor or debtor.

❒ In the balance sheet debtors and creditors are shown gross as the amount due includes VAT.

❒ Bookkeeping entries for VAT are simply:

Output Tax	Dr Customers	Cr Customs and Excise
Input Tax	Dr Customs and Excise	Cr Suppliers
Payment	Dr Customs and Excise	Cr Cash Book

❒ Businesses send in a VAT return quarterly, monthly or annually.

❏ VAT on items sold subject to settlement discount is calculated on the amount of the invoice less the discount.

Points to note

❏ The VAT included in a bad debt which is more than six months old and where the output tax has been paid and the debt has been written off in the accounts as a bad debt is recoverable from HM Customs and Excise.

❏ The VAT on a car bought for the business is in general not reclaimable.

❏ Some firms sell both exempt and non-exempt goods (e.g. a retailer may sell goods which are subject to VAT and sell them on an instalment plan which includes interest and interest is an exempt supply). Such firms are partially exempt and subject to special rules

❏ Domestic fuel is subject to VAT at a special rate of 5%. This is generally non recoverable as users are final consumers.

Exercises

1. (a) Enter the following items for the quarter ending 31.8.x7 in the double entry system of Gillian whose year end is 31.8.x7:
   (i) Show only the accounts for sales, purchases and Customs and Excise.
   (ii) Balance due to Customs and Excise at 1.6.x7 £2,900.
   (iii) Paid to Customs and Excise on 23.7.x7 £2,000.
   (iv) Sales invoices £17,600 + VAT at 17.5%.
   (v) Purchase invoices £8,280 including VAT at 17.5%.
   (vi) Cash sales £5,750 including VAT at 17.5%.
   (b) How much is due to Customs and Excise? When will this be paid? How will these items appear in the financial statements?
   (c) Complete a VAT return.

2. (a) Enter the following items for the quarter ending 28.2.x8 in the double entry system of Horne. You should show only the sales, purchases, motor expenses, and Customs and Excise Account.
   (i) Sales invoices £45,800 + VAT at 17.5%.
   (ii) Cash sales £8,970 including VAT at 17.5%.
   (iii) Purchase invoices £34,799 + VAT at 17.5%.
   (iv) Zero rated purchase invoices £360.
   (v) Motor expenses £830 + VAT at 17.5%.
   (vi) Zero rated motor expenses £200.
   (b) How much is due to Customs and Excise? When will this be paid? How will all these items appear in the financial statements if the year end is 28.2.x8?
   (c) Complete a VAT return.

3. In the final quarter of 19x3, Hugh found that output tax amounted to £13,000 and input tax to £6,300. He put these figures on his VAT return and made payment in January 19x4. Give the entries in financial statements for 19x3.

4. Hank sells 12 widgets to Marvin at £36 each less 10% trade discount. He offers a cash discount of 3% for payment in seven days. VAT is at 17.5%. Design an invoice and insert the figures.

5. The following data relate to Hugo, a VAT registered retailer, for the VAT quarter ending 31 March 19x7:

Sales to UK customers	243,300.00
VAT added to sales	42,056.32
Acquisitions from other EU countries	2,870.00
Input tax re UK purchases and expenses	27,475.00
UK purchases and expenses	189,540.89
Sales to customers in other EU countries	12,789.00

Required:

Complete the VAT return.

6. The following data relate to Harriet Ltd, a VAT registered retailer, for the VAT quarter ending 31 March 19x7:

Due to Customs and Excise at 31 December 19x6	61,800.00
Paid to Customs and Excise	61,800.00
Sales to UK customers	600,600.00
VAT added to sales	103,154.98
Acquisitions from other EU countries	27,867.00
Input tax re UK purchases and expenses	64,760.11
UK purchases and expenses	460,411.43
Sales to customers in other EU countries	29,500.66

Required:

Complete the VAT return.

7. Revisit the computer accounting exercise in Chapter 6 and use the financials + VAT option to prepare a VAT return.

Assignment

❑ *Penny is in business as a self employed taxi driver. Her annual turnover is just under the limit for VAT registration. She finds that the business is profitable but not excessively so as there is very strong competition from larger firms. She wonders if she could not make as much money going back to her old business of computer programming. She gave up computing because she prefers the human contact of taxi driving. She is considering working longer hours to make a larger turnover.*

Write a report to her outlining the financial effects of increasing her turnover.

16 Accounting for stocks and materials costing

The majority of businesses include among their assets stock. Measuring the quantity and value of this asset is difficult, subject to differing methods, time consuming and there is much potential for error.

This section considers stock under a number of headings:

(a) Stock and the matching convention.

(b) Types of stock.

(c) Inclusions in cost.

(d) Valuation methods, FIFO etc.

(e) Net realisable value and the prudence convention.

(f) Stocktaking.

(g) For cost accounting purposes.

The valuation of stock and work in progress is covered by Statement of Standard Accounting Practice Number 9 and much of this section reflects the requirements of this accounting standard.

Stock and the matching convention

1. Consider the accounts of a retailer in the illustration. The objective in this case is to match the cost of the goods sold with the sales made in the year. The cost of any unsold or unconsumed stocks will have been incurred in the expectation of future revenue and closing stock is included in the accounts in order to take out of the costs those costs which should be matched with sales of the following year. The problem is which costs relate to the following period and are thus taken out by the inclusion of closing stock.

A Retailer
Trading Account for the year ending 31 December 19x5

	£	£
Sales		134,820
Less cost of goods sold:		
Opening stock	20,871	
Purchases	86,382	
	107,253	
Less closing stock	24,693	
		82,560
Gross profit		£52,260

2. In the case of the retailer or wholesaler, the cost of his unsold stock is relatively straightforward and the stock takes out that part of purchases which relates to unsold stock.

    The matter is more complicated with a manufacturer because costs of manufacture of work in progress (goods in course of manufacture) and finished goods are not simply the bought in cost of goods but some of the other costs of production which are incurred in making goods and services. The idea to grasp is that closing work in progress and finished goods stock:

    (a) Take out those costs which relate to incomplete or unsold goods which can then be matched with sales of the following year.

    (b) Leave the sales of this year to be matched with the costs of producing the goods sold this year.

    We will consider the costs of **making** goods and services later in this chapter and how profit is measured in manufacturing businesses in the next chapter.

Types of stock

3. Stocks of incomplete, unsold or unconsumed items can be categorised as:

    (a) Finished goods held for resale.

    (b) Goods purchased for resale.

    (c) Work in progress.

    (d) Raw materials and components purchased for incorporation into products for sale.

    (e) Consumable stores – lubricants, cleaning materials, fuel, spare parts etc.

    The balance sheet should show the stock analysed into these categories either on the balance sheet proper or preferably in a note attached to the balance sheet.

Inclusions in cost

4. Stock is normally valued at cost. However, the term 'cost' needs some precise definition. In SSAP 9, cost is defined as:

    'That expenditure which has been incurred in the normal course of business in bringing the product or service to its present location and condition.'

    Cost should include:

    (a) Cost of purchase including import duties, transport and handling costs (e.g. carriage in) and any other directly attributable costs less trade discounts, rebates and subsidies.

    (b) Cost of conversion.

    Cost of conversion comprises:

    (a) Costs which are specifically attributable to units of production, ie direct labour, direct expenses (e.g. royalties payable on production) and sub-contracted work.

    (b) Production overheads.

    (c) Other overheads (e.g. of administration), if any, attributable to the particular circumstances of the business to bringing the product or service to its present location and condition. In practice, few of these costs are ever included.

Production overheads are overheads incurred for production, based on the normal level of activity. Overheads to be included are all those related to production (e.g. rent of factory, depreciation of machinery, salary of works manager) notwithstanding that these may accrue wholly or partly on a time basis.

This means that expenses such as rent which accrue strictly on a time basis can be taken out of production overheads by inclusion of part of the cost in the value of work in progress or finished goods. This subject is taken further in the chapter on overheads.

Valuation methods – FIFO etc

5. The cost of an item in stock should be measured as nearly as possible to the *actual historical cost* of that particular item. This is the fundamental requirement. Note it well!

   For example, in a shop there are in stock 160 widgets. The most recent purchases of widgets were:

Dec 4	150 at £25 each
Dec 13	50 at £26 each
Dec 19	90 at £30 each

   Thus 290 widgets were purchased and, as 160 remained, 130 were sold.

   How much did the 160 widgets cost? The answer clearly depends on which consignment the individual widgets arrived in and this may not be known as the widgets are indistinguishable one from another (the technical expression is that they are **fungible** assets).

6. In practice firms use one of the following methods of stock rotation for actually dealing with stock.
   (a) The oldest are used up first – obviously essential for perishable items like food-stuffs.
   (b) The latest arrivals are used first. This seems unlikely but if the goods are stacked in a bin as:

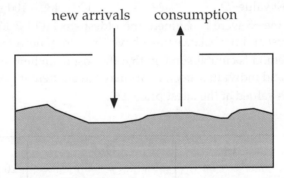

   new arrivals   consumption

   it will be seen that this can occur.
   (c) Consumption is from old and new stocks selected randomly. This happens with liquids as old and new stock mix up completely and selection for consumption must be of the mixture. It can also happen with solid items that are stacked randomly so that it is not known which is old and which is new.

7. For *valuation* of the year end stock, a method is selected which approximates to 6 (a), (b) or (c). The *method chosen may not actually follow precisely the reality* but it should do so as nearly as possible. The methods to correspond with 6 (a), (b) and (c) are:
   (a) First in, first out – FIFO
   (b) Last in, last out   – LIFO
   (c) Average cost   – AVCO

8. In *some* businesses, the amount and cost of stock is recorded continuously and we will illustrate FIFO etc as if it were so recorded. In practice, most businesses do not have continuous stock recording but stock must be valued following the same principles. For each illustration we will assume that 'consumed' can mean used in production or sold. Never use the sale price in these calculations.

	Stock item		small widgets
	Stock at	1.12.x5	– 20 at £5 each
	Purchases:		
		2.12.x5	– 30 at £6 each
	Consumed	9.12.x5	– 35
		18.12.x5	– 10

FIFO

Date	In		Out		Balance	
1.12.x5					20 at £5 =	£100.00
2.12.x5	30 at £6 =	£180.00			20 at £5 =	£100.00 }
					30 at £6 =	£180.00
9.12.x5			20 at £5 =	£100.00 }	15 at £6 =	£90.00
			15 at £6 =	£90.00		
18.12.x5			10 at £6 =	£60.00	5 at £6 =	£30.00

Notes:
(a) The account balances as to quantity: 20 + 30 – 35 – 10 = 5
    and cost value (£)   100 + 180 – 100 – 90 – 60 = 30
(b) When the 35 were consumed, the oldest stock (20 @ £5) were assumed to be used first and the balance must have come from newer stock.
(c) The method is cumbersome in that the cost of an item sold is a mix of different prices and individual stock items may have different prices.
(d) Stock is valued at the latest price (£6).

LIFO

Date	In		Out		Balance	
1.12.x5					20 at £5 =	£100.00
2.12.x5	30 at £6 =	£180.00			20 at £5 =	£100.00 }
					30 at £6 =	£180.00
9.12.x5			30 at £6 =	£180.00 }	15 at £5 =	£75.00
			5 at £5 =	£25.00		
18.12.x5			10 at £5 =	£50.00	5 at £5 =	£25.00

Notes:

(a) The account balances as to quantity: $20 + 30 - 35 - 10 = 5$

and cost value (£): $100 + 180 - 180 - 25 - 50 = 25$

(b) When the 35 were consumed, the newest stock (30 @ £6) were assumed to have been used and the balance only came from earlier purchases.

(c) The method is cumbersome in that consumption and stock can be at multiple prices.

(d) Stock is valued at the earliest price (£5).

(e) In times of inflation, LIFO gives a lower value to stock.

AVCO – weighted average cost

Date	In	Out	Balance	
1.12.x5			20 at £5 =	£100.00
2.12.x5	30 at £6 = £180.00		50 at £5.60 =	£280.00
9.12.x5		35 at £5.60 = £196.00	15 at £5.60 =	£84.00
18.12.x5		10 at £5.60 = £56.00	5 at £5.60 =	£28.00

Notes:

(a) On the purchase at 2.12.x5, a weighted average cost is calculated by dividing the total cost (£100 + £180 = £280) by the number of items in stock (20 + 30 = 50). This gives a cost of £5.60 which is part way between £5 and £6, but nearer £6 because more weight is given to the 30 items (at £6) than the 20 items (at £5).

(b) The calculation of average cost occurs only at purchases. In practice issues are much more frequent than purchase.

(c) Issues and stock are all at one price. This price changes only when a purchase is made.

(d) All the items in stock are valued at the same, average price.

(e) In times of inflation, weighted average cost gives a value of stock and profit, between that of LIFO and FIFO.

9. Other stock valuation methods are possible – unit cost, base stock, replacement cost, standard cost, adjusted selling price.

(a) **Unit cost.** Where the stock is divisible into individual units and the cost of each unit can be reasonably found then this cost should be used and approximations such as LIFO and FIFO are not required.

	PROFIT WITH AVCO AND FIFO AND LIFO				
		Trading Account 19x4			
	AVCO		LIFO		FIFO
Sales		100	100		100
Opening stock	10		10		10
Purchases	70		70		70
	80		80		80
Closing stock	15		13		18
		65	67		62
Gross profit		35	33		38

Notes:

(a) In periods of rising prices stock values under LIFO will be lower than AVCO prices which will be lower than FIFO values.

(b) The effect on profit can be seen in the examples. Instinctively, a lower asset value at the year end must mean a lower profit.

(c) When opening stock and closing stock are similar in size the effect of the different stock value methods becomes negligible.

(b) **Base stock**. This method assumes that a certain minimum stock is always held and that this minimum quantity should be valued at some historically based (and therefore low) fixed unit price. All stock held in excess of base stock will be valued on LIFO, FIFO or some other acceptable method.

Base stock is not acceptable under SSAP9.

(c) **Replacement price** should not be used as it does not measure the **cost** of the stock. However, it can be used in the special circumstances described in paragraph 10.

(d) **Standard cost** is a measure of cost arrived at as part of a system of management accounting called standard costing. A standard cost is a predetermined budgeted cost. It is not acceptable as an actual cost but frequently by applying variances (differences between budget and actual cost) actual cost can be approximated.

(e) **Adjusted selling price** can sometimes be used. In supermarkets the cost price is difficult to determine but selling price is of course marked on all items. If the stock is evaluated at selling price and then marked down by the normal gross profit margin, then actual cost is approximated providing all stock is fairly fast moving.

Net realisable value and the prudence convention

10. Most items of stock will be sold at a price higher than their cost. However, some items may have to be sold at prices which are lower than their cost. Reasons include damage, obsolescence, buying errors, deliberate policy (e.g. to clear out old stock), technological change, market changes etc.

Such items should be valued at net realisable value. Net realisable value of an item is defined as the amount which the item can be disposed of without creating either profit or loss in the year of sale. It is easier thought of as the:

estimated proceeds of sale
less all further costs to completion; and
less all costs to be incurred in marketing, selling and distributing directly related to the item.

Example

Widget A4 had cost £500 to place it in its present location and condition. However, a new model had been put in production and it is estimated that Widget A4 can only be sold for £450. Completion costs will be £45 and selling and distribution costs (including sales commission) directly related will be £64.

Net realisable value will be: 450 – 45 – 64 = £341

Each item in stock should be reviewed to determine if net realisable value is less than cost and, if it is, net realisable value should be the value used. Thus all items of stock are valued at the lower of cost and net realisable value.

The valuation of some stock items at net realisable value is an example of the use of the prudence convention, sometimes called the conservatism convention. The convention requires that:

'Revenue and profits are not anticipated, but are recognised by inclusion in the profit and loss account only when realised in the form either of cash or of other assets, the ultimate cash realisation of which can be assessed with reasonable certainty; provision is made for all known liabilities (expenses and losses) whether the amount of these is known with certainty or is a best estimate in the light of the information available.'

All this means, is that:

(a) Items not sold in a year are valued at cost.
(b) Items of stock that will be sold at a price less than cost must be valued at the net realisable value. Effect on profit:

	Stock at cost		Stock at lower of cost and n.r.v.	
	£	£	£	£
Sales		1,000		1,000
Less cost of goods sold:				
Purchases	800		800	
Less closing stock	200		170	
		600		630
		400		370

The lower profit is because of the lower valuation of stock.

(c) The expected profit (which will only be realised on sale in the next period) is not counted but any expected losses (b) are counted.

(d) Net realisable value is not always known with certainty and estimates have to be made.

In some cases a good surrogate (= substitute) for net realisable value is replacement price. If replacement price is used, it is being used not as the valuation method, but as a reasonable equivalent or surrogate for net realisable value.

Stock: cost or net realisable value?

200 good widgets:		
Cost £20 each	£4,000 }	Select cost as
Net realisable value (selling price) £30 each	£6,000	cost is lower
10 damaged widgets:		
Cost £20 each	£200 }	Select NRV as
Net realisable value £10 each	£100	as NRV is lower

Stocktaking

11. In practice, stock is difficult to determine both as to quantity and to value. Errors are easily made. The needs specifically are:
    (a) Identifying precisely each item of stock.
    (b) Counting, weighting or measuring accurately.
    (c) Entering the details on stock sheets.
    (d) Ensuring all stock sheets are included.
    (e) Determining cost for each item.
    (f) Extending quantity x price accurately to give value.
    (g) Identifying and valuing items which need to be valued at net realisable value.
    (h) Summing the values.
    (i) Ensuring accurate cut-off.

12. Good stocktaking procedures would include:
    (a) Good, early planning of the stocktaking operation.
    (b) Issue and discussion of instructions to staff.
    (c) Division of the stock into manageable areas for control purposes.
    (d) Proper instructions for counting, weighing, measuring and checking.
    (e) Two persons to be involved in counting each item.
    (f) Procedures for marking items which have been counted.
    (g) Control of movement during the stock take.
    (h) Cut off procedures.
    (i) Procedures for identifying damaged, obsolete and slow moving stock.
    (j) Identification of stock on the premises owned by third parties, and of stock held by outside parties.
    (k) Control over the issue of blank stock sheets and the return of completed and unused stock sheets.

Stock records and management accounting

13. Continuous inventory (keeping records of precisely what is in stock at all times) is very important in management accounting. Management accounting is the use of

accounting information for management purposes and continuous inventory provides a great deal of information for management. Some of the uses are:

(a) Where companies have a wide variety of items in stock which are for sale or for use in the manufacturing process, it is important to maintain adequate stocks of each item. Otherwise customers' needs cannot be met or the manufacturing process comes to a halt. It is possible to set a re-order level for each item so that when stocks go down to this level, the ordering process is triggered off. Having written records, regularly updated, of what is in stock, facilitates this process. Computerised stock records can set the re-order process going automatically. Setting the optimum re-order level is an interesting subject beyond the scope of this book.

(b) Customers enquire about buying items in stock. Having continuous stock records enables instant answers to be given about the availability of stock without physical inspection. Where stock is held at several locations, customer service is greatly helped by knowing instantly what is in stock and where it is. Similar benefits arise to production controllers who need to know what raw materials and components are in stock.

(c) When continuous inventory records also the cost of each item estimators can know the cost of the materials to use in preparing their estimates. For example, Dave is an estimator at Grainger Equipment Ltd. Cook, a customer, requires a price quotation for a widget of a particular specification and Dave has to collect the expected costs, add on an element of profit and quote a selling price. Dave can estimate the type and quantity of materials which will be needed. The continuous inventory assists him in informing him if the items are available in stock and what each cost. The costs are of course FIFO, LIFO or average costs and these costs may not be seen as being the best for this purpose. Some companies use other prices in making estimates. These include:

(i) HIHO – highest in highest out. The highest recorded input price is used.

(ii) NINO – next in next out. The estimator uses the price of the next delivery.

Clearly this information is not available from the stock records but is usually available from catalogues etc.

(d) Many firms collect the costs of all their products. The reason may be for comparison with expected or budgeted costs. Sometimes the cost collection process is carried out on double entry principles. Whatever method is used materials and other inputs must be valued at cost. With materials, this cost is based on LIFO, FIFO or AVCO and collected costs are thus a function of the recording process. Different costs will be given depending on whether LIFO, FIFO or AVCO is used.

(e) Management need to know the profit made by the enterprise overall as well as that made (see (d) above) on individual products. This is of course done in the annual accounts but management like to know the profit more frequently, perhaps monthly. The difficulty of measuring profit lies in the counting and pricing at cost of stock. Where continuous inventory is maintained at cost then (if computerised) the total stock at cost is available at the touch of a button.

Summary

❐ The objective of the valuation of stock (and work in progress) is to remove from costs of the year, those costs that relate to stocks at the year end in order to match the remaining costs with the sales of the year.

❐ Stock should be valued at the lower of cost and net realisable value.

❐ Cost is the expenditure incurred in bringing the stock items to their present location and condition.

❐ Cost includes cost of purchase and cost of conversion.

❐ Cost of conversion includes direct costs and a proportion of production overheads including costs which vary on a time basis.

❐ Valuation methods include FIFO, LIFO and weighted average cost.

❐ The valuation of stock at net realisable value is an example of the use of the prudence convention.

❐ Continuous inventory provides information for management including: re-order levels, what is in stock and where it is, costs for pricing and estimating, costs for cost collection and comparisons with budgets and standard costs, end of period total stock at cost.

Points to note

❐ The measurement of profit on a regular basis is highly desirable. For many businesses this is done infrequently, perhaps only once a year, because of the difficulty of stocktaking. However, computers have made stock recording within the reach of many more businesses.

A benefit of computerised stock records is that stock can be valued with relative ease at any time.

❐ You should note that a higher closing stock means a higher profit. This is sometimes difficult to see because of difficulty in visualising the double negative – 'less cost of goods sold' incorporating 'less closing stock'.

❐ The various alternative stock valuation methods are not all acceptable. SSAP 9 recommends FIFO or AVCO and condemns LIFO and base stock. LIFO is also not acceptable in the UK to the tax authorities and if LIFO is used, then adjustments have to be made to represent the Accounts using FIFO or AVCO. LIFO is commonly used by American companies.

❐ Students should note that adoption of say FIFO does not mean that goods are physically kept in that way but the method used should as far as possible, accord with what actually happens.

❐ Weighted average cost takes into account the differing quantities of stock at each price. An alternative is to use simple average cost, e.g. if prices are £2.50 and £3.50, simple average is £3.00. Weighted average is to be preferred.

❏ The use of LIFO can lead to stock being valued at prices which are many years old. In practice, stock varieties change and there are occasions when a stock line is reduced to nil, so that very old prices are rarely found.

❏ Different stock valuation methods lead to different profits. However, both opening and closing stocks must be valued using consistent methods. If opening and closing stocks are similar in value then the effect of different stock valuation methods is not usually significant except in the first and last periods of a business.

Self-testing questions

1. What is the relationship between stock and the matching convention?
2. What categories of stock can be found in a balance sheet?
3. Define 'cost' in relation to stock.
4. Define 'cost of conversion'.
5. What overheads should be included in stock, and on what basis?
6. What are fungible assets?
7. What should be the relationship between stock rotation and stock valuation methods?
8. What is (i) FIFO; (ii) LIFO; (iii) AVCO?
9. When should selling prices be used in stock recording systems using LIFO, FIFO etc?
10. Describe the stock valuation methods:
    (a) Unit cost.
    (b) Base stock.
    (c) Replacement cost.
    (d) Standard cost.
    (e) Adjusted selling price.
    When can these methods be used?
11. What is the relationship between net realisable value and the prudence convention?
12. Define net realisable value.
13. List the management accounting uses of continuous inventory.

Exercises

1. What is the correct valuation for the accounts, of the following items in stock:
   (a) 200 widgets invoiced at £40 each less 20% trade discount. The goods were delivered to head office with a carriage charge of £500 for the consignment. Since purchase, the goods have been transported to a branch at a cost of £405 and the widgets have been rust proofed at a cost of £3 each. The invoice from the supplier was paid less a settlement discount of 5%.
   (b) 40 brockets which had been invoiced at £30 each. They have been replaced in the catalogue and the proposal is to sell them off at £32. On sale, commission of 10% and a carriage charge of £1 each will have to be paid.
2. Show continuous stock records for the following on:
   (a) FIFO.
   (b) LIFO.
   (c) Weighted average costs methods.

		Business		
		A	**B**	**C**
1.1.x5	Stock	200 at £12	50 at £71	40 at £30
6.1.x5	Purchase	400 at £17	40 at £56	50 at £40
9.1.x5	Sale	300 at £30	20 at £100	80 at £65
15.1.x5	Sale	250 at £32	25 at £95	10 at £60
17.1.x5	Purchase	100 at £18	30 at £41	50 at £35
21.1.x5	Sale	60 at £32	5 at £60	10 at £70

3. Janet is preparing the estimated price to be quoted to Fred, a customer, for a special widget. The widget includes three boggets. On consulting the bogget record, she sees the following:

Boggets

1.	b/f			20 at £5 £100
2.2	In	30 at £5.50 £165.00		50 at £5.30 £265
6.2	Out		13 at £5.30 £68.90	37 at £5.30 £196.10
9.2	In	5 at £5.20 £26.00		42 at £5.29 £222.18

Required:

(a) What measurement methods for cost records does the company use?

(b) What cost should be included for the boggets if the company uses:

   (i) The stock record as it stands.

   (ii) HIFO.

   (iii) NIFO (the supplier has quoted £60 a dozen less 5% for orders greater than 10 dozen + delivery of £5 an order + VAT at 17.5%).

   (iv) FIFO.

   (v) LIFO.

4. What is the correct valuation for the accounts of the following items of stock?

150 frames which had been invoiced at £40 each, less a trade discount of 15%. The goods were delivered with a carriage charge of £500 the lot. Since purchase, the goods have been painted at a cost of £2 each and transported to stores at a cost of £700 the lot. The invoice was paid, less a settlement discount of 2%.

Note:

One frame was damaged in transit to the store and it is proposed to sell it for £30. This will involve expenditure of £5 for repairs.

Assignment

❑ *Rhian is taking stock in her motor parts retail business. She is not sure how to value the following items:*

   (a) 30 Wartburg exhausts; she originally purchased these in two separate assignments: 50 in January 19x8 at £50 each and 60 in March 19x8 at £60 each. There is a ready sale for these items at £100 each.

   (b) 12 sets of Clino brake linings. These cost £100 a set but she finds that they can now only be sold at £65 a set. She sells them through an agent who charges her 10% commission.

(c) 31 Bullnose steering wheels. She bought these for £20 each and they can be sold at £40 except four which are damaged. She will sell two of these at only £25 each and two at £15 each.

(d) 30 Panhard cylinder heads. She bought these at £25 each and can sell them for double that. She has now found a new supplier who will charge her only £18 each.

(e) 42 Ford springs. She bought 100 of these for £10 each and has had to spend £350 on heat treatment of them before she can sell them.

(f) 231 gallons of heating oil which cost £3.20 a gallon.

Required:

(a) How should these items be valued for the purposes of her financial statements? Her year end is June 19x8 and she uses FIFO.

(b) Using these items explain how using LIFO or AVCO for the fungible items would change her profit.

17 Labour costs

This chapter is concerned with the cost of labour – wages, salaries and other remuneration. We will look at the different types of labour, how labour is paid, and the classification of the cost of labour so that the labour of the cost of a product can be found.

Types of labour

1. Labour in a factory can perform many functions, e.g.:
    (a) On the shop floor:
        (i)   Making the product.
        (ii) Supervising the manufacture.
        (iii) Cleaning.
        (iv) Repair and maintenance of the machinery.
        (v)   Clerical.
        (vi) Transporting materials and products within the factory.
    (b) In the offices:
        (i)   Accounting both cost and financial.
        (ii) Management.
        (iii) Selling and marketing.
        (iv) Personnel work.
    (c) In other activities:
        (i)   Selling.
        (ii) Transport.
        (iii) Grounds maintenance.

    In other kinds of enterprise, similar kinds of classification of function can be made. For example in a hospital you might categorise activities as: medical staff, administrative staff, cleaning staff, porters, support staff (e.g. pathology, pharmacy), specialist staff (e.g. almoners, chaplain). In a school a division might be: teachers, management staff (e.g. head teacher), administrative staff, technicians, support staff (e.g. groundsman, cleaners, catering). This type of classification is often complicated because some people have more than one function – for example the Head may also teach.

Payment systems

2. How are people paid? There are basically three payment systems found in practice:
    (a) An hourly (or weekly or monthly) rate – so much an hour or so many £s a week.
    (b) Payment according to output – piece work, commission on sales.
    (c) Complex systems (based on a mixture of some or all of time work, profitability, group output, budget achievement and other quantities).

    Whatever method is used to calculate the wage or salary, payment has actually to be made to the employee. At one time, most employees were paid in cash. Some still are paid in cash but the common method now, is to pay through the banking system so that the pay is transferred directly from the employer's bank account to the bank or building society account of each employee. Normally each employee is informed of the amount of pay on a **payslip**. Here is an example:

MEGA CO. LTD PAY ADVICE		Name: May Jones Dept: 07	
		Employee No.: 126	
Date: W/E 27.1.x5		Tax code: 387L Week 42	
Payments		**Deductions**	
Basic pay	273.32	Income Tax	64.30
Overtime	54.20	Nat Ins	26.10
Gross pay	327.52	Union dues	1.98
Net pay	235.14	Total	92.38
Gross pay to date	12,200.90	Tax Paid this year	2,300.40
Taxable pay	9,650.20	NI Paid	901.76

This payslip is designed to inform the worker about the pay he or she is receiving. Some explanation is perhaps necessary:

(a) Ms Jones is paid weekly. This week is week ending 27.1.x5. It is also tax week number 42. The government year ends on 5 April and weeks start from 6 April.

(b) Her pay this week is the usual pay for a standard week (£273.32) + some overtime (£54.20). So her total pay for the week is £327.52. This is known as the gross pay.

(c) There are several deductions to be made before Ms Jones is paid. The first is Income Tax. This is calculated by a clever system called PAYE (= pay as you earn). This week the tax is £64.30.

(d) The second deduction is for national insurance. This is also effectively a tax and this week she has to pay £26.10. In addition she has elected to have her trade union dues paid by deducting them from her pay. The employer will then pay them to the union. The total deductions are £92.38.

(e) After deductions, her net pay is £235.14 and this will be paid to her either in cash or direct to her bank account. The net pay is colloquially known as take home pay.

(f) The other sums are data concerning the PAYE system.

Not all payslips are as informative as this but all should be!

3. The payslip is in itself a form of internal control. This is so because errors will be pointed out by the employee. However, errors in favour of the employee might not be! Several frauds are possible in the wages area. These include:

(a) Payments to non-existent employees.

(b) Inflation of the wage roll so that more is drawn from the bank than is required to pay the employees.

Controls that can be implemented include:

(a) Separate personnel records that can be (and at intervals are) compared with the wage roll.

(b) Formal procedures for engaging and dismissing employees and fixing wages rates.

(c) Supervised time recording systems.

(d) Formal output records which can be reconciled to actual production.

(e) Separation of duties amongst wages department personnel so that, for example, separate people are responsible for preparing the wage roll, summarising it, checking it, obtaining money from the bank, making up the wage envelopes, paying the wages to the employees.

Today, most employees are paid by transfer between bank accounts and most systems are computerised. These procedures may prevent some frauds (e.g. misappropriation of cash) but open up other possibilities.

Calculation of gross pay

4. (a) Time related pay. The contract of employment between the worker and his employer should indicate the pay. This may be expressed as an annual rate, a monthly rate or a weekly or hourly rate. Payment is usually weekly or monthly however the rate is expressed. Employees on an annual salary are usually paid 1/12 of it each calendar month. There are often arrangements for extra payments for overtime.

As an example of hourly pay including overtime, consider Hugh who is paid £4 an hour and time and one half for total hours greater than 40 on weekdays and double time for all work at weekends. He is required to record his arrival and departure times on a card stamped by a time clock. This is supervised to ensure he does not cheat. The card for week 18 showed:

Hugh	Number 238	Week 18	
Day	**Arrival**	**Departure**	**Hours**
Monday	0830	1900	10.5
Tuesday	0900	1600	7
Wednesday	0700	1500	8
Thursday	0930	1700	7.5
Friday	0830	1730	9
Saturday	0800	1200	4
Sunday	0900	1300	4
Weekday total	42	Weekend total	8

Hugh will be paid:

40 hours at £4	£160	
2 hours at £4 x 1.5	£12	
8 hours at £4 x 2	£64	
	£236	

(b) Performance related pay. This may be simply so much an item. For example, payment is 4p a pressing operation and, in the week, 4,800 operations were done. The gross pay will be 4,800 × 4p = £192. With salesmen, the method is often a commission based on a percentage of sales achieved. There is now a general movement towards performance related pay even in such difficult areas as the civil service and teaching.

(c) Many variations on these themes are found in practice and there are many other systems for calculating pay including profit sharing and other incentive schemes.

Product cost

5. Before considering the labour cost of specific products, we must consider costs in general and understand some ideas and the words that are used to express the ideas. The first idea is to realise that the cost of a product can be divided into three major parts or elements:

(a) Materials and component parts.

(b) Direct labour.

(c) Overheads.

Materials were considered in the last chapter and overheads are considered in the next chapter.

6. SSAP 9 considers product costs in terms of:

(a) Cost of purchase.

(b) Cost of conversion.

Essentially, the cost of purchase is the materials and components which are bought from suppliers to form part of the product. Examples are wood, screws, paint and brass fittings which form the physical substance of a piece of furniture. SSAP9 defines the purchase price as including import duties, transport and handling costs and any other directly attributable costs less trade discounts, rebates and subsidies. Generally this is not difficult to see in the case of manufactured products but can be more difficult with services. However consider the cost of an operation in a hospital. Materials are used – swabs, dressings, drugs, anaesthetic materials etc.

The cost of conversion is the cost of turning the raw materials and components into a saleable finished product. Costs of conversion are the direct labour and overheads.

Direct costs are those costs which can be directly identified with a job, batch, product or service. Direct costs can be contrasted with indirect costs (= overheads). To illustrate the difference, screws used in making a particular lock can be used only in that lock and the cost of the screws can be traced directly as a part of the cost of that lock. When the key to the lock is assembled from separate parts by means of an electric arc welder, a small amount of electricity is used and the cost of that electricity is technically a direct cost of producing the key. However, in practice, the cost of electricity is traceable only as a monthly charge for the whole factory and it is not feasible to trace the cost of electricity used to individual products. More obviously, the cost of cleaning the factory is clearly a part of the cost of production but it is not feasible to ascribe the cost of particular cleaning materials or cleaner's wages to particular products. The costs of cleaning are shared by all the products.

Thus: *Direct costs can be traced exclusively to particular products. Indirect or overhead costs are shared by more than one product.* Examples of direct costs include direct labour (e.g. the wages of a worker who is assembling a particular lock), direct expenses (e.g. the cost of hallmarking the cost of a particular piece of gold jewellery) and sub-contracted work (e.g. the cost of blister wrapping the finished lock which is done by local housewives in their own homes). In the case of the hospital operation, the direct labour costs can be seen as the pay of the surgeon, anaesthetist, technicians, theatre nurses etc. Some hospital staff costs are not direct but are overheads – administrative staff, cleaners, porters, gardeners etc.

Only labour which has direct contact with products can be considered to be direct. In Adam Smith's famous pin factory (in *The Wealth of Nations* 1776) the workers each did one only of eighteen distinct operations on the pin and the direct labour cost of each whole pin was thus easily determined. This division of labour still exists today, but many production processes are automated and a worker may control several machines so that it is difficult to trace his wage to particular products.

Collecting data

7. (a) Where direct labour is paid by reference to time, the problem for costing systems is to collect data on the time spent on each individual product. This can be achieved by time sheets and diaries. It would be necessary for the surgeons, nurses etc to record the time spent on each operation.

(b) Where payment is by piecework, collection of the data is relatively easy. For example, in a lock factory, the workers are often paid x pence per action performed. The number of actions performed can be entered in an record card signed by the worker and the foreman. Subsequently, the amount of work paid for should be reconciled with output.

(c) In complex systems it is much more difficult to collect the precise direct labour costs of each product.

The total cost of labour

8. The cost of labour is not as simple as may appear. In the UK and most other countries the gross pay (e.g. hourly rate x hours worked) is not the only cost. There is also the cost of national insurance and other social security and pension costs. We saw that National Insurance was deducted from the worker but that is the worker's share of NI. In addition there is the employer's share. In addition each worker costs extra for holiday pay and pay while absent during sickness and training. All these extra costs are generally regarded as indirect.

All work paid for does not result in work chargeable to particular products. Workers are paid also for idle time. Idle time arises for many reasons – getting from the gate to the workbench, toilet and refreshment breaks, machine breakdown, shortage of parts or work, illness at work, accidents etc. Idle time is usually regarded as an indirect cost. One of the advantages of piece work payment systems is that idle time is not paid for.

Overtime

9. Many workers work overtime. This presumes that there are standard hours established for work and that any hours worked beyond those hours are paid at a higher rate – for example, double time on Sundays. The overtime premium is the extra amount paid over the standard rate. For example if the standard rate is £4 an hour and time and a half is paid for Saturdays then the premium is £2 an hour. Overtime premiums are usually regarded as indirect costs. However, in special circumstances they can be direct costs. For example Jim wants his widget made in a hurry and Ron agrees to make it on a Sunday if Jim will pay a higher price. In this case the overtime is specific to the widget and is thus direct.

Income tax - PAYE

10. This is very complex in practice but essentially tax is paid at *specified rates* on gross income less any *allowances*. Suppose James earns £24,000 in a year. The first £4,045 of this is free of tax as a result of his personal allowances. Personal allowances vary from person to person. The remainder (£19,955) will be taxed as:

£3,900 at 20%	780.00
£16,055 at 24%	3853.20
	4633.20

However James pays his tax not at one go but each month as he is paid. The mechanism for this is that he is given a code number say 463L and each month a table called Table A is consulted for that month and the *free pay* for his code number found. The free pay is deducted from the gross pay to date (the total of gross pay for that financial year so far) and that gives the *taxable pay*. Another table - Table B - is consulted and that gives the tax to be deducted for that month.

National insurance

11. National insurance is in effect a tax payable on employees' wages but also on the self-employed and others.

The rates depend on a number of factors There are rates for payment by the employee and these payments are deducted from the employee and there are rates for payment by the employer.

The total PAYE and national insurance (employees' and employer's) is paid monthly to the Inland Revenue.

Summary

❏ Product costs can be divided into direct materials, direct labour and overheads.

❏ SSAP 9 considers product costs as being cost of purchase plus the cost of conversion.

❏ The cost of conversion is the cost of turning the product into a saleable product.

❏ Direct costs are those costs that can be reasonably traced to particular products.

❏ Indirect costs are all other costs. The essence of an indirect cost is that it is shared by more than one product.

❏ Labour costs can be direct or indirect. Only the wages paid to workers whose work can be directly related to particular products are direct.

❏ There are many payment systems. The simple ones are directly related to time worked or to output.

❏ The total cost of labour includes social security and holiday pay and idle time. Additions such as national insurance and holiday pay may be regarded as indirect costs as may idle time.

❏ The overtime premium is usually regarded as indirect.

Points to note

❏ Reference has been made in this chapter to products. In practice products may be made singly or may be made in batches. A product can thus be a single product (e.g. a set of double glazed windows for a customer), a particular job (e.g. the construction of a garage for a customer), a batch (e.g. a batch of yoghurts), or a service (e.g. the production of a set of accounts for a client or a surgical operation). In a University or college it may be a course given or a specific lecture.

❏ The distinction between direct and indirect costs is important because a particular cost will, if direct, be ascribed to a particular product and, if indirect, be shared amongst all the products (the next chapter explains how). This means that although the total costs are the same whether they are direct or indirect the total costs will be shared out amongst the products in ways which depend on the relative treatment of costs between direct and indirect. If a product cost is measured in different ways by different accountants then different decisions (e.g. on pricing) will be taken. Also the costs enter into the valuation of work in progress and finished goods and thus affect the measurement of profit.

❏ The measurement of product cost is simple in theory but exceptionally difficult in practice.

Self-testing questions

1. What payment methods can be used in practice?
2. Draft a payslip for a pieceworker.
3. What are the elements of cost?
4. State the view of product cost set down by SSAP9.
5. Define the cost of purchase.
6. What is the conversion cost?
7. Define direct costs.
8. What are indirect costs?
9. What labour costs can be considered as direct?
10. How can the labour cost of particular products be measured?
11. What costs are additional to hourly rate or piece work payments.
12. How are such costs treated?
13. How is overtime costed?
14. How are PAYE and NI calculated?

Exercises

1. Woad Ltd manufactures paint in standard batches of 1,000 tins. The direct labour employed on manufacture of a batch is:

    (a) Ron who is paid 20p a box to pack the tins in boxes of four tins.

    (b) Les and Doug who are paid £3.50 an hour each to mind the machines which produce the paint. Each batch varies in time of manufacture but batch 34 took four hours.

    (c) Hugh who is paid £6 an hour to set up the machines. Batch 34 took him 1.6 hours.

    Required:

    (a) What is the direct labour cost of batch 34:

       (i) Per batch?

       (ii) Per tin?

    (b) What other costs would be incurred in producing batch 34?

    (c) What would be the direct labour cost if batch 34 happened to be produced on a Saturday? Regular Saturday overtime is worked.

    (d) What would the direct labour cost be if batch 34 had been produced on a Saturday (time is paid at 1.5 times normal rate) in response to an order from a customer who agreed to pay extra for immediate delivery?

2. What is the direct labour cost of the meal provided at the Grand Hotel to teachers of the Sheinton Infants school on 20 December 19x4? There were eight teachers present and, that evening, there were 162 diners altogether. Data collected was:

    (a) Waiting staff: Janet engaged for the evening to wait exclusively on the teachers' party £18.00.

    (b) Cooks: there were four cooks on duty, each paid £22 an evening.

    You should consider what data would be needed to determine the direct cost of the cooks' time spent on the teachers' dinner.

3. What is the cost to be included in the closing stock of a part finished trailer whose costs had been:

    (a) Parts £32 + £4 carriage from Glasgow less 5% for payment within seven days.

    (b) Paint 2 gallons at £16 a gallon.

    (c) Direct labour: 4 hours at £5.20 an hour.

    (d) 32 operations at an average cost of 43.1p an operation?

    (ignore overheads).

4. Williams the Vet wishes to know the costs of doing operations on his client's animals. Consider what costs would be involved, distinguishing between direct and indirect costs. How might the costs be collected?

5. Which of the following are direct labour in a coffee plantation?

Bean pickers	Coffee plant planters	Truck drivers
The general manager	Drying machine minders	Irrigation workers
Canteen workers	Sacking machine operators	

6. Julie is employed by Amos Ltd. In the week ending 18 February 19x4 she worked 51 hours. Her hourly rate is £5 an hour up to 40 hours and time and one half for hours beyond that. Assume that she pays tax at 24% of all earnings over £70 a week. Her

employee national insurances is 8% of gross pay. The employer's national insurance is 9% of gross pay. The firm collects a weekly subscription of £1 for her Union by deduction from wages.

Complete a payslip for Julie and show how much will be due to the Inland Revenue in respect of Julie's employment that week.

7. Howard is employed by BK Ltd In the week ending 18 January 19x4 he worked 41 hours. His hourly rate is £7 an hour up to 35 hours and time and one third for hours beyond that. Assume that he pays tax at 24% of all earnings over £90 a week. His employee national insurance is 8% of gross pay. The employer's national insurance is 9% of gross pay. The firm collect £10 a week as a repayment of a loan made to Howard.

Complete a payslip for Howard and show how much will be due to the Inland Revenue in respect of his employment that week.

Assignment

❑ *Carlotta is employed by Daft Ltd. In the week ending 18 December 19x4 she made 463 widgets. Her piece work rate is £0.90 a widget. Assume that she pays tax at 24% of all earnings over £70 a week. Her employee national insurance is 8% of gross pay. The employer's national insurance is 9% of gross pay. Daft Ltd deduct £2 from her under a court order.*

Complete a payslip for Carlotta and show how much will be due to the Inland Revenue in respect of her employment that week. She is paid by BACS. Explain what this means and show the double entry for her pay.

The widgets cost £1.60 in basic materials and £1.20 for a special component as well as Carlotta's labour.

In the week she started 503 widgets but only 463 were accepted by quality control. The basic materials cannot be recycled but 50% of the special components can be used again if they are part of rejected widgets.

Required:

Calculate the materials and labour cost per good widget.

18 Overheads

The cost of manufacture of finished goods is defined in SSAP9 as the cost of purchase (materials) + the cost of conversion. Cost of conversion is:

(a) *Costs which are specifically attributable to units of production (e.g. direct labour, direct expenses and sub-contracted work).*

(b) *Production overheads.*

(c) *Other overheads – but only in certain circumstances.*

Overheads are shared among all the products made and it is difficult to assign an appropriate share to each product. Cost accountants have devised a method of doing this which is rather arbitrary. Students find this very difficult but it is not that impossible to grasp.

Production and other overheads

1. Overheads can be classified according to function. They can be:

   (a) Production.

   (b) Administration.

   (c) Selling and delivery.

   Whether an overhead is production, administration or selling is not always obvious. Consider the following expenses:

   rent of the premises   advertising

   the cost of the accounts department   interest

   production director's salary   audit fee

   If the premises consist of the factory (production), the offices (admin), the sales department and the transport section (delivery) then the cost of running the premises will have to be split in some way between the functions.

   Advertising is easier, it is obviously a selling overhead. Note that this means that it is not part of the cost of producing a product.

   The cost of the accounts department is also an overhead split amongst the functions. The accounts department will do at least the following:

   (a) Paying production wages and dealing with production purchases (production).

   (b) Dealing with the sales ledger (selling).

   (c) Preparing the annual accounts (admin).

   Interest is usually regarded as an administrative expense although a case can be made for part of it (say the interest on money borrowed to buy extensive stocks of raw materials) being production.

   The production director's salary appears to be a production expense but part of his time will be spent on general directorial matters and attending board meetings. These are administration matters.

   The audit fee is generally regarded as an admin expense.

   You will see that splitting overhead by function is not easy and different accountants may take different views. In that case the cost of products both for decision

213

making (e.g. pricing) and for inclusion in the annual accounts will differ, albeit marginally.

Production overheads and cost centres

2. The first step, as we have seen, is to classify overheads by function. We are then only concerned with the production expenses. The next step is to associate the production overheads with cost centres prior to assigning them to products.

The term cost centre can be defined as 'a location, function, or item of equipment in respect of which costs may be ascertained and related to cost units for control purposes'. For example, in a factory making galvanised sheeting the factory may be divided into departments as: the shearing shop (where sheet steel is cut into appropriate sizes, the pressing shop (where it is pressed into the required shapes), the galvanising shop (where it is coated with zinc), the packing shop (where it is packed ready for delivery to customers). In a hospital cost centres might be each ward, each operating theatre, the pathology department, the laundry, the kitchen, X-ray etc. Each department is regarded as a cost centre. These cost centres are locations. Functional cost centres may be appropriate in a merchant bank (which also produces a product – a service), e.g. share dealing, portfolio advice, corporate finance and venture capital. The number of cost centres in a business is a matter of opinion as much as a matter of fact. Some are regarded as having just a few (like the galvanising factory) but some have many. It is possible to regard each machine in a factory as a separate cost centre. The level of detail chosen affects the amount of work involved for the cost accounting staff.

Splitting overheads among cost centres

3. Suppose a factory has the following departments with some statistics about them also given:

	Area metres^2	Number of employees	Value of plant	Stores requisitions made
Press shop	25	36	£230,000	165
Assembly shop	37	51	£65,000	456
Packing shop	50	26	£10,000	341
Stores dept	40	12	£35,000	–
Maintenance dept	8	5	£21,000	138

Note that all these cost centres are to do with production but that stores and maintenance do not produce anything but provide services to those departments that do.

	Pr	As	Pa	St	Ma	Shared
Rates						38,000
Heating						26,000
Employer's liability insurance						2,500
Canteen costs						5,000
Labour – direct	15,400	25,100	12,000			
Labour – indirect	4,900	7,200	4,000	7,800	4,230	

Depreciation 12% pa on the value of plant

Notes:

(a) I have put in seven expenses – there would be many more in practice.

(b) The first four items are shared amongst the departments. The others are not. They are said to be **allocated** to the departments where the costs are incurred. The other first four items will need to be apportioned.

(c) I have included direct wages. This is not an overhead – it is a direct cost.

(d) These costs are expected or budgeted costs. Costs are useful if they can be foreseen and decisions made accordingly. After the event actual costs can be compared with budgeted costs and useful lessons learned.

The costs can be apportioned as follows:

Expense	Basis	Total	Pr	As	Pa	St	Ma
		£	£	£	£	£	£
Rates	metres^2	38,800	6,062	8,973	12,125	9,700	1,940
Heating	metres^2	26,000	4,062	6,013	8,125	6,500	1,300
EL ins	gross pay	2,500	652	989	490	239	130
Canteen	No of workers	5,000	1,385	1,962	1,000	461	192
Indirect labour	Allocated	28,130	4,900	7,200	4,000	7,800	4,230
Depreciation	Allocated	3,610	2,300	650	100	350	210
Total		104,040	19,361	25,787	25,840	25,050	8,002

Notes:

(a) Make sure your totals cross-cast.

(b) Rates have been apportioned on the basis of floor area. This is usual for rent, rates, building insurance and heat and light. However heat and light may be apportioned in other ways – volume, or number of workers or using special knowledge. For example, some shops may need no heating because heat is produced by the process.

(c) Employer's liability insurance premiums are based on the total payroll.

(d) Canteen costs have been apportioned using the number of workers in each department – this seems a rational procedure.

(e) Direct labour is excluded. It is included in product costs as a direct cost, not as a part of overheads.

(f) Depreciation is 1% on value as this is a one month period.

(g) You will realise that there are several very inexact areas here. Depreciation is an estimate. The apportionment bases are matters of opinion. Consequently, in practice, very elaborate apportionment schedules are no more 'accurate' than less detailed ones.

4. There is a further step. We must ascribe all production overheads to producing departments. So we further apportion the service departments to the producing departments as:

	Pr	As	Pa	St	Ma	Sum
From schedule	19,361	25,787	25,840	25,050	8,002	104,040
Stores	3,757	10,384	7,766	(25,050)	3,143	
Subtotal					11,145	
Maintenance	7,801	2,229	1,115		(11,145)	
Total	30,919	38,400	34,721			104,040

Notes:

(a) A rational way of apportioning the costs of the stores department is by reference to use by the other departments. A reasonable indication of use is the number of stores requisitions raised.

(b) The use by each department of maintenance is not easily determined. In examination questions the basis of apportionment is usually given to examinees. I have assumed that an investigation has revealed an apportionment on the basis of 7:2:1 as rational.

(c) You will note that some of the stores department costs have been reapportioned to the maintenance department. It would also be possible then to reapportion some of the maintenance department costs back to the stores. This would require further apportionment of stores to maintenance and from maintenance to stores ... This problem is called the reciprocal service department problem. There are several ways of solving it but I will refer you to a text specialising in costing for the solutions.

Overhead absorption

5. Now that we have all the production overheads allocated or apportioned to the production departments, we need to find out how much of these overheads is absorbed or shared by each product.

Suppose that in the press shop, the main activity is the pressing of the product into different shapes using machines. The machines are, of course, operated by workers but the use of the machines is the main determinant of product use of the department. Essentially, the more machine time is spent on a product, the larger share it has of the overheads.

If we estimate that in the month, there will be an average of 200 hours of usage out of each of the 20 presses. That is a total of 2,400 machine hours. So the overheads of the department are £30,919 and are spent to provide 2,400 machine hours. You can thus say that each machine hour costs £30,919/2,400 = £12.88 (or say £13 as the figures are full of assumptions, opinions and estimates). We say we have a machine hour rate of £13 and that is the overhead cost of using a machine for one hour.

With the assembly shop the primary purpose is to enable *direct labour* to work. Thus if we estimate that 45 of the employees in the assembly shop are direct labour and they will work on products for a total of 7,200 hours in the month then the overhead cost of each worker is £38,400/7,200 = £5.33. This is called a *labour hour rate*. The overhead cost of one direct worker for one hour in the assembly shop is £5.33. Note that is *in addition* to his/her wage.

Similarly, in the packing shop, if total direct labour hours are estimated to be 3,360 then the labour hour rate is £34,721/3,360 = £10.33.

6. These rates – machine hour and labour hour – are called absorption rates. If it takes say four machine hours in the press shop, five labour hours in the assembly shop and 3.5 labour hours in the packing shop to make a particular product then the total overhead cost or total overhead absorbed is 4 × £13 + 5 × £5.33 + 3.5 × £10.33 = £114.80. This information might be used in:

(a) Determining the price to be charged for the product.

(b) Controlling costs by determining, after the event, how many hours were actually used on manufacture.

(c) Assessing the cost of products in stock at the year end.

Product costs

7. In the factory discussed in the paragraphs above, a customer has made an enquiry for a product of a particular specification. The estimator discovers that the probable costs of manufacture will be:

	In the press shop	In the assembly shop	In the packing shop
Direct costs:			
Materials	£187	£31	£24
Labour	12 hours at £4	15 hours at £3.50	6 hours at £3.60
Overheads:			
Machine hours 15			

The company has a policy of charging cost + a profit sufficient to give a 25% gross profit on selling price.

Required:

Calculate the estimated selling price.

Answer:

The estimated selling price can be derived as:

				£
Material cost		£187 + £31 + £24		242.00
Direct labour costs				122.10
Overheads	: press shop	15 × £13	195.00	
	: assembly shop	15 × £5.33	79.95	
	: packing shop	6 × £10.33	62.00	336.95
Total cost				701.05
Profit margin 25/75 × £701.05				233.68
Estimated selling price (rounded)				935.00

Notice what a large proportion of the total cost is provided by overheads. This is a common experience.

Levels of activity

8. In the example above the level of activity chosen for the press department was 2,400 hours. This assumes that the department will be able to provide 2,400 hours and that there will be enough work available to need 2,400 hours. If less than 2,400 hours are worked – say only 2,100 hours of work were possible – then the machine hour rate would be £30,919/2,100 = £14.72. Thus all products will cost a little more as the overheads have to be divided over fewer products. SSAP 9 requires the level of activity taken to be *the normal level* of activity taken *one year with another*. In deciding upon *normal*, account should be taken of intended levels of production for which the facilities were designed and the budgeted level and the levels achieved in recent periods.

Summary

❐ The cost of a product at any given stage in its production is the costs incurred up to that point in bringing the product to its present location and condition.

❐ This cost is the cost of purchase (materials) + the cost of conversion.

❐ Cost of conversion includes direct costs and some appropriate proportion of the overheads or indirect costs.

❐ Only production overheads should normally be included in the cost of production of a product.

❐ Production overheads are allocated or apportioned to cost centres.

❐ A total overhead for each cost centre can be obtained.

❐ Service department costs are then apportioned to the producing departments.

❐ An absorption method is developed to share these overheads amongst the products. These methods include machine hour rates and labour hour rates.

❐ A product cost is the direct costs + the overheads absorbed.

❐ In deriving absorption rates, a normal level of activity should be used.

Points to note

❐ Production overheads include expenses which accrue on a time basis such as rent. Thus if rent is incurred in year 1 and the rent is included in the overheads of a cost centre and the overheads are a part of the cost of manufacturing widget x and the widget is in stock at the year end *then* part of the rent will become an expense of year 2.

❐ When overheads are absorbed into a product they are said to be *recovered*. This means in essence that the costs are recovered from the customer. If insufficient products are made to absorb all the overheads then those overheads are lost. For example, if the overheads of department Z are £20,000 and the expected machine hours are 5,000 then the recovery rate is £4 an hour. If only enough products are made to absorb 4,000 hours then only £16,000 is recovered and £4,000 is under-recovered or lost. Really, the absorption rate should have been £5 an hour.

❏ Remember that a *labour hour rate* is overheads. The wage paid is additional.

❏ I have covered only machine hour rates and labour hour rates. There are several others in use including:
   (i)   Percentage on materials (used in restaurants).
   (ii) Percentage on direct labour costs (used in garages).
   (iii) Percentage on prime cost (= materials + direct labour).

❏ This method of finding the *total cost* of a product is called *total absorption costing*. It contrasts with marginal costing which we will meet later. Total absorption costing is required by SSAP 9 for inventories.

❏ The value of 'cost' found in this way is subject to many uncertainties, opinions and estimates. It is thus very imprecise. Scientifically educated readers will recognise the concept of error in scientific experiment. Note that accountants never say 'the cost is expected to be £36 plus or minus £4.20'. We have an undeserved reputation for accuracy!

❏ Overheads other than production overheads can occasionally be included in costs but only in rare circumstances. For example, where firm sales contracts have been entered into for the provision of goods or services to a customer's specification, overheads relating to design, and marketing and selling costs incurred *before* manufacture, may be included in arriving at cost.

❏ The method of costing described in this chapter was originally developed for the manufacture of goods but it is used equally in the manufacture of services.

❏ Never include direct costs in overheads.

Self-testing questions

1.   Define cost of manufacture.
2.   What functions of a firm absorb overheads?
3.   What functional costs are included in the cost of production?
4.   Define cost centre.
5.   Suggest some bases of apportionment.
6.   Distinguish allocation from apportionment.
7.   What is the reciprocal service department cost problem.
8.   Explain the derivation of two absorption rates.
9.   Explain the derivation of a product cost.
10. What level of activity should be used in deriving the denominator in absorption rate calculations?
11. How does under recovery of overheads occur?
12. What other methods of overhead recovery exist?
13   Distinguish labour rates from labour hour rates.

Exercises

1. Which of the following costs are likely to be classified as:
    (a) Production?
    (b) Direct?
    >   (i)   Rates of the premises.
    >   (ii)   Travelling expenses.
    >   (ii)   Lubricating oil.
    >   (iv)   Royalties.
    >   (v)   Cleaning materials.
    >   (vi)   Paint.
    >   (vii) Lathe operator's wages.
    >   (viii) Packing materials.
    >   (ix)   Canteen subsidy.
    >   (x)   Foremen's wages.
    >   (xi)   Accounting software.
    >   (xii) Repairs to machinery.
    >   (xiii) Employer's national insurance.
    >   (xiv) Commissionaire's wages.

2. Deskout Ltd is a manufacturer of office furniture. Budgeted data for period 24 is:

Direct materials	£24,000
Direct labour 15,000 hours at £4 an hour	
Rates	£28,000
Machinery depreciation	£18,000
Electric power	£38,400
Supervision	£9,000

    Statistics about the three manufacturing departments (cutting, joining, finishing) are:

	Cutting	Joining	Finishing
Area in square meters	1,200	1,000	600
Machinery value	£600,000	£240,000	£60,000
Number of employees	40	20	15
Machine hours	12,000	6,000	1,200

    Required:
    (a) Prepare an overhead apportionment schedule for the three production cost centres.
    (b) Calculate a machine hour absorption rate for the cutting department.　　　(RSA)

3. The Widget Manufacturing Co Ltd make widgets to order.

    A customer has requested a price for a widget and you have been asked to prepare an estimate for that customer.

    You determine the following:
    (a) The widget will use 13 kilograms of Hedonite at £2.50 a kg, 4 metres of tube at £5.25 a metre and £9 worth of sundry material.
    (b) Direct labour costs will be:
    >   in the machine room – 18 hours at £3 per hour
    >   in the assembly shop – 6 hours at £2 an hour
    >   in the packing shop – 4 hours at £2.50 an hour.

(c) The manufacture of the widget will include five hours' use of a machine in the machine room.

(d) Overheads are absorbed as follows:

in the machine room, by a machine hour rate of £6.50

in the assembly shop, by a labour hour rate of £3

in the packaging shop at 150% of direct labour cost.

(e) A profit margin is to be added such that the profit margin is 33% of the selling price.

Required:

The estimated selling price which will be quoted to the customer. You should set out your answer in the form of a statement with sub-total of direct costs, overheads and total cost. (RSA)

4. The Leebotwood Sports Centre is losing money. The manager, Louise, feels that fees charged are incorrect. She thinks that some should be lower so that more customers are attracted. She thinks that some should be higher to reflect higher costs in some areas. She thinks that the way forward is to have a clear idea of the costs of each part of the Sports Centre. The Centre consists of a two swimming pools, two sports halls, a multigym, four squash courts, two football pitches, a hockey pitch, a cafeteria, an entrance hall with self service and gaming machines, a ticket office, changing rooms and offices. There are 10 full-time staff and some 50 part timers. Employees are groundsmen, cleaners, maintenance people, office staff, managerial staff, instructors, guards (swimming), security and caretaking.

Required:

Set out a procedure for finding the cost of each activity offered. You should consider the imprecisions in the process and the effects of volume of business done.

5. St Eata's is a new complex set up by a group of churches to provide accommodation for groups and for courses and conferences. It is essential that a fair system of charging is set up to enable costs to be recovered. There are six rooms and facts about them have been collected as follows:

Room	Area in m²	volume in m³	Average weekly use in hours
Refectory	80	400	70
Lecture room 1	30	90	30
Lecture room 2	20	60	20
Chapel	40	220	10
Conference room 1	50	200	60
Conference room 2	90	450	40

The annual overhead cost of running the complex is:

Expense	Amount	Method of apportionment
Rent	25,000	area
Insurance	4,000	area
Gas and electricity	12,300	volume × usage
Wages	11,200	usage
Cleaning contract	4,500	area × usage
Sundries	3,500	usage

Required:

(a) Prepare an overhead apportionment table and calculate an hourly rate for overheads for each room.

(b) Discuss how the management might establish a scale of charges based on these costs.

(c) Would it be possible to include special low rates for some particularly deserving groups? If so what would be the financial consequences?

Assignments

❏ *Infobuk Ltd runs a mail order business in computer equipment and commercial software packages. It also manufactures some metal furniture for use with its equipment. It is considering the introduction of a continuous inventory database for its mail order section including values at cost.*

Required:

(a) Detail the uses of such a database and how it will help the company to increase profits.

(b) Suggest which method (FIFO etc) should be used and explain the effect on (i) pricing when the sales department prepares estimates for the supply of computers and software for major customers, (ii) profit measurement (year end is 31 December) of the alternative methods. You may use as an example:

October 15	*Purchased 24 Jinx 486 computers at £560 each*
November 12	*Sold 12 Jinx*
December 3	*Purchased 24 Jinx at £470 each*
December 18	*Sold 8 Jinx*

(c) Describe how the stock of metal furniture, finished but unsold, should be valued for the annual accounts.

Notes:

You may use the following data to assist you:

The furniture is made in two successive shops: 1. metal forming (largely automated) and 2. assembly (largely manual work).

Data about the two shops is:

Shop:	1	2
Floor area (sq. m.)	*80*	*40*
Direct workers	*0*	*8*
Indirect workers	*6*	*4*

Data about product CZ:

Shop:	1	2
Direct materials	*£12*	*£8*
Direct labour	*0*	*4 hours at £4.50*
Overheads use (hours)	*8*	*4*

Monthly overheads of the two shops total:

	£
Rent and rates	*£660*
Production management	*£2,040*
Cleaning	*£300*
Power (treat as Shop 1)	*£280*

Monthly output for the two shops:

Shop 1	*800 hours*
Shop 2	*900 hours*

(d) Discuss the accuracy of the costs you have devised and indicate how the costs may be used.

❏ *The Sheinton District Hospital has been told that its funds will increase by only 1% for 19x7 and expects inflation to actually increase its costs by 4%. Economies are called for! The chief executive feels that there is much waste and loss in the system both in terms of materials and fixed assets. Loss includes thefts, drugs going out of date, fixed assets being unusable due to lack of certification, and delays and cancelled treatments due to breakdowns in equipment*

Required:

Explain how accounting may be organised to control materials and fixed assets and to assist in minimising waste and loss. Discuss also the cost of this accounting.

19 Manufacturing accounts

The objectives of a manufacturing enterprise are:

(a)   To make a saleable product.

(b)   To sell the product.

Activity (b) is the same activity as that carried on by the trader. The difference is that instead of buying in saleable products from outside suppliers, the manufacturer makes the products himself. The accountant therefore needs to substitute for purchases, the costs of goods manufactured. This cost is derived from an account called the manufacturing account and we shall begin with the preparation of a manufacturing account.

A special problem with manufacturing is the valuation of year end stocks of finished goods and work in progress. This was reviewed in the last chapter.

The manufacturing account

1.   The format of a manufacturing account is:

Richard, trading as The Widget Manufacturing Co
Manufacturing Account for the year ending 31 December 19x4

		£000
Raw materials and components		
Opening stock		26
Purchases		134
Carriage on purchases		6
		166
Closing stock		30
Issued to production		136
Direct labour		288
Other direct costs		16
Prime cost		440
Works overheads		
Rates	30	
Insurance	15	
Indirect labour	82	
Indirect materials, heat, light, power	16	
Repairs	14	
Miscellaneous	19	
Depreciation of factory	12	
Depreciation of plant	39	
		227
Factory inputs in the year		667
Add: Opening work in progress		19
		686
Less: Closing work in progress		24
Works cost of finished goods output		662

2. (a) Raw materials and components are those physical things which will actually form part of the finished product, e.g. wood, plastic, screws, glue, varnish, glass and cabinet fittings in a furniture factory.

   (b) Direct labour is the remuneration paid to production workers for work directly related to production. It will not include supervisory or clerical labour.

   (c) Other direct costs are costs incurred specifically for a particular product. Examples include royalties paid per unit for a copyright design and plant or tool hire charges for a particular job.

   (d) Prime cost is an important concept in costing and consists of direct materials, direct labour and other direct costs.

   (e) Direct costs are all those costs which can be directly identified with particular jobs, batches or products. For example, in the production of brass castings, direct costs are brass and the wages of the workers who tend the furnace, cast the brass, and clean, polish and pack the brass castings.

   (f) Works overheads are all those costs which are incurred in operating the works but which cannot be identified directly with a particular job, batch or product. The heating and lighting in a pin factory is clearly related to production in general but is in practice impossible to relate to particular pins or batches of pins.

   (g) Indirect labour will include remuneration paid to supervisors, clerks, maintenance people, cleaners etc.

   (h) Indirect materials will include lubricating oil, spare parts for machinery, cleaning materials, maintenance materials etc.

   (i) Work in progress. Some manufacturing processes are completed very quickly, for example, bread making or pin making. Some products take a long time to complete – we say that they have a long manufacturing cycle. Examples are aircraft, ships and heavy machine tools. Where the manufacturing cycle is longer than a day, there will always be some products at the day's end which are incomplete. These items are called work in progress. It is very difficult to value work in progress and the method of doing this by summing materials, labour and other direct costs and a proportion of production overheads, was outlined in the last chapter.

The trading account of a manufacturing business

3. In the previous section, the manufacturing account was used to build up and demonstrate the cost of the output of finished, saleable products from the factory. This output can be seen as being transferred to a warehouse where the goods are stored until they are sold.

   The format of a trading account is:

(continued from paragraph 1 – Richard)
Trading Account for the year ending 31 December 19x4

	£
Works cost of finished goods output transferred from the manufacturing account	662
Finished goods bought from outside supplier	104
Opening stock of finished goods	109
Available for sale	875
Less closing stock of finished goods	162
Cost of goods sold	713
Sales	1,138
Gross Profit	425

Finished goods bought from outside suppliers

4. Many manufacturers also sell goods made by other manufacturers or imported from abroad, in addition to their own product. The cost of such goods must be included in the trading account.

The profit and loss account of a manufacturing business

5. As a manufacturing business tends to be more complex in its administration than a purely trading business, non-manufacturing overheads are usually analysed into categories and sub-categories.

Here is a possible format:

	£	£
GROSS PROFIT		425
Administrative expenses		
Rates	6	
Insurance	4	
Salaries	28	
Telephone	14	
Miscellaneous	19	
Depreciation	3	
	74	
Selling expenses		
Salaries	26	
Commissions	31	
Advertising	43	
Motor expenses	16	
Depreciation of representatives' cars	26	
	142	

Distribution costs	£	£
Salaries	20	
Transport costs	41	
Depreciation of vehicles	30	
	91	
Financial costs		
Loan interest	8	
Discount allowed	14	
Discount received	(3)	
	19	
		326
NET PROFIT		£99

Note that this need to analyse and sub-divide overheads can also apply to retailers and wholesalers.

Exceptions, alternatives, difficulties

6. (a) **Physical parallels**

    The assumption that on completion, finished goods are transferred to a separate warehouse to await sale is useful but is not often an accurate reflection of reality.

    (b) **Apportionment of expenses**

    Some examination questions require apportionment of overheads between manufacturing and other overheads. For example, rates are £18,000 and 7/9 are factory, 1/9 are administrative and 1/9 sales administration. This does not present any particular difficulty but if this is combined with accruals and prepayments, care is required.

    Example:

    Insurance payments were £15,000. £1,500 insurance is outstanding and £2,500 of the cost is in advance. Insurance is considered to be 4/5 factory and 1/5 office.

    Solution:

    Total cost of the period is £15,000 + £1,500 − £2,500 = £14,000. Factory overheads will include £11,200. Office overheads will include £2,800.

    (c) **Separate profit centres**

    Some questions require the transfer of finished goods from the manufacturing account to the trading account to be at some arbitrary figure and not at cost. This transfer price may be based on some externally derived data such as the cost of competing products or it may be based on cost plus a percentage. Assuming the transfer is above cost, there will be profit in the manufacturing account and a reduced gross profit. The object of this process may be:

    (i) To compare the cost of production with some bench mark such as the possible buying in price.

(ii) To provide an incentive to the different sections of the enterprise.

(iii) To determine the separate contributions of the various sections to overall profit.

This approach is very artificial as the valuation is usually arbitrary. It also leads to difficulties as the stock will be valued at above cost. The profit element has to be taken out at some stage in order that the balance sheet shows stocks at cost.

Summary

❏ Profit measurement in a manufacturing business is achieved through a series of accounts viz:

(i) The manufacturing account.

(ii) The trading account.

(iii) The profit and loss account.

❏ Manufacturing costs include direct materials, direct labour and other direct costs which collectively are called the prime cost. Manufacturing costs also include works (production or, manufacturing, or factory) overheads or indirect costs.

❏ The preparation of a manufacturing and trading account involves the valuation of:

(i) Stocks of raw materials.

(ii) Work in progress.

(iii) Stock of finished goods.

❏ Non-manufacturing costs are usually categorised into types. A division into administration costs, selling costs, distribution costs and financial costs is one such categorisation.

Points to note

❏ I have included separate manufacturing, trading, and profit and loss accounts in this chapter to emphasise the stages in the measurement of profit. In practice, these accounts can be separate or joined together as:

Herman Engineering
Manufacturing, Trading and Profit and Loss Account for the year ending 31 March 19—

	£
Raw materials issued to production	x
Direct labour	x
Other direct costs	x
Prime cost	x
Works overheads	x
Total works input	x
Work in progress adjustment	x
Cost of finished goods produced	x
Finished goods bought in	x

...continued

	£
Finished goods stock adjustment	x
Cost of goods sold	x
Sales	x
Gross profit	x
Non-manufacturing overheads	x
Net profit	x

☐ Many accountants consider that a global summary of all manufacturing operations for a whole year as illustrated in this chapter is of little value. They would prefer the accounts to be broken down into separate manufacturing accounts for individual products or groups of products or for the individual departments. Examiners usually ask for global accounts but segmented accounts are sometimes asked for.

☐ The manufacturing account concept draws upon the framework developed by cost accountants. This framework assumes that costs can be categorised into:

(i) Direct costs.

(ii) Indirect costs.

☐ Very often the distinction is clear in theory but difficult to make in practice. For example, electricity to power a machine may, in theory, be directly related to a specific item made on the machine but finding the quantity of electricity used requires data collection methods which would cost more than any possible benefit.

☐ The framework also assumes that the indirect costs can be categorised into:

(i) Manufacturing overheads.

(ii) Non-manufacturing overheads.

In practice a manufacturing concern is very complex and the sections of the enterprise – manufacturing, warehousing, the offices, selling and distribution – are not as separate and distinct as the framework assumes. Many costs, for example, rent and rates, can only be categorised by arbitrary assumptions.

Self-testing questions

1. What is the relationship between purchases in a trading business and cost of goods manufactured in a manufacturing business?

2. Draft a manufacturing account.

3. What is the meaning of the phrase direct costs?

4. Give examples of indirect (i) labour, (ii) materials.

5. What is prime cost?

6. What are the difficulties involved in treating manufacturing and trading as separate profit centres?

7. What are the arguments against a global manufacturing account?

8. What assumptions underlie the preparation of a manufacturing, trading and profit and loss account?

Exercises

1. From the following data prepare manufacturing, trading and profit and loss accounts for the businesses of Terri, Vic and Aled:

	Terri	Vic	Aled
Stock of raw materials1.1.x5	134	68	219
Work in progress 1.1.x5	68	108	245
Finished goods stock 1.1.x5	234	27	160
Purchase of raw materials	764	453	865
Stock of raw materials 31.12.x5	237	55	189
Work in progress 31.12.x5	73	123	221
Finished goods stock 31.12.x5	255	64	178
Direct labour	324	541	132
Direct expenses	39	54	21
Plant and machinery cost	654	320	941
Accumulated depreciation	389	101	431
Indirect labour	106	238	98
Works overheads	254	381	120
Goods purchases for resale	103	76	642
Sales	2,500	2,720	2,800
Administrative overheads:			
Rent and rates	31	88	64
Salaries	91	56	78
Sundry	102	143	154
Selling and distribution:			
Advertising	221	129	35
Salaries	143	151	60
Transport	121	39	143
Sundry	74	32	78
Interest on loans	154	40	12
Bank interest	63	23	165

Notes:

For Terri
(a) There is an accrual of direct labour – £12.
(b) Depreciation is 15% on cost.
(c) Rent and rates includes £3 in advance.

For Vic
(a) Depreciation is 25% reducing balance.
(b) There is an accrual of £23 and a prepayment of £11 on rent and rates. 10% of the rent and rates should be regarded as selling and distribution.

For Aled
(a) Depreciation is 20% straight line.

Assignment

☐ *Set up a manufacturing, trading and profit and loss account on a spreadsheet and enter the figures for Aled in Exercise 1. Explore and print out the effects of changing opening stocks, closing stocks and depreciation rates.*

20 Construction industry

So far we have measured profit using the realisation convention. We have assumed that a profit is made when a product or service is sold. This is reasonable and defensible for retail, wholesale and many service companies (e.g. hairdressers, transport). However it presents difficulties in industries which engage in long-term contracts. For example, Welleymac PLC builds roads for the transport agency (really part of central government). The mode of business is to tender for any work going. It wins some contracts and starts about four major road contracts a year. Each contract takes up to three years to complete. Some years it may actually complete perhaps just one contract and other years it may complete perhaps as many as six. It is not always clear when completion has taken place. This is because a contract may be physically complete on say 31 March, but it has to rectify any faulty work for a 12 month period and does not get the final part (usually 5% of the total amount) until the work is fully rectified.

If the criterion for recognising a profit is the completion then it is a matter of chance whether none, one or six or seven contracts are actually completed in a year. As a consequence, the profit of some years would be nil and of other years very high. Yet each year, about the same amount of work is done.

The way round this is to change the accounting convention and to recognise a profit in a contract as it goes along. This chapter explains how this is done.

SSAP 9 – Stock and long-term contracts

1. SSAP 9 allows that when the outcome of contract can be foreseen with reasonable certainty a portion of the expected profit can be included in the profit. Conversely, if it is expected that a loss will be incurred on a contract then the whole expected loss should be accounted for straight away. This is a consequence of the prudence (or conservatism) convention.

2. Some examples: (All figures in £'000)

Project	A	B	C
Total costs incurred	564	730	35
Value of work done	620	720	45
Cumulative payments on account received	430	525	–
Expected costs to completion	240	134	920
Contract total price	915	835	1,200

Notes to all three contracts:

(a) The figures are as at a year end when each contract was still in progress.

(b) The contract price is as tendered and is for the whole contract.

(c) Total costs incurred are all the costs incurred on the contract to the year end.

(d) It is possible to value the work done to date. This is at selling price. That is, it is that part of the contract price already completed. Valuation is by quantity surveyors.

(e) It is customary for the client (the highways agency, local authority or other body or company) to pay on account as the work progresses.

(f) It is possible to estimate the total costs yet to be incurred, from the current state to the end of the contract.

Project A

This project is about 2/3 through and appears to be profitable. So a portion of the profit can be taken to profit and loss account. You will see that the remainder of the contract price (£295) is greater than the cost of work to be done (£240). Thus:

Include in turnover in the profit and loss account	£620
Include in cost of sales	£564
Thus profit taken =	£56
Include in debtors £620 – £430	£190

Note that in accordance with SSAP 9 the part finished contract, which is expected to make an overall profit, is included in turnover and debtors and not as work in progress.

Project B

This contract is expected to make a loss overall and so (prudence) the whole expected loss must be include in the profit and loss account.

Include in turnover	£720
Include in cost of sales £730 + £19	£749

(The £19 is the expected loss on the contract being £835 – (£730 + £134) – £10 already taken.)

Thus include in the profit and loss account a loss of £29.

Include in the balance sheet as debtors £720 – £525	£195
Include in balance sheet as accrual/provision for loss	£19

Project C

This contract has hardly started so no profit can be taken as the outlook for the contract cannot reasonably be foreseen so early. The cost of the work done £35 should be included in long term contract balances, in stocks.

3. Note that in project A, the amount to be included in the turnover (i.e. in sales) is the value of the work done to date. This can normally be ascertained on a long-term contract. The profit to be included is the profit earned to date, that is, the value of work done to date less the cost of carrying out that work. Ultimately, the remaining turnover and profit on the contract will be included in the years when the work is done. The value on the balance sheet (in debtors) is the work done to date less money already received. It is usual for customers to pay for long-term contracts as they go along and not wait until completion.

In project B, the contract is expected to make a loss of £29 and the whole of this loss, not just the £10 lost so far, must be included in the profit and loss account.

Summary

❏ Long-term contracts should be valued to include that part of the expected profit which has been earned to date as attributable profit. This should occur only if the outcome of the contract can reasonably be foreseen.

❏ If an attributable profit is included then the work done to date should be included in turnover and (the cost + attributable profit – amount received to date) should be included as a separate item in debtors.

❏ If a loss is expected on a contract then the whole expected loss should be included in the accounts. The work done to date should be included in turnover and the value of work done less the cash received on account should be included in a separate item in stocks. Further, the provision for the loss should be included in current liabilities.

Points to note

❏ In estimating costs to completion, all expected costs must be considered including rectification and guarantee work and bearing in mind the effects of inflation on future costs.

❏ Many contracts are agreed at a total price for the job and a sale price, for the work done so far, can only be estimated. However some jobs do have separate prices for separate stages and usually, for stage payment purposes, quantity surveyors certify the value of the work done. It is customary for contractors to tender high prices for the first part of a contract and low prices for the latter parts. This way, they receive the actual profit on the contract in the earlier stages!

❏ SSAP9 states that if the stage payments received exceed the value of work done (this seems unlikely) then the excess should be separately included in current liabilities as payments on account.

Self-testing questions

1. When will SSAP 9 permit a portion of the profit to be made on an uncompleted contract, to be included in the profit and loss account?
2. Explain how the figures will be shown in the financial statements for a profitable contact which is half complete.
3. Explain how a loss making contract should be shown.

Exercises

1. What should be included in the accounts for the following long term contracts?

	A	B	C	D	E
Total contract price	2,000	386	375	750	843
Value of work done	650	300	200	80	500
Cost of work done to date	450	305	160	74	450
Estimated cost of work to completion	1,059	100	120	?	480
Payments on account	400	230	300	nil	450

2. What should be included in the accounts for the following long term contracts?

	A	B	C	D	E
Total contract price	754	643	385	900	376
Value of work done	390	180	325	50	200
Cost of work done to date	351	170	284	45	190
Estimated cost of work to completion	299	420	40	?	220
Payments on account	350	200	280	nil	170

Assignment

❑ *Write a report explaining the timing of recognition of profit in trading businesses. Contrast the method of recognising profit in construction companies and include a report on how expected losses are dealt with in trading companies and construction companies.*

21 Departmental accounts

Some businesses are essentially two or more businesses. For example, a departmental store is really a collection of separate businesses – toiletries, ladies fashions, perfumes, furniture etc. In this book you have learned to prepare income statements to measure and demonstrate the profit earned by a business. Usually the income statement is prepared for the whole business. However, management finds it useful to know the profit earned by each department or section of the business if there are separately identifiable sub-divisions of the enterprise. There are a few difficulties with this process so this chapter shows how to prepare departmental accounts and how these might be useful.

Preparing departmental accounts

1. The primary difficulty in preparing departmental accounts is that many expenses are *shared*. For example, in the business of John, there are two sections – books and toys. Many of the expenses are shared – rent, rates, insurance and general management. A possible format for departmental accounts might be:

John – Trading and profit and loss account for year ending 31 December 19x7

	Books	Toys	Total
Sales	68	54	122
Cost of goods sold	48	37	85
Gross profit (a)	20	17	37
Other direct costs (b)	7	6	13
Contribution (c)	13	11	24
Shared overheads (d)			15
Net profit			9

Notes:

(a) It is relatively simple to keep separate records of the sales, purchases and stocks of the two departments and so separate gross profits can be calculated.

(b) Some overheads can be considered to be direct costs of one or other of the departments. For example, the wage of an assistant who only works in the book department is wholly an expense of the book department.

(c) Contribution is a management accounting term – it means the sale price of an item less the direct costs attributable to that item – we shall meet it again. Note that if the book department was closed down the business as a whole would not have to spend £7,000 (the direct expenses) and would thus be worse off by the contribution £13,000. (However, this is not quite all the story and we will discuss this further later.)

(d) No attempt has been made to split shared overheads between the two departments.

Shared overheads

2. In the example of John, the shared overheads were not split between the two departments but this can be done if some rational means can be found. In the above example, the shared overheads were:

Rent, rates and insurance	9.3
Telephone	1.1
Motor expenses	2.6
Other expenses	2.0
	15.0

It is felt that these costs can be split as:

(a) Rent etc on floor area occupied (53 m^2:37 m^2).

(b) Telephone ($\frac{2}{3}:\frac{1}{3}$) – more to books as they have more telephone contact with customers.

(c) Motor expenses ($\frac{1}{4}:\frac{3}{4}$) mostly to toys as toy supplies are often bought at cash and carry warehouses and have to be transported back to the shop.

(d) Other expenses – equally.

Thus the income statement may now appear as:

	Books	Toys	Total
Gross profit	20.0	17.0	37.0
Allocated costs	7.0	6.0	13.0
Apportioned costs:			
Rent etc	5.5	3.8	9.3
Telephone	0.7	0.4	1.1
Motor	0.7	1.9	2.6
Other	1.0	1.0	2.0
Net profit	14.9	13.1	28.0
	5.1	3.9	9.0

Notes:

(a) This profit and loss is more traditional in that it distinguishes the gross profit and then shows the overheads in detail. The additional words (allocated and apportioned) do alert the reader to the artificial nature of the split of the apportioned expenses.

(b) The management can now see the overall profit of £9,000 came from books £5,100 and toys £3,900. However, this division of profit is artificial and different accountants may well have apportioned the overheads differently and got a different division of the profit.

(c) One decision that could be made is to close down one department – say toys. What would the effect of this be?

   (i) Loss of gross profit £17,000.

   (ii) Saving of direct costs £6,000.

   (iii) Saving of some of the shared costs ?.

It is not clear what shared costs would be saved if the toys department was closed down. The rent and rates etc would not change unless the space vacated by the toy department could be let. The motor expenses include a number of fixed costs (e.g. tax and insurance) which would not be saved.

Finally, some customers come into the shop to buy toys and then buy a book as well. This trade would be lost to the book department if the toy department were closed down.

Thus, the departmental accounts, whether in the first form shown or in the second, do not show the effect of closing down one of the departments. They do however, help in any real analysis of the effects of a closure of a department.

Decision making

3. As many businesses are compartmentalised and prepare departmental accounts, one must suppose that such accounts are useful. One such use has been identified (the closure decision) and the matter has been seen to be rather more difficult than appears at first sight. Other uses include:

    (a) Knowing which part of a business is more profitable. Suppose Sid has a business which is divided into (i) stamp dealing and (ii) publishing a monthly magazine about stamp dealing. It is really essential to know which part of this dual business is more profitable. This enables decisions about expansion and contraction of parts to be made.

    (b) Paying commissions or shares of profits to management or staff of the separate departments based on departmental profits.

    (c) In many partnership businesses, one section is run by one partner and one by another (up to any number of partners) and partnership profit sharing may use a formula taking into account departmental profits.

Shared overheads and the not-for-profit sector

4. In not-for-profit enterprises like colleges, there is a shortage of finance and a need to ensure that overall income at least equals overall expenditure. A problem is that with some activities income is less than expenditure and for others income is greater than expenditure. The difficulty is knowing which activities have surpluses and which have deficits. It is possible to retain deficit activities if that is the college's policy but it is essential to know which activities are in deficit so that the extent of cross subsidy can be managed.

    The preparation of departmental accounts is clearly a good start. However dividing a college into separate activities is not at all simple. Decisions have to be made on whether the 'activities' which will be separately accounted for are the separate academic departments or individual courses or what. Many college activities are not directly concerned with teaching. For example: general management, administration, libraries, refectories, student accommodation, computing facilities, games facilities, student facilities. Finding the cost of these is difficult and then ascribing the cost of them to the actual academic departments or courses is even more difficult. However the basic ideas of apportioning costs on an area occupied or some other simple approach is usually adopted. We will take this matter up again in a later chapter.

Summary

☐ Some businesses are divisible into separate parts or departments or sections or divisions.

☐ It may be of use to break down the overall profit departmentally.

☐ This can be done by showing separate gross profits or separate contributions with shared overheads also broken down or not broken down.

☐ Decisions about expansion and contraction, closing down divisions or starting new divisions, partner or management remuneration, can be made.

Point to note

☐ Goods can be transferred between departments. Such transfers should normally be made at cost by a Dr to purchases of the transfer-in department and a Cr to purchases of the transfer-out department.

☐ In this chapter I have talked of departments, divisions and sections. Other words are classes of business, components of the business and segments of the business. I have also used the expression shared costs. It is also possible to use the term common costs.

☐ It is possible to have a departmentalised balance sheet but this is not usually of great use. However, some managements like to know the separate fixed assets and working capital employed by the departments.

☐ Business is now very competitive. It is not possible for commercial enterprises to have one part of the business in profit and another part making a loss. Even the privatised electricity boards are finding that electrical supply subsidising retail shops is unacceptable – to the shareholders as well as to competitors in the retail trade. Consequently the idea of departmental accounting is assuming increased importance. Management needs to know how well each segment of the enterprise is performing so that appropriate decisions can be made. For example, the reduction in the subsidy to a professional symphony orchestra may lead the management to review the inputs (costs) and outputs (benefits) of the orchestra for each activity – public concerts, tours, recording, schools, education, broadcasting, commissioning and playing new music, etc. Accountants who measure the inputs and outputs are well aware that the outputs can be actual revenue (seats sold, fees from recording etc) and more intangible benefits (education, international goodwill etc). Accountants are also well aware that:

    (i) Apportioning shared costs among different activities is fraught with difficulty and leads to much arguments amongst the persons affected.

    (ii) Departments are rarely 'stand alone' but have subtle interactions with each other that are not usually understood.

Self-testing questions

1. What are the main difficulties in preparing departmental accounts?
2. What are the difficulties in making decisions based on departmental accounts?
3. What decisions might be made?

Exercises

1. Prepare departmental accounts for Simone's business which has two parts – letting caravans and selling caravans:

	Letting	Selling	Unspecified
Sales	135,000	264,700	
Purchases		137,000	
Stock 1.1.x4		43,600	
Stock 31.12x4		58,700	
Caravans at cost 1.1.x4	145,000		
Depreciation on caravans to 31.12x3	60,300		
Land at cost			220,000
Buildings at cost			146,000
Depreciation of buildings at 31.12.x3			37,000
Wages	43,000	34,000	13,300
Rates etc			15,000
Other overheads	24,700	20,100	12,800

Notes:

(a) During the year some caravans which had been let were sold. These had cost £50,600 and had been depreciated by £15,600.

(b) Depreciation policy is 20% straight line on caravans and 4% straight line on the buildings.

(c) The manager of the caravan sales department is entitled to a commission of 10% of the net profit of the department after charging the commission.

(d) The buildings are estimated to be used 4/5 by caravan sales and 1/5 by letting.

(e) Unspecified wages and other expenses are to be divided equally.

Required:

(a) A departmental profit and loss account.

(b) Assess the impact of closing down either department.

(c) Would you be happy with the accounts if you were the manager of the caravan sales department?

2. Fingle is in business as a DIY Superstore. He has three departments, A, B and C. His figures for 19x7 were: (in £'000)

	A	B	C	Common
Stocks 1.1.x7	120	84	100	
Stocks 31.12.x7	158	76	130	
Purchases	689	840	562	
Sales	1,031	1,150	954	

	A	B	C	Common
Labour	104	60	101	48
Occupancy costs				215
Buildings at cost				870
Administration expenses	23	15	30	129
Equipment at cost	123	53	120	160

Notes:

(a) Depreciation is 15% on cost for equipment and 5% on cost for buildings.

(b) Common depreciation is to be divided in proportion to other equipment.

(c) Occupancy costs are to be divided in proportion to sales.

(d) Common administration costs are to be shared equally.

(e) Each department head is entitled to a commission of 5% of gross profit + 3% of net profit after deducting both types of commission.

Required:

(a) Prepare a departmental profit and loss account.

(b) Comment on the apportionment methods.

Assignment

❏ *Leaven owns a bakery. He has shop (1) in a modern town centre precinct. The back of the shop is used to bake the bread and the front to retail the bread. He also rents a lock up shop (2) in a suburban shopping parade. He also sells his bread to other bakery shops in the area. For the year ending 31 December 19x5, he has collected the following data:*

Equipment in bakery cost	28,700	Rent – town centre	8,800
Depreciation to 31.12.x4	7,300	Rent (2)	2,600
Equipment etc (1) cost	8,520	Rates – town centre	6,500
Depreciation to 31.12.x4	2,740	Rates (2)	1,900
Equipment etc (2)	10,400	Insurance – town centre	2,190
Depreciation to 31.12.x4	5,170	Insurance (2)	900
Stock of flour etc 31.12.x4	1,200	Other overheads – town centre	4,100
Stock of flour etc 31.12.x5	1,700	Other overheads – (2)	2,900
Debtors	2,900	Common overheads	6,230
Creditors for flour etc	3,600	Drawings	9,000
Sales (1)	98,000	Van at cost	8,000
Sales (2)	53,700	Van depreciation to 31.12.x4	4,000
Sales to other bakery shops etc	37,500	Van running costs	2,120
Wages – bakery	18,200	Bank overdraft	900
Wages – shop (1)	10,500	Capital 31.12.x4	33,610
Wages – shop (2)	8,600	Electricity (2)	760
Electricity – town centre	4,700	Van driver's wages	5,100
Purchases of flour etc	90,000		

Notes:

(a) Depreciation is over five years straight line for all equipment (with nil salvage value) and four years straight line for the van (also with nil salvage value).

(b) The stock of flour at 31.12.x5 is valued at cost. However several sacks (which cost £300) are damaged and about 50% of the flour will be unusable.

(c) The debtors are all for other bakery shops and include £200 from Crust who has closed down and disappeared.

(d) Accruals are: Rent (2) £400, Common overheads £270, Electricity (town centre) £300.

(e) Rates (2) include rates for the six months to 31.3.x6 of £810.

(f) Floor area of the town centre promises is divided 70% bakery and 30% retail.

(g) The electricity in the town centre is 90% bakery.

(h) The van is used to transport bread from the bakery to shop (2) (1/3) and to other bakery shops (2/3).

(i) Sales to other bakeries are at retail selling price less 25%.

(j) Insurance in the town centre is 80% bakery.

Required:

(a) Prepare financial statements for the year ending 31 December 19x5, showing separately the profits from the different activities as far as possible (baking, shop 1, shop 2, sales to other bakeries)

(b) Leven is concerned about the low profits earned by the business and wonders if he should close down any part of the business or buy in bread or services instead of baking himself and using employees. Write a report on what he might do and how the figures might change if he makes such changes. Make such assumptions as are consistent with the data.

22 Incomplete records

In the real world, many enterprises do not keep very good records and accountants have had to develop the special skill of preparing financial statements from such evidence as exists. The process is analogous with that of the detective and is often frustrating but usually interesting. In the somewhat different but no less real world of accounting exams, incomplete records questions are favourites of examiners if not of examinees. Note that some teachers call this subject single entry.

Method

1. The ideal method for preparing the annual final accounts for a business is from double entry records.

   The method, where records are incomplete is to create some summary accounts and workings in double entry form.

Examination technique

2. Before working an example, consider the following points:
   (a) Incomplete records questions present a large amount of unsorted information.
   (b) This information has to be used to prepare specific financial statements.
   (c) An essential intermediate stage is the preparation of working papers in which:
       (i) Proper headings must be given.
       (ii) The work is neat.
       (iii) All amounts must be adequately described.
   (d) It is essential to concentrate on one matter at a time.
   (e) Be patient, thorough and painstaking.

   An example

   Mr T Bone runs a butcher's shop. All his takings are in cash, which he pays into the bank after deducting:
   (a) £50 per week in drawings.
   (b) Wages and expenses also paid in cash. During the year to 30 June 19x5 these were as follows:

	£
Assistants' wages	4,420
Sundry expenses	1,050

   A summary of his bank account for the year revealed the following:

	£		£
Balance b/f 1 July 19x4	850	Rent	2,900
Shop takings banked	29,270	Rates	1,020
		Electricity	490
		Sundry expenses	280
		New fittings	4,800

... continued

	£			£
		Purchases		19,400
		Balance c/f 30 June 19x5		1,230
	30,120			30,120

You discover the following additional information:

	30 June 19x4	30 June 19x5
	£	£
Fittings at cost	6,300	?
Accumulated depreciation	2,900	?
Accrued electricity	50	60
Prepaid rates	100	140
Stock	1,820	2,600
Debtors	530	880
Creditors for meat	1,380	1,934
Cash in the till	100	90

Depreciation of fittings is at 20% on the reducing balance basis.

Required:

(a) Prepare a statement of Mr Bone's capital as at 1 July 19x4.

(b) Prepare a trading and profit and loss account for the year ended 30 June 19x5.

(c) Prepare a balance sheet as at 30 June 19x5.

3. **Answer**

(a) Statement of Mr Bone's capital at 1 July 19x4:

	£	£
Assets		
Fittings at cost		6,300
Less Depreciation		2,900
Net book value		3,400
Stock		1,820
Debtors		530
Prepaid rates		100
Balance at bank		850
Cash in hand		100
Total assets		6,800
Liabilities		
Creditors	1,380	
Accrued electricity	50	1,430
Capital		5,370

Notes:

(a) This statement is usually called a 'statement of affairs'. It is essentially a balance sheet without the trimmings.

(b) The statement is produced by searching all the data for matters which give information on assets and liabilities at 1 July 19x4.

(c) Before the profit and loss account and balance sheet can be prepared, working schedules must be drawn up:

Cash in the till

Receipts	£	Payments	£
Balance at 1.7.x4	100	Drawings 52 × 50	2,600
From customers (a)	?	Wages	4,420
		Sundry expenses	1,050
		Payments into bank	29,270
		Balance 30.6.x5	90
	37,430		37,430

Notes:

(a) Mr Bone started with £100 in his till. During the year, his customers paid him some unknown amount. From this he paid out £2,600 to himself, £4,420 as wages, £1,050 for cleaning and put £29,270 into the bank. He still has £90 in the till at the year end.

(b) The amount he must have received to do all this is the balance of the account (a). You can calculate this. It is £37,330.

(c) We now have cash received from customers in the year.

Customers

Due from customer	£	How the customers settled	£
Balance at 1.7.x4	530	Cash	37,330
Sales made (b)	?	Balance at 30.6.x5	880
	38,210		38,210

Notes:

(a) Customers owed £530 at the beginning of the year. Sales were made in the year of some unknown amount.

(b) As the customers paid £37,330 and still owed £880 at the year end, the sales must have been the balance of the account (b) which you will calculate at £37,680.

(c) We now have the figure of sales for the trading account.

Suppliers

How Bone settled	£	Due to suppliers	£
Payments	19,400	Balance at 1.7.x4	1,380
Balance at 30.6.x5	1,934	Purchases (c)	?
	21,334		21,334

Notes:

(a) This account is similar to the account for customers but appears on opposite sides.

(b) The balance on the account (c) is the amount purchased during the year £19,954 and this figure is required for the trading account.

We are now ready to prepare the trading and profit and loss account:

T Bone – Butcher
Trading and profit and loss account for the year ending 30 June 19x5

	£	£
Sales		37,680
Less Cost of goods sold:		
Opening stock	1,820	
Purchases	19,954	
	21,774	
Less Closing stock	2,600	19,174
Gross Profit		18,506
Less Expenses:		
Assistants' wages	4,420	
Sundry expenses (a)	1,330	
Rent	2,900	
Rates (b)	980	
Electricity (c)	500	
Depreciation (d)	1,640	11,770
Net profit		£6,736

Notes:

(a) Some sundry expenses were paid by cash £1,050 and some by cheque £280, the total is £1,330. Marks will be deducted if these figures appear separately in the profit and loss account.

(b) Rates is calculated as:

	£		£
Prepayment b/f	100	Expense of year	?
Cheques	1,020	Prepayment c/f	140
	1,120		1,120

(c) Electricity is similarly calculated:

	£		£
Cheques	490	Accrual b/f	50
Accruals c/f	60	Expense of year	?
	550		550

(d)

	£
Net book value of fittings at 1.7.x4	3,400
Additions in year	4,800
	8,200
Depreciation at 20%	1,640

The balance sheet can now be prepared as:

T Bone – Butcher
Balance sheet as at 30 June 19x5

Fixed assets	£	£
Fittings at cost		11,100
Less Accumulated depreciation		4,540
Net book value		6,560
Current assets		
Stock	2,600	
Debtors	880	
Prepayments	140	
Cash at bank	1,230	
Cash in hand	90	4,940
		11,500
Less **Current liabilities**		
Trade creditors	1,934	
Accruals	60	1,994
		9,506
Capital:		
as at 1 July 19x4		5,370
Add Net profit		6,736
		12,106
Less Drawings		2,600
		9,506

Summary

❐ Not all businesses keep perfect records on double entry principles. Many traders have incomplete records. Preparing accounts from such records poses the accountant with logical problems which may tax his ingenuity.

❐ Such problems are overcome by patience, concentration on one item at a time, and careful recording of all steps taken.

❑ The steps to be taken are:
   (i) Prepare opening statement of affairs.
   (ii) Prepare working schedules.
   (iii) Prepare accounts.

Points to note

❑ Students find incomplete records difficult. The only way of mastering the subject is constant practice and rigid following of the steps in paragraph 3. Neat work with adequate descriptions of all figures is essential.

❑ There are a number of computer packages on the market which assist with the preparation of accounts from incomplete records.

Self-testing questions

1. List the stages on the preparation of financial statements when proper bookkeeping methods are employed.
2. When financial statements are prepared from incomplete records what working papers may be required?
3. What is a statement of affairs?
4. What will appear in the 'Cash in till' working paper?
5. What is the relationship between sales in the trading account and cash received from customers?
6. What are the essential requirements for success in incomplete records preparation?

Exercises

1. The following data relates to the businesses of Hugh, Heather and Munro at 31 December 19x4:

	Hugh	Heather	Munro
Stock	23,670	146,549	23,211
Debtors	13,652	98,762	35,327
Cash in hand	2,543	1,548	Nil
Creditors	42,411	69,820	28,567
Bank	Dr 21,783	Cr 2,540	Cr 1,321
Fixed assets at cost	54,844	38,700	50,050
Accumulated depreciation	17,540	21,734	41,450
Accrued electricity	641		105
Prepayment of rates		1,580	

Calculate for each the capital at 31 December 19x4.

2. The following relate to the businesses of Alan, Beth and Claire:

	Alan	Beth	Claire
Debtors at 31 December 19x2	12,650	34,678	20,800
Sales 19x3	102,650	?	102,500
Cash received from debtors	98,500	41,820	?
Discounts allowed	4,300	830	1,762
Contras	2,699		–1,004
Debtors at 31 December 19x3	?	36,391	22,500

Required:

Calculate the amounts labelled '?'.

3. The following relate to the businesses of Leon, Mary and Sue

	Leon	Mary	Sue
Cash in till at 31 December 19x4	1,600	Nil	2,490
Payments into bank in total in 19x5	102,564	96,450	64,237
Payments into bank which were not from customers	10,000	6,400	2,000
Total sales	114,004	99,700	?
Cash payments from till for expenses	7,400	4,320	3,100
Cash in till 31 December 19x5	1,350	1,500	800
Drawings in cash	?	6,800	8,000
Debtors at 31 December 19x4	Nil	7,500	2,431
Debtors at 31 December 19x5	Nil	?	2,800

Required:

Calculate the items labelled '?'.

4. The following data relates to the business of Geoff, Winnie and Ron:

	Geoff	Winnie	Ron
Sales in 19x8	100,060	?	154,800
Stock 31 December 19x7	23,859	14,542	32,692
Stock 31 December 19x8	?	16,740	27,750
Purchases in 19x8	74,610	?	?
Gross profit/sales ratio	25%	30%	?
Creditors 31 December 19x7	Nil	28,590	16,560
Creditors 31 December 19x8	Nil	31,562	18,630
Payments to creditors in 19x8	74,610	176,932	92,400

Required:

Calculate the items labelled '?'.

5. Hunter is a wholesaler of furniture. A balance sheet of his business at 1 January 19x9 showed the following figures:

	£		£
Capital	9,420	Fixed assets – cost	6,000
Furniture suppliers	2,300	Depreciation	2,500
Rent	100		3,500
		Stock	6,200
		Debtors	1,500
		Bank	620
	11,820		11,820

Proper books were not kept but an analysis of his bank statements revealed:

£

Lodgements

From customers	15,180
Legacy	1,100
Sale of motor car	400

249

Cheques drawn

To suppliers	9,730
Rent	700
Other overheads	2,050
Drawings	2,200
New car	2,600

A small black book was kept and this showed that before banking the cash and cheques received from customers, £1,000 was paid out for purchases and £200 for personal drawings.

Rent is £1,000 a year.

At 31 December 19x9, the following figures were computed:

Debtors	£2,300
Stock	£7,800
Creditor for furniture	£3,950

Depreciation is at 15% on the reducing instalment method. The original cost of the car sold was £1,500 and its written down value was £500.

Required:

(a) A trading and profit and loss account for the year ending 31 December 1979.

(b) A balance sheet as at that date.

(RSA)

Assignment

❒ *Examine again the figures in exercise 3 for Leon who is a greengrocer. The Inspector of Taxes is suspicious of the methods adopted and feels that Leon has made more profit than that revealed by preparing a profit and loss account using the figures in the exercise. Explain how Leon might establish these figures more convincingly and suggest how he might keep proper books which would provide convincing evidence of the correctness of the figures.*

23 Income and expenditure accounts

Retailers, wholesalers, manufacturers and other commercial and industrial organisations have, as a primary objective, the making of a profit. The profit (or loss) is measured in the profit and loss account. For clubs, societies and charitable bodies, the objectives are not to make profits, but to supply a service to members or the beneficiaries of the charity.

Nonetheless, clubs, societies and charitable bodies must have, at least in the long term, sufficient income to meet expenditure and annual (or more frequent) accounts must be produced to show members and others, the financial affairs of the organisation. Frequency of production of accounts depends on the club rules.

The format for reporting financial affairs of a club, society or charitable body is:

(a) An Income and Expenditure Account.

(b) A Balance Sheet.

The income and expenditure account, which is the equivalent of the profit and loss account of a business, contain sub-divisions such as a bar trading account.

Preparation of accounts

1. Here is an example:

    The Tettenhall Accountants Club was formed on 1 January 19x4 to provide an opportunity for accountants to meet together and also to amass sufficient money to endow a scholarship fund for accounting students without grants.

    At the end of the first year the treasurer summarised the bank account as follows:

Receipts	£	Payments	£
Members' subscriptions	1,250	Purchase of 10 years lease of building	2,000
Donations to scholarship fund	1,180	Rent for first 15 months	560
Grand draw receipts	1,425	Bar purchases	1,934
Bar takings	2,763	Overheads	620
Interest on Building Society Account	12	Deposited in Building Society	1,000
Loan at 10% on 1.1.x4 from wealthy		Equipment	340
member	2,000	Books for library	147
		Grand Draw prizes	710
		Part time bar staff – wages	290
		Grants made to students	580

You ascertain that:

(a) The equipment should last at least five years.

(b) At 31 December 19x4:

	£
Bar stocks	325
Creditors – bar purchases	327
Accrued overheads	13
Subscriptions in arrears	20
Subscriptions in advance	60

(c) The profit on the grand draw is to be credited to the scholarship fund.

Required:

(a) Income and expenditure account for the year ending 31st December 19x4.

(b) Balance sheet as at 31 December 19x4.

2. **Answer**

The Tettenhall Accountants Club

Bar Trading Account for the year ending 31 December 19x4

	£	£
Sales		2,763
Less Cost of goods sold:		
Purchases (a)	2,261	
Less Closing stock	325	1,936
Gross profit		827
Wages – bar staff		290
Net profit		£ 537

Notes:

(a) Purchases is obtained from payments (£1,934) and year end creditors (£327).

(b) This account is drawn up on conventional lines. It is clearly important for the members to know the financial contribution made by the bar and for them to apply elementary appraisal techniques such as computing the gross profit percentage (30%) to see that it is reasonable.

Income and Expenditure Account for the year ending 31 December 19x4

	£	£	
Income			(a)
Net profit on bar		537	
Subscriptions		1,210	(b)
Building Society interest		12	
		1,759	
Expenditure			(c)
Rent	448		
Overheads	633		
Books for library	147		(d)
Amortisation of lease	200		(e)
Depreciation of equipment	68		(f)
Interest on loan	200	1,696	
Surplus of income over expenditure for year		63	(g)

Notes:

(a) In the Accounts of clubs etc, there are usually several sources of income, unlike businesses where gross profit is the main source of income.

(b) Subscriptions must be the subscriptions for 19x4 and receipts have to be adjusted for receipts in arrear and in advance.

(c) Expenditure categories are included using the accruals convention. In this example:

    (i) Rent is adjusted for a prepayment.

    (ii) Overheads are adjusted for an accrual.

    (iii) No interest has been paid on the loan but interest has accrued over the year and is thus an expense of the year.

(d) It is arguable that as the books will be of use over more than one year, their cost could be capitalised (= treated as a fixed asset) and depreciated over their useful life. In practice most accountants would write them off (= treat them as an expense in the year of purchase).

(e) Lease depreciation is traditionally termed lease amortisation.

(f) I have adopted a depreciation policy of straight line with no salvage value.

(g) Since the club does not have as a primary aim the making of a profit, the difference between income and expenditure for the year is called a surplus, or, if expenditure exceeds income, a deficit.

Income and Expenditure Account of Scholarship Fund for the year ending 31 December 19x4

		£	£
Income			
Donations			1,180
Grand draw:	Receipts	1,425	(b)
	Prizes	710	715
Expenditure			1,895
Grants to students			580
Surplus for the year			1,315

Notes:

(a) The club has two principal aims, a social one and a philanthropic one. In this case, it is desirable to measure the income and expenditure of each separately because:

    (i) Social section income must, in the long run, exceed or equal social section expenditure.

    (ii) The amount of grants which can be made depends on there being sufficient income for this purpose.

(b) Members could be interested in knowing:

    (i) The income from the draw.

    (ii) The outlay on prizes.

    (iii) The surplus achieved.

The Tettenhall Accountants Club Balance Sheet as at 31 December 19x4   (a)

Fixed Assets	Cost £	Accumulated Depreciation £	Net Book Value £
Leasehold premises	2,000	200	1,800
Equipment	340	68	272
	2,340	268	2,072

Current Assets			
Bar stocks		325	
Subscriptions in arrear		20	
Prepayments		112	
Building society deposit		1,000	
Cash at bank		449	1,906
			3,978

Less Current Liabilities			
Bar creditors		327	
Accruals		213	
Subscriptions in advance		60	600
			3,378

Less Long term Liabilities			
Loan at 10%			2,000
			1,378

Accumulated Fund:			
Surplus for year			63 (b)
Scholarship Fund:			
Surplus for year			1,315 (c)
			£ 1,378

Notes:

(a) The balance sheet is drawn up on conventional lines as far as assets and current and long-term liabilities are concerned. The sections, accumulated fund and scholarship fund are peculiar to clubs and societies and charitable bodies.

(b) This is equivalent to 'capital' in a business balance sheet.

(c) The idea of separate funds is not easy to grasp. The club has assets of £3,978 and liabilities to specific external persons of £2,600 so that the net assets are £1,378. Of the net assets, £1,315 is held so that grants may be paid to students. Only the remainder of the net assets £63 properly belongs to the members.

Theory

3. The accounts of many clubs, societies and charitable bodies consist simply of a *receipts and payments account*. This has the merit of simplicity and is easy for non-accountants to prepare and for non-accountants to understand. Where the organisation has few assets other than cash in hand and at bank, this approach is acceptable.

4. When an organisation has assets other than cash, a simple receipts and payments account fails to give the relevant information which members are entitled to and leads to lack of comparability between successive years as income and capital items are not separated.

5. In consequence, clubs, etc, in their accounts normally adopt an income and expenditure account which uses the accounting conventions:

   (a) **Realisation** – for bar trading.

   (b) **Matching** – income of a year is matched with expenditure of the year.

   (c) **Accruals** – receipts and payments are adjusted for accruals and prepayments.

   (d) **Going concern** – as the organisation is expected to continue into the foreseeable future, the fixed assets can be valued at unamortised cost.

   (e) **Prudence** – this convention can be applied to value stocks and also to debtors (subscriptions in arrears for example) whose collectibility is in doubt.

6. Finally, there is the item of net assets being divided into separate funds indicating that the net assets are held or owned for different purposes.

Problems in implementation

7. **Life members**. Subscriptions are often received from *life members*. Life members pay a once and for all subscription which entitles them to membership facilities for the rest of their lives. Clearly, the accounting convention of matching requires that such subscriptions should be credited to income and expenditure, not as they are received, but over the *lifetimes* of such members.

   In practice, if life member subscriptions are small, they are credited to income as received but if they are significant in amount, then they should be credited in equal parts over the *estimated active* club membership of such members.

8. **Entrance fees**. Similar problems are encountered with *entrance fees*. In practice, most accountants take entrance fees to income and expenditure account as they are received.

9. **Separate activities**. In the example chosen, the bar represents a *separate activity* of a fairly complex nature and a separate account is drawn up to measure the income from the source. It is possible that other activities (e.g. the grand draw) may be sufficiently complex to require a separate account away from the income and expenditure account proper. In all cases where sources of income have associated expenditures, the income and expenditure should be put together and the surplus or loss on that particular activity should be shown.

10. **Separate funds and separate investment**. In the example chosen, the monies received for the benefit of the scholarship fund were paid into the general club bank account and assets acquired therefrom for general club use. The effect of this is that, although the scholarship fund stands at £1,315, actual cash is not available to make grants of that amount.

To prevent monies given or raised for a particular purpose being used for other purposes, it is possible to invest such sums in specific investments. In such cases, a choice can be made between:

(a) Showing the fund and its associated investments in separate parts of the general balance sheet.

(b) Having a separate balance sheet for the fund and its associated investments.

Restricted and unrestricted funds

11. A new concept for charities is the idea of restricted and unrestricted funds. Charities raise money for:

(a) The general purposes of the charity.

(b) Specific projects

If money is raised for a specific project its use is restricted to that project. Money raised for the general purposes of the charity is unrestricted and can be used for any allowable purpose of the charity

The accounts of charities

12. Charities are now ruled by Statute (The Charities Act 1993) which prescribes accounting and audit regulations. These regulations imply that accounting and audit must follow the rules of the Financial Reporting Standards, Statements of Recommended Practice (accounting recommendations for particular sectors) and Auditing Standards.

The Charities Act now requires that charities:

Requirement	Income not over £1,000	Neither income nore expenditure over £10,000	Income not over £100,000	Neither income nor expenditure over £250,000	Income or expenditure over £250,000
Receipts and and payments account	if preferred	if preferred	if preferred	no	no
Accruals accounting	if preferred	if preferred	if preferred	yes	yes
External scrutiny of accounts	none	not generally required	audit or independent examination	audit or independent examination	audit
Annual returns to Charity Commission	not applicable	yes; in simplified form	yes	yes	yes
Annual report & accounts to Charity Commission	not applicable	only if requested	yes	yes	yes

Notes:

(a) The making of an annual report and the making of a return to the Charity Commission is only required of *registered* charities. Registration is voluntary unless annual income is greater than £1,000 or there is a permanent endowment or it has the use or occupation of land.

(b) An audit must be by a registered auditor.

(c) An independent examination must be by a competent person but need not be by a qualified accountant.

(d) All charities must maintain and retain proper accounting records.

(e) All charities must make their accounts available to the public on written request.

(f) Some charities are registered under other Acts of Parliament (e.g. The Companies Act) and must also obey the rules therein required.

Summary

❏ Clubs, societies, charitable bodies and other organisations that do not trade with a view to profit, must prepare annual accounts to present to members and other interested parties.

❏ The financial statements produced are:
   (i) An Income and Expenditure Account.
   (ii) A Balance Sheet.

❏ The income and expenditure account may be supported by separate accounts such as a bar trading account.

❏ The *capital* of a business balance sheet is, in a non-trading body, called the accumulated fund.

❏ Where the net assets are held or earmarked for specific purposes, the balance sheet may show separate *funds* in addition to the accumulated fund.

Points to note

❏ Clubs, society and charity accounts, are examples of *stewardship* accounting. The committee, council, trustee or whatever the management are termed, receive, spend and invest monies belonging to others and it is right they should give an account of their dealings with the funds entrusted to their care.

❏ Members of a club or society or a person concerned with a charity, can appraise the performance of the management body in many ways. Financially this may include:
   (i) Assessing the bar trading account for adequacy of gross profit margin, appropriateness of pricing or sufficiency of contribution to the organisation's finances.
   (ii) Assessing income and expenditure to determine whether, taking one year with another, income matches expenditure. Note that, in these organisations, non-recurring income or expenditure can occur and regular income should be sufficient to meet regular expenditure.

(iii) Assessing future policy on such matters as subscription levels and charitable giving.

❏ Receipts and payments accounts are often presented horizontally as:

Dr   Receipts   Payments   Cr

Some income and expenditure accounts are also presented horizontally, in which case the two sides are the reverse of those of receipts and payments:

Dr   Expenditure   Income   Cr

❏ In examination questions, workings must be given, preferably in double entry form. For example, if the calculation of subscriptions for the year is complex:

Subscriptions Account

Dr				Cr
Subscriptions in arrear b/f	110	Subscriptions in advance b/f		286
Income and Expenditure A/c	?	Cash receipts		3,240
Subscriptions in advance c/f	813	Receipts by cheque		4,860
		Subscriptions in arrear c/f		140
	£8,526			£8,526

From this account, the subscriptions for the year can be calculated as £7,603.

❏ There are innumerable clubs, societies, charities, churches, associations etc. All of them prepare accounts. Sometimes the accounts are excellent and drawn up using accrual accounting and presenting information informatively. Others are less satisfactory! You should try to see as many sets of club etc accounts as you can. Be critical of them but do not voice your criticisms out loud. The treasurer is doing his or her best but is probably an engineer or bank manager and does not fully understand accounts.

Self-testing questions

1.   What are the objectives of clubs, societies, and charitable bodies?
2.   What financial requirements do such bodies have?
3.   What financial statements should be produced by such bodies?
4.   What is the term used for the capital of a non-trading body?
5.   What is the relationship between 'funds' and 'net assets'?
6.   Contrast a Receipts and Payments Account with an Income and Expenditure Account.
7.   How should (i) life member subscriptions and (ii) entrance fees be accounted for?
8.   Distinguish between separate funds and separate investment.
9.   How can a member of a club use the financial statements to appraise the performance of the management body?

Exercises

1.   The following is the receipts and payments account of Twood Climbing Club for the year ending 31.12.x7.

Receipts and Payments Account of Twood Climbing Club
for the year ending 31.12.x7

	£		£
Subscriptions	5,600	Clubhouse overheads	4,540
Bar takings	4,530	Bar Purchases	3,180
Donations	100	New equipment	1,200
Annual Dinner tickets	850	Cost of Annual Dinner	1,070
Collection for Prize Fund	970	Prizes purchased	865
		Petty cash	100
b/f	1,030	c/f	2,125
	13,080		13,080

Balances at 31.12	19x6	19x7
	£	£
Subscriptions in advance	135	240
Subscriptions in arrear	200	320
Bar stocks	780	543
Bar purchases creditors	650	728
Prize fund	1,600	?
Clubhouse overhead accruals	238	143
Clubhouse overhead prepayment	100	57
Equipment at cost	3,600	?
Equipment accumulated depreciation	1,400	?
Prize stock	300	327
Petty cash	30	51

One quarter of the clubhouse overheads is apportionable to the bar.

Depreciation is at 30% reducing balance.

Petty cash is used only for postage and stationery.

Required:

Bar trading account; income and expenditure account; balance sheet; a commentary on the results and on treasurer's proposal to increase subscriptions by 5%.

2.   The Anglo India Cricket and Hockey Club has two sections – cricket and hockey. Its receipts and payments account for the year ending 31.12.x7 showed:

	£		£
Subs – Hockey 67 x £30	2,010	Bar purchases	4,600
Subs – Cricket 58 x £40	2,320	Hockey dinner costs	623
Dinner – Hockey section	456	Cricket dance costs	520
Dance – Cricket section	561	Barman's salary	1,100
Bar takings	6,790	Development fund raffle prizes	200
Raffle for development fund	880	General overheads	3,100
		Hockey section costs	1,168
		Cricket section costs	653
		Government Bonds	2,000
b/f	1,543	c/f	596
	14,560		14,560

Balances at 31 December were:		19x6	19x7
Bar debtors		132	247
Bar creditors		780	903
Bar stocks		580	435
		19x6	19–7
Subs in advce	– hockey	3 mbrs	2 mbrs
	– cricket	12 mbrs	18 mbrs
Subs in arrear	– hockey	5 mbrs	12 mbrs
	– cricket	0 mbrs	1 mbr
General overheads creditors		120	238
General overheads prepmts		100	350
Stock of raffle prizes		140	138
Club premises at cost		24,000	24,000
Premises accumulated depreciation		3,000	?
Development Fund balance		4,700	?
Hockey section balance		2,170	?
Cricket section balance		2,305	?
Loan on mortgage		13,000	13,000

Note: The cost of the clubhouse (£20,000) is being depreciated over 20 years. The bar profit is credited 50% to the hockey section and 50% to the cricket section. Depreciation and general overheads are debited similarly.

Required:

Prepare income and expenditure account and balance sheet. Comment on the club's financial affairs.

Assignment

❏ *The Sheinton Club presents you with the following data for the year ended 31 December 19x7.*

Receipts	£	Payments	£
Subscriptions received	40,000	Rates	1,100
Concert takings	12,000	General expenses	14,000
		Concert expenses	9,500
		Wages	18,800

You are also advised that:

	31.12.x6	31.12.x7
	£	£
Subscriptions owing	800	950
Subscriptions pre-paid	250	nil
Premises (at cost of £80,000)	50,000	?
Fixtures and fittings (at cost of £20,000)	9,000	?
Bank	870	?

Notes:

(a) *Depreciation of buildings (cost £60,000) is straight line over 24 years.*

(b) *Depreciation of fixtures is 20% reducing balance. Just before the year end, a snooker table was traded in for a new one. The new one cost £5,000 and £800 was allowed on the old one. The old one had cost £3,000 in 19x2. The payment was made in January 19x8 but the transaction properly belongs to 19x7.*

(c) *40% of the subscriptions in arrear at the end of 19x7 are expected to be uncollectible.*

Required:

(a) *Prepare financial statements for 19x7.*

(b) *Prepare forecast financial statements for 19x8 based on the following predictions:*

(i) *A concert will be held again but the profit is forecast as only £1,000.*

(ii) *Rates will be £1,300.*

(iii) *General expense are expected to rise by 5%.*

(iv) *Wages will increase by 4%.*

(v) *No subscriptions will be in advance or in arrears at the end of 19x8.*

(vi) *In 19x7 the subscription was £60 a member, you are to suggest a suitable subscription for 19x8. Membership is expected to decline by 4%.*

(c) *Prepare your treasurer's address to the members at the 19x8 AGM presenting the 19x7 financial statements and the 19x8 forecasts and suggesting a subscription.*

24 Partnerships

This chapter introduces partnership: what a partnership is, how partners come to a partnership agreement, how profits and losses are shared, accounting for partnership and the appropriation, capital and current accounts, the dissolution of partnerships, goodwill and changes in partnerships.

Definition

1. The Partnership Act 1890 defines partnership as:

    'The relationship which subsists between persons carrying on a business in common with a view to profit.'

2. Thus:
    (a) Partnership is a relationship. In fact it is a relationship requiring the utmost trust and co-operation between the partners.
    (b) Partnership, in this manual, is a business relationship. It is concerned with two or more people who jointly own and manage a business.
    (c) The objective of the partnership is to make a profit which has to be shared in some ways by the partners.

The agreement

3. The essence of a partnership is the *agreement*. Partners must agree about all aspects of the conduct of the business and of the relationship between the partners. Some of the aspects which must be covered by the agreement are:
    (a) Who the partners are.
    (b) How much each should contribute to the partnership capital.
    (c) When the partnership should commence.
    (d) How long the partnership should last.
    (e) How profits should be shared.
    (f) How much each partner may draw from the business.
    (g) Hours of work, holidays etc.
    (h) What happens if a partner dies, retires, becomes bankrupt, medically incapable or insane.
    (i) The extent to which partners can engage in other business activities.
    (j) Commercial matters – products, premises, rate of expansion, employment policy etc.

4. The agreement may be a formal one – a deed drawn up by a solicitor and signed by all the partners – or it may be written less formally, perhaps in the form of the exchange of letters or minutes of a meeting, or it may merely be the conduct of the parties.

    The assumption behind the latter is that the agreement is what the partners do.

For example, if the written partnership agreement says that the partners may take two weeks' holiday each a year but they actually take four weeks each, then their agreement is not what the written agreement says but what they do.

5. In practice, failure to agree in advance on some aspect of the partnership affairs may lead to acrimony and even collapse of the partnership. I recall two partners who differed in their opinion of the length of the working day. No agreement was reached in advance and it became impossible for the ambitious partner who wished to work a 14-hour day to continue in partnership with his partner who felt that eight hours were sufficient.

The law

6. Partnership law is a considerable subject and I do not intend even to outline it. It is sufficient for our purposes to know that the general law was codified in the Partnership Act 1890 and that relations between partners are governed by their partnership agreement whether this be expressed, or implied by the conduct of the parties.

7. The number of partners in a partnership permissible in law is restricted to 20 except for certain professional partnerships – accountants, doctors, solicitors, chartered loss adjusters etc.

8. A section of the Partnership Act 1890 of particular interest to accounting students is Section 24 which states how profits are to be shared in the absence of agreement. This will be discussed in the next section.

Profit sharing

9. Partners can share the profits of their business in any way they like. Many partnerships share profits in ways which reflect the differing contributions made by the partners to the business, for example:
    (a) Capital invested.
    (b) Time spent on partnership business.
    (c) Expertise or experience.
    (d) Seniority.

10. Some profit sharing arrangements are complex. For example, in the partnership of Dick, Eddie and Fred they agreed that:
    (a) Each should have a part of the profit equivalent to 10% of their capitals at the beginning of the year. This reflects the different amounts of capital each has tied up in the partnership business.
    (b) Dick should have £7,000 of the profit to reflect the fact that he alone works full time on the business and thus foregoes the salary he could have earned elsewhere.
    (c) Eddie should have a share of the profit equal to 2% of the sales to reflect the special expertise he has in obtaining customers.
    (d) Any remaining profit should be shared equally.

The appropriation account – division of profit

11. We will demonstrate this with an example.

Andrew, Guy and Martin are in partnership as camping equipment retailers. Their trial balance at 31.12.x3 was:

Dr		£	Cr	£
Fixed assets at cost		24,300	Depreciation provision 31.12.x2	4,750
Stock 31.12.x2		16,720	Sales	112,220
Debtors		1,340	Andrew – Capital 31.12.x2	12,020
Overheads		7,105	Guy – Capital 31.12.x2	7,001
Purchases		78,626	Martin – Capital 31.12.x2	1,000
Drawings:	Andrew	4,800	Creditors	9,820
	Guy	7,100		
	Martin	5,600		
Bank		1,220		
		146,811		146,811

Notes:

(a) Stock at 31.12.x3 was valued at £22,300.

(b) Depreciation is at 20% a year on the reducing balance.

(c) The partnership agreement provides that profit shall be shared:

Interest on capital 15%

Salaries: Guy £3,000, Martin £2,000

Balance: 5:4:3

Required:

Prepare trading and profit and loss and appropriation accounts for the year ending 31.12.x3.

Answer

Andrew, Guy and Martin

Trading and Profit and Loss Account for the year ending 31 December 19x3

	£	£
Sales		112,220
Less Cost of Sales:		
Opening stock	16,720	
Purchases	78,626	
Available for sale	95,346	
Closing stock	22,300	73,046
Gross profit		39,174
Overheads	7,105	
Depreciation	3,910	11,015
Net profit		£28,159

Appropriation Account

	Andrew	Guy	Martin	Total
	£	£	£	£
Interest on capital	1,803	1,050	150	3,003
Salaries	–	3,000	2,000	5,000
Balance	8,398	6,719	5,039	20,156
	10,201	10,769	7,189	28,159

Notes:

(a) The first stage in these questions is to prepare the trading and profit and loss account in exactly the same way as with the accounts of a sole trader.

(b) With a sole trader, all of the profit belongs to the sole trader, but in a partnership the profit is shared among the partners. Consequently an additional account is required to show the appropriation of the profit among the partners.

(c) The profit is shared in accordance with the agreement.

Note that despite reference to interest on capital and salaries these are not interest on capital or salaries, they are part of the profit sharing formula.

(d) In this case the profit sharing formula divides the profit among the partners as Andrew £10,201, Guy £10,769 and Martin £7,189.

12. The profit sharing *formula* agreed on by Andrew & Co divided the profit of £28,159 in a unique way. But suppose the business had a bad year and the profit earned was only £7,000. How would this be divided? There are at least two possibilities:

(a)

	Andrew	Guy	Martin	Total
	£	£	£	£
Interest on capital	1,803	1,050	150	3,003
Salaries	–	3,000	2,000	5,000
Balance (loss)	(418)	(334)	(251)	(1,003)
	1,385	3,716	1,899	7,000

(b)

	Andrew	Guy	Martin	Total
	£	£	£	£
Interest on capital	1,803	1,050	150	3,003
Salaries	–	2,398	1,599	3,997
	1,803	3,448	1,749	7,000

The salaries have been reduced so that total salaries absorb the remainder of the profit. Each salary has been reduced proportionately. Another alternative would be to give priority to salaries over interest on capital.

Whichever is correct, depends on a legal interpretation of the partnership agreement. To avoid difficulties of this sort, the wording of the formula must be precise and unambiguous and be able to cover all sizes of profit or loss.

Profit sharing in the absence of an agreement

13. It may be that the partners in a business failed to agree in advance how they should share profits. This is not necessarily a problem, as they could come to an agreement in arrear. However, if they are still unable to agree, the Partnership Act 1890, Section 24 provides that:

    (a) 5% interest on loans to the partnership by partners.

    (b) No interest is to be allowed on capital.

    (c) Balance of profit to be divided equally.

    Notes:

    (a) Loans to the partnership by partners are possible but normally any monies put into the business by a partner are regarded as part of that partner's capital.

    (b) Section 24 is rarely invoked in practice.

Capital and current accounts

14. Some partnerships have capital and current accounts. Some have only capital accounts.

    (a) **Capital accounts where there are also current accounts**

    At the formation of a new partnership, the partners may agree to put into the partnership from their private resources, cash and/or other assets to an agreed value. The amount of such resources put in by a partner is his capital. Usually the partners agree that no partner will withdraw resources from the partnership in such a way that the capital is reduced. A partner's capital account will only change by agreement or on the occurrence of events such as a change in the profit sharing ratio or on the death or retirement of a partner or the admission of a new partner.

    (b) **Current accounts**

    If a profit is made by a partnership, it means that the net assets of the partnership have increased by the amount of the profit. Each partner's share of the profit is credited to his current account. The balance standing to the credit of a partner's current account represents the maximum amount that the partner can withdraw from the partnership assets. Thus a partner can only make drawings up to the amount of his accumulated share of profits. The current account represents undrawn profits.

    (c) **Capital accounts without current accounts**

    Many partnerships simply have capital accounts without partners' current accounts. In these cases, the capital account represents a mixture of capital subscribed and undrawn profits. There is therefore no maximum put on partners' drawings by the division between capital and current accounts and restriction of another sort has to be agreed upon. (Perhaps a weekly amount and an annual drawing when profits have been calculated.)

    In the question in paragraph 11, the partners' capital accounts would appear thus (in columnar form as is usually asked for in examinations):

	Andrew	Guy	Martin		Andrew	Guy	Martin
	£	£	£		£	£	£
31.12.x3 Drawings	4,800	7,100	5,600	31.12.x2 Balance	12,020	7,001	1,000
31.12.x3 Balance	17,421	10,670	2,589	31.12.x3 Profit	10,201	10,769	7,189
	22,221	17,770	8,189		22,221	17,770	8,189

Formats

15. Formats for a partnership *trading and profit and loss account* are the same as for sole traders. The additional feature for partnerships is the *appropriation account* and a suitable format has already been given in paragraph 2.

An alternative is:

	Interest	Salary	Balance	Total
	£	£	£	£
Andrew	1,803	–	8,398	10,201
Guy	1,050	3,000	6,719	10,769
Martin	150	2,000	5,039	7,189
	3,003	5,000	20,156	28,159

Other formats are possible but any format should show the total share of profit given to each partner.

16. The *balance sheet* formats of a partnership are the same as for sole traders. The difference is that instead of a single capital account for the proprietor, there are several accounts (and perhaps current accounts), one for each partner. In simple cases, the full accounts can be given, showing separately, opening balance, share of profit, drawings, closing balance. But in more complex cases, the detail is usually put in a separate *schedule* and only the final balances put on the balance sheet.

An example

Katie and Brennan are in partnership as tree surgeons sharing profits 3:2. Their trial balance after computing profit at 31.12.x4 showed:

	£		£
Fixed assets at cost	20,000	Creditors	6,280
Debtors	15,400	Capital: Katie	10,000
Cash at bank	1,100	Brennan	7,000
Stock	8,400	Current a/c 31.12.x3 Brennan	3,100
Current a/c 31.12.x3 Katie	180	Loan at 15% Brennan	10,000
Drawings: Katie	4,600	Profit 19x4	10,200
Brennan	5,200	Depreciation 31.12.x4	8,300
	54,880		54,880

Note: During 19x4, each partner had subscribed an additional £3,000.

Required:

Draw up the balance sheet at 31.12.x4.

Katie and Brennan
Schedule of Capital and Current Accounts
year ending 31 December 19x4

	Katie	Brennan	Total
	£	£	£
Capital Accounts			
As at 31.12.x3	7,000	4,000	11,000
Additions in 19x4	3,000	3,000	6,000
As at 31.12.x4	10,000	7,000	17,000
Current Accounts			
As at 31.12.x3	(180)	3,100	2,920
Profit share in 19x4 (3:2)	6,120	4,080	10,200
	5,940	7,180	13,120
Drawings in 19x4	4,600	5,200	9,800
	1,340	1,980	3,320
Total interest in the net assets of the partnership at 31.12.x4	11,340	8,980	20,320

Balance Sheet as at 31 December 19x4

Fixed Assets at cost		20,000
Less Accumulated depreciation		8,300
		11,700
Current Assets		
Stock	8,400	
Debtors	15,400	
Cash at bank	1,100	
	24,900	
Current Liabilities		
Creditors	6,280	18,620
		30,320
Partners' interests – as schedule		20,320
Long-term liability		
Loan at 15%		10,000
		30,320

Note: The schedule is often expressed as being attached to and forming part of the balance sheet.

17. To complete the chapter and to show a balance sheet format without a schedule, we will complete the question in paragraph 11.

Andrew, Guy and Martin
Balance Sheet as at 31 December 19x3

	£	£
Fixed Assets at cost		24,300
Less Accumulated Depreciation		8,660
		15,640
Current Assets		
Stock	22,300	
Debtors	1,340	
Bank	1,220	
	24,860	
Current Liabilities		
Creditors	9,820	15,040
		£30,680

Capital Accounts

	Andrew	Guy	Martin	Total
	£	£	£	£
as at 1.1.x3	12,020	7,001	1,000	20,021
Net profit share	10,201	10,769	7,189	28,159
	22,221	17,770	8,189	48,180
Drawings	4,800	7,100	5,600	17,500
	17,421	10,670	2,589	30,680

Dissolution of partnership

18. The dissolution of partnerships may be caused by many factors including:
    (a) Insolvency – the inability to continue because the partnership cannot meet its financial obligations.
    (b) A decision of the partners not to continue, in order perhaps that each may go his own way.

    There is a special, but exceedingly rare, situation when a partner owes money to the partnership in dissolution and is unable to pay. The matter was dealt with in the legendary case of *Garner v Murray 1904* which is the concluding subject in this section.

The realisation account

19. The dissolution of a partnership involves the disposal (= realisation) of the assets. Inevitably the amounts realised will differ from the book value and a profit or loss will result. The bookkeeping is:
    (a) Open an account to be called the realisation account and debit it with the book values of the assets being realised. The credit will be the asset accounts and the entry will close the asset accounts.

(b) Credit the realisation account with the creditors who will be paid off. This will close the creditors' accounts.

(c) Credit the realisation account with the proceeds of disposal of the assets and debit the cash book (or other asset account, if the proceeds are not in cash form).

(d) Debit the realisation account with the amount paid to creditors and credit the cash book.

(e) The balance on the realisation account now represents the profit or loss on the disposal or realisation of the assets and any gain or loss on paying off the creditors. This profit or loss has to be divided up amongst the partners in profit or loss sharing ratio (but ignoring interest on capital and salaries).

(f) Distribute the overall difference (profit or loss) among the partners in the profit sharing ratio. This will close the realisation account.

(g) Complete the dissolution by paying to partners the balances on their capital/current accounts.

20. **Example:**

The balance sheet of Vanessa and Julie at 31.12.x4 showed:

	£		£	£
Capital accounts		Fixed assets		14,000
Vanessa	10,000	Current assets		
Julie	9,000	Stock	6,800	
Current accounts		Debtors	4,750	
Vanessa	1,900	Cash	150	
Julie	1,700			11,700
Creditors	3,100			
	£25,700			£25,700

The partnership was dissolved at 1.1.x5.

(a) The motor cars included in fixed assets were taken by the partners at agreed values as Vanessa £2,000, Julie £3,000.

(b) The remainder of the fixed assets were sold for £12,000.

(c) The stock was sold at auction for £4,300.

(d) The debtors realised £4,600.

(e) The creditors were paid off less a 5% discount.

(f) Expenses of realisation were £250.

(g) The profit sharing formula is: 10% interest on capital, balance 3:2.

Required:

Show relevant accounts in the dissolution.

Answer

Realisation Account

	£		£
Fixed assets	14,000	Car taken by Vanessa	2,000
Stock	6,800	Car taken by Julie	3,000
			...continued

	£		£
Debtors	4,750	Proceeds of sales of fixed assets	12,000
Creditors	2,945	Proceeds of sales of stock	4,300
Expenses	250	Debtors	4,600
Profit on realisation:		Creditors	3,100
Vanessa	153		
Julie	102	255	
	£29,000		£29,000

Cash

	£		£	£
Balance b/d	150			
Proceeds from fixed assets	12,000	Creditors		2,945
Proceeds from stock	4,300	Expenses		250
Proceeds from debtors	4,600	Vanessa	10,053	
		Julie	7,802	17,855
	£21,050			£21,050

Capital account

	V	J		V	J
	£	£		£	£
Cars	2,000	3,000	Capital b/f	10,000	9,000
Cash	10,053	7,802	Current accounts b/f	1,900	1,700
			Share of profit on realisation	153	102
	£12,053	£10,802		£12,053	£10,802

Notes:
(a) Assets to be realised are debited to the realisation account. This closes the fixed asset, stock and debtors accounts.
(b) The proceeds of the realisation are credited to the realisation account and debited to cash or in the case of the partners' cars to the partners.
(c) Creditors are usually put through the realisation account if a profit or loss is involved, as here.
(d) There are often some expenses of realisation.
(e) The profit/loss is shared in profit/loss sharing ratio – the interest on capital part of the formula is irrelevant as no effluxion of time is involved.
(f) There is no need to show the account of the assets realised as they are simply (e.g.):

Stock

	£		£
Balance b/f	6,800	Transfer to realisation a/c	6,800
	£6,800		£6,800

(g) The capital and current accounts are put together in a dissolution since their difference is no longer relevant. As a going concern capital accounts are not payable to partners as they are permanent capital. Current accounts are payable to partners as they are undrawn profits. In a dissolution, the business is clearly not a going concern!

(h) When all the assets have been realised and the creditors paid off, there are only three balances left:

An asset – cash		£17,855
Two liabilities:	Vanessa	£10,053
	Julie	£7,802

The asset just matches the liabilities and can be used to pay them off, leaving no balance at all in the double entry system. Note this well – students frequently distribute the cash in profit sharing ratio!

Garner v Murray

21. A complication arises in dissolution when one partner finishes up in debit (i.e. owing the partnership money) and has no assets.

Example

Tom, Roger, and James are in partnership sharing profits equally. Their balance sheet at 31.5.x4 was:

	£		£
Tom	4,000	Fixed assets	6,006
Roger	3,000	Stock	9,500
James	416	Debtors	7,800
Creditors	6,250		
Overdraft	9,640		
	£23,306		£23,306

On 1 June 19x4 the partnership was dissolved and the following happened:
(a) The assets were sold to RPH Ltd for £20,000 only.
(b) The creditors were settled for £6,103.
(c) James was declared bankrupt with no assets.

Answer

Realisation Account

	£		£
Fixed assets	6,006	RPH Ltd – Cash	20,000
Stock	9,500		
Debtors	7,800	Creditors	6,250
Cash paid to creditors	6,103	Loss on realisation	
		Tom	1,053
		Roger	1,053
		James	1,053
			3,159
	£29,409		£29,409

Cash

	£		£
RPH	20,000	b/f	9,640
		Creditors	6,103
		Tom	2,583
		Roger	1,674
	£20,000		£20,000

Partners' Accounts

	T	R	J		T	R	J
	£	£	£		£	£	£
Share in loss	1,053	1,053	1,053	b/f	4,000	3,000	416
G v M	364	273		G v M			637
Cash	2,583	1,674					
	4,000	3,000	1,053		4,000	3,000	1,053

Notes:

(a) The first step is to open a realisation account and transfer to it all the assets and the creditors.

(b) The proceeds of the sale £20,000 are credited to the realisation account and debited to cash.

(c) Cash is credited and the realisation account debited with the payment to the creditors.

(d) The loss on realisation is credited to the realisation account and debited in equal shares (the profit/loss sharing ratio).

(e) James's account is in debit, meaning that he owes the partnership £637. As he is bankrupt he cannot pay it so the debit balance has to be written off. This is done by debiting the remaining partners in accordance with the rule in Garner v Murray 1904. Thus the amount is apportioned in the ratio of their last agreed capital accounts (£4,000:£3,000). The rule is not followed in all countries and in the USA and elsewhere the loss would be debited in profit/loss sharing ratio.

(f) The only remaining balances are Cash Dr £4,257 and the capital accounts of Tom Cr £2,583 and Roger Cr £1,674. The books are cleared by payments to the partners.

Goodwill

23. Goodwill has been judicially described as 'the probability that the customers of a business will continue to patronise the business on a change of ownership'. Goodwill can be personal to the proprietor, in which case customers will cease to patronise the business on a change of ownership.

That goodwill has value can readily be seen by an example. Cooper is a newly qualified accountant who wishes to commence private practice. He could do so by renting some offices and advertising his services in the press. However, finding clients is difficult and takes time. It may be that Price has a block of clients and wishes to retire. Clearly it would pay Cooper to buy the clients from Price. The intention of the clients to patronise a particular accounting practice is known as the goodwill of the practice. Such intention is usually transferable and hence has value.

Goodwill, like any other scarce commodity, is worth what a willing buyer will pay a willing seller. The value, or price if it is to be sold, is normally reached by negotiation or in cases of dispute by independent arbitration.

Although the value of goodwill is reached by agreement after negotiation amongst the interested parties, there are some guidelines as to how the value may be estimated in certain industries and also in general. These include:

(a) n times the gross annual fee income – accounting practices (n is usually 1 to $1\frac{1}{4}$).

(b) x times the annual gallonage of beer sold – public houses.

(a) n times the average net profit. This is often described as n years' purchase of the average annual net profit.

When a change occurs in a partnership which is a going concern such that goodwill has value then the following procedures are required:

(a) Agree on the value of goodwill.

(b) Write up the goodwill account, by debiting goodwill and crediting the pre-change partners in the pre-change profit/loss sharing ratio.

(c) Write down the goodwill to nil, by crediting the goodwill account and debiting the post-change partners in the post-change profit/loss sharing ratio.

(d) Assets other than goodwill are sometimes involved and are treated in the same way.

Example 1: Change in profit sharing ratio

The partners, Graham and Keith of Truckbits, share profits equally and the partnership balance sheet at 30.6.x4 was:

		£		£
Capital:	Graham	30,000	Fixed assets	35,000
	Keith	18,500	Current assets	28,000
Current liabilities		14,500		
		63,000		63,000

On 1.7.x4, the partners agreed that as Graham wished to take a smaller part in the partnership business, the profit sharing ratio should change to 2:3 with a salary of £5,000 a year to Keith. For the purpose of the change only, goodwill was agreed at a value of £30,000 and fixed assets at a value of £47,000. These changes in value were not to be incorporated in the books.

Answer

Goodwill Account

	£		£
Graham (a)	15,000	Graham (b)	12,000
Keith (a)	15,000	Keith (b)	18,000
	30,000		30,000

Fixed Assets

	£		£
b/f	35,000	Graham (b)	4,800
Graham (a)	6,000	Keith (b)	7,200
Keith (a)	6,000	c/f	35,000
	47,000		47,000

Capital Accounts

	Graham	Keith		Graham	Keith
	£	£		£	£
Goodwill (b)	12,000	18,000	b/f	30,000	18,500
Fixed assets (b)	4,800	7,200	Goodwill (a)	15,000	15,000
c/f	34,200	14,300	Fixed assets (a)	6,000	6,000
	51,000	39,500		51,000	39,500

Notes:
(a) Goodwill and fixed assets are written up to their agreed values (£30,000 and £47,000) by credits to the partners' accounts in the old profit sharing ratio (equal shares).
(b) Goodwill and fixed assets are written down to their continuing book values (nil and £35,000) by debits to the partners' accounts in the new profit sharing ratios (2:3).
(c) The salary part of the profit sharing formula is irrelevant for this purpose.

Example 2: Introduction of a new partner

Jonathan and Diane are in partnership sharing profits equally and with a balance sheet at 31.7.x5 as:

		£		£
Capital:	Jonathan	60,000	Net assets	100,000
	Diane	40,000		
		100,000		100,000

On 1.8.x5 Tina was admitted to the partnership and brought in £30,000 cash. Profit sharing was to be in equal shares. It was agreed that goodwill was worth £24,000 and that no goodwill account was to be maintained in the books.

Answer

Goodwill Account

	£		£
Jonathan	12,000	Jonathan	8,000
Diane	12,000	Diane	8,000
		Tina	8,000
	24,000		24,000

Capital Accounts

	J £	D £	T £		J £	D £	T £
Goodwill	8,000	8,000	8,000	b/f	60,000	40,000	
c/f	64,000	44,000	22,000	Goodwill	12,000	12,000	
				Cash			30,000
	72,000	52,000	30,000		72,000	52,000	30,000

Note: If the business was dissolved then Tina would receive the amount of her share of the net assets (= her capital) plus her share of the proceeds of the sale of the goodwill i.e. £22,000 + £8,000 = £30,000 which she put in. Always check answers this way.

Retirement of a partner

24. In theory, the retirement of a partner from the partnership involves the dissolution of the partnership and the setting up of a new partnership of the non-retiring partners from the old partnership. In practice the assets and liabilities of the old partnership are usually carried through to the new partnership and the books continued.

The steps required on the retirement of a partner are:
(a) Determination of the value of the goodwill.
(b) Writing up the value of the goodwill as:
   Dr Goodwill
   Cr Partners in their profit sharing ratio
(c) Charging any assets taken by the retiring partner to his account.
(d) Making any required adjustments to the value of any assets or liabilities with corresponding entries on the capital accounts of any profits/losses in profit sharing ratio.
(e) Writing down the value of goodwill to nil by:
   Dr Capital accounts of remaining partners
   Cr Goodwill
   in new profit sharing ratio.
(f) Re-titling the capital (together with current account) of the retiring partner as a loan to the new partnership.

Example of retirement of a partner

Bill, Moon and Hartland are in partnership sharing profits equally. On 31 December 19x1 their balance sheet showed:

		£		£
Capital	Bill	31,100	Plant and vehicles	28,000
	Moon	17,000	Stock	14,000
	Hartland	11,900	Debtors	21,700
Creditors		10,500	Cash at bank	6,800
		70,500		70,500

On 1 January 19x2, Bill retired and it was agreed that, in accordance with the partnership agreement:

(a) Goodwill was valued at £33,000.

(b) Bill should take a car (written down value £2,800) at a valuation of £4,000.

(c) Bill should take £5,000 immediately and leave the balance on loan bearing interest at 10%. Repayment would be in two instalments at the ends of 19x2 and 19x3.

The new profit sharing ratio between the remaining partners was to remain in equal shares.

Required:

Show:

(a) The capital accounts and loan account in the books of the old partnership.

(b) The balance sheet of the new partnership after the retirement.

(c) Capital and loan accounts in the books of the old partnership.

We will begin with an account to show the realisation of the car which is taken by Bill and the write up of goodwill:

Realisation Account

	£		£
Car at book value	2,800	Goodwill	33,000
Profit on realisation Bill	11,400	Transfer to Bill	4,000
Moon	11,400		
Hartland	11,400		
	37,000		37,000

Partners' Capital Accounts

	B	M	H		B	M	H
Car	4,000			b/f	31,100	17,000	11,900
Cash	5,000			Realisation gain	11,400	11,400	11,400
Transfer to loan a/c	33,500						
Goodwill		16,500	16,500				
Balances c/f		11,900	6,800				
	42,500	28,400	23,300		42,500	28,400	23,300

The new Balance Sheet:

Capitals – Moon	11,900	Plant and vehicles	25,200
– Hartland	6,800	Stock	14,000
Loan – Bill	33,500	Debtors	21,700
Creditors	10,500	Cash	1,800
	62,700		62,700

Notes:

(a) Goodwill is written up by a credit to realisation account.

(b) The gain on the car is also credited to the realisation account.

(c) The net gain on realisation is credited to the partners in the profit sharing ratio.

(d) The balance on Bill's capital account is renamed as a loan since he is no longer a partner.

(e) The goodwill balance is written off to the new partners in profit sharing ratio.

Theory

25. The theory on the treatment of goodwill in partnership changes can be summarised as:

(a) Profit is any increase in the net assets of a business other than from an injection of capital.

(b) In a partnership profits are credited to capital accounts in profit sharing ratio.

(c) The net assets of the partnership are equal to the sum of the partners' capital accounts.

(d) There is usually an asset, goodwill, which is not normally included in the net assets on the balance sheet.

(e) The recognition of this asset (and any other incorrectly valued asset or liability) would, in a dissolution, involve a credit to the partners' capitals in profit sharing ratio. Effectively the creation of a new asset is a profit, and profit is shared in the partnership profit sharing ratio.

Summary

❏ Partnership is defined in the Partnership Act as the relationship which subsists between persons carrying on a business in common with a view to profit.

❏ The rules governing partnership are found in the partnership agreement. This may be expressed in a written agreement or implied by the conduct of the partners.

❏ The number of partners in a partnership is limited to 20. Some professional partnerships are exempted from this rule.

❏ All partnerships must have some arrangement for sharing profits and this may be complex, to reflect the differing contributions of the partners.

❏ In a partnership, profit is shared amongst the partners in accordance with the formula in the agreement.

❏ The computation of the profit sharing is demonstrated in the appropriation account.

❏ In cases of dispute where there is no agreement on how to share profit, Section 24 of the Partnership Act 1890 gives directions.

❏ Partnerships may distinguish between permanent capital and undrawn profits by keeping separate capital and current accounts for each partner. Alternatively the partners may maintain only capital accounts for each partner.

❏ The balance sheet of a partnership may show movement on the capital accounts of the partners in detail in the balance sheet. Alternatively, the capital (and current accounts if kept) may be summarised in a separate schedule which is attached to and forms part of the balance sheet.

❏ Partnerships may dissolve when the following happens:

(i) The assets are realised, usually at a profit or a loss.

(ii) The external liabilities (creditors etc) are settled.

(iii) The balance of cash or other assets remaining are distributed to the partners by settling the balances on their capital accounts.

❏ In a dissolution, assets are debited to a realisation account and the proceeds of disposal credited. Any difference is debited or credited to partners' capitals in the profit/loss sharing ratio.

❏ If the account of a partner finishes up as a debit balance and the partner has no assets, the balance is written off to the debit of the other partners' account in the ratio of their last agreed capital accounts following the rule in Garner v Murray 1904.

❏ Partnership changes may include:

(i) Changes in profit/loss sharing ratio.

(ii) Introduction of a new partner.

(iii) Retirement of a partner.

❏ Goodwill is the value to be placed on 'the probability that the customers of a business will continue to patronise the business on a change of ownership'.

❏ The value of goodwill is a matter of agreement between a willing buyer and a willing seller, but there are some recognised methods of arriving at such a value.

Points to note

❏ It is important to realise that partners' salaries and interest on capital are not salaries and interest but part of the profit sharing formula.

❏ Consequently, partners' salaries and interest on capital do not appear in the profit and loss account. Interest on partners' loans, if any, will appear as an expense in the profit and loss account.

❏ Partners' drawings have nothing to do with the profit and loss account or the appropriation account.

❏ The format of a balance sheet is a matter of the best means of carrying information from the accountant who prepares it to the partners and others who need it. As a general rule, a partnership balance sheet (in conjunction with a schedule if desired) must clearly show separately fixed assets, current assets, current liabilities, the net total of all these and how this was financed by showing long-term liabilities and the net interest each partner has in the net assets of the business.

❏ Partnership is entirely a matter of mutual trust and agreement among the partners. This is well illustrated by the famous story of business ethics. A partner in a retail business received £100 overpayment from a customer due to a misunderstanding. The ethical problem is: should he tell his partner?

❑ Note the information conveyed by a partnership balance sheet. It shows the assets and liabilities to outside parties as do all balance sheets. The net assets are the substance of the business. How this substance is shared among the partners is shown by the capital (and current) accounts.

❑ Be careful to maintain double entry in these cases. The debits and credits are equal in the opening balance sheet and care should be taken to ensure all debit entries have corresponding credit entries and vice versa.

❑ The distinction between capital and current accounts is no longer relevant in dissolution.

❑ The profit and loss on realisation is shared between the partners in profit/loss sharing ratio ignoring interest on capital, partners' salaries etc.

❑ At the conclusion of the dissolution, the remaining assets (usually just cash) is paid to the partners to settle their capital accounts. Students who distribute the remaining cash in profit/loss sharing ratio are advised to take up manual work!

❑ The Garner v Murray rule applies to a type of situation which is exceedingly rare in practice. However, knowledge of the case distinguishes accountants from other people.

❑ A complication of there being final assets other than cash (for example, shares in a company) is common in partnership dissolution questions. The question should indicate how the asset is to be distributed to the partners.

❑ The value of goodwill is relevant only when a business or an interest in a business (e.g. a partnership share) changes hands. In such cases, the value is a matter of agreement between the parties concerned.

❑ However, there are a number of accepted methods of achieving a first estimate of value which is then subject to negotiation. In this chapter, a number of methods of arriving at the first estimate have been discussed.

❑ In examination questions, the usual approach is either:
(i) To give the value.
(ii) To explain how the value is to be derived.

❑ One common method is to give the profits (or super profits) for recent years and to base the calculation on a weighted average of these profits, e.g.

	19x0	19x1	19x2
	£	£	£
(i) Profits	24,200	26,900	30,400

(ii) Goodwill is to be valued at two years' purchase of the weighted average of the three years' profits.

Calculation

		£
19x0	1 × 24,200 =	24,200
19x1	2 × 26,900 =	53,800
19x2	3 × 30,400 =	91,200
	6	£169,200

$$£$$

$$\text{Weighted average} = \frac{169,200}{6} \qquad = £28,200$$

$$\text{Two years purchase} = 2 \times £28,200 \qquad = £56,400$$

Note that *more* weight has been given to the later years.

Self-testing questions

1. Define partnership.
2. What matters might be included in a partnership agreement?
3. What factors may influence profit sharing arrangements?
4. What is the maximum number of partners in a partnership? What partnerships does the rule not apply to?
5. What information will appear in a partnership appropriation account?
   (b) In what part of the profit and loss account of a partnership should partners (i) interest on capital, (ii) salaries, appear?
   (c) Which section of which Act applies in the absence of agreement among partners?
   (d) Distinguish between partners' capital and current accounts.
9. How are capital and current accounts expressed on a partnership balance sheet?
10. What factors may lead to the dissolution of a partnership?
11. List the accounting procedures required in a dissolution.
12. What is the relevance of capital and current account separation in a dissolution?
13. How should the final cash balance be distributed among the partners?
14. When does the rule in Garner v Murray 1904 apply?
15. How is the rule applied?
16. What changes in partnerships can occur?
17. What is goodwill?
18. How should goodwill be valued?
19. What methods are found in practice to assess the value of goodwill?
20. List the accounting procedures on a change in a partnership.
21. What is the relationship between capital, net assets, goodwill and profit?
22. What is a weighted average?

Exercises

1. Alice, Brenda and Carla are meeting together to discuss the formation of a partnership between them. The business would be the importation of expensive textiles from Europe and selling them to fashion manufacturers in England. Payment would be required for the goods immediately on importation to the UK, substantial stocks would be carried and customers would on average take some two to three months to pay.

   Alice, a retired lecturer in fashion, is 67 years old, has some £20,000 of capital available, has a good pension, speaks several European languages and loves travel. She does not wish to work full time in the business as she likes to spend time with her dogs.

   Brenda is 34 and has passed some of the Certified Accountants exams and works with a firm of export/import agents. She has agreed to give three months' notice to her employers. She has an overdraft facility with her bank for £3,000 and her current overdraft is £600. She likes hard work.

Carla, who is 44, is a partner in a fashion shop and wishes to retain this connection at least part time. Her former employment was with a firm of fashion manufacturers as a buyer. She is married with three children. She has £2,000 in a building society account and her husband is a wealthy man with inherited capital.

Required:

Draw up a partnership agreement. (In class this exercise could be used as a role play exercise.)

Hint: use the ideas in paragraph 10 as a start to this question.

2.   Gordon, Frank and Ed are considering going into business as specialist car kit makers.

Gordon is already doing this successfully but on a very small scale. He could only bring in the net assets of the business worth about £3,500. He is 58 and has a heart condition.

Frank is 24, is well-known in the car racing and rallying world, receiving a good salary. He has no capital. He is a good rally driver and receives a good fee for entering rallies with works cars.

Ed is 37 and has recently been made redundant from his job as a works manager. He has £20,000 in cash from his savings and redundancy money. He is married and has four children.

Required:

Draw up a possible partnership agreement.

3.   Why do partnerships need an agreement?

4.   List the heads of agreement between the prospective partners of a firm of Certified Accountants.

5.   Gaynor, Amanda and Samantha started in partnership as office cleaners on 1.1.x7. Their verbal agreement was:

(a) 10% interest on capitals.

(b) 5% commission on turnover to Gaynor to reflect her ability to get business.

(c) A salary to Amanda of £3,000 to reflect her longer work time on partnership affairs.

(d) Balance of profit to be divided 2:2:1.

At the end of the first year turnover was found to be £40,000 and net profit £14,640.

Capitals were:

	Introduced 1.1.x7	Introduced 30.6.x7	Withdrawn 30.6.x7
Gaynor	£2,000	£6,000	
Amanda	£6,000		£1,000
Samantha	£5,000		

Drawings were: Gaynor £2,400, Amanda £2,300, Samantha £2,000.

Required:

(a) The partnership appropriation account for the year ending 31.12.x7.

(b) The partners' capital AND current accounts for the same period.

(c) Recast (a) and (b) on the basis that the interest on capital was at 7%.

    (d) Recast (a) and (b) on the basis that profit was not £14,640 but only £2,600.

    (e) Recast (b) on the basis that all transactions go through the capital accounts. How would this affect the profit sharing?

6.   Karl and Stanley have formed two separate partnerships. Their profit sharing agreements and other information are:

	Partnership 1	Partnership 2
Interest on capital	10%	15%
Interest on loans	15%	12%
Salary – Karl	2,000	
Salary – Stanley		4,000
Capital – Karl 1.1.x8	15,000	6,000
Capital – Stanley 1.1.x8	7,000	2,000
Profit 19x8 after loan interest	26,500	23,980
Loan from Karl	20,000	
Drawings 19x8 – Karl	6,500	4,700
Drawings 19x8 – Stanley	3,000	4,100
Residual profit share:		
– Karl	3/5	2/5
– Stanley	2/5	3/5

Required:

(a) Appropriation account for 19x8 for each partnership.

(b) Capital accounts for each partner. No current accounts are kept.

(c) Recast (a) and (b) on the basis that the profit before interest was – Partnership 1 £4,000, Partnership 2 £6,000.

7.   Eric and Janet are in partnership sharing profits 3:1 after a salary to Janet of £4,000 and interest on their capital at the beginning of the year of 15%.

At 31.12.x7 the capitals were Eric £32,500 and Janet £18,400.

In 19x8 the profit was £33,635.

Drawings in 19x8 were Eric £9,254 and Janet £8,709.

Required:

(a) Show the appropriation account and the partners' capital accounts.

(b) Repeat the exercise with a profit of £8,200 and a loss of £2,865.

8.   John and Mary are in partnership sharing profits equally. Their balance sheet at 31.5.x5 showed:

	£		£
John	15,352	Fixed assets	16,435
Mary	11,530	Stock	8,762
Creditors	12,465	Debtors	12,900
		Bank	1,250
	£39,347		£39,347

On 1.6.x5 they dissolved the partnership and one of the following events occurred: (note these are independent – this is really three questions).

	A	B	C
	£	£	£
The fixed assets were sold for	15,000	18,000	22,000
The stock was sold for	7,500	10,200	3,600
The debtors realised	12,450	12,600	8,600
The creditors were paid off for	12,200	12,100	13,700
The expenses of realisation were		200	680

Required:

All accounts to close the partnership books in each case. Discuss why the assets and liabilities are not realised at exactly their book values.

9. Harry, James and Roger are in partnership sharing profits 3:2:1. Their balance sheet at 1.10.x4 showed:

	£	£
Fixed assets		23,875
Stock		24,567
Debtors		13,546
		61,988
Current liabilities:		
Creditors	38,970	
Overdraft	13,456	
		52,426
		£9,562

Partners' accounts

	Capital	Current	
	£	£	£
Harry	3,000	102	3,102
James	4,000	860	4,860
Roger	1,000	600	1,600
	£8,000	£1,562	£9,562

The partnership was dissolved on 2.10.x4 when the following events occurred:

	£
The fixed assets were sold for	20,000
The stock was sold for	18,000
The debtors realised	13,000
The creditors were paid off for	38,965

Note: Roger has no private assets and is therefore unable to contribute to the assets of the partnership.

As an alternative, the partnership was dissolved on 2.10.x4 when the following occurred:

	£
The fixed assets were sold for	22,000
The stock was sold for	16,000
The debtors realised	12,800
The creditors were paid off for	38,500
Expenses of realisation were	2,400

This time Harry is bankrupt and is only able to contribute £2,000 to the partnership assets. Both Roger and James are wealthy men and can pay into the partnership whatever may be required.

Required:

All accounts to close the partnership books.

10. Alec and Ben are in partnership as bakers. Their profit sharing formula is Alec – salary £5,000, the balance to be shared equally. Their balance sheet at 31.12.x4 was:

		£		£
Capital:	Alec	23,000	Goodwill	5,000
	Ben	22,000	Other net assets	40,000
		45,000		45,000

As from 1.1.x5, the profit sharing ratio is to be Alec – salary £10,000, Ben 2% commission on sales, balance 3:2. Goodwill at 1.1.x5 was agreed at £30,000. After 1.1.x5, the goodwill account is to be written out of the books.

Required:

(a) Alec and Ben's capital accounts.

(b) Goodwill account.

11. Felix and Gemma are in partnership sharing profits equally. Their balance sheet at 31 May 19x8 is:

		£		£
Capitals:	Felix	35,000	Net assets	58,920
	Gemma	20,000		
Current accounts:				
	Felix	3,100		
	Gemma	820		
		58,920		58,920

(a) From 1 December 19x8, profit sharing is to be – Felix, salary £6,000 a year, remainder Felix 3/5, Gemma 2/5.

(b) Profit in the year ending 31 May 19x9 was £24,000. It accrued evenly during the year.

(c) Goodwill is to be valued at £20,000 and no account is to be maintained for goodwill in the books.

(d) Drawings in the year to 31 May 19x9 were Felix £12,700, Gemma £9,250.

Required:

(a) Prepare the appropriation account for the year ending 31 May 19x9.

(b) Show capital and current accounts for the same period.

(c) What are the net assets at 31 May 19x9?

12. Louise, Manuel and Nathan are in partnership sharing profits 2:2:1 with balance sheet at 31 October 19x8:

	£		£
Louise	14,300	Net assets	26,300
Manuel	6,800		
Nathan	5,200		
	26,300		26,300

(a) On 1 November 19x8, Manuel retires on the basis that his share of the goodwill is credited to him and the balance of his capital account is transferred to a loan account carrying interest at 15% with repayments of the loan being as soon as possible but no later than 31.12.x5.

(b) Goodwill is valued at £36,000 but no account is to be maintained in the books.

(c) As from 1 November 19x8, Louise and Nathan will share profits as 10% interest on capital, remainder 3/5:2/5.

Required:

Show the capital and loan accounts of the partners at the retirement of Manuel.

(a) On 31 October 19x9, the partnership had made a profit of £28,400 before interest to Manuel.

(b) On 30 April 19x9, £3,000 had been paid to Manuel together with interest to that date.

(c) The partners had drawn: Louise £6,200, Nathan £4,100.

Required:

Show the appropriation account for 19x8/x9, the current accounts of the partners and the balance sheet as at 31 October 19x9.

13. Windle and Zengle are in partnership sharing profits 7:3 with balance sheets at 31.12.x7 as:

	£		£
Windle	24,620	Net assets	43,350
Zengle	18,730		
	43,350		43,350

(a) On 1 January 19x8, Windle retired and goodwill was valued at £11,000.

(b) Zengle borrowed from his bank to pay half the amount due to Windle.

Required:

Show the balance sheet of Zengle after these transactions.

14. Lorraine, Steel and Wilkes are in partnership sharing profits – 10% interest on capital and balance 5:5:4. Their balance sheet at 31.1.x8 showed:

	£		£
Lorraine	31,000	Net Assets	61,300
Steel	23,500		
Wilkes	6,800		
	61,300		61,300

(a) On 1 February 19x8, Barker was admitted as a partner and the profit sharing was changed to 15% interest on capital and the balance in equal shares.

(b) Goodwill was valued at £28,000 but no goodwill account was to be maintained in the books.

(c) Barker bought in £20,000 as his capital and his share of the goodwill.

Required:

Show their capital accounts.

At the end of the year ending 31 January 19x9, profit was £58,000, drawings were: Lorraine £7,300, Steel £12,200, Wilkes £8,700 and Barker £5,350.

Required:

(a) The appropriation account for the year.

(b) The partners' capital accounts for the year.

15. James and John are in partnership sharing profits equally. Their balance sheet at 31.5.x7 shows:

	£		£
James	2,400	Net Assets	6,700
John	4,300		
	6,700		6,700

On 1.6.x7 Mary is admitted to the partnership bringing in £2,000. The new profit sharing ratio is to be James 2/5, John 2/5 and Mary 1/5. Goodwill is to be valued at £5,000 but no account is to be maintained on a permanent basis in the books.

Required:

(a) Capital accounts of the partnership, and the balance sheet after admission of Mary.

(b) Repeat under a new profit sharing ratio of equal shares.

16. Dwin and Dell are in partnership sharing profit 3/5:2/5 with Dwin having a salary of £6,000.

Their balance sheet at 30.6.x7 shows:

		£		£
Capitals			Net assets	25,700
	Dwin	13,000		
	Dell	10,000		
Current a/cs				
	Dwin	1,400		
	Dell	1,300		
		25,700		25,700

On 1.7.x7 Gain is admitted bringing in £6,000 so that the partnership profit sharing ratio is 4:3:3, with all partners having 10% interest on capital and Gain having a salary of £4,000.

Goodwill is valued at £12,000.

In the year ending 30.6.x8 the profit was £28,000 and drawings were Dwin £6,800, Dell £8,300, Gain £7,200.

Required:

(a) The balance sheet of the partnership at 30.6.x8.

(b) Repeat under the basis that the new profit sharing ratio is equal shares with no interest on capital or partnership salary.

Assignment

❑ *Al, Beth and Cilla start in partnership as traders in reproduction furniture on 1.1.x4. They agree to share profits 3:3:2 with Al receiving a salary of £10,000.*

On 31.12.x4, they found they had made a profit of £40,800.

Requirement (a): Explain how this profit will be shared. In the year the partners have drawn: Al £16,000, Beth £7,000 and Cilla £7,000. Explain the relationship between profit, profit sharing and drawings.

On 1.1.x5, the partners decided to change the profit sharing ratio to equal shares with no salaries.

Requirement (b)

Invent and explain a scenario which might have made the change desirable. The partners are unable to agree on the value of goodwill. Suggest ways in which goodwill might be valued and why its valuation is necessary. Eventually valuation was agreed at £24,000. Explain the accounting entries necessary on the change in profit sharing ratio.

On 1.1.x6, Al retired from the partnership and Doe was admitted on the basis of profit sharing Cilla 3/8, Beth 3/8 and Doe 1/4. Goodwill was valued again at £24,000. Al agreed to have his capital account repaid over a period of six years and Doe agreed to bring in £15,000 as his share of the capital.

Requirement (c)

Explain how these changes would be accounted for. Explain (using invented facts) why Al cannot be paid out immediately and why Doe is expected to bring in cash to the partnership.

Requirement (d)

Draw up a possible balance sheet for the partnership (invent figures) and explain its structure and what information each item conveys to a reader.

25 Limited companies

A business can be owned by an individual personally (a sole trader), several people in common (a partnership), or by a company registered under the Companies Act. These are the common forms of ownership. However there are some other forms of ownership (trusts, Royal Charter etc) and some organisations are governed by other Acts of Parliament (e.g. the Charities Acts). This chapter reviews some of the vocabulary used in company law and accounting, considers the preparation of company financial statements for internal use and explains share premium, bonus issues, rights issues, preference shares and their redemption, and reserves. The law relating to companies is immense and this chapter is concentrates only on the accounting aspects.

Characteristics of limited companies

1. These include:

    (a) **Legal personality**. A company is regarded as having separate legal personality. It is an *artificial* person that can own property, make contracts, sue and be sued. The company is a separate entity distinct from those who own it. It is owned by its shareholders (also known as its **members**).

    (b) **Perpetual succession**. As a company is a separate entity, its ownership can change without changing the company itself. Shares in companies quoted on the Stock Exchange are continually bought and sold.

    (c) **Limited liability**. The owners of a company (its *members* or *shareholders*) are not liable for the debts of the company. With sole traders and partnerships the creditors of a business will look first to the assets of the business to receive payment If the business has insufficient assets to satisfy their claims they can look to the private assets of the sole trader or partners. So, a sole trader with a failing business is at risk of losing his house, car, furniture, everything. With a company the creditors of the company can only look to the assets of the company. The shareholders do not normally have any personal liability to the creditors of the company. There is therefore some incentive for a businessperson to set up the business, not as a sole trading, but as a limited company. However there are some drawbacks to this, including the need to comply with a lot of complicated legal requirements and a requirement to make at least some accounting information available to the general public.

Some legal requirements

2. Legal requirements relating to companies are numerous. The main Act of Parliament regulating companies is the Companies Act 1985 as modified by the Companies Act 1989 and numerous subsequent Regulations and Orders. Administratively there is a Registrar of Companies in Cardiff. This office maintains a file on every company and this file is open to inspection by the public. Here are a few requirement for companies:

    (a) Every company must have a set of rules governing it. These are known as the **memorandum and articles of association.** The memorandum usually has five clauses. These state the name of the company (ending in Limited or Public

Limited Company), the domicile of the registered office, e.g. in England (this is simply to indicate whether English or Scottish law is applicable), the objects of the company (usually running to several pages and allowing the company to do almost anything), a statement that the liability of the members is limited, and a statement of the share capital of the company (e.g. £100 shares divided into 100 shares of £1 each). A public company (PLC) also has a clause stating that it is a public company. The articles contain regulations on such matters as the issue of shares, the appointment and duties of directors, voting at meetings etc. Many companies adopt a model set of Articles known as Table A with modifications – see Companies (Table A to F) Regulations 1985.

(b) A company may have many members (some large companies number their members in the hundreds of thousands) or as few as just one (two for public companies). Every company must have a Board of Directors (at least one director for a private company and two directors for a public company). The directors are elected by the members. Every company must have a secretary who may not also be the sole director and must be suitably qualified if the company is a PLC.

(c) Every company must maintain certain books known as the statutory books. These include a register of members, a register of directors and secretaries, a register of charges (see later on the subject of debentures), and minute books. Also the company has to maintain the books of account specified in the Companies Act 1985 sections 221 and 222.

These sections say that all companies must maintain proper accounting records which record:

(i) Entries from day to day of all *sums of money* received and expended and the matters about which these receipts and payments took place, i.e. a cash book.

(ii) *Assets* and *liabilities*.

(iii) Where the company *deals* in *goods* then:
   – Statements of stock held at each financial year end.
   – Statements of stock takings from which these were prepared.
   – Except for retail sales, statements of all *goods bought and sold* with names of buyers and sellers, i.e. purchase and sales daybooks and ledgers.

The books must be sufficient to show, with reasonable accuracy, at any time the financial position of the company and enable the directors to ensure that any profit and loss account or balance sheet produced both shows a *true and fair view* and complies with the requirements of the Companies Acts.

(d) Companies are required to prepare annually certain financial statements:
   (i) A profit and loss account.
   (ii) A balance sheet.
   (iii) Notes attached to forming part of, and amplifying (i) and (ii).
   (iv) A directors' report with specific content.
   (v) The auditors' report.

In the case of non-trading companies (e.g. clubs), an income and expenditure account is required instead of a profit and loss account.

These accounts must be *laid* before the members at each Annual General Meeting. Normally they are circulated in advance with other documents in the Annual Report and Accounts.

The accounts must also be *delivered* to (filed with) the Registrar of Companies in Cardiff.

Both these presentations must be within 10 months (for private companies) or seven months (for other companies), of the accounting reference date (= company year end).

The accounts must give a *true and fair view* and comply with the accounting requirements of the Companies Act. What is true and fair is a difficult subject. Essentially the content must be true (e.g. the cash on hand shown in the balance sheet must be right) and fair (e.g. the depreciation policy must be appropriate to the circumstances and the stock valuation method must be within the acceptable list in SSAP 9 and appropriate to the circumstances).

(e) The financial statements must be audited by an independent approved auditor. For more information on auditing, see Auditing, also by your author and published by DP Publications.

(f) Every company must have an Annual General Meeting of its members.

(g) Every company must file an Annual Return with the Registrar of Companies in Cardiff. The Annual Return contains details of directors, members, secretary, registered office etc and includes a copy of the annual accounts. The company's file including the annual returns can be inspected by members of the public.

3. **Different types of company**

   (a) **Public companies**

   A public company is one which:

   (i) States in its memorandum that it is a public company.

   (ii) Ends its name with 'public limited company' or PLC.

   (iii) Has a minimum share capital of £50,000.

   (b) **Private companies**

   A private company is any company which is not a public company. Private companies end their names with the word 'limited'.

   The differences between the two types of company are numerous. As examples:

   (i) Public companies must have at least two directors and private companies need only have one but in that case must have a different person as secretary.

   (ii) A private company cannot offer its shares or debentures to the public and thus cannot obtain a stock exchange listing.

   (c) **Small, medium and large**

   To be small or medium sized, a company must satisfy *two or more* of the following criteria:

	Small	Medium sized
Turnover not exceeding	£2.8m	£11.2m
Balance sheet total not exceeding	£1.4m	£5.6m
Average number of employees does not exceed	50 or less	250 or less

Note: m = £1million

Small and medium sized companies are permitted to file modified accounts, giving less information, with the Registrar of Companies and a number of other Companies Act regulations are relaxed including the requirement to hold AGMs.

(d) **Unlimited companies**

These are relatively rare private companies where the liability of the members is unlimited.

(e) **Companies limited by guarantee**

Most companies have a share capital. A company may instead have the liability of its members limited by the Memorandum to such amounts as the members may guarantee to contribute to the assets of the company in the event of its being wound up. Guarantee companies are usually trade associations, professional associations or clubs or societies.

(f) **Quoted (also called listed) companies**

These are public companies whose shares are traded on the stock exchange. As shares are bought and sold on the stock exchange, the shareholders change and thus the ownership of the company is continually changing.

Share issues

4. A company is owned by its shareholders. A shareholder becomes a shareholder by buying shares in the company. A person can buy a share in a company in two ways:

(a) He can buy it from an existing shareholder. In this case the only recording the company has to do is to record the new shareholder in the *register of members*.

(b) He can buy it from the company. This does require some bookkeeping by the company. Suppose the company decides to sell 1,000 shares with a nominal value of £1 each for £1.45 each. The sale is advertised and applications are invited. The amount payable is in three instalments; £0.50 on application on March 18 19x8, £0.50 on allotment (including the premium) on 31 March 19x8 and £0.45 one year later. Applications are received for 1,500 shares on 19 March and each applicant is allotted 2/3 of the number applied for. The amount paid on the shares not allotted is held against the sum due on allotment. The remaining payments are received on the day after the due date. The entries are:

Share capital

18 March x8	A and A a/c	500
31 March x8	A and A a/c	50
31 March x9	1st Call	450
		1000

Share premium

31 March x8	A and A a/c	450

Application and Allotment Account

18 March x8	Share capital	500	19 March x8	Cash	750
31 March x8	Share capital	50	1 April x8	Cash	250
31 March x8	Share premium	450			
		1000			1000

First Call Account

31 March x9	Share capital	450	1 April x9	Cash	450

Cash book

19 March x8	Application	750
1 April x8	Allotment	250
1 April x9	Call	450
		1450

Notes:

(a) We begin by opening an account called the *application and allotment account*. The first sum expected is £500 (1,000 x £0.50) and we credit this to share capital and debit it to applications and allotment account. This account is in effect a debtor account and shows a sum due to the company.

(b) Applications are received from persons wishing to become shareholders. More shares were applied for than were available but in any case the cheques are cashed and the sum of £750 (1,500 x £0.50) is debited in the cash book and credited in the applications and allotment account. In this case the surplus is held by the company because more is required on allotment. Suppose Alan applied for 30 shares. He would send a cheque for £15. As he gets only 20 shares he need have paid only £10 and the extra £5 is held by the company because he owes £10 (20 x £0.50) on allotment. Allotment simply means assigning or granting him the shares. If he had been given no shares (this might happen as some companies might draw lots to decide who gets the shares!) then the sum paid would be returned to him.

(c) The sum due on allotment is 1,000 x £0.50 and this is debited to the applications and allotment account and credited to share capital and share premium. Note that the total sum due on each share is £1.45 but the nominal value of the share is only £1 so that the extra 45p is called a share premium.

(d) The sum due on allotment is paid and this is £250. It would of course be 1,000 x £0.50 = £500 but part has been paid from the surplus paid on application.

(e) At this point nothing happens for a year. We have £1,000 in the bank and share capital of 1,000 x £0.55 = £550. This is described as 1,000 ordinary shares of £1 each 55p paid. This is *called the called up share capital* and the shares are partly paid.

(f) A year later the rest of the money is due and a new account called the *first call account* is opened. It is debited with the sum due (1,000 x £0.45 = £450) and share capital is credited.

(g) The cash is received and the cash book debited and the first call account credited. The latter account is then closed.

(h) The share capital now stands at £1,000 and is known as 1,000 ordinary shares of £1 each fully paid.

(i) If a shareholder fails to pay the sum due on the call, his shares will be *forfeited* and will be sold to someone else. He then loses the sum he has already paid.

Financial statements of companies for internal use

5. Almost every company has to prepare a profit and loss account every year. The only exceptions are non-trading companies (such as charities and clubs) which prepare an income and expenditure account and dormant companies (companies which do not trade because they have ceased to do so or have never started).

6. The first stage is to produce a detailed profit and loss account for internal purposes. This may take the form of a manufacturing, trading and profit and loss account or a trading and profit and loss account. These are very much like the income statements of sole traders and partnerships but do exhibit special features which I will discuss. Some exam syllabuses only require company profit and loss accounts for internal purposes.

The next stage is to shorten the internal profit and loss account to accord with the Companies Act requirements for laying accounts before the shareholders and filing them with the Registrar of Companies. We will see how to do this in the next chapter.

Profit and loss account for internal use

7. We will use an example. Here are the balances in the books of Belswardine Ltd, which operates a bookshop from owned premises as at 31 December 19x7:

Purchases	470,600	Sales	602,000
Wages	23,700	Trade creditors	67,200
Rates etc	21,542	Share capital (20p shares)	20,000
Other overheads	19,490	Profit & loss account 31.12.x6	10,110
Debenture interest	1,400	10% debentures	28,000
Bank interest	1,398	Bank overdraft	13,200
Fixtures etc at cost	16,600	Depreciation fixtures to 31.12.x6	7,100
Premises at cost	150,600	Depreciation premises to 31.12.x6	18,120
Stock 31 December 19x6	32,000		
Stock 31 December 19x7	33,200		
Debtors	2,700		
Directors' remuneration	23,700		
Interim dividend	2,000		

Notes:

(a) The second half year's debenture interest is due.

(b) Corporation tax is estimated to be payable on the 19x7 profits at £8,050.

(c) A final dividend is to be recommended of 4p a share (ignore ACT).

(d) Depreciation policy on the fixtures etc is 30% reducing balance.

(e) Depreciation policy on the premises is: on the land – nil, on the buildings (cost £90,600) over 30 years straight line with nil salvage value.

8. The financial statements for internal use may appear like this:

Trading and Profit and Loss Account

Sales		602,000
Less Cost of goods sold:		
Opening stock	32,000	
Purchases	470,600	
	502,600	
Closing stock	33,200	469,400
Gross profit		132,600
Wages	23,700	
Rates etc	21,542	
Other overheads	19,490	
Depreciation fixtures	2,850	
Depreciation buildings	3,020	
Directors' remuneration	23,700	94,302
Net profit before interest		38,298
Interest		4,198
Net profit before tax		34,100
Taxation		8,050
Net profit after taxation		26,050
Dividends		6,000
Retained profit		20,050

Balance Sheet

Fixed assets		136,110
Current assets:		
Stock	33,200	
Debtors	2,700	
	35,900	
Current liabilities:		
Creditors	67,200	
Accrual	1,400	
Overdraft	13,200	
Taxation	8,050	
Dividend	4,000	
	93,850	
Net current liabilities		57,950
Total assets less		
Current liabilities		78,160
Debentures		28,000
Net assets		50,160
Capital and reserves		
Share capital		20,000
Profit and loss account		30,160
		50,160

9. Much of these financial statements will be familiar to you – the trading account, the expenses, depreciation, fixed assets, current assets and liabilities and, perhaps others. However some of the words will be new. We will try and explain them:

(a) **Directors' remuneration**

Directors are regarded as *employees* of the company and as such their remuneration is an *expense* in the same way as any wages and salaries are expenses. This applies even if the shareholders and directors are the same people. Directors' remuneration may be in the form of salary, bonus, fees, commission, pension contributions, compensation for loss of office and there are other possible terms. It is sometimes called directors' emoluments.

(b) **Debentures and debenture interest**

Companies can borrow money. When they do, they often issue a piece of paper called a debenture. This is simply a written acknowledgement of the loan. The loan itself is often called a debenture although, strictly speaking, the debenture is the piece of paper.

Loans can also be called loans, debentures, notes, bonds (in the USA) or other terms. They can be:

(i) Unsecured ('naked debentures'). This means that debenture holders have the same rights in a liquidation as any unpaid supplier of goods or services. Liquidation means that the company is wound up or terminated, the assets sold and the proceeds of sale are distributed among the creditors and shareholders in a strict order. Liquidation and receivership is a very specialised subject.

(ii) *Secured* by a *fixed charge* on a *specific asset*. These loans are often called *mortgage* debentures.

Example:

A Ltd wishes to buy a property for £100,000. The company can find £20,000 and to obtain the balance, it borrows £80,000 from the Ineffective Assurance Co PLC, giving the assurance company a fixed charge (or mortgage) on the property.

The effect of the charge is:

The deeds of the property will be deposited with the assurance company.

–   This means that the property cannot be resold by A Ltd, without first paying off the loan.

–   If A Ltd fails to pay the interest on the loan or due instalments of the capital, then the assurance company can seize the property (technically it appoints a *receiver* to act for it), sells it and uses the proceeds of sale to repay the loan due to it. Any surplus is returnable to the company where it can be used for the benefit of other (unsecured) creditors.

–   Thus, as long as the value of the security (the property) exceeds the loan, a lender with a fixed charge cannot lose. A fixed charge can be taken over any asset, but in practice fixed charges are taken only over interests in land, ships and aircraft. This is, of course, the same idea as mortgages given on domestic property.

(iii) *Secured* by a *floating charge* over the *assets generally*.

Example:

B Ltd borrows £20,000 from the Muddy Bank PLC who evidenced the loan with a debenture giving a floating charge on the assets. This means that if B Ltd defaults on the interest or capital payments then the bank can seize (or appoint a receiver to do this for it), all the assets of the company, sell the assets and use the proceeds to repay the loan. Any surplus goes to the company for the benefit of unsecured creditors. Thus, as long as the company has assets with a value greater than the loan, the bank cannot lose. However, unlike the holder of a fixed charge who can prevent the company disposing of the subject (property) of the fixed charge, the holder of a floating charge can only hope that the assets he seizes will be sufficient. The floating charge is said to crystallise on the occurrence of an event (default on payment etc) foreseen in the debenture deed.

Note that Belswardine Ltd has given a fixed charge to the debenture holders and a floating charge to the bank to secure the overdraft. Any trade creditor of the company may wonder if Belswardine will be able to pay the sum due. He or she may look at the balance sheet like this:

- What will the assets fetch if they are all turned into cash?
- The debenture holders and the bank will have to be paid off first together with some of the other creditors who, in law, are preferential (these include unpaid wages, VAT and PAYE).
- Will there be anything left for me?

In liquidation the shareholders are last in the queue but receive all that is left.

(c) **Corporation tax**

Companies are required to pay a tax called *corporation tax* on their profits. The computation of the tax payable is complicated and outside the scope of this manual. In questions, the amount of corporation tax payable on the profit of the year is normally given, as it is here. Note that the corporation tax is not regarded as an expense, but as an *appropriation* of profit. Thus the net profit is calculated first, the corporation tax follows and the difference is shown as the net profit *after* tax. Corporation tax is normally paid nine months after the year end. At the year end it is shown as a current liability, as here.

(d) **Dividends**

The owners of companies (the shareholders) do not have drawings. They receive dividends.

The mechanics of dividend payments are:

(i) The directors decide whether a dividend should be paid and the amount. The decision is based on whether the company has made a profit, the amount of previous dividends and other criteria.

(ii) In the case of *interim* dividends (those paid before the end of the year), the directors *declare* that a dividend should be paid and it is then paid.

(iii) In the case of final dividends, the directors *recommend* a dividend and the recommended dividend is *approved* by the members at the AGM. Dividends are also *appropriations* of profit and appear in the Profit and Loss Account after the Net Profit after Tax. The final dividend is paid after the year end, and at the year end, appears in the current liabilities, as here.

(iv) In modern practice, a dividend is always x pence a share. So that if a dividend is 2.5p a share and if a shareholder has 100 shares, he will receive £2.50.

(e) It is modern practice to show several lines and figures as the profit. This follows the requirements of the Companies Act, of which more in the next chapter. You will see that there is a profit before interest, a profit before tax, a profit after tax and a retained profit. So which is The Profit? The answer is that it is always essential to specify the profit before interest or before tax etc. The famous bottom line is somewhat elusive!

(f) **Fixed assets**

These are much the same as in any balance sheet. The Companies Act requires that cost, accumulated depreciation, and net book value should all be shown. These are not shown on the face of the balance sheet but in a note attached to and forming part of the balance sheet. The note might appear as:

Fixed assets:	Cost	Accumulated depreciation	Net book value
Land	60,000	–	60,000
Buildings	90,600	21,140	69,460
Fixtures	16,600	9,950	6,650
	167,200	31,090	136,110

In practice, figures would also appear of additions and disposals in the year and of the corresponding figures for the previous year.

(g) **Current assets**

These are as in any balance sheet.

(h) **Current liabilities**

These are styled in the Companies Act as 'Creditors: amount falling due within one year'. They include the items found in any balance sheet plus the final dividend and corporation tax. We have already discussed these items.

(i) There are two lines which we do not always include in non-company balance sheets. Net current liabilities (or more frequently net current assets) and total assets less current liabilities. The Companies Act requires them. I think they are self-explanatory.

(j) **Long-term liabilities**

These are styled in the Companies Act 'Creditors: amounts falling due after more than one year'. You will find loans in this section, as here.

(k) **Capital and reserves**

So far, the company balance sheet should have presented you with few problems. The next section – Capital and Reserves – is more difficult. We will take it bit by bit.

(g) **Ordinary share capital**

When a company is formed by its *promoters*, it has no assets or liabilities. On its incorporation, the *memorandum* allows or *authorises* the company to *issue* any number of *shares* in the company up to the maximum stated in the memorandum. Issue means giving the new shareholders shares in the company in exchange for valuable consideration. The consideration can be in the form of cash or other assets, for example, a business.

Suppose Belswardine Limited was formed on 1 June 19x0 and issued 100,000 ordinary shares of 20p each, for cash, then its balance sheet would show:

Assets:	£
Cash	20,000

Liabilities:	
Ordinary share capital	20,000

When it starts to trade, the cash will be changed into fixed assets, stock etc but the ordinary share capital will remain as 100,000 ordinary shares of 20p each – £20,000 in successive balance sheets unless more shares are issued.

What does it mean?

(i) The company is divided into 100,000 shares or parts. Any particular share-holder can own one or more shares. In effect the owner of one share owns 1/100,000th of the company.

(ii) The company owes the shareholders collectively £20,000 because that was the amount they originally subscribed for the shares. This is thus a liability of the company to the shareholder. It is however a rather peculiar liability in that the company are not allowed (except in special circumstances) by company law to pay the liability. This is part of the doctrine of capital main-tenance which, in order to protect creditors, prevents companies from repaying capital.

(iii) The company has been financed by the shareholders giving the company £20,000 in exchange for shares. Note that the '20p' records the amounts paid on the share in the past, it does not indicate the value of the share. The value depends on the balance of supply and demand for the share. The 20p is known as the nominal value or par value. It need not be 20p but can be any value – 10p, 25p, £1 or any amount.

(m) **Reserves**

This word has caused more misunderstandings than any other in accounting. Abandon *all* of your present understandings of the word (perhaps you think of something being held back for future use or for emergency use). In accounting the words means: 'the amount by which assets exceed specific liabilities'.

Reserves are *not* assets but are *represented* by assets – some part of the fixed and current assets.

Remember that Belswardine started with net assets of £20,000 cash. Our balance sheet shows that it now has net assets of £50,160. How did the extra £30,160 of net assets get there. The answer is that Belswardine has traded prof-itably since its formation and has made retained profits of £10,110 up to 31 December 19x6 and an additional retained profit of £20,150 in 19x7. Thus:

– the profit and loss account figure on the balance sheet shows the accumu-lated retained profits since the start of the company. Retained profits are the profits after tax and dividends. In our case, the reserves are simply the profit and loss account balance or retained profits. There can be others as we will see.

(n) You will see that each share has a nominal value of 20p. The total share capital is £20,000, so there are 100,000 shares in issue. The net assets have a book value (actual value is unknown) of £50,160 and that indicates that the asset value of each share is £50,160/100,000 = approximately 50p. Clearly the value of the share will be nearer 50p than 20p but valuation of shares is a difficult area. The interim dividend cost the company £2,000. This means the dividend was £2,000/100,000 = 2p a share. The final dividend is 4p a share.

Share premium

10. A share with a *nominal* value of £1 will normally be sold *by the company* at that price on the formation of the company and will remain on the balance sheet as a liability of the company of £1. If the company is successful, then the *market* value of the share may be much higher. You should realise that the market value is the *real* value of the share and the *nominal* value is fundamentally of historical interest only and yet it is the nominal value which appears in the balance sheet.

If a successful company later wishes to issue more shares, it will be able to sell its £1 shares at a price in excess of £1. The excess is called the *share premium*. Thus if Belswardine Ltd's shares had a market value of 60p each, the company could sell *new* shares at that price. If 10,000 were so sold, the changes to the balance sheet would appear as:

	£
Assets – Cash (10,000 × 60p)	6,000
Share capital	2,000
Share premium	4,000
	6,000

Notes:

(a) The buyers of the new shares have bought something worth 60p. It is right that they should pay more for their shares than the original shareholders.

(b) The extra over the nominal value of the share is called the share premium, here it is 40p a share. 'Share premium' is a liability of the company to *all* its ordinary shareholders.

(c) Like share capital, share premium is a liability which cannot be paid because of the doctrine of capital maintenance.

(d) The capital and reserves will now be:

Share capital (110,000 shares of 20p each)	22,000
Share premium	4,000
Profit and loss account	30,160
	56,160

Net assets are now £56,160 as the assets now include £6,000 from the sale of the shares. Specifically the overdraft will now be £7,200.

Rights issues

11. In practice companies do not sell shares to third parties except in specific circumstances – see later. The shareholders own the company and to sell shares to non-shareholders (who then become shareholders) would change the ownership. To avoid this the Stock Exchange and Section 89 of the Companies Act require that new issues should be offered to all existing shareholders *pro rata* (= in proportion) to their existing holdings. Thus if a shareholder has 10% of the new shares she will be offered 10% of any new ones issued. In practice, PLCs call new issues *rights issues* and price the new shares somewhat below the market price. The right to buy at

under market price has value and if the shareholder does not want to take up her rights, she can sell them to somebody else. Exceptions to this rule include incentive shares offered to employees and directors, shares issued in exchange for consideration other than cash (e.g. a business or a whole company). The memorandum and articles of a private company are permitted to exclude the rights requirement.

The entries in the balance sheet and the books are as in the issue of shares at a premium. A company is not normally allowed to issue shares at a discount.

Bonus issues

12. It is possible for a company to increase its share capital by *giving* new shares to its existing shareholders. Suppose that A Ltd has an authorised share capital of 100,000 ordinary shares of £1 each and a balance sheet as:

	£
Ordinary share capital	60,000
Profit and loss account	123,000
	183,000
Net assets	183,000

The company makes a bonus issue of 30,000 new ordinary shares of £1 each. Each shareholder will be given one new share for every two held. This is called a one for two issue. George who has 24 shares will be given 12 new shares and finish up with 36 shares.

The effect on the balance sheet will be:

	£
Ordinary share capital	90,000
Profit and loss account	93,000
	183,000
Net assets	183,000

Notes:

(a) The share capital has increased from £60,000 to £90,000.

(b) The net assets remain unchanged. The shares have been *given* and the shareholders have paid no money to the company. Contrast a bonus issue with a rights issue where the shareholders pay for their new shares.

(c) Since the balance sheet must balance, the reserves must be reduced by the amount of the increase in the share capital. The effect on the ability of the company to pay dividends is that the legal maximum dividend is reduced from £123,000 to £93,000. £30,000 of the payable liability to shareholders (profit and loss account) has been changed to an unpayable liability to shareholders (Share Capital).

13. The reasons why a company make a bonus issue may include:

(a) To bring the intrinsic value of each share nearer to its nominal value. In this case the net assets per share were £3.05 and after the bonus issue they had become £2.03.

(b) To fix the net assets representing the profit and loss account in the company. In theory the company could have paid a dividend of £123,000. Now the company can only pay £93,000. This means that creditors are sure that the assets less liabilities of the company to which they can look for now has a larger irreducible minimum. New and potential lenders may be more inclined to lend if this happens.

(c) By tradition the announcement of a bonus issue is a 'bull' point. It means that the directors are signalling to investors that the company has good prospects and, perhaps, implying that the existing rate of dividend will be maintained on the enlarged capital.

Bonus issues are also called Capitalisation issues, Scrip issues and, in the United States, Stock (= share) dividends.

The effect on the market price

B PLC has a share capital of 50,000 shares of 25p each quoted at £2.10 each. A bonus issue of one for two is made, the total value of the company before the bonus issue was 50,000 × £2.10 = £105,000. After the bonus issue, the value of the company remains at £105,000 but as the company is now divided into 75,000 shares, each share will be worth, and hence the quotation will move to, £105,000/75,000 = £1.40. John who has 14 shares worth £2.10 each with a total value to his investment of £29.40 will, after the bonus issue have 21 shares worth £1.40 each worth in all £29.40. In practice the share price will probably change a little as an effect of the bonus issue but the actual change is unpredictable and difficult to untangle from ordinary movements of the share price.

Bonus issues effect very little change and yet they are common and shareholders receiving free shares are usually very pleased. Probably they do not understand the empty nature of the happening. Because of the negligible effect, bonus issues have been jokingly called bogus issues.

A bonus issue always involves an equivalent transfer from reserves to share capital. Any reserves whether capital (unpayable such as share premium) or revenue (payable such as profit and loss account) can be used for this purpose. See later for the meaning of transfer.

Preference shares

14. The ordinary shareholders are in effect the owners of the company. But some companies also issue preference shares. Preference shareholders are technically part-owners of the company but their interest in the company is more like that of lenders than owners.

Preference shareholders are entitled to a fixed rate of dividend which is specified in the memorandum. Suppose a company has 100,000 7% preference shares of £1 each. Then a dividend at the rate of 7% will be paid. This means that the owner of a £1 preference share would receive a dividend of 7p a year and all the preference shareholders together would receive £7,000 which is 7% of £100,000.

Ordinary and preference shares compared

15.

	Ordinary Shares	Preference Shares
Risk	Will receive high dividends if the company does well or no dividend if the company loses money.	Dividend is at a fixed rate (but usually not payable if company makes a loss).
Right to vote at meetings	Yes	Usually not
Rights to dividend	As declared by the company. Rate will vary, inter alia, with profit.	A fixed rate of dividend which must be paid before any ordinary dividend can be paid.
Rights in a liquidation	Right to all that is left (if anything) after all other claims have been met.	Rights to return of capital subscribed after all claims except those of the ordinary shareholders have been met.

Notes:

(a) Some preference shares are participating, that is they have some claim on profits in addition to their fixed dividend.

(b) Preference shares are normally cumulative. That is if in a year no profit is made, and no dividends (preference or ordinary) are paid then before any ordinary dividend can be paid in future years the arrears of preference dividend must be made good.

(c) Some investors prefer the lower risks attached to preference shares and are content with the more limited prospect of rewards. Thus a company may issue preference shares to obtain access to funds available from such investors.

Redeemable shares

16. A company can issue *redeemable* shares. These can be preference or equity (ordinary) shares. The capital maintenance concept means that share capital is a non-payable liability and redeemable means that share capital will be paid back to the shareholders. In practice the capital maintenance concept is not infringed as we will see. The legislation is in the Companies Act 1985 and there are some restrictions:

(a) Authorisation must be given in the articles.

(b) There must always be some non-redeemable share capital (or the company could have no share capital).

(c) Only fully paid up shares can be redeemed.

(d) Payment must be made at the same time as the redemption. Thus redemption cannot take place without simultaneous payment.

(e) Redeemable shares may only be redeemed out of distributable profits or out of the proceeds of a fresh issue of shares made for the purposes of redemption.

(f) Any premium on redemption must be paid out of distributable profits.

(g) Where the redeemable shares were issued at a premium, any premium payable on redemption may be paid out of the proceeds of a fresh issue up to the lesser of:

(i) Premiums received on the issue of the shares redeemed.

(ii) The current balance on share premium account.

17. Thus, the assets representing the original capital subscribed by the redeemable shareholders cannot be paid back to them, but:

(a) The capital can be replaced by a new issue of shares.

or

(b) The assets representing profits can be paid to the redeemable shareholders.

Where profits are so used, the portion of the reserve 'profit and loss account' (a payable liability) used must be renamed 'capital redemption reserve' (a non-payable liability).

Balance sheet entries on redemption of share capital

18. The capital and reserves of Thin Ltd is:

	£
500 ordinary shares of £1 each	500
1,000 redeemable preference shares of £1 each fully paid	1,000
Share premium account	100
Profit and loss account	3,800
	5,400

On 1 January 19x5, the redeemable shares were redeemed at par out of:

(a) A new issue of 200 ordinary shares of £1 each at £1 each.

(b) Profits.

The entries are:

(a) New issue: Cash – add: £200. So net assets increase by £200. Capital and reserves increase by £200 also and they do so as ordinary shares increase by £200.

(b) Redemption: Cash – pay out £1,000. So net assets go down by £1,000. The preference shares have gone so they disappear and capital and reserves go down by £1,000.

(c) The transfer to capital redemption reserve. This is simply saying profit and loss account goes down by £800 (debit profit and loss account) and the capital redemption reserve goes up (credit capital redemption reserve).

The balance sheet capital and reserves will now be:

	£
Ordinary share capital	700
Share premium	100
Capital redemption reserve	800
Profit and loss account	3,000
	4,600

Check that the new issue and the redemption mean that the net assets are also £4,600.

This transaction may seem odd to you. For now, just learn the entries, understanding may come in due course!

Fixed asset revaluation reserve

19. Suppose the book value of a property on the balance sheet of A PLC is at Cost less accumulated depreciation £480,000. The property is valued at £700,000 by a chartered surveyor and the Board decided to change the book value to £700,000. The entries are:

  Net assets – increase by £220,000.

  Capital and reserves – increase by £220,000 by including a new figure 'Fixed assets revaluation reserve £220,000'.

Transfers to reserves

20. You will have noticed that, in certain circumstances, reserves can be renamed. The Board might look at the capital and reserves section which has figures thus:

Share capital	20,000
Share premium	10,000
Profit and loss account	140,000
	170,000

By now you will realise that the net assets are also £170,000 but net assets means assets less liabilities. Perhaps the company has lots of assets like stock, premises, debtors, plant but no cash. And perhaps the liabilities include a large bank overdraft.

Some shareholders, lacking understanding of balance sheets, might see the balance on the profit and loss account and ask for a large dividend. To avoid this the Board might decide to rename the profit and loss account (or part of it) as 'general reserve' thus changing capital and reserves to:

Share capital	20,000
Share premium	10,000
Profit and loss account	35,000
General reserve	105,000
	170,000

This has no effect on *anything*. This meaningless practice has virtually died out in the real world.

Summary

❐ Companies provide a mode of ownership of a business whereby a company owns the assets, owes the liabilities and is in turn owned by its shareholders.

❐ The characteristics of a company include:
  (i) Legal personality.
  (ii) Perpetual succession.

(iii) Limited liability on the part of its shareholders.

❒ Companies are regulated by the Companies Act 1985 as modified by the Companies Act 1989.

❒ The Registrar of Companies in Cardiff maintains a file on every company. Each file contains information about the company including the accounts and is available to the public.

❒ Every company has a Memorandum and Articles of Association, members, directors and a secretary.

❒ The Companies Act requires companies to maintain or prepare:
  (i) Proper accounting records – receipts and payments, assets and liabilities, stock-takings, suppliers' and customers' ledgers.
  (ii) Statutory books.
  (iii) Annual accounts consisting of:
    – A profit and loss account (or income and expenditure account).
    – A balance sheet.
    – Notes attached to and forming part of these two documents.
    – A directors' report.
    – The auditors' report.
    – An annual return.

❒ There are public companies, private companies, quoted (= listed) companies, small, medium and large companies, unlimited companies, and companies limited by guarantee.

❒ Companies are required to prepare financial statements as required by the Companies Act. The first stage is to prepare financial statements for internal use.

❒ A company balance sheet is much like any balance sheet but contains a number of words which require explanation. These include: corporation tax, dividend, share capital, reserves, debentures, charges securing debentures, fixed charges, floating charges.

❒ A company profit and loss account is also much like that of any business but contains some words needing explanation. These include: directors' emoluments, debenture interest, corporation tax, dividends both interim and final, retained profit.

❒ Shares can be issued at a premium. The share premium appears in the capital and reserves.

❒ Companies can make rights issues. These are simply issues of new shares but have to be offered to all existing shareholders pro rata to their holdings. Rights usually have value and the shareholder can subscribe for the shares or sell the rights to some other person.

❒ Companies also make bonus issues which are free issues of shares to the shareholders pro rata to their holdings.

❏ Preference shares can also be issued. They usually have a fixed rate of dividend which is cumulative.

❏ Preference shares are usually redeemable. To the extent that the redemption is not out of a new issue of shares made for that purpose, there must be a transfer to capital redemption reserve.

❏ Companies sometimes revalue upwards the carrying value of properties. This requires the creation of a reserve called the fixed assets revaluation reserve.

❏ Some companies rename profit and loss account or part of it as general reserve or some other name such as reserve for asset replacement or reserve for old stocks. Such renamings or transfers are devoid of meaning.

Points to note

❏ Companies range in size from the very small, the corner shops, to the very large, the multi national companies. Many small companies are owned by a man who has 99 shares and is the sole director, and his wife with one share. In such cases ownership and management are in the same hands. In public companies there are typically many thousands of shareholders with a board of directors who themselves own a negligible number of shares.

❏ There are many times as many private companies on the register as there are public companies. However, many of the private companies are subsidiaries of (they are owned by) public companies.

❏ The Companies Act regulates the formation, conduct, and liquidation of companies with two principal objectives:

   (i) To protect creditors of the companies.

   (ii) To protect investors.

❏ The requirement to file information and accounts at Companies House has led to the saying 'public disclosure is the price paid for limited liability'.

❏ The government of public companies is currently a subject of some discussion. A recent report (known as the Cadbury report) has suggested a number of guidelines, which many companies have now adopted. Another contentious issue is that the reality of public companies is that new directors are elected by the Board rather than the members. Directors then tend to pay themselves inflated salaries and have contracts which, when they are forced out because of incompetence or failure, oblige the company to pay them indecent sums in compensation.

❏ The Greenbury committee has recently reported on the relationship of directors to their companies and on disclosure of remuneration and other matters. Companies should now abide by two codes of conduct - the Cadbury code and the Greenbury code.

❏ Loans can be issued at a discount (e.g. £100 of debenture can be sold for say £95) or at a premium (e.g. £100 can be sold for say £105). The repayment will still be £100 (although the repayment might also be at a premium or a discount).

❑ Debentures can be sold (i.e. money borrowed) to a single lender or many lenders.

❑ Debentures are contracts which contain clauses on repayment, interest, charges etc.

❑ Capital and reserves includes share capital, capital reserves and revenue reserves.

For example:	Ordinary shares of £1 each	30,000
	Preference shares	10,000
	Share premium	15,000
	Capital redemption reserve	25,000
	Fixed asset revaluation reserve	10,000
	Profit and loss account	56,000
		146,000

❑ The first five are non-payable and the profit and loss account is payable. What does this mean? Payment means payments to shareholders in the form of dividends. Essentially the maximum dividend that could be paid here is £56,000. If a bonus issue of one for one out of profit and loss account was made then the ordinary share capital would become £60,000. The profit and loss account would be reduced to £26,000 and the maximum dividend would be reduced also to £26,000. Why do this if the company has no intention of paying any such dividend? Although the company has no such intention (and probably no liquid resources), the potential is still there. Bankers and creditors would rather see the potential removed and this is often done.

❑ Dividends are traditionally paid by cheque (or these days by transfers through the banking systems). However most companies are reluctant to pay out money so they offer shareholders the option of new shares instead. A proportion of the shareholders take up this offer.

❑ Revaluing fixed assets makes the balance sheet more realistic as some of the values on the balance sheet become nearer market values. However the effect on profit is often not appreciated. SSAP 12 – depreciation – requires that depreciation should be based on book values. Thus if the book value is increased then so is depreciation. The effect of revaluing fixed assets is to decrease profits!

Self-testing questions

1. List and explain three characteristics of limited companies.
2. Give another name for shareholders.
3. What act of parliament regulates companies?
4. Who elect the directors of a company?
5. What are the documents called that regulate a particular company?
6. What clauses appear in the memorandum of a company?
7. What accounting records must a company keep?
8. What are the time restrictions on the laying and delivery of accounts?
9. What financial statements must be prepared by companies annually?
10. What is meant by laying and delivering?
11. Distinguish public, private and quoted companies.

12. State the criteria for defining small and medium sized companies.
13. Which companies are required to prepare annual financial statements?
14. Explain:

Directors' emoluments	Debentures	Secured loans	Floating charges
Fixed charges	Liquidation	Receivership	Corporation tax
Dividends	Final	Interim	Appropriation
Bottom line	Share capital	Reserves	Retained profits
Par and nominal value	Market value		

15. Distinguish the nominal price of a share, its issue price and its market value.
16. What is the effect on a balance sheet of the sale of shares at a premium?
17. What is a rights issue? Why does the law require new issues to be rights issues? Why are some issues exempt from this requirement?
18. What are the effects of a bonus issue on a balance sheet? What practical effects does a bonus issue have?
19. Why do companies make bonus issues?
20. What might be the effect on share price of a bonus issue?
21. Contrast preference shares with ordinary shares.
22. What are the rules on redemption of redeemable shares?
23. Give the balance sheet entries on redemption of preference shares.
24. Give the balance sheet entries on the revaluation of fixed assets.
25. Explain the effect on the bank balance of a transfer to general reserve.

Exercises

1. Explain the following terms:

Companies Act	Company	Delivered to
Act of Parliament	Legal personality	Protection of creditors
Limited liability	Members	Perpetual succession
Memorandum	Articles	Shareholders
Audit	Income & expenditure	Director
Registrar of Companies	Domicile	AGM
Public company	Authorised capital	Objects clause
Limited	Private company	Table A
Unlimited	Listing	PLC
Accounting records	Guarantee	Quoted
Register of Members	True and fair	Statutory books
Minute book	Secretary	Small & medium
Laid before	Annual Return	Annual accounts

2. Why should A and B who are in partnership as importers of toy guns wish to incorporate their business into a company? Note that their mode of business is to buy the goods for cash (using an overdraft) as they are landed in the UK, hold them in stock until sold and then sell on credit to retailers.
3. Discuss why limited companies are tightly regulated when partnerships are not.

4. Tulip Ltd is inviting applications for the issue of 20,000 ordinary shares of £1 each at £1.80, each payable on application (12 April 19x7) £0.50, on allotment (30 April 19x7) £1 including the premium, and the balance on 30 April 19x8. Applications for 40,000 shares were received and the applicants received half of their applications. Overpayments on application were retained by the company. The amounts due on allotment and call were received on time.

    Show all these items in double entry accounts and how the balances would appear in the balance sheets at 31 December 19x7 and 19x8.

5. Daff Ltd is inviting applications for the issue of 30,000 ordinary shares of £1 each at £2.80 each, payable on application (12 April 19x7) £1, on allotment (30 April 19x7) £0.80, being the premium and the balance on 30 April 19x8. Applications for 60,000 shares were received. Applicants for 15,000 shares were refused and the sums paid returned to them. The remainder of the applicants received 2/3 of their applications and their over-payment was retained by the company. The amounts due on allotment and call were received on time.

    Show all these items in double entry accounts and how the balances would appear in the balance sheets at 31 December 19x7 and 19x8.

6. Primrose Ltd is inviting applications for the issue of 100,000 ordinary shares of £1 each at £3 each, payable on application (12 April 19x7) £0.50, on allotment (30 April 19x7) £2, being the premium and the balance on 30 April 19x8. Applications for 120,000 shares were received and the applicants for 20,000 were refused and their money returned. The amounts due on allotment and call were received on time except for the sum due on the 100 shares owned by Tom, who had been made bankrupt. These were forfeited and sold to Dick for £4 each on 31 May 19x8

    Show all these items in double entry accounts and how the balances would appear in the balance sheets at 31 December 19x7 and 19x8. Note that the total amount paid on a share (including that paid by the original owner and the subsequent buyer for the company) over the nominal value goes to share premium.

7. Here are the balances in the books of Garmston Ltd, which operates a wholesale ware-house from rented premises, as at 31 December 19x7:

Purchases	880,000	Sales	1,240,000
Wages	82,000	Trade creditors	90,100
Rent, rates etc	51,000	Share capital (10p shares)	50,000
Other overheads	47,000	Profit & loss account 31.12.x6	1,580
Debenture interest	2,000	8% Debentures	50,000
Motor expenses	48,700	Bank overdraft	12,200
Fixtures, vehicles, etc at cost	60,100	Depreciation fixtures to 31.12.x6	35,320
Stock 31 December 19x6	80,300		
Stock 31 December 19x7	102,300		
Debtors	140,000		
Directors' remuneration	80,200		
Interim dividend	5,000		
Bank interest	2,900		

Notes:

(a) Six months' debenture interest is due.

(b) Corporation tax is estimated to be payable on the 19x7 profits at £9,200.

(c) A final dividend is to be recommended of 5p a share, (ignore ACT).

(d) Depreciation policy on the fixtures etc is 20% straight line with nil salvage value.

(e) A bonus is payable to the directors of 10% of the profit before interest.

Required:

(a) Prepare financial statements for internal use.

(b) A comment by the trade union representative on seeing the accounts is 'the capital and reserves amount to over £67,000 and capital £50,000, the company have reserves of £17,000. They can use the reserves to pay a large bonus to the staff'. Comment on this statement.

(c) The bank has a floating charge on all the assets. Comment on the rights of the ordinary creditors and the bank in a liquidation.

8. Here are the balances in the books of Shirlett Ltd, which operates an agricultural machinery business from rented premises, as at 31 December 19x7:

Purchases	780,000	Sales	1,196,000
Wages	102,000	Trade creditors	140,100
Rent, rates etc	71,000	Share capital (50p shares)	1,000
Other overheads	57,000	Profit & loss account 31.12.x6	99,950
Debenture interest	3,000	10% debentures	30,000
Motor expenses	48,700	Hire purchase commitments	6,320
Fixtures, vehicles, etc at cost	120,800	Depreciation fixtures to 31.12.x6	30,800
Bills receivable	6,400	Discounts receivable	6,230
Stock 31 December 19x6	130,000		
Stock 31 December 19x7	114,000		
Debtors	120,000		
Directors' remuneration	60,400		
Interim dividend	6,000		
HP interest	2,100		
Cash at bank	3,000		

Notes:

(a) The HP is over 24 instalments. Five months' instalments have been paid so far.

(b) Corporation tax is estimated to be payable on the 19x7 profits at £9,600.

(c) A final dividend is to be recommended of £7.50 a share (ignore ACT).

(d) Depreciation policy on the fixtures etc is 25% reducing balance.

(e) A bonus is payable to the staff of 10% of the profits.

(f) Motor expenses include licences of £6,000 for the year to 31 August 19x8.

(g) Of the debtors, £1,100 are considered bad and £3,100 of the remainder are very doubtful.

Required:

Prepare financial statements. Comment on the dividend and the staff bonus.

9.   Wallis PLC has a balance sheet as at 31.12.x7 as:

	£		£
Ordinary 20p (10p paid)	60,000	Net assets	240,000
Profit and loss account	180,000		
	240,000		240,000

The following transactions occurred:
(a) The company issued 80,000 50p preference shares at 90p each.
(b) The company issued 40,000 16% debentures at 105.
(c) The company called up the amount unpaid on its ordinary shares at par.
(d) The company redeemed 20,000 of its preference shares.
(e) The company revalued its property upwards by £30,000.

Required:
Prepare successive balance sheets to show the effect of these transactions.

10.   Jimboy Limited has a balance sheet as at 31.12.x7 as:

	£		£
Share capital		Net assets	31,600
Ordinary 10p	10,000		
10% preference £1	8,000		
Share premium	2,600		
Profit and loss account	11,000		
	31,600		31,600

The following transactions occurred:
(a) A rights issue of 1 for 4 was made at 24p a share on the ordinary share capital.
(b) A bonus issue of 1 for 5 was made on the enlarged ordinary share from profit and loss account.
(c) The company issued 6,000 14% debentures at 98.
(d) The company redeemed half the 10% preference shares at par out of:
    (i) A new issue of 2,000 8% preference shares at par.
    (ii) Profits.

Required:
Prepare successive balance sheets to show the effect of these transactions.

11.   Mouldy Breads Ltd had a balance sheet as at 31.12.x7 as:

	£'000		£'000
Ordinary shares (20p each)	240	Net assets other than cash	980
Preference shares (£1)	100		
Share premium	60		
Profit and loss	510		
Overdraft	70		
	980		980

The following occurred:

(a) A bonus issue of one ordinary share and one preference share for every six ordinary shares held was made.

(b) A rights issue of one new ordinary share at 60p for every seven ordinary shares held was made on the enlarged capital.

(c) The preference shares were redeemed at a premium of 5% partly out of the proceeds of the rights issue and partly out of the profits. An overdraft was obtained for the purpose.

(d) The costs of the various issues and redemptions was £20,000 and was paid by cheques.

Required:

Show this series of transactions by (a) successive balance sheets, or (b) journal entries or (c) double entry accounts. Prepare a balance sheet at the end.

12. The following are balances in the ledger of Gooee Soups Ltd at 31.12.x8:

	£	£
Land & buildings at cost	23,567	
Plant & vehicles at cost	45,800	
Provision for depreciation on land etc		6,580
Provision for depreciation on plant etc		17,540
Investments at cost	3,000	
Stocks	11,654	
Debtors and provision for doubtful debts	22,500	1,500
Cash in hand	1,200	
Bank balance		4,351
Trade creditors		14,300
Accruals and prepayments	2,400	3,100
Proposed dividends		5,200
Provision for corporation tax		3,600
Profit and loss a/c at 31.12.x7		9,400
Ord share capital in 20p shares		30,000
6% preference share capital in 20p shares		1,000
Retained profit for 19x8		1,550
Share premium		2,000
General reserve		10,000

An error occurred, in that the provision for doubtful debts should have been 5% of debtors.

Required:

Correct the error with a journal entry, then prepare a balance sheet in good form.

13. Using the data in question 12 only:

(a) Show journal entries for the following transactions:

(i) Purchase by cheque of a vehicle for £6,000 (note that the marketing director has requested that this comes out of the general reserve).

(ii) Issue of 5,000 ordinary shares at 35p each to rank pari passu (equal in all respects) with the existing shares.

(iii) Issue of £10,000 16% Debentures at par.

(iv) Revaluing the land and buildings at £33,000.

(b) Produce the revised balance sheet.

Assignment

❑ The trial balances of Periwinkle Limited at 31.12.x7 show:

(Note that all amounts including the notes are in £000).

	Dr	Cr
Share Capital Ordinaries £1		50
7% Preference shares of 20p		100
Share premium account		34
Profit and loss account		8
Land and buildings at cost	200	
Land and buildings depreciation		30
Plant at cost	204	
Plant depreciation		71
Stock 1.1.x7	90	
Debtors and creditors	120	180
Provision for doubtful debts		7
Purchases and sales	380	556
Discounts	12	14
Carriage in	18	
Wages	53	
Overheads	46	
Interim ordinary dividend	10	
General reserve		6
Bank balance	23	
10% Debentures 2010/2013		100
	1,156	1,156

Notes:

(a) Stock is valued at 125.

(b) Depreciation is at 2% on the buildings (150 at cost).

(c) Depreciation is 20% reducing balance on the plant.

(d) The doubtful debts provision is to be made equal to 5% of debtors.

(e) There is a wages accrual of 5.

(f) No interest has been paid on the debentures during the year.

(g) During the year a bonus issue of one for five was made to the ordinary shareholders. This has not been entered into the books.

(h) The proposed dividends are: preference 7% and ordinary 10p a share. The bonus shares do not rank for dividend until the following year.

(i) The company acquired the goodwill but no other assets of a similar business for 30. The consideration was 20,000 ordinary shares. These shares also do not rank for dividend. This transaction has not been entered in the books.

(j) Transfer 3 from general reserves back to profit and loss account.

Required:

(a) Prepare financial statements for internal use.

(b) Write a report to the Board on items d, g, h, i and j, explaining why the transactions were entered into and the effects on the financial statements.

26 Interpretation of accounts

This chapter attempts to show how accountants and other persons can read a set of financial statements and obtain useful information therefrom. It also contains warnings that this is a difficult area and it is very easy to draw entirely the wrong conclusions. It discusses who are the users of financial statements and how they might go about making sense of accounting information; introduces the traditional accounting ratio analysis of liquidity, reviews the performance ratios.

Performance analysis

1. Financial statements for a business are produced to provide information to people who have contact with the business. The information is of an historical nature and is in a summarised form (e.g. net book value of plant is £x, but not a list of items of plant), and is highly selective (e.g. net book value of plant is given but not its market or replacement values).

2. Despite these disadvantages, financial statements are frequently used:
   (a) As a guide to the future.
   (b) As a basis for action.

Users and their information needs

3. Financial statements of an enterprise are used by many categories of people who have contact with the business. This table shows the types of user and lists their particular needs.

Users

Owners who are also managers	(i)	Assessment of past performance.
	(ii)	Whether to cease business, continue as before, expand, etc.
	(iii)	As a basis for detailed future planning.
	(iv)	To show to potential buyers of the business.
Owners who are not managers e.g. shareholders in companies	(i)	To assess the performance of the management.
	(ii)	Whether to support or change the management.
	(iii)	Whether to remain as an owner, dispose of the investment or invest still more etc.
Management who are not also owners, e.g. company directors	(i)	To assess their own performance.
	(ii)	In the case of companies, to decide on what dividends to recommend.
	(iii)	As a basis for detailed future planning.
Inspectors of taxes	(i)	To assess the taxation which is due.
	(ii)	To determine if all income has apparently been included.

Banks and other lenders	(i)	To assess the management's performance to decide whether lending should be abandoned, reduced, continued or increased.
	(ii)	To determine the terms and conditions of any lending (e.g. if security should be offered, if guarantees should be sought from owners, repayment times etc).
Potential buyers of the business	(i)	Whether the business should be bought or not.
	(ii)	The price it is reasonable to pay.
	(iii)	What detailed actions will need to be taken if the business is bought (e.g. changing premises, buying new plant, paying off workers etc).
Actual and potential suppliers	(i)	How long the business takes to pay its suppliers.
	(ii)	Whether it is likely to stay in business long enough to pay.
	(iii)	What credit limit is reasonable.
Actual and potential customers	(i)	An appreciation of the size of order to be placed compared with the whole turnover of the business.
	(ii)	Appraisal of the long and short term ability of the business to fulfil orders placed.
Employees and potential employees and trade unions	(i)	Ability of the business to pay higher wages and salaries.
	(ii)	Ability of the business to survive in the long term.

4. Each category of user has his own particular information needs. Some of these information needs can be met from financial statements. Many needs cannot be so met.

The information that users attempt to gain from financial statements is under general headings:

(a) **Liquidity** – the ability of the business to pay its way and survive in the long run.

(b) **Performance** – the quality of management and the rightness of decisions made.

(c) A guide to the **future**.

Analysis of financial statements

5. Investigation, analysis and appraisal of the figures in a set of accounts is carried out by:

    (a) Examining each figure and comparing it with:

        (i)   The corresponding figure in previous accounts.

        (ii) The figure which was forecast or budgeted.

        (iii) The same figure in other similar businesses.

    (b) Computing ratios (e.g. gross profit to sales percentage) and comparing them with:

        (i)   The corresponding ratio in previous accounts.

        (ii) The ratios of forecast or budgeted accounts.

        (iii) The ratios found in the accounts of other businesses.

Why use ratios?

6.   Suppose we compare the accounts of two hairdressing businesses. We can do this line by line and the first line of the profit and loss account will be turnover or sales (both for 19x7):

Business A	Business B
Sales 80,000	160,000

What can we deduce from this? Only that business B is twice as big or does twice as much business as business A. Let us add a second line and two years for both.

	Business A		Business B	
	19x6	19x7	19x6	19x7
Sales	64,000	80,000	155,000	160,000
Wages	36,000	43,000	94,000	95,000

Just looking at the numbers does not easily tell us anything. Let us try a few ratios (the relationships between numbers) and see what happens.

Ratio	Business A	Business B	How to calculate
Growth in sales	25%	3.2%	(19x7-19x6)/19x7 $\times$ 100
Wages to Sales 19x6	56.25%	60.64%	Wages/Sales $\times$ 100
Wages to Sales 19x7	53.75%	59.37%	

So how have ratios helped? The management of business B can now see that they have very sluggish growth compared with business A. Perhaps they could study business A to see how they did it. Business A has lower wages to sales ratios especially in 19x7. The management of business B might wonder why. Perhaps business A staff are paid less or business A's prices are higher or business A's staff have less idle time. Ratios do not tell us why things are as they are but they do make us aware of differences between businesses or years or from budget to actual. Once we are aware of a difference we can look for reasons.

An example of accounts appraisal

6.   Pete owns a chain of hardware shops in suburban shopping centres. Each shop is managed by a manager who makes his own decisions on buying, pricing, employment of staff etc. Some buying is done jointly to obtain the advantages of bulk discounts.

Each year, a trading and profit and loss account and balance sheet is produced for each shop and Pete studies these carefully to make assessments of:

(a) The performance of the managers.

(b) Whether to maintain the shop as it is, expand it or close it.

The trading account of the shop in Smalltown showed:

	19x3		**19x4**	
	£000		**£000**	
Sales		110		95
Less Cost of goods sold:				
Opening stock	18		21	
Purchases	72		75	
	90		96	
Closing stock	21	69	30	66
Gross profit		41		29

Pete notices that:

(a) Sales in money terms have reduced from £110,000 to £95,000, a reduction of 13.6%, which is even greater in *real* terms.

(b) The gross profit to sales ratio has reduced from $\frac{41}{100} \times 100 = 37.3\%$ in 19x3 to 30.5% in 19x4.

(c) Stock as a proportion of cost of sales is $\frac{21}{69} \times 100 = 30.4\%$ at the end of 19x3 and 45.5% at the end of 19x4.

At first sight, the manager's performance is very poor – sales have declined, the profit element of each sale is smaller and stocks have increased. Pete feels inclined to:

(a) Dismiss the manager; and/or

(b) Close the shop.

However, Pete asks the manager for an explanation of the results and discovers:

(a) During 19x4, a cut price competitor opened nearby and therefore, sales were lost to this competitor.

(b) Prices had to be reduced to meet the competition.

(c) An extensive housing area near the shop has been demolished under an urban renewal scheme.

The manager maintained that he had done well in the circumstances. He also pointed out that:

(a) At the end of 19x4, the competitor had become bankrupt and had closed his business.

(b) A new housing estate was under construction in the urban renewal area.

(c) He had bought large stocks at the end of 19x4 to take advantage of the new custom available from the new estate and the collapse of his competitor, and he had bought most of the stock of his competitor at a very low price.

You will see that the apparent poor performance with a bad prognosis for the future was in fact completely wrong!

Ratio analysis is used to assess performance and liquidity and to forecast the future by extrapolating trends. However, as our example has shown, things are not always what they seem. Ratio analysis should not be used as a basis for decisions but rather as a guide to what questions to ask.

Liquidity ratios

8. There are a number of ratios which are traditionally calculated. These are often divided into liquidity ratios and performance ratios. Liquidity is the term used to describe the extent to which a business can pay its debts as they fall due. Insolvency is the state of being *unable to pay debts as they fall due*. Insolvency leads to the collapse of the company and the appointment of a receiver or a liquidator. Investors are unwilling to buy shares in or lend money to a company which is insolvent and traders are unwilling to supply goods on credit to companies which are or are likely to become insolvent. The distinction between liquidity ratios and performance ratios is not very helpful and some ratios (e.g. stock turnover) give information on both.

Actual and potential investors and trade suppliers need to assess the liquidity of a business to determine if it is or is likely to become insolvent. Assessing the financial statements of a business to assess its liquidity is in practice difficult and inconclusive. This is because:

(a) Financial statements are historical. Liquidity assessment is concerned with the future.

(b) Financial statements are static displays. Liquidity is concerned with *flows* of resources.

(c) Financial statements are not designed to give the information required for an accurate liquidity assessment of a business.

(d) Financial statements are summaries. Effective liquidity assessment requires a detailed breakdown of such items as debtors and stocks.

(e) Financial statements omit information on important areas such as overdraft facilities agreed but not taken up.

(f) Year ends are often chosen at dates when balance sheet items had untypical sizes. For example, a shop may choose a year end when stock is usually low, perhaps when winter goods have almost gone and spring goods have not yet arrived.

(g) Some managements engage in 'window dressing' – see later.

Despite the inherent difficulties, the assessment of liquidity is a very common activity. It is usually done by means of ratios, some of which are:

(a) Debtors' payment period.

(b) Creditors' payment period.

(c) Stock turnover.

(d) Current ratio.

(e) Acid test ratio.

The examples of calculations of ratios in this chapter are taken from the accounts of Bingo Manufacturing Co Ltd. on the following page.

Debtors' payment period

9. This ratio purports to measure the average length of time that credit customers take to pay. The ratio is calculated for 19x3 as:

$$\frac{\text{Debtors}}{\text{Credit sales}} \times 12 = \frac{900}{4,800} \times 12 = 2\frac{1}{4} \text{ months}$$

Alternatively, 365 could be used instead of 12 to give the answer in days – 68 days.

For 19x4 and 19x5, the figures are 2.8 months and 1.95 months.

Bingo Manufacturing Co Ltd
Profit and loss account for the years ending 31 December

	19x3	19x4	19x5
	£000	£000	£000
Sales	4,800	5,050	5,340
Less Cost of sales	2,600	2,800	3,050
Gross profit	2,200	2,250	2,290
Distribution costs	460	530	495
Administration expenses	1,140	1,220	1,300
Net profit	600	500	495
Taxation	150	160	85
Profit after tax	450	340	410
Dividends	150	150	170
Retained	300	190	240

Balance sheets as at 31 December

	19x3	19x4	19x5
	£000	£000	£000
Fixed assets	1,560	1,753	2,448
Current assets			
Stock – raw materials	200	240	180
Work-in-progress	250	280	210
Finished goods	460	475	560
Debtors	900	1,190	870
Prepayments	54	56	60
Cash in hand	45	32	47
	1,909	2,273	1,927
Creditors – due within 12 months			
Trade creditors	560	760	900
Accruals	70	86	60
Corporation tax	150	160	85
Dividends	150	150	170
Bank overdraft	479	620	670
	1,409	1,776	1,885

...continued

	19x3	19x4	19x5
	£000	£000	£000
Net current assets	500	497	42
Net assets	2,060	2,250	2,490
Share capital – 25p shares	600	600	600
Reserves	860	1,050	1,290
Due to shareholders	1,460	1,650	1,890
Creditors due more than 12 months	600	600	600
	2,060	2,250	2,490

10. The ratio is an indication and should be used with care because:
    (a) The debtors are as at the year end, average debtors over the *whole* year are unknown. The year end figures may not be typical.
    (b) The debtors may include debtors which are not trade debtors (e.g. loans to employees).
    (c) The turnover may include *cash sales*. Only credit sales should be included.
    (d) Turnover is net of VAT, debtors include VAT.
    (e) Sales may not be uniform over the year. If sales are smaller than average in the last quarter, the debtors will be from those sales and should be compared with the last quarter's sales and not the sales of the whole year.

Interpretation of the debtors' payment period

11. The ratio on its own indicates very little. It can be compared with:
    (a) Credit period granted to customers – say 30 days. Customers rarely pay within the time allowed.
    (b) The ratios of other similar businesses. If other companies persuade their debtors to pay more quickly, perhaps Bingo needs to see if it can improve its performance.
    (c) Trends – the ratio has worsened between 19x4 and 19x5 and improved between 19x5 and 19x6. Any change indicates not satisfaction or despair, but a search for explanations, which might be:
        (i)   A genuine change in credit control and credit management.
        (ii)   Deliberate policy to seek sales from less or more credit worthy customers.
        (iii) Commencement or abandonment of settlement discount offers.
        (iv)   Changes in the seasonal patterns of sales.
        (v)   Averages may conceal changes in the composition of sales and/or debtors.
        (vi)   Window dressing. Window dressing is a procedure where managers engage in business practices, not for commercial reasons, but to bolster up the appearance of the accounts. In this case the company may deliberately date sales invoices before the year end but allow longer credit. The effect is the same commercially but the accounts show a different position.
        (vii) Some other reason not apparent from the published figures.

Creditors' payment period

12. This ratio measures the average time taken to pay suppliers. It is a very important ratio because:
    (a) Potential suppliers will want to know how long it will be before they get paid.
    (b) Significantly long payment time may mean that the business is about to fail because if creditors sense impending failure or become impatient with waiting, they may sue the company. If material numbers of creditors sue, the company will be unable to pay. Alternatively unpaid creditors may refuse to supply further goods on credit.
    (c) It is the most sensitive indicator of liquidity.

    It is measured by taking annual supplies on credit. This is generally not revealed on financial statements. The figure is not 'Cost of sales' since much of this is wages and other costs not supplied on credit. Let us assume that the figure is one half of cost of sales plus one half of distribution costs namely 1,300 + 230 = £1,530,000.

    The ratio is $\dfrac{\text{Creditors}}{\text{Credit inputs}} \times 12 = \dfrac{560}{1,530} \times 12 = 4.4$ months

    Alternatively, 365 could be used to give the answer as 134 days.

Difficulties in measurement

13. These include:
    (a) Supplies on *credit* are not stated separately in financial statements.
    (b) Profit and loss account items are exclusive of VAT. Trade creditors on the balance sheet include VAT.
    (c) Trade creditors at the year end may not be typical of the whole year.
    (d) Supplies on credit may be seasonal or not uniformly distributed through the year for other reasons.
    (e) The management may window dress the accounts. For example, reducing creditors by increasing bank overdraft *in appearance only* by drawing cheques but not sending them.

Interpretation of the creditors' payment period

14. (a) This ratio can be compared with that indicated by other businesses.
    (b) A more useful interpretation is from examining trends. Bingo Ltd seems to be deteriorating. Care should be taken to investigate the reasons, which might be:
        (i)   A deliberate policy of financing new investment (note increase in fixed assets) by postponing payment of suppliers.
        (ii) A change in policy on settlement discounts.
        (iii) Changes in the seasonal patterns of supply.
        (iv) Inclusion in creditors of large amounts of special items (e.g. capital expenditure) made late in the year.
        (v)   Averages may conceal changes in the composition of creditors or suppliers.
        (vi) Some other reason, not apparent from the financial statements.

(c) This is one statistic which does give information in itself. Taking nearly six months to pay suppliers is very dangerous. Collapse of the company may be imminent.

Stock turnover

15. This ratio is usually given as an indicator of liquidity and indeed *changes* in stock turnover may give indications of better or worse liquidity. It is also a useful indicator of management performance.

The stock turnover rate measures the average length of time that stock is stored before use. In the case of work-in-progress it measures the average length of time between commencement and completion of items produced.

Calculation

16. To determine the stock turnover of finished goods stock, the formula is:

$$\frac{\text{Stock}}{\text{Cost of goods sold}} \times 12 = \frac{460}{2,600} \times 12 = 2.1 \text{ months}$$

Alternatively use 365, to give 65 days.

The ratios for 19x4 and 19x5 are 2 and 2.2 months.

An alternative measure using the same data is:

$$\frac{\text{Cost of goods sold}}{\text{Average of year end stock}} = \frac{£2,600,000}{£460,000} = 5.6$$

This is expressed by saying that the stock is turned over 5.6 times a year.

Work-in-progress turnover is measured in the same way by comparing work-in-progress with average monthly throughput of sales at cost price, namely cost of sales.

The figures are:

	19x4	19x5	19x6
Months	1.1	1.2	.8
or on the alternative measure			
Times a year	10.4	10	14.5

Raw materials turnover is also measured in the same way by comparing the raw material stock with average monthly raw material usage. This is not given in published accounts but will be included in a full manufacturing account. Assume in Bingo that raw material usage is:

	19x4	19x5	19x6
	1,300	1,400	1,525

Then the raw material stock represents

	19x4	19x5	19x6
Months usage	1.8	2.0	1.4
or on the alternative measure			
Times a year	6.5	5.8	8.4

Interpretation of the stock turnover

17. **Management performance**

    (a) As a single statistic, the appropriate level of stock is difficult to evaluate. Sales and production management like large stocks to ensure that customers' requirements can be met and production is not halted by shortages. Financial managers like small stocks because stock:

    (i) Deteriorates with storage.

    (ii) Costs money to store.

    (iii) Ties up capital.

    (b) Comparison with other businesses is useful. If Bingo's management discovered that a rival company had only one month's requirement of finished goods, that might be an indication that Bingo's finished goods stock was higher than necessary.

    (c) Trends. The trends indicated here are:

Raw materials	– a rise in 19x4 and a substantial fall in 19x5.
Work-in-progress	– a rise in 19x4 and a substantial fall in 19x5.
Finished goods	– a small fall in 19x5 and a considerable increase in 19x6.

    The causes of these changes might be:

    (i) Deliberate changes of policy, e.g. to reduce raw materials and work-in-progress and increase finished goods stock.

    (ii) A build up of finished goods stock during 19x5 caused by an imbalance between production and sales followed by a reduction of output leading to lower raw material stocks and work-in-progress.

    (iii) Improvement in management performance in that production time, as evidenced by lower work-in-progress, has shortened.

    (iv) Random fluctuations caused for example by consignments in or out arriving or departing by chance either just before or just after the year end.

    (v) Inflationary effects – the same *quantity* of stock may be held but at a higher *cost*.

    ### Stocks and liquidity

    Any increase in stocks decreases liquidity – simply because more money is tied up in stocks. Thus an increase in activity and turnover at the same stock turnover rate will reduce liquidity. Slower stock turnover at the same level of activity will reduce liquidity.

    The effects on liquidity of stock turnover changes in the case of Bingo are substantial.

Current ratio

18. This ratio simply compares the relative sizes of *current assets* and *current liabilities*.

    In the case of Bingo, the current ratio at 31.12.x3 is:

    $$\frac{\text{Current assets}}{\text{Current liabilities}} \times \frac{1,909}{1,409} = 1.35$$

    The corresponding ratios at 31.12.x4 and 31.12.x5 are 1.28 and 1.02.

325

Interpretation of the current ratio

19. **As a single statistic**

It has, since the 1890s, been a tradition that the current ratio of a business ought to be at least two. This idea came about because it was felt that current assets would, in liquidation, be used to pay off current liabilities and as on forced sales current assets would 'shrink' then credit or loans should only be granted up to a limit of a current ratio of two. It was then felt that fixed assets were to be considered as giving unknown support to credit or loan applications.

In practice 'the current ratio must be at least two' idea is surely an illogical measure of liquidity because:

(a) In the event of liquidation, all assets and all liabilities must be taken into account in assessing whether or not a particular creditor will be paid in full.

(b) The possibility that a company may fail is a function of all its assets and liabilities and also of dynamic not static factors. Cash flows are measured over time – debtors' payment period, creditors' payment period and stock turnover are better predictors of failure.

(c) Business A with excessive stocks and slow paying debtors would apparently have a better current ratio than business B with a fast turnover of stocks and efficient credit management. Yet business A is clearly more likely to fail.

(d) The bank overdraft factor. Bank overdrafts normally appear among the current liabilities. Note that:

  (i) The bank may have advanced the money to pay for capital expenditure.

  (ii) The existence of bank overdraft finance is a random factor. Some businesses may obtain medium term finance, some may use bank overdraft finance, some (which will then have a better current ratio) may be unable to obtain an overdraft.

  (iii) The figure in the balance sheet may be much less than the overdraft facilities (maximum overdraft allowed) granted by the bank.

20. **Comparisons with other businesses**

Some types of business are likely to have low current ratios. For example, a shop which sells largely for cash will have few debtors. Some types of business will have very high current ratios. For example, civil engineering contractors will have very large work-in-progress. Only comparison of the current ratios of a particular business with others of the same type can give indications of liquidity problems.

21. **Trends**

Downward changes in the current ratio may indicate liquidity problems. However, causes which are not indicative of liquidity problems include:

(a) An overdraft increase to acquire fixed assets.

(b) An overdraft increase to finance increased business which will result in higher stock and debtors.

Suppose company AB Ltd had a large current ratio but the management felt that:

(a) The stock was too high.

(b) The customers took too long to pay.

(c) The creditors were paid unnecessarily quickly.

So began a campaign to reduce stocks, reduce debtors and take a longer time to pay customers. Having succeeded in this, the current ratio is now much smaller. This is good. So interpreting a downward trend in current ratio as bad can simply be wrong!

Acid test ratio

22. This ratio is: $\dfrac{\text{All current assets except stock}}{\text{Current liabilities}} = \dfrac{999}{1,409} = .71$

Ratios for 31.12.x4 and 31.12.x5 are .72 and .52.

This ratio is also historically regarded as a good indicator of liquidity. Many old textbooks suggested that the ratio ought to be at least one, in which case Bingo Ltd appears to be inadequate. However, the arguments against using the ratio in this simple manner are similar to those described for the current ratio.

Interpretation of the acid test ratio

23. Indications of liquidity problems arising from the acid test ratio include:
   (a) Comparison with other businesses. If other businesses in the same industry have higher acid test ratios then this may indicate poor liquidity.
   (b) Trends. If the ratio has a downward trend then this again may be an indication of future liquidity difficulties but remember the lesson of AB Ltd above.

Overtrading

24. Normally businesses that increase their sales at profit earning prices are rightly considered successful. However, paradoxically success may lead to failure due to liquidity problems caused by overtrading, that is, by doing too much business.

Jan 2   Buy goods in anticipation of increased sales.
Feb 28   Pay for them.
Mar 4   Sell the goods on credit.
May 8   Customer pays.

Assume that the goods are over and above normal levels of business then cash must be found to make the payment on 28 February.

Unless a new source of cash is found, e.g. by borrowing, then the cash used will have to be diverted from some other use. This other use might be payment of creditors in the normal way. Failure to pay may lead to the creditor suing for payment or cutting off supplies.

Indications of overtrading include:
(a) Higher turnover.
(b) Increasing debtors.
(c) Increasing stocks.
(d) Longer payment period for creditors.

Performance ratios

25. The purpose of producing financial statements is to measure the profit earned over the period and the capital employed at the end of the period. The purpose is not to enable ratio analysis to be done! However, the owners of an enterprise, whether or not they also manage the enterprise, will use the financial statements to appraise the success of the business over the period and other parties will do so also.

The owners of the enterprise may then take action based upon their appraisal.

The actions may be:

(a) Enquire further.

(b) Support, chastise or fire the management.

(c) Expand, maintain or close down the enterprise.

To assist in the appraisal:

(a) The figures may simply be compared with those of previous periods, budgets and forecasts and those of other businesses.

(b) Ratios may be prepared and compared with those of previous years, budgets and forecasts and other businesses.

This chapter gives examples of profitability analysis of:

(a) The trading and profit and loss account of a retail business.

(b) The return on capital employed of a small business owned and managed by a sole trader.

(c) The return on capital employed of a company.

Trading and profit and loss account analysis

26. Steve owns a newsagency business selling newspapers, magazines, books, records, stationery, tobacco, ice cream, toys and confectionery. His trading and profit and loss account for the three years to 31 December 19x4 shows:

	All in £000		
	19x2	19x3	19x4
Sales	135.0	158.0	178.0
Cost of sales	95.0	116.0	135.0
Gross profit	40.0	42.0	43.0
Occupancy costs (rent, rates etc)	6.2	8.3	10.4
Wages and national insurance	14.3	15.9	17.1
Motor expenses	2.7	2.4	2.6
Other overheads (telephone, audit fee etc)	3.8	4.4	4.9
	27.0	31.0	35.0
Net profit	13.0	11.0	8.0

Steve is concerned that his net profit has declined from £13,000 to £8,000 over the three years and wishes to analyse his trading and profit and loss account to seek possible causes of the decline and to determine what measures can be taken to arrest the decline.

The first step is to calculate the proportions of all items to sales by computing percentages. Restating the data:

	19x2 £000	%	19x3 £000	%	19x4 £000	%
Sales	135.0	100.0	158.0	100.0	178.0	100.0
Cost of sales	95.0	70.4	116.0	73.4	135.0	75.8
Gross profit	40.0	29.6	42.0	26.6	43.0	24.2
Occupancy	6.2	4.6	8.3	5.2	10.4	5.8
Wages	14.3	10.6	15.9	10.1	17.1	9.6
Motor expenses	2.7	2.0	2.4	1.5	2.6	1.5
Other overheads	3.8	2.8	4.4	2.8	4.9	2.8
Total overheads	27.0	20.0	31.0	19.6	35.0	19.7
Net profit	13.0	9.6	11.0	7.0	8.0	4.5

The significant variables should also be compared with the corresponding figures for previous years. Again restating the figures:

	19x2	% Increase	19x3	% Increase	19x4
Sales	135.0	17.0	158.0	12.7	178.0
Gross profit	40.0	5.0	42.0	2.4	43.0
Occupancy	6.2	33.9	8.3	25.3	10.4
Wages	14.3	11.2	15.9	7.5	17.1
Motor expenses	2.7	(11.2)	2.4	8.3	2.6
Other overheads	3.8	15.8	4.4	11.4	4.9
Total overheads	27.0	14.8	31.0	12.9	35.0
Net profit	13.0	(15.4)	11.0	(27.3)	8.0

Studying the data, the following observations can be made:

(a) Sales have increased by 17% and 12.7% which is above the rate of inflation and appears to be satisfactory. However:

    (i) Percentage increases always seem large if they are from a low base, i.e. if 19x2 was a poor year.

    (ii) An increase may seem good but opportunities may have existed for even larger increases.

(b) Gross profit has increased each year (but by only 5.0% and 2.4%) but the gross profit portion of sales revenue has declined from 29.6% in 19x2 to 26.6% in 19x3 and 24.2% in 19x4. This clearly is the major cause of the decline of net profit and the reasons must be sought. Possible explanations include:

    (i) Excessive pilfering of money and/or goods by staff or 'customers'.

    (ii) Change of sales mix, so that a larger proportion of low margin items (e.g. cigarettes) are being sold.

(iii) Scrapping of unsaleable items e.g. magazines.

(iv) Reductions in selling prices.

(c) Occupancy costs have risen by 33.9% and 25.3% so that they went from 4.6% of sales in 19x2 to 5.8% of sales in 19x4. These are significant increases. The causes are probably unavoidable increases in rent and rates and electricity tariffs.

(d) Wages have increased by 11.2% and 7.5% but as a percentage of sales, they have declined.

(e) Motor expenses seem to be under control.

(f) Other overheads have increased in absolute terms but have remained the same proportion of sales revenue.

(g) Overall, overheads have increased by 14.8% and 12.9% but have declined as a proportion of turnover.

(h) The effect overall is a serious decline in net profit.

An examination of past achievements and historical accounting data is without point unless indications for future action are found and followed. The remedies might be:

(a) Careful buying to avoid stocking unsaleable items.

(b) Attention to pricing so that optimum prices can be obtained.

(c) Control over security of stock and cash.

(d) Concentration on high profit lines.

Note that some costs increases (e.g. rent and rates) are out of the control of the business. The effect of such increases may be to make the business unviable or to inspire the proprietor to greater efforts in increasing turnover and margins and reducing overheads.

Return on capital employed of a small business owned by a small trader

27. Return on capital employed is calculated by:

$$\frac{\text{Income derived from the use of capital (the return)}}{\text{The capital used}} \times 100\%$$

Consider the simple case of an investment in a building society of £100 invested on 1 January. If this will yield £8 interest by 31 December, then the return on capital employed is:

$$\frac{8}{100} \times 100 = 8\%$$

For a business, the calculation is complicated by several factors:

(a) The 'return', the profit, can be calculated in many different ways (e.g. by using different depreciation methods).

(b) The capital employed is not a simple building society deposit but a complex mix of assets and liabilities.

(c) The valuation of the assets can be accomplished in many different ways (e.g. different depreciation methods or FIFO or AVCO stock valuation methods).

(d) The 'capital' of the business is not constant but is varied as profit is made, new capital is introduced and drawings are made.

(e) The profit is not wholly a reward for investing capital. It is also:

(i) A reward for the proprietor's time in managing the enterprise.

(ii) A reward for the proprietor's 'risk' in engaging in entrepreneurial activity.

28. Vic is the proprietor of Vic's ice cream parlour. His balance sheets at 31 December were (in £000):

		19x3		19x4
Fixed assets				
Properties		51		55
Equipment		14		17
Vehicles		10		13
		75		85
Current assets				
Stock	6		8	
Debtors	5		9	
Cash	1	12	1	18
		87		103
Current liabilities				
Creditors	15		18	
Overdraft	3	18	14	32
		69		71
Capital				
At 1 January		65		69
Net profit for year		19		22
		84		91
Drawings		15		20
		69		71

Vic is concerned about the profitability of his business and is seeking a measure to indicate this. He estimates that:

(a) Alternative employment is available to him at about £9,000 a year.

(b) If the business were wound up, the assets sold and the liabilities paid off, he could invest the remainder at an interest rate of 10%.

Thus, the profit for 19x4 of £22,000 can be seen as:

	£
(a) A reward for Vic's labour in managing the business full time	9,000
(b) A reward for investing his capital in business assets $10\% \times \dfrac{(69 + 71)}{2}$	7,000
(c) The balance a reward for entrepreneurial endeavour	6,000
	£22,000

Notes:

(a) The notional reward for Vic's time and the 10% interest rate adopted are *opportunity costs*, that is the best rewards foregone by engaging in business.

(b) The capital employed throughout 19x4 has been taken as the average of the opening and closing figures. In practice it rarely makes much difference whether the opening figure, the closing figure or the mean of the two is taken.

Return on capital employed of a company

29. Bev PLC has a balance sheet at 31 December as (in £'000):

	19x3	19x4
Fixed assets	4,300	4,550
Net current assets	3,200	3,380
	7,500	7,930
Ordinary share capital (£1)	1,000	1,000
Reserves	3,500	3,930
Due to shareholders	4,500	4,930
10% unsecured loan stock	3,000	3,000
	7,500	7,930

The profit and loss account for 19x4 showed:

	£
Net profit before interest	1,030
Interest on loan stock	300
Net profit after interest	730
Dividends	300
Retained profits	430

Calculation of the return on capital can be:

(a) Return on capital employed by *all long term suppliers of capital*.

(b) Return on capital employed by *ordinary shareholders*.

(a) Return on capital employed by all long term suppliers of capital

$$= \frac{\text{Return gained from the use of capital}}{\text{Capital employed}} \times 100\%$$

$$= \frac{1,030}{\left(\dfrac{7,500+7,930}{2}\right)} \times 100\% = 13.35\%$$

(b) Return on capital employed by ordinary shareholders

$$= \frac{\text{Return gained from the use of capital}}{\text{Capital employed}} \times 100\%$$

$$= \frac{730}{\left(\dfrac{4,500+4,930}{2}\right)} \times 100\% = 15.48\%$$

Notes:

(a) I have taken the average of opening and closing capital employed. In practice, the opening or the closing figure might be used. It would make little difference.

(b) Capital employed can be seen here as the assets used in the business less all liabilities except those for whom we are measuring the return. Thus in measuring the return to all long term suppliers of capital (ordinary shareholders and loan stock holders), we take: Fixed assets + Net current assets and for return on capital of ordinary shareholders we take: Fixed assets + Net current assets – the unsecured loan stock, which is by definition equal to share capital + reserves.

(c) The net profit before interest is taken for calculation (29a) because this sum is the sum to be used to reward both loan stock holders (with £300,000) and ordinary shareholders (with £730,000).

(d) The net profit after interest is taken for calculation (29b) because only this is available to ordinary shareholders even though £300,000 only is to be paid to them as dividends.

Interfirm comparison

30. Many industries and trades have set up interfirm comparison schemes, whereby:

(a) Member firms send in details of their financial statements.

(b) Ratios and other significant data are abstracted and the mean and spread of ratios and other data is calculated. Spread can be measured by standard deviation or the use of quartiles or deciles.

(c) The mean and spread of the ratios and other data is communicated to member firms. The name of member firms is kept confidential.

As an example, the Institute of Chartered Accountants in England and Wales runs a confidential annual interfirm comparison in which data calculated includes:

(a) Operating and gross profit as a percentage of fees.

(b) Salaries as a percentage of fees.

(c) Overheads as a percentage of fees.

(d) Profit and remuneration per partner.

(e) Inflation adjusted profit per partner.

(f) Growth in fee income.

(g) Debtors and work-in-progress as a percentage of fees.

(h) And many others.

The major difficulty with interfirm comparisons is that all firms do not use precisely uniform accounting practices in preparing their financial statements. Most schemes detail exactly how financial statements are to be prepared to overcome this problem.

An item by item comparison of a firm's data with the average data of firms in the industry will:

(a) Enable management to identify variations from the average.

(b) Direct management to seek causes for variation.

(c) Direct management to take corrective action.

Summary

❑ Financial statements contain information which is used by several categories of people having an interest in the business including owners, managers, lenders, suppliers, customers, the taxman and employees.

❑ The utility of this information is limited because accounts are:

(i) Historical.

(ii) Summaries.

(iii) Selective as to content.

❑ Users of accounts seek information on:

(i) Liquidity and the survival prospects of the business.

(ii) Performance of the management.

(iii) Future prospects of the business.

❑ Financial statement analysis is carried on by comparing detailed figures and ratios with:

(i) Previous accounts.

(ii) Budgets and forecasts.

(iii) Other businesses.

❑ Misleading or false conclusions can be drawn from ratio analysis. Ratio analysis should be used as a pointer to further enquiries rather than a source of data for decision making.

❑ Liquidity is the extent to which a business can pay its debts as they fall due.

❑ Insolvency describes the inability to pay debts as they fall due.

❑ Investors and trade suppliers are often concerned to assess a business's liquidity from its financial statements.

❑ Investors and trade suppliers are also concerned to detect impending failure of businesses which may come about for illiquidity reasons.

❑ Ratios can be used in assessing liquidity.

❑ Debtors' payment period is the average time credit customers take to pay. It is measured by

$$\frac{\text{Year end debtors}}{\text{Turnover}} \times 12 \text{ (months) or} \times 365 \text{ (days)}$$

❏ Creditors' payment period is the average time taken to pay suppliers on credit. It is measured by:

$$\frac{\text{Year end creditors}}{\text{Credit supplies}} \times 12 \text{ (months) or} \times 365 \text{ (days)}$$

❏ Stock turnover measures the average time goods are in stock before sale. It is measured by:

$$\frac{\text{Average stock}}{\text{Annual throughput}} \times 12 \text{ (months) or} \times 365 \text{ (days)}$$

or by

$$\frac{\text{Average throughput}}{\text{Annual stock}}$$

❏ Stock turnover is a measure of liquidity and also a measure of management performance. High stocks indicate poor control over stocks, low stocks may indicate difficulties in continuing production or meeting customers' demands.

❏ The current ratio is simply: $\dfrac{\text{Current assets}}{\text{Current liabilities}}$

❏ The acid test or quick ratio is measured by: $\dfrac{\text{Current assets (less stock)}}{\text{Current liabilities}}$

❏ Overtrading, or doing too much business, can lead to liquidity difficulties and very often to business failure.

❏ Ratios can be used by:
  (i)   Considering the ratio in isolation and with budgets.
  (ii) Comparing the ratios with those of other, similar companies.
  (iii) Examining trends.

❏ Owners and managers of businesses use financial statements to assess the performance of the business and its management in order to make decisions about the business's future.

❏ Each item of expense and net profit can be expressed as a percentage of sales and the percentage compared with corresponding percentages:
  (i)   In previous years.
  (ii) In budgets and forecasts.
  (iii) In other similar businesses.

❏ Changes in corresponding items in the profit and loss accounts of successive years can be converted into percentages to determine trends.

❏ The profit of the business of a sole trader who also manages the business is:
  (i)   A reward for the use of the capital employed in the business.
  (ii) A reward for the time and expertise spent in management.
  (iii) The residue being a reward for entrepreneurial endeavour.

❑ The return on capital employed in a company can be measured as:

    (i) The return on the capital employed by all long term suppliers of capital. This is

$$\frac{\text{Profit } before \text{ interest}}{\text{Equity} + \text{debt}} \times 100\%$$

    where equity is the sum due to the shareholders (share capital + reserves) and debt is long term loans.

    (ii) The return on capital employed by the ordinary shareholders. This is

$$\frac{\text{Profit } after \text{ interest}}{\text{Equity}} \times 100\%$$

Points to note

❑ In appraising financial statements, the figures considered by themselves are rarely useful. The basis of appraisal is the comparison of figures and ratios and the determination of trends.

❑ The *static* ratios – the current ratio and acid test ratios – are widely used but are unreliable. The *dynamic* ratios are better indicators. A comparison is often made with a reservoir. Does water level really indicate water surplus or shortage? What determines surplus or shortage is the supply (from rainfall) and demand (from consumers) over time.

❑ In all ratio analysis be careful to compare *like* with *like*. For example:

    (i) Debtors (at selling prices) with sales (also at selling prices).

    (ii) Stocks (at cost) with cost of sales.

    Where debtors are inclusive of VAT and sales are exclusive, an adjustment should be made but rarely is!

❑ I have computed the dynamic ratios in months. It is equally correct to calculate them in days, e.g.

$$\frac{\text{Debtors}}{\text{Sales}} \times 365 \text{ days}$$

❑ Ratios should not be calculated with excessive precision as the underlying data is not precise.

❑ In the case of private businesses and partnerships, trade creditors must take into account that the private assets of the proprietor and partners are also available to creditors.

❑ Limited companies that are part of groups may have access to group resources.

❑ The stock turnover ratio requires the average stocks. Average means the average over the whole year. The use of an average of beginning of year and end of year stocks is unlikely to be nearer the average than the year end stock.

❑ The stock turnover ratio can be computed by reference to purchases or annual consumption. There is not usually a material difference.

❑ Window dressing does occur but should be prevented by a competent auditor.

❏ Overtrading is caused involuntarily by inflation. Each sale of an item of stock requires a replacement at a higher price.

❏ The assessment of a business's liquidity is immensely difficult in practice. Beware of assuming that the calculation of a few ratios gives any conclusive answers.

Self-testing questions

1. What are the disadvantages of financial statements to persons seeking information about a business?
2. List the categories of persons seeking information about a business.
3. How can investigation, analysis and appraisal of financial statements be carried out?
4. How should ratio analysis be used?
5. Define liquidity.
6. Define insolvency.
7. Why is the assessment of the liquidity of a business carried out?
8. What are the limitations of using financial statements in assessing liquidity?
9. How is the debtors 'payment period calculated?
10. List some explanations for a change in the debtors' payment period.
11. How is the creditors' payment period calculated?
12. State two measures of stock turnover.
13. What criteria are there for deciding on optimum stock levels?
14. Why is the current ratio a poor tool for assessing liquidity?
15. How is the acid test ratio calculated?
16. What is overtrading?
17. Why does overtrading lead to illiquidity?
18. What are the purposes of calculating profitability ratios?
19. What comparisons can be made using a particular ratio?
20. Are ratios, in themselves, indicative of malaise or well-being within the business?
21. What rewards to a sole trader does his business profit represent?
22. What is meant by 'opportunity cost'?
23. How is the return on capital employed by all long term suppliers of capital calculated?
24. How is the return on capital employed by ordinary shareholders calculated?
25. Why should share capital plus reserves be taken as capital employed by shareholders?
26. What are the difficulties of interfirm comparison?
27. What are the benefits of interfirm comparison ?

Exercises

1. Hicks is a foreman in the foundry shop of Wenfield Engineering PLC. From his point of view and from the point of view of the company discuss whether or not accounting information should be given to Hicks by the company. What information might be given?
2. Wibble PLC is considering the purchase of the whole share capital of Advourd Ltd, an advertising agency and of Reelail Ltd, a small brewery. Discuss the utility of financial statements in evaluating each potential purchase.

3. N Ltd is a new wholesale company operating from rented premises with very few fixed assets and a small staff. Its first three years' figures showed (in £'000):

	19x3		19x4		19x5	
Sales		110		192		360
Opening stock	–		15		51	
Purchases	100		180		315	
	100		195		366	
Closing stock	15	85	51	144	94	272
Gross profit		25		48		88
Overheads		12		22		45
Net profit		13		26		43
At year end						
Debtors		27		56		120
Creditors		26		60		131
Overdraft		10		15		26

Required:

(a) Calculate five liquidity ratios for all three years.

(b) What problems of liquidity might N Ltd be facing?

4. Flotsam Limited is a retail carpet store and Jetsam Limited is a manufacturer of catering equipment. Their working capitals at 31 December 19x8 were:

	Flotsam £'000	Jetsam £'000
Stock – Raw materials and components	–	33
Work in progress	–	41
Saleable goods	104	98
Debtors	13	180
Creditors	200	43
Overdraft	90	231
Dividend	20	20
Taxation	30	32
Turnover in 19x8	1,000	1,000
Purchases on credit in 19x8	600	500

Calculate suitable liquidity ratios and comment on their meaning for:

(a) a potential supplier to either company.

(b) a potential maker of an unsecured loan to either company.

5. Your company is considering supplying goods on credit to T Ltd. You have the accounts of T Ltd for two years and calculate the following:

	19x4	19x5
Debtors/sales ratio	2.4 months	2.9 months
Creditors/credit purchases ratio	3.1 months	3.8 months
Stock turnover	4.0 times	3.4 times
Current ratio	1.4	1.2
Acid test ratio	0.8	0.7

(a) Would you sell on credit to T Ltd?

(b) Each ratio is 'worse' than the previous year. Give explanations for each change which puts the company in a favourable light.

6. The balance sheet of the businesses of Abel, Ben, Cain and Darren show (all in £000 and all retailers of fashion goods):

	A	B	C	D
Premises	50	–	76	–
Fixtures and vehicles	26	41	52	12
Stock	62	87	60	21
Bank	4	–	–	–
Creditors	46	54	40	11
Overdraft	–	39	22	13
Profit and loss account:				
Net profit	24	26	12	18

Note: Abel, Ben and Darren all work full time in the business. Comparable inputs of time, expertise etc would probably cost at least £15,000 a year. Cain employs a manager and lives in the Bahamas. Abel's premises are at recent valuation but Cain's are now worth £100–£120,000.

Required:

Calculate a measure of profitability for these businesses.

7. Amanda owns and manages a retail jewellers shop and Sandra owns and runs a leather goods shop.

Their figures for 19x6, 19x7 and 19x8 were (in £000):

	Amanda			Sandra		
	19x6	19x7	19x8	19x6	19x7	19x8
Sales	165	169	174	102	124	142
Cost of sales	92	98	110	50	62	69
Gross profit	73	71	64	52	62	73
Occupancy	16	19	23	12	15	16
Wages	24	20	18	14	16	18
Motor expenses	3	3	4	2	3	3
Advertising	4	5	3	7	12	14
Other overheads	9	9	10	6	7	7
Net profit	17	15	6	11	9	15

Required:

Make observations on the profitability of their two businesses.

8. Shoe Man PLCand Mock Asin PLC are both manufacturers of footwear. Their accounts for the year ending 31 December 19x8 show (£000):

	Shoe Man	Mock Asin
Fixed assets	280	900
Current assets	149	460
	429	1,360
Current liabilities	86	380
	343	980
Share capital	120	150
Reserves	123	630
16% Debentures	100	200
	343	980
Net profit after interest	53	115
Taxation	17	40
Dividend	15	20
Retained	21	55

Calculate:

(a) Return on capital supplied by all suppliers of capital (before tax).

(b) Return on capital supplied by equity (i) before tax (ii) after tax.

Assignment

❐ *Charlie and Davina are both Certified Accountants in sole practice in Loamshire. They belong to an Interfirm Comparison Scheme operated in their county. Their figures and the means of the sole practitioners in the county are: 19x8 (£000)*

	Charlie	Davina	Mean
Fixed assets (excluding vehicles and premises)	18	4	12
Work in progress	5	10	4
Debtors	9	11	6
Current liabilities	9	12	5
Fees	68	80	50
Salaries	31	27	20
Occupancy	12	6	5
Other overheads	7	12	8
Net profit	18	35	17

Required:

Comment on Charlie's and Davina's performance and how they conduct their businesses.

27 Gearing and investment ratios

This chapter is concerned with the way companies are financed and the proportions of capital provided by risk taking shareholders and by lenders to the company.

Gearing

1. Companies are usually *financed* by:
   (a) Short-term methods, e.g. trade credit (paying for goods a short time after obtaining possession and use of the goods) and bank overdrafts.
   (b) Long-term borrowing e.g. by issuing, in exchange for loans, loan stocks or debentures which are pieces of paper acknowledging the loans and containing terms for repayment etc. Such borrowings are known as *debt*.
   (c) Obtaining money from persons or institutions who become shareholders. Remember that in effect, shareholders also contribute to the company's funds by allowing profit which belongs to them, to be *retained* by the company. The funds supplied by shareholders by direct subscription and by *retained* profits are called *equity*.

2. The proportions of capital raised by *debt* and *equity* is the subject of gearing. Gearing is called *leverage* in the USA and this term is becoming used also in the UK. Companies who engage in gearing give an *advantage* to their shareholders in that (see Bev PLC in the previous chapter):
   (a) Money (£3,000,000) can be borrowed.
   (b) The money can be invested in assets to produce a profit of 13.35% = £400,000.
   (c) Interest is payable to the lenders at 10% – £300,000.
   (d) Thus extra profit is produced of £400,000 at a cost of only £300,000. The £100,000 belongs to the shareholders.

3. There is a disadvantage:
   (a) Money (£3,000,000) can be borrowed.
   (b) The money can be invested in assets to produce a profit of 13.35% = £400,000, but this may not happen. Suppose that the extra profit produced is only £200,000.
   (c) The funds becoming available to pay interest £300,000 are only £200,000. This can lead to the company failing.

4. Gearing can be measured by: $\dfrac{\text{Debt capital}}{\text{All long term capital}} \times 100\%$

   In the case of Bev PLC (see previous chapter), this is (19x4 figures):
   $\dfrac{3,000}{7,930} \times 100\% = 37.8\%$

5. Companies with a *high* proportion of their capital in debt form are said to be *high geared*. Companies with a small proportion of their capital in debt form are said to be *low geared*. No gearing ratio can be considered high or low in general. To determine if a particular company is high or low geared, comparison has to be made with the gearing ratios of other similar companies.

Income gearing

6. It is possible to calculate a measure of gearing to the income of a geared company. For example:

Puddle PLC

Profit and Loss Account year ending 31.12.x7

	£000
Net profit before interest	2,400
Interest on debenture	600
Net profit after interest	1,800

A measure of gearing might be $\dfrac{\text{Interest}}{\text{Net profit before interest}} \times 100 = 25\%$

This interest takes up 25% of income, leaving 75% of income for shareholders. In appraising the company, commentators would note that a fall in income of say 10% (£240,000) would reduce the shareholders' portion of income by $13\frac{2}{3}\%$. (£240,000 is $13\frac{2}{3}\%$ of £1,800,000).

Investment ratios

7. The financial statements of quoted companies are appraised by investors and their advisers in order to make investment decisions like buying more of the shares or holding on or selling out. Such decisions are assisted by calculating ratios, and such ratios are calculated and given as well as the quotation for the share, against every share, daily, in the Financial Times and other newspapers.

Ratios

8. The ratios are (using Bev PLC 19x4 figures):

Bev PLC balance sheets

	19x3	19x4
	£000	£000
Fixed assets	4,300	4,550
Net current assets	3,200	3,380
	7,500	7,930
Ordinary share capital (£1)	1,000	1,000
Reserves	3,500	3,930
Due to shareholders	4,500	4,930
12% unsecured loan stock	3,000	3,000
	7,500	7,930

Profit and loss account for 19x4

	£
Net profit before interest	1,030
Interest on loan stock	300
Net profit after interest	730
Dividends	300
Retained profits	430

(a) **Price earnings ratio**

This is simply the: $\dfrac{\text{Price of one share}}{\text{Profit attributable to one share}}$

The price of a share is the price at which *small parcels* of the shares are bought and sold on the Stock Exchange. The price changes continually according to supply and demand for the shares. Let us assume that Bev PLC ordinary shares are quoted at £9.20 each. The earnings per share is:

$$\frac{\text{Total profit available to ordinary shareholders}}{\text{Number of shares}} = \frac{£730,000}{1,000,000} = 73p$$

In practice, there is no need to calculate the earnings per share (eps) as it is given in all published profit and loss accounts.

Thus the price earnings ratio for Bev PLC is: $\dfrac{£9.20}{73p} = 12.6$

The price of a share is 12.6 times the annual profits attributable to that share.

What this means is beyond the scope of this manual, but a high PE ratio (12.6 is fairly high) means that investors expect the profits of the company to grow.

(b) **Dividend yield**

This is simply: $\dfrac{\text{Dividend per share}}{\text{Share price}} \times 100\%$

In Bev PLC's case: $\dfrac{£300,000 \big/ 1,000,000}{£9.20} \times 100\% = 3.26\%$

An investor who buys one share at £9.20, the current market price, will receive a dividend of 30p which is equivalent to a return or yield of only 3.26%. This is substantially below the yield obtainable for investing in a building society. The yield is low because investors expect the rate of dividend per share to grow.

(c) **Dividend cover**

This is: $\dfrac{\text{Profits available to ordinary shareholders}}{\text{Dividend paid}}$

In Bev PLC's case, this is $\dfrac{£730,000}{£300,000} = 2.43$

This is expressed as the dividend being 2.43 times covered by the profits. This is an indication that:

(i) Profits will have to fall very substantially before the dividend is less than the profit.

(ii) A majority of the profit is retained rather than paid out to shareholders as dividends.

(iii) As the company is retaining the larger part of its profit, the company is growing and this will lead to growth in prospects and dividends in the future.

Summary

❒ Companies are financed by:

(i) Risk taking shareholders – equity.

(ii) Lenders to the company – debt.

❒ The different proportions of the company's capital supplied by equity shareholders and lenders is the subject of gearing.

❒ Investment ratios are used by investors in evaluating the shares of quoted companies as potential investments.

❒ The price earnings ratio (PE ratio) is: $\dfrac{\text{Quoted price of the share}}{\text{Earnings per share}}$

❒ The dividend yield is: $\dfrac{\text{Dividend per share}}{\text{Quoted price per share}} \times 100\%$

❒ The dividend cover is: $\dfrac{\text{Profits after tax available to ordinary shareholders}}{\text{Total dividends for the year}}$

Points to note

❒ Gearing is measured by the 'debt/equity ratio'. There are several ways of calculating this but the simple way is:

$$\frac{\text{Debt}}{\text{Debt} + \text{Equity}} \times 100$$

Note that shareholders' equity must include reserves.

❒ The dividend cover is also known as the payout ratio.

❒ The calculation of the price earnings ratio involves a calculation of earnings per share. This can be very complicated and is covered by Statement of Standard Accounting Practice No 3 and FRS 3 Reporting Financial Performance.

❒ Interpreting investment ratios is not easy and should be approached with care. However some general points may be made:

(i) Earnings per share can be compared from year to year in the same company. It cannot be compared across companies.

(ii) High price earnings ratios generally suggest that growth is expected.

(iii) High dividend yields generally indicate a static company.

(iv) Low dividend cover suggests the company has problems and dividends may fall.

(v) Single year data may not be indicative of long-term performance or prospects.

❑ Calculating the dividend yield may, as a first step, require the calculation of dividend per share. Dividend per share is simply Total Dividend (Interim + final, if there are two in a year) divided by Total Number of Shares. Total number may be given or may be calculated from Share Capital in £ divided by nominal or par value of share. Example: Total dividend £20,000, Ordinary Share Capital £40,000, par value of each share 20p. Dividend per share –10p.

Self-testing questions

1. How can companies be financed?
2. What is gearing or leverage?
3. What are the (i) benefits, (ii) disadvantages of gearing?
4. How can gearing be measured?
5. In measuring gearing, should reserves be included in shareholders' equity?
6. Why are investment ratios calculated?
7. What is the price earnings ratio?
8. How is the dividend yield calculated?
9. How is dividend cover calculated?
10. What are earnings per share?

Exercises

1. The Accounts for 19x8 of three companies show: (in £000).

Balance sheet	Boring plc	Risquee plc	Happee plc
Share capital	1,000	100	1,300
Share premium	100	400	200
Preference shares 7%	–	300	–
Reserves	200	250	600
Debentures 16%	100	400	800
Net assets	1,400	1,450	2,900
Profit and loss			
Net profit after interest	340	400	420
Preference dividend	–	21	–
Ordinary dividend	150	80	100
Retained	190	299	320

Required:
Calculate measures of gearing for the companies. Which companies are high geared?

2. 'A high geared company is a high profit company.'
'A high geared company is a high risk company.'
Comment.

3. I like to save up for things both at home and in my business.
Comment.

4.   Luvabull PLC is considering the financing mix for its debut as a quoted company. Possible arrangements are:

	(a)	(b)	(c)
Ord shares of 20p each	1,500,000	2,500,000	1,000,000
Share premium and reserves	1,000,000	1,000,000	1,000,000
15% debentures	1,000,000	–	1,500,000

Profits are expected to be £600,000 before interest.

Required:

(a) Calculate:
  (i) A gearing ratio.
  (ii) Profits available for dividend in each case.

(b) Assume a 10% reduction in profit before interest. Calculate the percentage change in profit available for dividend in each case.

5.   Data about:

	Proton plc	Neutron plc	Positron plc
	£000	£000	£000
Share capital in 20p shares	4,000	3,000	12,000
Net profit after tax	1,200	600	4,700
Dividend per share	3p	2p	5p
Share price	60p	32p	96p

Required:

Calculate:

(a) Earnings per share.
(b) Price earnings ratio.
(c) Dividend yield.
(d) Dividend cover.

Anticipate PLC wishes to make a bid for Proton PLC. If it offered 60p a share, do you think Proton's shareholders (or at least 50% of them) would accept the offer?

6.   Data in the Financial Times for Pullitt PLC and Chick PLC shows:

	Pullitt	Chick
Share price	80p	78p
Price earnings ratio	10	13
Dividend cover	2.5	4

The share capital is 1,000,000 ordinary shares of 20p each in each case

Required:

Calculate:

(a) Earnings per share.
(b) Net profit.
(c) Total dividend payable.
(d) Dividend per share.

Assignment

❐ *The following balance sheets as at 31 December relate to Pick PLC wholesale security products merchants.*

	19x5 £'000	19x6 £'000
Fixed assets at cost	740	920
Less depreciation	423	390
	317	530
Stock	80	105
Debtors	102	120
Bank	65	–
	564	755
Trade creditors	(90)	(111)
Taxation	(20)	(32)
Dividend	(15)	(15)
Overdraft	–	(24)
	439	573
10% debenture stock	(50)	(155)
	389	418
Issued share capital (20p shares)	100	100
Profit and loss account	289	318
	389	418

The trading and profit and loss accounts showed:

Sales (all on credit)	740	960
Gross profit	340	425
Overheads	290	340
	50	85
Interest	5	9
	45	76
Tax	20	32
	25	44
Dividends	15	15
	10	29

The Trade Association has published average figures compiled from returns submitted by all members of the Association, in respect of the year 19x6. Some of these are:

(i) rate of stock turnover	6 times
(ii) debtors' average credit time	60 days
(iii) percentage gross profit to turnover	42%
(iv) percentage net profit (before interest) to turnover	10%
(v) return on capital employed	19%
(vi) creditors' average payment time	56 days

Pick's share price on the stock exchange is 120p.

Required:

(a) Calculate a series of accounting ratios, giving in each case the formula used.

(b) Comment on the ratios including a comment on the difference between the years and the trade association average ratios.

(c) Give an overall assessment on what the firm did in 19x6 and suggest how the firm might seek to improve.

28 Service sector and public service accounting

Much of this book has been concerned with profit and capital measurement in retail, wholesale amd manufacturing firms. Indeed the methods of preparing financial statements were largely developed for these types of organisations.

In recent years, there has been a decline in manufacture and a rise in employment in the service sector. The service sector is those undertakings which provide a service, rather than a product, to their customers. I use the word service, although it has become common jargon to use the word product when service is actually meant. Insurance companies tend to talk about their products when inviting you to buy a policy. Customer is now the preferred word for some service industries including railway companies and some educational establishments. Other service industries describe their customers as patients or clients.

Accounting for service industries is relatively straightforward compared to the complexities of manufacturing industry. However, there is now a strong emphasis on financial statements in not-for-profit enterprise. There is no real theory about how to produce financial statements in the not-for-profit sector.

Profit and loss accounts in a service industry

1. Service industries are those in which the enterprises supply, not a good or commodity but a service. Examples are professional services (accountants, lawyers etc); personal services (hairdressing, driving schools); transport; insurance; financial services; entertainment; travel and holidays; restaurants and hotels. It is probable that service industries will grow rapidly in the future as manufacturing declines.

2. A suitable format for the profit and loss account of an accounting practice might be:

	£000	£000
Fees invoiced		440
Less		
Costs and expenses:		
Wages and salaries	180	
Rent, rates, insurance	46	
Professional indemnity insurance	8	
Motor and travelling	31	
Printing and stationery	36	
Sundries	12	
	313	
Work in progress at beginning	38	
	351	
Less work in progress at end	44	307
Net profit		133

Notes:

(a) There is no gross profit stage to the statement. Gross profit as an idea is difficult to define precisely, but might be considered to be goods or services supplied less the direct cost of the goods or services supplied. Net profit can then be derived by deducting overhead expenses which are not part of the direct cost of the goods or services supplied.

(b) In an accounting practice, it is impossible satisfactorily to distinguish between which expenses are part of the cost of service supplied and which are overheads, not directly related to the service.

(c) The matching convention which underlies the profit computation requires that revenue dealt with in the profit and loss account is matched with associated costs and expenses by including in the same account the costs incurred in earning them.

(d) The objective of including work in progress is to eliminate from the costs and expenses those costs and expenses, which although incurred in the year, should be matched with revenue of the following year. The problem is how to value work in progress.

(e) In this case work-in-progress is valued at all the costs so far incurred on the jobs concerned.

3. A suitable format for a travel agent might be:

	£000	£000
Commissions earned:		370
Less Costs and expenses		
Wages and salaries	104	
Rent, rates, insurance	59	
Telephone	34	
etc, etc	52	249
Net profit		121

In this case, there would be no work in progress.

4. In some service industries, the activities can be divided into *segments*. For example, a hotel may offer room lettings, a dining room and a bar. The gross profit on the bar can be determined but a gross profit on a dining room is more difficult. The cost of the goods offered, meals, is not simply the material cost, but the cost of labour in waiting and serving the meal and the cost of providing the dining room and kitchen facilities.

5. In most service industries, an approach to devising an appropriate and informative profit and loss account might:

(a) Consider if the activities can be segmented.

(b) Consider if the concept of a gross profit is appropriate for all or any of the activities.

(c) Consider what categories and sub-categories the overheads can be analysed into.

(d) Consider if work in progress exists and how it might be measured.

Accounting policies

6. In all businesses, a profit has to be measured for each separate accounting year. The accounting conventions are recognised as the way in which decisions are made about which accounting year the profit or loss on a particular transaction is entered.

   Examples are the realisation convention which indicates that profits are taken on all items sold in a year whether or not cash has been realised in the year, and the prudence convention which requires that expected losses, but not expected gains, are taken into account in the year that loss expectations are recognised.

7. Many expense items relate, not to particular revenue earning transactions, but to revenues in general. For example, the depreciation process is required to allocate fixed asset consumption to specific time periods and the accruals convention allocates revenue expenses (e.g. rent) to specific accounting periods.

8. There are many revenues and expenses where the application of the conventions requires the adoption of a choice among a limited selection of possible accounting *policies*. For example, depreciation of plant can be based upon any of the following depreciation *policies*:

   (a) Straight line.
   (b) Sum of digits.
   (c) Reducing instalment.
   (d) Usage as a proportion of maximum lifetime usage etc.

9. The problem of *annual* profit measurement in terms of accounting *policy* selection is illustrated by the following question:

   On 1 January 19x3, Meg Tape started in business as a software designer and computer bureau operator. She started her business bank account with £2,500 taken from her building society account and £6,200 borrowed at 20% from her brother. Her first year transactions were:

   (a) On 1.1.x3 she purchased the remaining 60 years of a lease on an old property for £20,000 taking a mortgage of £18,000 at 16%. Instalments with interest were due on 30 June and 31 December and in 19x3 were met on time. The capital part of each instalment was £1,000.

   (b) Computing and other equipment was bought for £10,000 using a temporary overdraft. Expected life of the equipment is very uncertain because of the probability of obsolescence.

   (c) Sundry overheads of £26,300 were paid of which £200 was in advance at 31.12.x3. A further £1,280 was outstanding at 31.12.x3.

   (d) Drawings were £4,400.

   (e) She paid various independent programmers £4,800 to write programs for her including £2,600 for a program which can be sold to numerous potential clients. No sale of this program has yet been made.

   (f) She wrote various programs for clients including one suite of programs which has general applicability and of which 20 copies have already been sold to clients.

   (g) Sales of £46,000 were made of which £5,300 was outstanding at 31.12.x3.

Required:

(a) The cash book summary for 19x3.

(b) Profit and loss account for 19x3.

(c) Balance sheet at 31.12.x3.

(d) A statement of accounting policies to accompany the accounts. You should select policies which accord with generally accepted accounting principles. Any assumptions made should be stated.

Part (a) is relatively simple:

Dr		Cash Book Summary 19x3	Cr
	£		£
Cash introduced by proprietor	2,500	Lease	20,000
Loan from brother	6,200	June mortgage instalment	2,440
Mortgage	18,000	December mortgage instalment	2,360
Sales receipts	40,700	Computing equipment	10,000
Balance c/f 31.12.x3	2,900	Sundry overheads	26,300
		Drawings	4,400
		Programmers	4,800
	70,300		70,300

Part (b) requires the development of appropriate accounting policies in the following areas:

(i) **Depreciation of lease**. Many businesses do not amortise (= depreciate) leases with more than 50 years to run. However we will select a policy to amortise the cost of the lease on a straight line basis.

(ii) **Depreciation of computing equipment**. Estimation of life and salvage value is exceedingly difficult in industries with fast changing technology. In addition several depreciation policies are possible. A prudent policy may be to use the reducing balance method at say 50% a year.

(iii) **Independently written programs**. It appears from the question that £2,200 (£4,800 − £2,600) was for work done that is to be matched with some of the revenues (£46,000) and is, therefore, an expense of 19x3. The £2,600 cannot be matched with 19x3 revenues. But can it be carried forward to 19x4 and subsequent years? The answer depends on the likelihood of future revenues and these are uncertain. A prudent policy may be to regard all such expenses as expenses of the year in which they are incurred. We will do so.

(iv) **Programs written in-house**. The ideal accounting policy here would be to determine the cost of the suite of programs (say £2,000) and charge that sum in the profit and loss accounts in those years when copies were sold. If for example, sales were 20 in 19x3, 30 in 19x4, 40 in 19x5 and 10 in 19x6, then the costs (£2,000) would appear in the accounts as:

	Sales (Units)	Costs (£)
19x3	20	400
19x4	30	600
19x5	40	800
19x6	10	200
		£ 2,000

In practice, two problems arise:

(a) What are the cost of the programs? Presumably a proportion of the overheads, depreciation of equipment etc. But estimating this is both difficult and arbitrary.

(b) At the end of 19x3, it is not known what sales would be made in later years.

Thus, the prudent policy is to allow all the costs of production of the suite of programs to fall into 19x3.

Meg Tape
Profit and Loss Account for the year ending 31 December 19x3

	£	£
Sales		46,000
Less Costs and expenses:		
Amortisation of lease	333	
Mortgage interest	2,800	
Depreciation of computing equipment	5,000	
Sundry overheads	27,380	
Programs written	4,800	
Loan interest	1,240	41,553
Net profit		£ 4,447

Balance Sheet as at 31 December 19x3

Fixed Assets	Cost £	Depreciation £	Net £
Lease	20,000	333	19,667
Equipment	10,000	5,000	5,000
	30,000	5,333	24,667
Current Assets			
Debtors		5,300	
Prepayments		200	5,500
			30,167
Current Liabilities			
Creditors		1,280	
Loan interest accrued		1,240	
Bank overdraft		2,900	5,420
			£ 24,747

353

		£	£	£
Capital	Introduced			2,500
	Profit for year			4,447
				6,947
	Drawings			4,400
				2,547
Loans	– Mortgage		16,000	
	– Brother		6,200	22,200
				£24,747

Statement of Accounting Policies

(a) Leasehold property is amortised on the straight line basis over its remaining life of 60 years.

(b) Computing and other equipment is depreciated on the reducing balance method at the rate of 50% a year.

(c) Costs of programs written by independent programmers are written off as the expenditure is incurred. The costs of programs created internally are also written off as incurred.

10. The profit for 19x3 has been measured at £4,447, but this is after charging all the costs of producing programs which, without further cost, may produce revenue in succeeding years. Thus, if the programs mentioned in notes (e) and (f) produce large sales in 19x4, the split of profit earned in the two years to 31 December 19x4 will be distorted.

Financial statements in the not-for-profit sector

11. Preparing financial statements in the not-for-profit sector is just as important as in the profit seeking sectors. Resources are entrusted to managers for use in supplying services in much the same way. In the profit seeking sector, the managers are called directors or partners. But in the not-for-profit sector they might be The Committee, the local council, the government, the Regional Health Council, The Governors or whatever. The theory is that whoever is responsible for the service is a *steward* of resources and it is desirable that an account of the stewardship is given to interested parties. How this accounting is done depends on a number of factors. There may be statutory requirements, there may be a SORP or there may be no specific requirements. Whether or not there are specific requirements, there is a need to use the Accounting Standards and generally accepted accounting principles.

12. We have seen, in another chapter, the financial statements of clubs and societies. The methodology for these is well established but for many organisations the methodology is only now beginning to evolve. In this section we will look at one set of financial statements and attempt to derive some principles of general application from it.

An example from education

13. Sheinton College is a small higher education college and its accountants have produced a set of financial statements as follows:

a.		**Income and Expenditure Account**
b.		**for the year ending 31 July 19x6**

		£'000
c.	**Income**	
d.	Recurrent grant from HEFCE	4,400
e.	Release of capital grant	250
f.	Education contracts	980
g.	Tuition fees	5,135
h.	Research grants and contracts	180
	Residences and catering operations	1,542
	Other income generating operations	260
	Other income	231
		12,978
j.	**Expenditure**	
	Academic departments	5,600
	Academic support services	630
	Other support services	289
	Administration and central services	897
	General educational expenditure	190
k.	Premises	2,340
	Other income generating activities	243
	Research grants and contracts	168
	Residences and catering operations	1,510
l.	Depreciation	739
m.	Interest payable	82
	Total expenditure	12,688
n.	Surplus before interest receivable	290
o.	Interest receivable	34
	Surplus for the period	324
p.	Transfers from reserves	70
q.	**Retained surplus for the period**	394

Balance Sheet as at 31 July 19x6

r.	**Fixed Assets:**		28,260
s.	**Current Assets:**	1,907	
t.	**Creditors – amount due within one year**	1,732	
	Net Current Assets		175

			£'000
Total Assets less Current liabilities			28,435
u. Creditors - amounts due after more than one year			6,190
Total Net Assets			22,245
v. Capital Reserves			21,660
w. Restricted Reserves			120
x. General Reserves	Revenue	220	
y.	Specific	245	465
Total Funds			22,245

Notes:

(a) As with any organisation not seeking to make a profit, this is the usual title.

(b) The year end date is a matter of choice. Colleges usually choose 31 July as this is the end of the academic year.

(c) Income should be subdivided into headings which are suitable for the enterprise or required by a SORP. With all income, the accruals convention is applied so that the income is placed in the right year irrespective of date of receipt.

(d) The main source of income is from central government via the Higher Education Funding Council for England.

(e) Capital grants (from central government) are often received for capital expenditure. The amount received is regarded as deferred income. The amount is released to income and expenditure account over the economic life of the relevant assets and may be the same as the depreciation charged on that part of the fixed assets paid for by grant. The amount of capital grant received but not yet released to income and expenditure account is divided into two parts – to be released within one year (in the balance sheet under current liabilities) and to be released after more than one year (in the balance sheet under long-term liabilities). The treatment of capital grants depends on conditions attached to the grants and requirements of SORPs. The treatment here is a common one.

(f) These can be from many and various bodies. An example may be the Department of Silly Walks who uses the College to train its staff.

(g) These can be for home, overseas or EU students. They may be from individuals or supporting institutions such as local education authorities.

(h) The remaining income sources are self explanatory. You will note that there are expenditures to match against these items in the expenditure section. It might be better to show these income against the expenditure and show a surplus or deficit and colleges may do this in a note. However showing both income and expenditure gross is the preferred option.

(j) Expenditure is itemised as is appropriate. Further categorisation may occur in notes. Expenditure on Other income, Research grants and Residences does not include any apportionment of depreciation or overheads.

(k) This is current expenditure on pay, maintenance, services etc on the premises

(l) Depreciation is provided in the same way as in any business.

(m) The college can borrow and can thus pay interest.

(n) A surplus every year is not essential but in the longer term, income must exceed expenditure. See the press for institutions that, in desperation, have to close departments etc to avoid deficits.

(o) Colleges sometimes have surplus funds which are invested and earn interest.

(p) The College allows departments who spend less than budget to spend the extra in the following year. If they fail to spend in the following year than the amount is lost to them.

(q) Note how, as with company profit, the definition of surplus has to be specified.

(r) Fixed assets are entered into the books at cost and then depreciated. This is the same process that you are very familiar with. However, many colleges and other institutions have periodic revaluations. The method of valuation can be open market value. However that is only suitable for assets that could be sold in the normal way. Assets that have no obvious market (primarily buildings like colleges and hospitals) can be valued at *depreciated replacement cost.* This means that the cost of replacing the buildings at prices ruling at the date of valuation is estimated and then an allowance is made for elapsed life, as they are not new. Depreciation is applied in the usual way once the valuation has been incorporated in the books. Note that depreciated replacement cost is usually higher than original cost so that the revaluation raises depreciation and thus reduces surpluses in the income and expenditure account.

(s) Current assets will be the usual set – stocks, debtors, cash, short term investments.

(t) These will be the usual set – accruals, creditors, short-term loans but will also include some deferred income. Deferred income includes grants and fees etc which are received in advance and this will then be the unexpired portion. I hope you now understand the accruals principle under which income is placed in the appropriate year. Please see also note (e) above.

(u) The College can borrow and these are the outstanding loans. See also note (e) above.

(v) Primarily this comes from two sources:
   (i) The value of assets transferred from the local authority when the College became independent of local authority control.
   (ii) Revaluations of fixed assets. The treatment is the same as in company accounting

(w) These are trust funds and prize funds which the College can only spend on the purposes of the trusts or on prizes. Note that there are no specific assets held for these purposes.

(x) Non-specific revenue reserves represent the value of that part of the net assets which the College can spend as it likes provided it keeps within its rules and regulations.

(y) Specific revenue reserves include:
   (i) Unspent budget allocations within the departments – see (p) above.
   (ii) Major capital projects which the College intends to fund from its own resources.

14. The above example is fictitious but you will find that most colleges publish similar financial statements. However, they are normally amplified by:

(a) Comparative figures for the previous year.

(b) A list of accounting policies.

(c) Notes expanding the detail and giving explanations.

(d) Other financial statements. These are usually: a Statement of Movement on Revenue Reserve: a Note of Historical Cost Surpluses and Deficits; a Cash Flow Statement; a Statement of Total Recognised Gains and Losses.

An example from the health service

15. The income and expenditure accounts of two hospital trusts for the years ending 31 March 19x7 and 19x8 showed the following figures: (in £'000)

	Barset		Womble	
Income	**19x7**	**19x8**	**19x7**	**19x8**
Health authorities	43,000	44,500	28,200	29,400
General practice fundholders	5,100	6,300	2,600	3,450
NHS trusts	870	1,024	240	230
Private patients	176	280	270	440
Other income	1,230	1,420	890	1,350
Expenditure				
Services from other NHS bodies	2,600	2,750	1,400	1,590
Staff costs	32,600	33,400	20,700	23,300
Supplies	6,050	6,400	3,700	3,950
Establishment	820	930	450	495
Premises	2,100	3,240	1,390	1,420
Depreciation	1,940	2,020	1,430	1,650
Other costs	1,800	1,900	1,320	1,440

Notes:

(a) These accounts are extracts only and are of course fictitious. There would be a lot more detail in a real set. They would be prepared under the National Health Service Act 1977 using forms approved by the Secretary of State for Health.

(b) Understanding them requires some knowledge of health service finance. Hospitals are run by hospital trusts which are autonomous as to finance. Fundamentally most income comes from the government (ultimately from you and I from taxation) via local health authorities or from local doctors who are given a sum of money to spend on patient care in hospitals. Hospital trusts do some work for each other so there is income from and costs charged to other trusts. Finally there are usually some other sources of income including private patients.

(c) Costs are analysed to show the main categories and you can see what these are. More details of these costs are usually given in notes including the number and type of staff.

(d) Analysis of these figures and calculation of ratios can be revealing. I will leave you to do this. But to start you might care to :

(i) Calculate the surpluses (income less expenses)

(ii) Calculate percentages of each category of income to total income and make comparisons

(iii) Calculate percentages of each category of expense to total income and make comparisons.

(e) Copies of NHS trusts' accounts can be obtained from the hospitals on request.

General rules for preparing not-for-profit financial statements

16. There are a great number of Institutions which are in the not-for-profit sector – schools, colleges, universities, charities, hospitals and other health service bodies, government agencies, local authorities etc. Each could have a large accounting manual on its own and I cannot begin to discuss them comprehensively. Some general rules can be discerned:

(a) There is often a SORP to give guidance.

(b) The Accounting Standards and generally accepted accounting principles usually apply.

(c) The income statement is usually called the income and expenditure account.

(d) The accounting conventions – accruals, going concern, prudence, consistency etc – apply.

(e) Income and expenditure should be categorised as appropriate.

(f) Fixed assets are usually valued at cost and depreciated in the normal way.

(g) Revaluation is common. This may be at open market values but may be at depreciated replacement cost. Depreciation is applied to the revalued amounts.

(h) Some income may be deferred and appear in short or long term liabilities before it is amortised to the credit of income and expenditure account.

(i) Capital and reserves will usually be subdivided into capital and revenue reserves.

Summary

❒ There are service industries as well as trading, manufacturing and non-profit organisations.

❒ The format of the profit and loss account of a business providing a service, may or may not include a 'half way stage' in terms of measuring a gross profit.

❒ Gross profit is an elusive idea which implies that costs and expenses can be separated into those directly incurred in creating a good or service and those not related or apportionable to the product.

❒ In businesses where two or more different services are provided, segmented profit measurement is desirable.

❏ In many service industries, the preparation of annual profit measures requires careful selection of appropriate accounting policies to relate revenue and expenses to particular financial years.

❏ The Committee/Council/ Board of Governors/whatever who has responsibility for an Institution has a duty to publish financial statements annually to report its stewardship of resources to all persons with an interest in the Institution.

❏ Every type of Institution needs tailor made income and expenditure accounts, balance sheets and other financial statements. However some general principles can be discerned.

Points to note

❏ The two stage income statement – gross profit and then net profit – is firmly established in the practice of preparing accounts for trading and manufacturing businesses. It does not usually work so well in service industries and you should be very sure that costs are distinguishable between those directly concerned with a product and those which are not, before deciding to compute a gross profit.

❏ Many of the accounting policy problems relate to the idea of work in progress. For example, in the accounting practice (paragraph 2), work in progress has been included. This means that, that part of the salaries, motor expenses etc, which relate to work done but not invoiced until the following year, has to be taken out of the profit and loss account as closing work in progress. The conceptual problem of valuing work in progress is very difficult. Very often an arbitrary approach of say 50% of selling price is taken.

❏ All published accounts include a list of accounting policies used. It is a good idea to look at some.

❏ The problems of accounting measurement and the selection of suitable accounting policies is common to all businesses. However, the problem is most frequently met within service industries.

❏ The owners of profit seeking bodies, such as companies, are primarily interested in the profit. To a considerable extent, the success of the undertaking can be measured in financial terms and, what is more, in one figure – the profit. Not-for-profit undertakings need to balance income with expenditure and the financial statements certainly give a useful account of the stewardship of resources. However, the effectiveness with which the undertaking carried on its mission is not really measurable in money terms. Other statistics of a numerical type may be more important – numbers of diplomas/degrees awarded, number of operations done or patients treated, number of grant applications processed etc. Non-numerical data may be even more relevant – the quality of treatment or education or rehabilitation of offenders given custody etc. These will perhaps be within the remit of the accountant of the future!

Self-testing questions

1. List some examples of service industries.
2. When can a gross profit be calculated?
3. When is segmental reporting desirable?
4. What is an accounting policy?
5. What is the purpose of a statement of accounting policies?
6. Why do institutions publish financial statements?
7. Explain: income and expenditure account, treatment of capital grants, depreciated replacement cost, capital reserves, revenue reserves, deferred income.
8. What other financial statements may be published and what additional information may be given?
9. enumerate some general principles used in preparing financial statements of not-for-profit bodies.

Exercises

1. The balance sheet of Sparks, a Certified Accountant in private practice was, on 31.12.x8:

	£		£	£
Capital	11,433	Equipment at cost	3,900	
Creditors	1,367	Depreciation	1,500	2,400
Bank overdraft	10,800	Car at cost	8,000	
		Depreciation	2,800	5,200
		Work in progress		9,800
		Debtors		6,200
	23,600			23,600

His cash book summary for 19x9 showed:

Receipts		Payments	
	£		£
From clients	50,700	Staff costs	28,590
Legacy from Aunt	5,000	Drawings	12,600
		Taxation – Schedule D	3,611
		Office occupancy costs	5,620
		Motor and other overheads	6,300

At 31.12.x9, his work in progress was valued at £12,800 and debtors amounted to £8,800.

He is depreciating his car, which he bought in 19x6, over five years on the straight line basis and his equipment at 20% reducing balance.

Creditors are all for office occupancy costs and the corresponding figure for 19x9 is £1,230.

Required:

(a) Prepare an income statement and a balance sheet.

(b) What do you think are Sparks' problems?

(c) Could you design an income statement for Sparks with an intermediate or gross profit?

(d) How would Sparks value his work in progress?

2. Partridge bought 40 acres of farmland and turned the estate into a series of boating and fishing lakes to provide amenities for tourists who came by the day or stayed in his farmhouse. Most day visitors also ate in his farmhouse restaurant/cafe. He charged for the use of all facilities and also made money from the sale of fishing and boating gear and souvenirs.

He spent large sums on building additions to the farmhouse, roads, excavating the lakes, and planting trees.

At the end of the first year he is very concerned to know if the venture is profitable and if any part should be further developed or any part reduced.

Required:

(a) Design a suitable sectionalised income statement.

(b) Consider suitable depreciation policies and rates for the capital expenditure.

3. Cressage House Trust is a charity set up to run a residential home for sufferers from Harbridge's disease. The charity was set up on 1 January 19x7 and the balance in the books after the first year included:

Building work on the house at cost	164,000	Loan	80,000
Equipment and furniture at cost	121,000	Charges to patients	53,500
Salaries and wages	28,600	Bank overdraft	6,280
Heat, light, rates and insurance	32,100	Capital grant	170,000
Interest paid	3,780	Legacies	34,900
General overheads	12,200	Donations	10,200
		Fund raising	6,800

Notes:

(a) Cressage House was given to the Trust by a well wisher. It was valued professionally at land £30,000 and building £111,000. It was resolved to write off the building, including the new work, over 25 years.

(b) At the year end, building work completed but not paid for amounted to £50,000.

(c) Furniture and equipment should be depreciated over five years straight line with nil salvage value.

(d) Accruals were: salaries £3,290, heating £1,700.

(e) Prepayments were insurance £670, general overheads £320.

(f) The loan bears interest at 8% beginning on 1 April 19x7. It is repayable in five annual instalments beginning on 1 April 19x9. Interest has been paid to 30 September 19x7.

(g) Charges to patients in arrear at the year end amounted to £4,780.

(h) The capital grant is not repayable.

Required:

(a) Prepare appropriate financial statements for 19x7.

(b) Explain your treatment of the capital grant, the gift of Cressage House, capital and revenue reserves.

(c) Discuss the relevance of any surplus or deficit shown.

(d) Explain why depreciation of buildings is necessary.

4. Find some published reports and accounts of not-for-profit organisations (your own college, a local authority, a charity) and write a report on the treatment in the financial statements of interesting assets, liabilities, revenues and expenditures.

5. St John's College, Uffington and New College, Pongwardine are two higher education colleges of similar size. After publication of their annual financial statements both principals are concerned to compare the performance of the two colleges. Some details are:

	St John's	New
	£'000	£'000
Funding council grants	17,200	9,600
Full time student fees	7,100	3,200
Part time student fees	1,030	890
Short course fees	475	1,132
Residence, catering and conferences	10,900	6,400
	36,705	21,222
Staff costs	21,580	9,600
Depreciation	1,840	1,600
Residence and catering consumables	3,200	2,200
Academic consumables	2,100	1,540
Other operating expenses	6,800	3,400
Interest	1,600	880
	37,120	19,220
Deficit/Surplus	415	2,002
Staff numbers:		
Academic	420	170
Non academic	598	310

Depreciation policies on buildings are 1% a year on the revalued amounts by St John's and 4% on the revalued amounts by New College. The colleges have similar policies for fixtures etc.

Required:

(a) Compare the performance of the two colleges as well as is possible. You may find using ratios assists.

(b) The principal of St John's is worried about the deficit and is concerned to reconsider the College's policies for the coming year. Using comparisons between the two colleges suggest some changes that St John's may adopt to improve financial performance.

Assignment

❐ *The Sheinton Housing Association (this is a not-for-profit body which owns properties and lets them to suitable tenants – it is partly supported out of public funds) are preparing annual accounts. Questions have arisen on the following matters:*

(a) The Association is a company limited by guarantee

(b) The Association have commissioned a valuation of their properties

(c) The Association receive grants from the Housing Corporation for a proportion of the cost of their properties.

Required:

(a) Write a report to the management committee on the effect on financial statements of these matters and also the matters in paragraph 16.

(b) The Association sets rents at a level which covers all its costs. What costs do you think should be included. Explain your reasoning.

29 Decision making

Introduction

This chapter is a very brief introduction to some uses of accounting in decision making. It is very important that books of account are kept, both for routine activity like sending out statements of account to customers and for the preparation of financial statements. However accounting has a high cost and to make the best use of this expensive service, organisations need to use the accounting data generated, in decision making. Increasingly accounting is being seen as a vital function in all areas of activity – manufacturing, trading, service providing and not-for-profit activities. Decisions are made in many fields – what to make or what service to provide, how to make the product or provide the service, how to make the best of limited resources, how to deal with peaks and troughs in activity and many others. Many decisions are made entirely on financial grounds and all have, at least, a financial component.

Marginal costing

1. Costs can be categorised in many ways. We have already considered categorisation into materials, labour and overheads, into production, marketing and distribution and general administration and into direct and indirect costs. Another very useful categorisation is into fixed and variable costs. Another word for variable is marginal and the subject of marginal costing is concerned with this categorisation. Variable and marginal costs are similar but have different definitions which we will deal with later.

2. The division of costs into fixed and variable categories enables a number of decisions to be made rationally. We will briefly look at some of these.

Fixed and variable costs

3. A *fixed cost* is one which, within certain output limits, tends to be unaffected by variations in the level of activity.

   A *variable cost* is one which tends to vary in direct proportion to variations in the level of activity.

   Examples of fixed costs are rent and rates. Examples of variable costs are materials, labour paid on piece rates and power consumption.

   A good way of thinking about which category a cost falls into is to consider a particular level of activity (say an output of 5,000 widgets a month) and then to see which costs would change if output was increased (to say 6,000 widgets a month). The rent and rates of the factory would not change although if production was to rise very substantially additional premises would need to be taken on. However, rent and rates tend to be fixed for likely output levels and in the short term. Labour costs are likely to increase pro rata to output if the workers are paid piecework and possibly also if extra hours have to be worked by workers paid an hourly rate. In practice it is difficult to determine the effect on other costs. Would the telephone costs or heating costs be different at different levels of output?

Marginal costs

4. Marginal cost is the additional cost incurred by the production of one extra unit. This idea is related to the division between fixed and variable costs. If a factory was producing 4,000 widgets in a period, what would be the *additional* cost of producing just one more. The extra cost may be in materials, piecework labour and perhaps a tiny amount of electricity, lubricating oil and other manufacturing costs. Many costs (salaries, rent, rates, insurance etc) will stay the same.

Contribution

5. An important idea in marginal costing is contribution. Contribution is simply sales value less variable cost of sales. Consider a bookshop. Each book has a cost to the bookshop (say £6) and also a selling price (say £9). The difference is £3 - the contribution. Suppose 10,000 books were sold in a year then the total contribution is the sum of the individual contributions made from each book sale. The bookshop has overheads which are mostly fixed - wages, rent, rates, depreciation etc. The important thing for the bookshop is that, in a period, the total contribution amounts to more than the total of overheads. The word contribution in fact means the amount contributed by a sale towards the overheads and profit. To illustrate:

Total sales	100,000
Total variable cost	64,000
Total contribution	36,000
Total overheads	24,000
Net profit	12,000

You will see that total variable cost in the case of a bookshop is simply the cost of goods sold or the cost of the books and similarly the total contribution is the gross profit or the sales margin.

The idea of contribution can also be used in more complex situations. In manufacture contribution is the sales price of a product less the variable cost of manufacture. Remember that variable costs in manufacture can be materials, some labour and some overheads. In service industries a sale often gives a contribution which is the same as the sale price as there are likely to be only negligible variable costs. Imagine you are a customer of the Badland Bank and the financial adviser persuades you to insure your house with the Unwilling Insurance company. You pay the premium to the Bank and it passes it on to the insurance company less its commission. From the Bank's point of view there is no variable cost as the costs of doing the transaction, which might be the financial adviser's salary, advertising, a share of the cost of the Bank's premises etc, are all fixed costs which would be incurred anyway even if you did not insure your house this way. Sometimes there are variable costs. Possibly the Bank may pay the financial adviser a bonus or commission based on the sales he makes. In that case the contribution is the commission from the insurance company less the commission paid to the financial adviser. There may be negligible variable costs as well (e.g. extra telephone calls) but these are usually regarded as fixed costs.

Contribution to sales ratio

6. This is another useful idea. It is defined as:

    $$\frac{\text{Revenue less all variable costs}}{\text{Revenue}} \times 100$$

    In the case of the bookshop above you will see this is:

    $$\frac{36,000}{100,000} \times 100 = 36\%$$

    It is the same idea as gross profit to sales ratio but in cost accounting we prefer the use of the word contribution. It is useful in product planning. For example if we know the desired profit, the total fixed overheads and the contribution ratio we can work out the total sales needed to achieve the desired effect. Suppose the profit desired was £20,000, the fixed overheads £44,000 and the contribution ratio was 40%. then the required sales are:

    $$\text{Required sales} = \frac{\text{Total contribution}}{\text{Contribution ratio}} \times 100 \text{ or } \frac{£20,000 + £44,000}{40} \times 100 = £160,000$$

    Note that the lower the contribution ratio, the more sales are needed to cover fixed overheads and profit. Try the effect of different ratios in the equation. The idea of contribution ratio leads us onto the next idea - break-even.

Break-even

7. This can be defined as the level of activity at which there is neither profit nor loss. For example:

Sales	110,000
Variable costs	66,000
Contribution	44,000
Fixed costs	44,000
Profit	nil

    You will see that at the level of activity - sales £110,000 - fixed costs = contribution and there is neither a profit nor a loss. It is a useful idea in that a businessperson can know that if the break-even sales level is achieved then the business is at least not making a loss. Suppose a concert is proposed by the Club Committee. The ticket prices are £5 each and the variable cost is £2 (a fish and chip supper supplied by an outside caterer). So the contribution per attendee is £3. If the fixed costs are £240, how many people need to attend to break-even? The answer is 80 as 80 contributions is 80 x £3 = £240 which just covers the fixed costs. Note that every sale of a ticket over 80 tickets brings in extra contribution and hence profit of £3. Knowing the fixed costs, the contribution ratio and the level of activity or sales, it is possible to calculate the profit or loss:

    Profit/loss = Total contribution - fixed overheads

    This brings us onto another useful idea - the break-even chart.

Break-even charts

8. These are designed to show the approximate profit at different levels of sales volume within a limited range. Here is an example based on the concert discussed above:

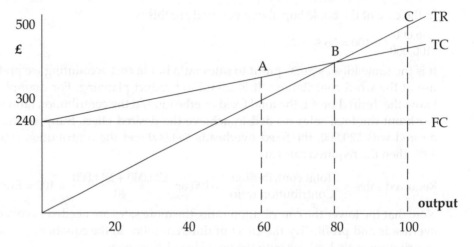

Notes:

(a) The vertical axis is in pounds sterling.

(b) The horizontal axis is a measure of output. In this case it is tickets sold but it might be total sales revenue.

(c) The line TR shows the total sales revenue. For example at point B (80 tickets sold) the total revenue is 80 x £5 = £400.

(d) The line FC shows the fixed costs (which are £240). It is horizontal because fixed costs are the same at all levels of output.

(e) The line TC is total cost and is Fixed costs + Variable costs. For example at point B (80 sales) the total cost = £240 + (80 x £2) = £400.

(f) At point A (60 tickets sold) the concert shows a loss calculated as:

Total sales - total variable cost - fixed costs = (60 x£5) – (60 x £2) – £240 = £60.
You may see that this is the same as: Total contribution (60 x £3) – £240 = £60.

(g) At point C (100 sales) the concert shows a profit of £60 (100 x £3 – £240).

(h) In fact 100 is the expected or forecast sales. Then difference between the forecast sales (point C) and the break-even point (point B) is known as the *margin of safety*. The margin of safety is the level by which sales have to fall before break-even is reached. It can be measured as a ratio: the *margin of safety ratio* and is equal to:

$$\frac{\text{forecast turnover - break-even turnover}}{\text{Forecast turnover}} \times 100$$

Here it is $\dfrac{100 - 80}{100} \times 100$

This is a measure of risk; the lower the ratio, the greater the risk of sales falling below break-even level.

(i) The chart shows output levels from nil to something over 100. The range shown is known as the *relevant range*. It is only necessary to show the output from the lowest likely to the maximum possible. I have shown it from a nil output - in practice this is extremely improbable. The maximum in this case depends on the maximum seating in the concert venue.

(j) The fixed cost line FC is horizontal here. In some cases it may be stepped like this

This is because the fixed costs may remain the same up to some level of output, e.g. 100 ticket sales. Above that level the fixed costs may be higher. As an example the fixed costs may be £240 up to 100 ticket sales. Above that and up to the level of venue capacity (120), the fixed costs may rise as 20 extra chairs have to be hired at £2 each. So from 100 to 120 the fixed costs will be £280.

(k) I have shown TR, FC and TC on my chart. You may prefer not to show the FC line. The profit, loss and break-even can still be read off.

(l) Some break-even charts show two lines only: Fixed Costs and Total Contribution. The profit, loss and break-even can still be read off in the same way.

Why use break-even charts?

9. They are useful because:
   (a) They are a useful way of clarifying thinking about the relationship between cost, volume and profit.
   (b) They are a useful way of demonstrating this relationship.
   (c) They enable the break-even point to be determined and also the profit or loss at different levels of output.
   (d) They show the margin of safety in a dramatic way.
   (e) They make the drawer of the chart think about the relevant range.

   They have some limitations:
   (a) They show straight lines. Relationships (e.g. between output and sales revenue) are often not that linear; few costs are truly fixed or truly variable and yet a break-even chart makes this assumption.
   (b) It assumes that there is a single product or a single constant mix of products. In our case there is a single product, ie a ticket. It would be more difficult to consider a situation where there were say three products, e.g. different prices for the waged, the unwaged and children.
   (c) They are really a simplification of what is usually a fairly complex situation.

Marginal costs and decision making

10. Knowledge of marginal costs is very useful in decision making. In this section we will look at four decisions that can be made using this costing approach.
    (a) **How to make**
       P Ltd can make its widgets on a labour intensive method (the L method) or by a capital intensive method (the C method). Figures are:

	L	C
Selling price per item	£20	£20
Variable cost per item	£12	£8
Total fixed cost	£20,000	£60,000

You will notice that labour intensive methods tend to have high variable costs. This is because labour tends to be the main component of cost and can be varied because payment is by hourly rate or piecework. Capital intensive methods involve a high amount of depreciation which is generally considered to be a fixed cost.

How should the item be made if output is expected to be:

(i) 4,000 units?

(ii) 12,000 units?

The approach is to work out the *contribution* in both cases. Contribution is simply selling price less variable costs. In this case it is £8 for the L method and £12 for the C method.

Profits will be:

	4,000 output		12,000 output	
	L	C	L	C
	£	£	£	£
Total contribution	32,000	48,000	96,000	144,000
Fixed costs	20,000	60,000	20,000	60,000
Profit (loss)	12,000	(12,000)	76,000	84,000

Clearly at 4,000 units the labour method is the most profitable but at 12,000 units the capital method gives higher profits. The reason is that as output rises, there are more contributions but fixed costs remain the same.

A useful idea is the **break-even** point. This is where total contribution equals fixed costs and no profit or loss is made. In the case of the L method:

If break-even output is y then: for the L method $8y = £20,000$ and $y = 2,500$. Whereas for the C method: $12y = £60,000$ and $y = 5,000$. At 4,000 units of output, output has not reached break-even point for the C method.

(b) **Limiting factor**

G Ltd has a choice of making either or both of two products A and B.

Facts are:	A	B
Contribution	£24	£40
Usage of scarce labour	$\frac{1}{2}$ hour	1 hour

There are only 400 hours of the *limiting factor* or scarce resource available. What should be made if sales are unlimited?

The technique is to calculate the *contribution per unit of scarce resource*. This is £48 an hour for A and £40 an hour for B. Thus if an hour of the scarce labour is used to make an A the contribution will be £48 and if making a B then it will be £40.

It is obviously more profitable to make As and a total of 800 As should be made as this will exactly use up all the limited labour available.

If only 700 As could be sold then output should be 700 As using 350 hours and 50 Bs to use up the remaining hours.

In some cases there are two or more constraints (= limiting factors) and to solve the output problem *linear programming* methods are required. These are beyond the scope of this book.

(c) **Special orders**

Grue Ltd has been asked to quote for the supply of 100 of their unique widgets to a company in Sweden. The price needs to be extremely low to land the order. The cost of each widget is:

	£
Materials	15
Direct labour	13
Variable overheads	8
Fixed overheads	6
	42

The normal home price is £55 and this will be unaffected by the export order if that order is received.

If the order is accepted, there will need to be a payment to a supervisor of £400 for the time he spends on the manufacture. There will also be an extra packing cost of £1 an item.

The *marginal* cost of the 100 widgets will thus be:

		£
Materials	100 × £15	1,500
Direct labour	100 × £13	1,300
Variable overheads	100 × £8	800
Packing	100 × £1	100
Supervisor		400
Total cost		4,100

Notes:

(a) The costs calculated above are marginal costs. They are extra costs that will be incurred by the firm if the 100 widgets are made.

(b) Any selling price above £4,100 will be of benefit to the firm.

(c) In this calculation, the fixed costs can be ignored as they will be incurred if Grue makes the widgets or if it does not.

(d) Selling at marginal costs can be dangerous, in that although the firm may receive more than it pays out as a result of a low price sale, other customers who are paying full price may want a reduction also.

(d) **Make or buy decisions**

Trater Ltd manufactures a flinge which costs:

	£
Materials	51
Direct labour	40

...continued

	£
Variable overheads	23
Fixed overheads	39
	153

It has been quoted £105 each for the supply of the flinges from a firm in Korea. Transport costs will be £5 an item. There will be a saving of £2,000 a year in fixed costs if the flinges are not manufactured by Trater. Output is 1,000 a year. The reduction in costs if the 1,000 flinges are not made will be:

$1,000 \times (51 + 40 + 23) + £2,000 = £116,000.$

The costs of importing the 1,000 items will be:

$1,000 \times (£105 + £5) = £110,000$

Thus it is more profitable to import than to manufacture. Note however, that there are many other arguments – continuity of supply, price variations due to exchange rates and other factors, delivery problems etc.

Decision making in the service sector

11. Decision making in the service sector is much the same as in the manufacturing sector. Financial considerations are extremely important and the accountant is expected to provide financial information which will assist management in making decisions. In the next section we look at cost categorisations which are helpful in the context of a number of types of service-providing enterprises.

Total absorption costing

12. The ideas of total absorption costing were developed primarily for the manufacturing business but apply equally well in services. As an example we will look at a branch office of a firm of solicitors. The firm occupies very expensive offices in a city centre. It employs 10 fee-earning staff (solicitors and legal executives) and 15 non-fee earning staff (office staff, accounting staff etc). Total overheads are budgeted at:

Salaries	£225,000
Occupancy etc	£165,000
Total	£390,000

Total fee-earning hours are budgeted at 13,000. Thus the average overhead is £30 an hour.

The direct cost depends on the fee-earner involved. The calculation of annual salary divided by chargeable hours varies from £15 to £53 an hour. Remember that a fee earner may work 40 hours a week but not all will be chargeable to clients as some time will be spent on administration, sickness, training, travelling etc. The firm aims to add 25% to cost to find a selling price. The charge out rate will thus vary from (£30 + £15 = £45 + 25%) £56.25 to (£30 + £53 = £83 + 25%) £103.75 per hour.

Uses of total absorption costing

13. Using total absorption cost to derive a charge out rate in this way, is justifiable and logical (unlike the law!). It ensures that all work is charged to clients at a price which is sufficient to cover all direct and indirect costs and to make a profit. It does imply that all the available chargeable hours are in fact charged out to clients. In times of recession, and with over supply in the legal profession, this may not always be so. The approach may also be used to value work in progress at the year end – at cost (say £30 + £15 = £48) not including a profit element.

In practice, pricing is subject to the market and the balance of supply and demand. It may be possible to exact much higher fees from some clients and some types of work. On the other hand it may only be possible to charge lower fees for some work.

This global approach to costs is relatively easy to do but a more exact calculation is possible if the firm is divided up into cost centres and an overhead cost derived by apportionment and allocation of costs on a rational basis to each cost centre. Cost centres used may be activity based – typing, photo-copying, reception, archiving etc or may be person centred. For any work done by a fee earner it will be necessary to identify the cost centres used in earning particular fees.

How to create the service

14. In service industries, as in manufacturing, there is often more than one way of producing the product. We will take, as an example, the holiday tour industry. Kosy coach tours is a new venture. Its way of operating is to put together coach tours including travel and hotel accommodation, and to advertise these in the hope of filling each tour to capacity. It has a choice of buying its own coaches and employing full time drivers. Alternatively, it can charter coaches from other coach firms. Which method is used depends on many factors – control, quality of coach, quality of driver, availability of coaches, back up service etc. But it also depends on financial factors. The problem is that the success of the advertising, and hence the number of tours which will actually run, is not known. The accountant might be asked to determine the fixed and variable costs on each alternative. For the buying-own-coaches approach, the costs will have a very high fixed element. For the hiring-other-people's-coaches approach, the costs will mainly be variable. Suppose that, if most tours actually run, the cheapest alternative will be to own their own coaches. If many tours do not actually run, then the cheapest is hiring.

The directors of the firm can now make a decision based on:

(a) Their estimate of how many tours will run (note that the cheaper alternative means lower charges and probably more sales).

(b) The non-quantifiable benefits/disbenefits of having their own coaches as against hiring coaches.

Without the financial input of knowing the probable cost of each tour based on alternative ways of supplying the product, the decision on what to charge customers and which way to supply the service may be sub-optimal – less than the best.

Limiting factors

15. Beverley has a hairdressing business in a very small town in the country. She has five chairs and four assistants plus two trainees. She is the only hairdresser in the town and is busy most of the time. She offers hairdressing services to women, men and boys. At the beginning of 19x6, a new housing estate was built at the edge of the town and business suddenly became very brisk. It became impossible to offer all the services she had offered hitherto. She decided to stop offering one or two of the services. The problem was – which?

    She solved the problem by calculating:

    (a) The contribution from each service (not just women, men, boys but also cut, shampoo, perm, restyle etc for each). This was calculated simply as the price charged less a small number of variable costs – mainly materials.

    (b) The average time taken for each service.

    (c) The total number of hours available from the five chairs.

    This enabled her to calculate the contribution per hour from each type of service. The total number of hours is a limited resource given the new demand for her products and the best strategy is to offer the service giving the highest contribution per hour.

    This is a short-term problem. In the long term, the higher population will induce other hairdressers to enter the market and she will have to decide if she wants to acquire additional premises and expand. Ponder on the effects of adopting the best strategy (just doing ladies' hair) on her long and short term prospects.

Special orders

16. For this area we will consider 'The King's Head', a pub on the edge of town. Large expenditure has been incurred on building and equipping a modern kitchen. This means that the business of selling meals has large fixed costs. The variable costs are largely labour (low paid and part time) and materials (very cheap considering the prices charged by the pub). Business has gone well but there is still some spare capacity at lunch time. The manager, Manuel, is highly enterprising and has identified a market for his spare capacity in the neighbouring industrial estate – taking meals to the firms for working lunches etc. Before doing this he notes that there is already a supplier of this service (one man and a van) and that the rival's prices are very low. He has to consider the financial benefits of this service. He calculates:

    (a) The marginal costs of supplying each meal – materials, labour, motor expenses.

    (b) The fixed costs of entering this market – some equipment and advertising.

    (c) How many meals he expects to sell.

    This tells him the cost per meal. He then calculates the minimum charge he can make per meal which is cost plus a small percentage. He then compares this with the prices charged by his rival.

    Should he go ahead? There are many imponderables – the response of his rival, the cost of each meal depends on how many he sells (as there is an element of fixed cost), he may be in competition with himself (firms' staffs may now choose to go to the pub or stay at work and still eat pub meals), higher profit in-pub sales may be turned away if he contracts to sell outside. Accountants give an essential service in calculating costs but business is really about commercial judgement and the balance of risks.

The not-for-profit sector

17. The not-for-profit sector includes undertakings that exist to provide a service but do not in general make a charge for it. These include charities, the health service, local government and central government. Income for these bodies includes trading (Oxfam has more branches than any other retailer), charges to users (e.g. admissions to National Trust houses, swimming pool charges, prescription charges), sponsorship, donations, legacies, investment income (the Church Commissioners are noteworthy here), local taxes (council tax, business rates), central taxes (income tax, VAT etc).

Local government

18. In all of these bodies, management accounting is practised to a greater or lesser extent. In local government, government imposed financial restriction has led to very careful assessment of costs so that:
    (a) Maximum **economy** is achieved by acquiring goods and services at the lowest possible cost.
    (b) Maximum **efficiency** is achieved in converting goods and services into an output (e.g. administering housing or running a home help service).
    (c) Maximum **effectiveness** is attained in achieving the goals of the service (e.g. by keeping delinquent youths away from parked cars).

19. Over the last 15 years the Government has obliged local councils to engage in compulsory competitive tendering. This means that the supply of a service (paid for by the local council) must be put out to tender so that the lowest bidder (subject to satisfactory quality and other factors) wins the contract and supplies the service. Initially this requirement was for works of construction and maintenance. It has now been extended to street cleansing, refuse collection and grounds maintenance and, most recently to specific percentages of white collar services such as legal services, finance, personnel and housing management. The council's existing employees are able to band together to tender for the contracts. Some are more successful than others. As an example Wolverhampton has awarded 92% of its contracts to its own employees and only 8% to private sector contractors.

20. Management accounting is well established in local government and the achieve-ment of the **three Es** requires a thorough understanding of costs. This is especially true of economy and efficiency but the basic problem of measuring effectiveness will always remain. Consider a council examining an area such as refuse collection and disposal. The following points may be made:
    (a) Maximum economy in the provision of the collection service must be achieved. If the internal tender is to win, the least possible costs must be found. This means evaluating labour intensive methods as against capital intensive methods and many other costing techniques.

(b) Maximum efficiency must be found in disposing of the rubbish. This may be tipping or burning or a mixture. Costs and benefits of extracting ferrous metals from rubbish before tipping or burning need to be evaluated.

(c) Whether the service achieved is effective is rather a matter of opinion. It may seem satisfactory that the rubbish is simply disposed of. However, tipping may lead to long-term problems (fires, blighted land, leaks of toxic substances etc). Burning may lead to addition to the greenhouse effect, release of toxic gases, smells and other problems. Also the ecological benefits of recycling paper, metals and possibly organic matter for animal feed may be important.

The important thing for accountants is to realise that councils have a need to know the cost of all sorts of activities and alternative activities. Once costs and benefits have been estimated in money terms, it is for politicians to make decisions. These are often perverse!

Central government

21. Historically accounting has not been a major concern of central government and the Civil Service. It was always felt that a lengthy education in non-relevant subjects was a better qualification for the Civil Service than professional qualifications. However all that has now changed and accountants are making a real impact on central government. A new technique recently introduced is **resource accounting and budgeting (RAB).** Essentially this is just the accruals accounting which this manual has used throughout. The idea is that accruals accounting (as against simply cash in and cash out) enables organisations to determine the full costs of *when* and *where* resources are consumed (for example – people, materials, *depreciation*) and to link these costs to outputs (services provided, roads built, embassies conducted, justice done etc).

22. It is for the Government to decide if a service is to be provided (e.g. defence, education, police, social security, health, pensions) and also to decide the extent of it (should nursery education be provided for all?). The decision on how it should be provided is subject to the ideas of the three Es. Clearly the cost of all the alternative methods of supply need to be determined and evaluated. A requirement for tendering is often a good way of elucidating the cheapest possible effective supply method.

Charities

23. Charities, like central and local government, tend to be short of money but not short of ways of spending it. Policies have to be chosen on what services can be provided and to what extent and how these services can be provided. Costs of different alternatives need to be evaluated so that policy makers can make an informed choice.

Consider the Church of England. Should every council estate have its own Church premises or should better premises be provided but in fewer places? Should every council estate have its own full-time minister or should fewer be employed with wider territorial responsibilities? What would be the effect of each policy on numbers of attenders and their giving? What to do is a matter of opinion and judgement and it may be suggested that the intrusion of sordid financial considerations is inappropriate. However the accountant can assist with decisions on spending limited resources by determining the costs and benefits of all possible strategies.

I do not suggest that hourly cost of a clergyman (probably about £8 to £12 an hour) should be a consideration in whether a minister should spend four hours visiting a hospital 20 miles away in order to visit a sick parishioner. On the other hand, a knowledge of costs is often worth at least a passing thought in deciding between alternative actions.

Summary

❑ Fixed costs remain the same at different levels of activity or output – at least within certain output levels and in the short term.

❑ Variable costs tend to vary in direct proportion (= linearly) to variations in levels of activity.

❑ A marginal cost is the additional cost of producing one more of a product.

❑ Marginal costs can be usefully employed in decision making – how to make, using scarce resources, special low price orders, make or buy.

❑ Service industries have need of cost determination for decision making.

❑ Cost calculation can be total absorption. This involves similar measures to those used in manufacturing – allocation and apportionment of costs to cost centres and the adoption of measures for recovering such costs.

❑ Calculation of marginal costs and contribution can also be useful in many areas of decision making including how to supply, limited resource situations and special orders.

❑ Local government has a long tradition of management accounting. The costs of various courses of action are an essential input to the decision process.

❑ Economy, efficiency and effectiveness are essential in local government provision of services.

❑ Compulsory competitive tendering is a requirement for many local government services.

❑ It is very difficult to measure the output of local and central government.

❑ Central government departments and agencies are now adopting conventional accounting practices and calling them resource accounting and budgeting.

❑ Charities also have to live within their resources and need management accounting information to enable them to choose between alternatives.

Points to note

❑ Direct costs, variable costs and marginal costs can be equivalent. However, some variable costs (e.g. power) are often not included in direct costs because of the diffi-culty of measurement. Variable cost is a term used to describe the behaviour of costs. Marginal costs are strictly as defined in the summary. In practice some people are very particular about terminology but it is perhaps more important to understand the concepts and use them intelligently.

☐ In practice the behaviour of costs is very difficult to determine. Even direct materials are not strictly linearly variable as quantity discounts may be obtained.

☐ Many textbooks consider the effect on profit measurement of valuing stocks at marginal cost. I will not do so, as this practice has largely died out in the UK. Since the mid seventies, stocks and work in progress, for balance sheet purposes, are required by SSAP 9 to be valued at full (= total absorption) cost (i.e. including overheads, some of which may be fixed). In view of this, it seems pointless to discuss how profit may be different if stocks were valued at marginal cost.

☐ The techniques, outlined in this section, are simple but business is complex. Other factors will complicate all decisions. For example, it may pay to make best use of a scarce resource, but customers may demand a mix of goods or not buy at all. Financial effects and costs are important and must enter into business decision making but management has to take in many more factors in making actual decisions.

☐ Management accounting is about providing management with financial information, together with techniques for using the information, for decision making. The information is often obtained from past experience but is essentially about the future. The future is unknowable and so decisions about the future are always of uncertain effect. The accountant can provide information but it is management's job to make the decisions based on judgement and assessments of risk.

☐ Management accounting in the service sector has a smaller literature than that of the manufacturing sector but is just as important. All the main techniques of management accounting can be applied.

☐ In business, there is an essential requirement to make a profit in order to survive. Efficiency is a goal sought by all firms. Management accounting provides ways of considering the costs of alternative courses of action and costs and revenues are all important. In not-for-profit undertakings, other considerations are often given more importance. Political ideology rules over financial correctness. However the hard world of scarce resources and ever increasing demand for services has led all not-for-profit bodies to have regard for costs and active cost finding regimes are now in place in many areas.

☐ The assessment of output in commercial firms is easy. Measurement is of turnover in money terms. Measures of output in not-for-profit undertakings are subjective. A simple monetary total needs to be replaced by a discursive essay.

Self-testing questions

1. Define fixed and variable costs.
2. Define marginal costs.
3. What is a contribution?
4. What is a break-even point?
5. What are the benefits of using total absorption costing in service industries ?

6. What influences exist on pricing in the service sector?
7. What other factors in addition to highest contribution per unit of scarce resource can apply in deciding on output in limiting factor situations?
8. What other factors apply similarly in special order situations?
9. What are the three Es of local government finance?
10. What is compulsory competitive tendering?
11. What is resource accounting and budgeting?

Exercises

1. Describe the behaviour of the following costs:
   Fire insurance, employers' liability insurance, depreciation of plant, repairs to buildings, cleaning materials, telephone, metered water.
2. Doe makes his socks by labour intensive methods and his costs are:
   Materials £30, direct labour £60, variable production costs £10 (all these are for 200 pairs), fixed production costs £40,000 a year. If output is:
   (a) 400,000 pairs;
   (b) 600,000 pairs;
   would it pay him to employ capital intensive methods if fixed production costs increased to £110,000 a year and direct labour fell £30 for 200 pairs? The selling price is 70p a pair.
   Would your answer be different if (i) getting sales was very difficult (ii) sales were expanding fast?
3. Hong can make three products whose contributions and potential sales and usage of scarce resource F are:

Product	J	K	L
Contribution (per unit)	£24	£16	£60
Potential sales (units)	20,000	16,000	5,000
Usage of F (per unit)	14	10	32

   Supply of F is limited to 300,000 units.
   What should he make?
4. Saeed makes a gong which costs – prime cost £39 + variable overheads £11 + fixed overheads £26. He sells it for £100. He has been asked to quote very keenly for the supply of 4,000 of these to a wholesaler (he normally supplies retailers). He reckons the extra sales will add £40,000 to his fixed costs but will reduce his prime costs to £37 for all his output (viz: his normal output of 30,000 + the 4,000).
   What is the lowest price he can accept?
5. Facts as in 4 above but ignore the extra 4,000 items. Saeed has been offered a supply of gongs at £62 each. Acceptance of the supply will halve his fixed overheads. Should he make or buy?
6. Rubb Industrial Polishes Ltd manufactures to order. The cost estimation department has costed an enquiry received from Orca Ltd at £30,500 on a total absorption cost basis and has suggested a selling price of £36,000. Orca states that this price is too high and suggests that it was expecting a price of about £27,000.

Discuss this problem from the point of view of Rubb. You might suggest alternative costing principles that might be useful in negotiating with Orca. It is unlikely that either company has said their last words on the potential deal.

7. Bluebeard owns and runs an old people's home. The home is large and he takes in a range of people from those living in one-room flatlets who do their own catering to persons requiring 24 hour nursing care. Most are permanent residents but he also takes in short-stay people (one night to two weeks).

Required:

(a) Outline a costing system to determine the full cost of putting up each type of resident.

(b) How might this total absorption cost help in price determination and what other factors might be relevant?

8. Lois owns and runs a bus company. She runs a scheduled service on four routes and a school bus service which employs three buses at relevant times. All these activities are profitable. A local museum has asked her to quote a very low price to run visitors between the three sites of the museum. She is unable to buy or lease more buses because of financial restraints and lack of garage and cleaning and service space.

Required:

Detail how you might determine the price she might quote the museum and indicate factors for and against accepting a long-term contract from them. Suggest terms she might require in the contract.

9. The Cressage Hospital Trust is considering the purchase of a new diagnostic machine. The costs will be:

(a) Construction of building to house the machine and its operators £250,000.

(b) Purchase and installation of the machine £340,000.

(c) Four full-time staff £68,000 a year.

(d) Other fixed overheads £70,000 a year.

At the present time the machine would be used for about 1,000 hours a year. This will probably double over the next few years. An alternative to buying the machine would be to rent time on a neighbouring Trust's machine at £140 an hour. This would involve transporting the patients to the neighbouring Trust hospital.

The Trust feels that the diagnosis by such a machine is essential for its patients.

Required:

Prepare a report, making reasonable assumptions and in numerical terms, on what to do.

Assignment

☐ *The Savant Educational Trust is a charity which runs correspondence courses in a variety of subjects. These are normally charged out at cost + 20%. The profit margin exists to increase resources available for developing the services of the Trust. The courses are mainly written by outside experts for a fee but some are written by full-time staff. Production and printing is done in-house at the Trust's owned premises by full-time staff. Administration of the courses is also carried out by the full-time administrative staff. Marking of scripts is done by outside experts on a piece-work basis but some are marked by full-time academic staff. Outside* experts are paid a fee per course and an additional fee per student to advise students over the telephone.

Required:

(a) Explain in detail how the cost of a course might be established in order to fix the selling price.

(b) The Trust has received an enquiry from an East European country to sell a particular course but the price must be very low indeed.

Facts established are:

(i) Take up of the course proved less than expected in the UK. As a result some 200 copies are in store. These cost £30 each to print and set up costs apportioned to the course (writing and editing) were £20 a course. The course will not be offered again in the UK as a new course has been produced. The Ruritanians have indicated that the old course is satisfactory for them.

(ii) Some changes have to be made to the course and these will cost £600 as a fee to the expert and printing the amendments will cost £400.

(iii) Most of the assignments will be marked by the Ruritanians but each final assignment will need to be marked by a member of the full-time staff. The salary of the staff member is £20,000 + 15% for national insurance. He is contracted to work 1,800 hours a year and overheads attached to him (provision of office space, secretarial assistance, telephone, computer, stationery, motor expenses etc) are £15,000 a year. He is very busy and the marking of the Ruritanian scripts will need to be done in overtime for which he is paid double time. He will take an hour over each script.

(iv) Administrative costs for sending out the courses to Ruritania and dealing with the final assignments will be (per course):

        apportioned fixed overheads £20

        variable costs £13

Calculate the minimum price per course to be charged to the Ruritanians on the assumption that they take up I. 100 courses or II. all 200 courses. Explain your reasoning.

(c) Explain how a marginal costing approach to pricing the new course would enable the Trust to supply the Ruritanians with the latest course at a lower price than that charged to UK students.

(d) Selling the courses world wide even at discount prices would enable the Trust to lower its average cost and hence its prices. Comment on this idea.

30 Forecast cash flows and financial statements

Introduction

1. Before starting a business it is now best modern practice to prepare cash flow forecasts. Cash flow forecasts are simply forecasts of the amounts and timing of future receipts and payments and balances in hand. Remember that we are talking about the state of the bank account, which can go into overdraft. So negative balances are possible if the bank manager agrees. Here is a simple example for a poor writer of novels.

2. **Cash Flow Forecast for Homer Shakespeare for the Six Months to June 19x9:**

	Jan	Feb	Mar	Apr	May	Jun
Inflows:						
Royalties from publisher	150	4,500		1,300	360	
Fees for magazine articles		200		650		
Total inflows	150	4,700		1,950	360	
Outflows:						
Household expenditure	800	730	600	1,200	800	650
Photocopying etc	100	340	280	200	100	200
Holiday					1,800	
New computer		1,800				
Total outflows	900	2,870	880	1,400	2,700	850
Balance at beginning	1,210	460	2,290	1,410	1,960	–380
Balance at end	460	2,290	1,410	1,960	– 380	–1,230

Notes:

(a) The balance in the bank at the beginning of the period is £1,210. This is known, but all the other figures are forecasts and estimates (both as to amount and timing) and so could turn out to be wrong!

(b) It is usual to make the forecasts on a monthly basis (as here) but shorter or longer intervals are possible.

(c) The receipts in January are forecast as £150 and the payments as £900. Thus the expected balance at the end of the month is £1,210 + £150 – £900 = £460. The balance at the end of the month is of course also the balance at the beginning of the next month.

(d) Shakespeare sees that if all goes according to plan he will be in overdraft at the ends of May and June. This is useful information for him as he can now make appropriate plans. For example he might:

(i) Approach the bank and ask for an overdraft to be allowed up to say £1,500. He needs plenty of time to arrange this. As a result of the forecast, he knows well in advance of his need to arrange overdraft facilities. Note that the right to overdraw at the bank is called an overdraft **facility**.

(ii) Change his plans in some way to avoid going into overdraft. One possibility might be to borrow the money from some other source to avoid paying out of his bank account for the computer. This could be done at very high interest rates on Access or Visa but future payments would then be needed to repay, with interest, any loan received. Another possibility might be to postpone or cancel the holiday or to take a cheaper one. A third possibility might be to generate more income by, say, writing more magazine articles.

A business example

3. Here is a more complicated example. We will begin by assembling some information before actually writing out the example. Andrea intends to start trading as a wholesaler of widgets (a widget is any product you want it to be!) at the beginning of January 19x9. She assembled the following estimates:

(a) She will start the bank account with £3,000 – her life savings.

(b) She hopes to make sales of : January £3,000, February £4,000, March and subsequent months £5,000 a month. She sells on credit and expects her customers to pay two months after the actual sales (i.e. January sales will be paid in March).

(c) She will buy an initial stock of widgets at a cost of £5,000 and thereafter will replace stock as it is sold. She sells at a mark-up of 100% so that the sales of widgets in February for £4,000 will require purchases from her suppliers at a price of £2,000. She receives one month's credit from her suppliers so that purchases in January (£5,000 + 50% of £3,000 = £6,500) will be paid for in February.

(d) Overhead expenses (rent, insurance, electricity, transport etc) will be £1,500 a month.

(e) She will take £800 a month from the business bank account to pay her household bills.

The forecast should show:

Andrea – Cash Flow Forecast for the Six Months to June 19x9:

	Jan	Feb	Mar	Apr	May	Jun
Inflows:						
From Andrea	3,000					
From customers			3,000	4,000	5,000	5,000
Total inflows	3,000		3,000	4,000	5,000	5,000
Outflows:						
Suppliers		6,500	2,000	2,500	2,500	2,500
Overheads	1,500	1,500	1,500	1,500	1,500	1,500
Andrea – drawings	800	800	800	800	800	800
Total outflows	2,300	8,800	4,300	4,800	4,800	4,800
Balance at beginning	nil	700	–8,100	–9,400	–10,200	–10,000
Balance at end	700	–8,100	–9,400	–10,200	–10,000	–9,800

Notes:

(a) As before, the forecast is composed of estimates. Andrea may not achieve the sales forecasted and the customers may take longer than two months to pay. Overheads may be more or less and have different timings. In practice, actual achievement usually turns out to be somewhat different from the forecasts.

(b) Clearly Andrea is going to need a bank overdraft facility of at least £10,200. Note that a facility of that amount would allow the bank account to go into overdraft up to that amount. The actual overdraft at any one time would hopefully be less than that.

(c) In practice banks only grant overdraft facilities when they see some reasonable prospect of the overdraft being repaid. The evidence for this is usually a cash flow forecast. In this case the overdraft is probably going to rise until April and then begin to decline through May and June. The banks have special forms for cash flow forecasts with spaces for the most likely headings for receipts and payments and usually covering 12 months.

Preparing forecast financial statements – an example

4. Kallagan Ltd trades in hot air balloons and has just received the accountant's report on its first year of operation:

Trading and profit and loss account for year ended 31 March 19x5

	£	£		£	£
Opening stock	40,000		Sales – cash	50,000	
Purchases	180,000		Sales – credit	150,000	200,000
	220,000				
Less Closing stock	80,000				
		140,000			
Gross profit c/d		60,000			
		200,000			200,000
Administration expenses		20,000	Gross profit b/d		60,000
Selling & distribution exps		9,000			
Depreciation		21,000			
Net profit before tax c/d		10,000			
		60,000			60,000
Tax at 50%		5,000	Net profit before tax b/d		10,000
Net profit after tax c/d		5,000			
		10,000			10,000

Balance sheet as at 31 March 19x5

	Cost £	Depr'n £	Net £
Fixed assets	140,000	21,000	119,000
Current assets:			
Stock		80,000	
Debtors		50,000	
		130,000	
Less Trade creditors:		45,000	
Taxation		5,000	
Overdraft		4,000	
		54,000	
			76,000
			195,000
Financed by:			
Share capital (50p shares)			190,000
Net profit			5,000
			195,000

The Chairman of Kallagan Ltd, Arthur Gillscar, and his board have produced the following guidelines for 19x5/x6:
(a) Double turnover.
(b) Expect tax to remain at 50%.
(c) Increase gross profit to sales margin by one fifth.
(d) Increase administration costs by £10,000.
(e) Reduce stock by 25% at the end of the year.
(f) Maintain the ratio of cash:credit sales.
(g) Maintain the depreciation policy at 15% straight line at its present level.
(h) No fixed assets are to be bought or sold.
(i) Reduce the average collection period by one month.
(j) Take three months to pay creditors.
(k) Increase selling and distribution costs by 30% and add £20,000 for advertising.
(l) Declare a dividend of 5p a share.
You are asked to prepare budgeted accounts for 19x5/x6 incorporating the above decisions.

5. **Answer:**

Kallagan Ltd

**Budgeted trading and profit and loss account
for the year ending 31 March 19x6**
a

	£	£	
Sales		400,000	b
Less Cost of sales:			
Opening stock	80,000		
Purchases	236,000		f
	316,000		
Closing stock	60,000	256,000	e, d
Gross profit		144,000	c
Administration expenses	30,000		g
Selling and distribution expenses	31,700		h
Depreciation	21,000	82,700	i
Net profit before tax		61,300	
Taxation at 50%		30,650	j
Net profit after tax		30,650	
Proposed dividend		19,000	k
Retained profit for the year		11,650	

Kallagan Ltd.
Forecast balance sheet as at 31 March 19x6

	Cost	Depr'n	Net	
	£	£	£	
Fixed assets	140,000	42,000	98,000	
Current assets:				
Stock		60,000		
Debtors		75,000		l
Cash at bank		?		n
		217,300		
Current liabilities:				
Creditors		59,000		m
Dividend		19,000		
Taxation		30,650		
		108,650		
			108,650	
			206,650	

... continued

	Cost	Depr'n	Net
	£	£	£
Financed by:			
Share capital			190,000
Retained profits			16,650
			206,650

Notes:

(a) Forecast or budgeted statements must be so labelled.

(b) Gross profit margin in 19x4/x5 was $\frac{60}{200} \times 100 = 30\%$.

Gross profit margin in 19x5/x6 will be $30\% + \frac{1}{5} = 36\%$.

Gross profit in 19x5/x6 will be $36\% \times 400,000 = £144,000$

(d) Cost of sales is computed by deducting gross profit from sales.

(e) Closing stock is 25% less than last year.

(f) Purchases are obtained by deduction.

(g) Administration costs are £10,000 more than last year.

(h) Selling expenses are $130\% \times £9,000 + £20,000$.

(i) Depreciation is 15% of cost of fixed assets.

(j) Tax is 50% of net profit.

(k) Dividend is 5p a share on 380,000 shares.

(l) Collection period in 19x4/x5 was $\frac{50,000}{150,000} \times 12 = 4$ months

Collection period in 19x5/x6 will be three months.
Debtors will be $\frac{3}{12} \times 300,000 = £75,000$.

(m) Creditors will be $\frac{3}{12} \times 236,000 = £59,000$.

(n) The cash at bank is the balancing figure on this balance sheet. You will calculate it as £82,300.

Summary

❐ The forecasting, recording and management of cash flows is an important facet of the management of all enterprises.

❐ Cash can mean notes and coin but, more commonly in business, it is used to mean the bank account.

❐ Before commencing, any enterprise (whether profit seeking or non-profit) should forecast its cash flows on a monthly basis for at least the first year. This will enable the enterprise to ensure that cash flow patterns are satisfactory. A need for an overdraft facility may be seen in advance and arrangements negotiated. Alternatively changes may be made in the timing and amounts of cash flows.

❐ A major determinant of the balance at the bank is the amount of credit given and taken. In practice, it is difficult to forecast when customers will pay and continuous efforts need to be made to persuade them to pay including reminders, telephone calls and, if all else fails, threats to cut off supplies or legal action. The timing of payments to suppliers is under the control of the business but unreasonable delays in payment can lead to supplier bad will, cutting off of supplies and ultimately legal action.

❏ The majority of accounting paper questions are concerned with the preparation of historical accounts.

❏ Increasingly, the same techniques used to prepare historical accounts can be used to prepare forecast or budgeted financial statements.

❏ The effect of different trading and other policies can be tried out by determining the resulting trading and profit and loss accounts and balance sheets.

Points to note

❏ Enterprises are advised to prepare cash flow forecasts for at least their first year. Banks always want to see this if an overdraft facility is asked for. It is good management for all enterprises to prepare a cash flow forecast at the beginning of every financial year.

❏ This applies to all enterprises not just for those engaged in profit seeking activities. For example, my local primary school, Anglican Church and charitable old people's home all prepare forecasts each year. The information gained can be very useful. As an example the school governors may decide that a pupil recruiting drive and /or economies are required (if outflows are expected to exceed inflows) or that an extra part-time teacher can be afforded (if inflows are expected to exceed outflows).

❏ Care must be taken to include only actual cash flows and to include them at the right time. For example depreciation of a motor car is not a cash flow but the purchase of a new motor car is. However this may be outright (if cash is paid at time of purchase for the whole cost) or say by monthly instalments if it is on Hire Purchase.

❏ A primary purpose of a cash flow forecast is to assist in an application for a loan from a bank to start a business. Banks are notorious for not lending unless they are very sure of getting their money back. Consequently before lending, the bank wishes to see what cash flows are forecast to enable it to be sure that, if all goes according to plan, the loan can be repaid. Very often the loan agreement has specific dates stated for repayment and for payment of interest. Interest is often added monthly and it should be included in the forecast as it adds to the overdraft. Similarly repayments should be included. It is not easy to forecast the amounts of interest because the amount of the overdraft is likely to fluctuate and interest rates vary from month to month. If the forecast shows that a credit balance is expected then interest may be earned on the balance and the interest should be included in the forecast.

❏ Banks do not simply see a cash flow forecast and, on that alone, decide to make a loan. They see the forecast as an essential element in a battery of evidence. This evidence will include an assessment of the viability of the business, an assessment of the borrower, the existence of guarantors and the availability of security.

❏ Value added tax is a complication in cash flow forecasts. If trader is registered for VAT, then most receipts and payments on a forecast should include a VAT element. In addition, the VAT is paid over to Customs and Excise at intervals (usually quarterly) and the payment should be included also. Not all items are subject to VAT and accounting can be one of several schemes. As a result I have ignored the issue in this book. You should not do so in practice.

❏ Budgeting properly belongs to a work on management accounting. However, the preparation of projected financial statements and cash flow forecasts is increasingly common in financial accounting papers. The techniques used are largely those of financial accounting.

❏ The profit and loss account and balance sheet can be thought of as models of the firm. Trying out possible trading and other policies using these models is a fast growing technique, now that appropriate computer software is available.

❏ In working questions involving forecasts in examinations, remember:

(i) There are no short cuts – work everything out.
(ii) Focus on one thing at a time.
(iii) Prepare and submit good workings.
(iv) Ensure that the requirements of the question have been met.

Self-testing questions

1. What is a cash flow forecast?
2. What can be meant by cash?
3. List the benefits of cash flow forecasting.
4. What can be done if the forecast flows are unsatisfactory?
5. Why do actual cash flow commonly differ from forecasts?
6. How can financial accounting be used for planning?

Exercises

1. James is a student at Ironbridge University. Before the beginning his fourth term he decides to forecast his cash flows for the three months of the term – October, November and December. He forecasts:

(a) He will start the term with £200 in the bank. His grant (£450) will be received in October. His parents will give him a cheque for £700 in October.

(b) He will have to pay a monthly rent of £160 in advance for his share of the house he shares with three other students. Household services (telephone, heat etc) will cost £300 a month for the house (to be shared). He will need to pay £180 for books and equipment at the beginning of term. Food, travel and entertainment will cost £170 a month. He needs a new coat (cost £150) and two trips home to Dover will cost him £30 each.

Required:

(a) Prepare a cash flow forecast for the three months.
(b) List items that may differ from forecast.
(c) List options open to him to contain the forecast deficit.

2. The profit and loss account for 19x7 of Bangle Limited, a wholesaler of novelty goods with also a retail outlet, is:

	£			£
Administration	44,000	Sales – credit		140,000
Selling and distribution	8,000	Sales – cash		100,000
Depreciation	8,000			240,000
Advertising	6,000	Opening stock	31,000	
Directors' remuneration	20,000	Purchases	155,000	
Net profit	10,000		186,000	
		Closing stock	42,000	144,000
	96,000			96,000

A dividend of 20p a share will be paid.
The balance sheet shows:

	£			£
Share capital (10p)	2,000	Fixed assets:		
Reserves	23,000	Cost		40,000
Loan from a director	20,000	Depreciation		24,000
Creditors	26,000			16,000
Overdraft	18,000	Stock	42,000	
Dividend	4,000	Debtors	35,000	77,000
	93,000			93,000

The loan is interest free.
In 19x8 plans are to:
(a) Increase cash sales by 40% by volume but prices will be reduced by 5%. Advertising will increase by £5,000 to achieve the cash sales and to achieve an increase in credit sales of 15% at 19x7 prices.
(b) Reduce administration costs by 10%.
(c) Allow selling and distribution costs to rise by 25%.
(d) Increase directors' remuneration by 10%.
(e) Pay £15,000 off the loan.
(f) Reduce stock by 10%.
(g) Campaign to reduce debtors to two months.
(h) Maintain the creditors' credit payment period.
(i) Spend £10,000 on new fixed assets. Depreciation is 20% straight line. No assets have been completely written off.
(j) Pay a dividend of 25p a share.
Required:
Prepare forecast accounts.

3. (a) Use a spreadsheet program to prepare trading and profit and loss accounts and balance sheets for the first three years of Humbug's business given that:
   (i) Sales will be £100,000 in the first year and grow at 15% compound.
   (ii) Gross profit will be 25% of sales.
   (iii) Debtors at year end will be two months of annual sales.
   (iv) Stock at year ends will be three months of annual cost of sales.
   (v) Creditors will be 1.5 months of purchases.
   (vi) Overheads (excluding depreciation) will be £6,000 and grow at 10% compound a year.
   (vii) Fixed assets will cost £30,000 at the beginning of the first year.
   (viii) Depreciation will be 25% reducing balance.
   (ix) Drawings will be £10,000 a year.
   (x) Initial capital will be £12,000.
   (b) Repeat the exercise as (each is separate):
   (i) Sales in the first year of £150,000.
   (ii) Sales growth at 4% compound.
   (iii) Debtors at three months.
   (iv) Creditors at one month.
   (v) Stocks at four months.
   It is possible to do this exercise by hand!

4. Take the financial statements of Kallagan Ltd given in this chapter and prepare forecast financial statements using the following separate sets of predictions:

	Prediction 1	Prediction 2
(a) Increase turnover by	30%	50%
(b) Tax to be at	30%	45%
(c) Gross profit margin to be	35%	27%
(d) Admin costs to be	£25,000	£32,000
(e) Stock to be (as %age of throughput)	40%	30%
(f) Credit sales: cash sales ratio	70%	80%
(h) Purchases of fixed assets	£20,000	£30,000
(i) Debtors average collection time	3 months	2.5 months
(j) Creditors payment time	4 months	3 months
(k) Dividend per share	4p	3p
(l) Increase selling and distribution cost by	20%	25%
(m) Maintain same depreciation policy.		

Assignments

❑ *A. Helen intends to start her catering business from 1 Jan 19x3. Her forecast is:*
   (a) *She will put £2,000 into a business bank account from her savings.*
   (b) *She will rent a small workshop at a rent of £3,000 a year, payable on the usual quarter days in arrears.*
   (c) *She will have to pay rates of £1,200, payable £380 in March and £820 in September.*

(d) *She will equip the workshop at a cost of £6,400 payable in February.*

(e) *She hopes to make cash sales and credit sales of:*

Quarter	March	June	September	December
Cash	3,000	4,000	5,000	7,000
Credit	6,000	8,000	9,000	10,000

She expects 30% of credit sales in a quarter to be outstanding at the end of the quarter.

(f) *Materials will cost 30% of the sales in a quarter. She expects still to owe 25% of the purchases in a quarter at the end of the quarter.*

(g) *Labour will cost £1,200 a month.*

(h) *She will draw £400 a month for herself.*

(i) *On 1 January, she will borrow £2,000. This will be repaid by two instalments of £1,000 each on 30 June and 30 September, together with quarterly interest at a rate of 12% a year.*

(j) *She will spend about £300 a month on other expenses (advertising, energy etc).*

(k) *She will buy an estate car to use in the business. This will cost £6,000 and will be financed by trading in her old car at £2,000 and the rest by hire purchase with instalments at £165 a month beginning in February.*

Required:

(a) *Prepare a cash flow forecast for the four quarters of 19x3.*

(b) *How much overdraft should she ask for?*

B.   *The actual cash flows in 19x3 were as forecast except:*

(a) *Cash sales were 5% lower than expected.*

(b) *Credit sales were 10% higher than expected.*

(c) *The September loan repayment was not made until 31 December.*

(d) *Her credit customers paid her more slowly so that 40% of a quarter's credit sales were outstanding at the end of each quarter.*

(e) *Materials were paid for more slowly also so that 30% of a quarter's purchases were outstanding at the end of each quarter.*

(f) *Other expenses cost £350 a month.*

(g) *She drew £500 a month from July onwards.*

Required:

(a) *Enter the actual receipts and payments in a cash book and bring down the balances at the end of each quarter. (In reality each receipt and payment would be entered in detail but you can enter the amounts received under each heading for each quarter.)*

(b) *Write a commentary on the effect of each difference, between actual and forecast, on the overdraft requirement. Discuss the probable effect of increasing sales by 50%.*

31 Published company accounts

Company accounting is highly regulated. The primary regulation is in The Companies Act 1985 and subsequent Acts and Regulations. We begin with these Regulations, considering the balance sheet and explaining the profit and loss account. We then move to the accounting standards, elucidating the profit and loss account as required by Financial Reporting Standard (FRS) 3 – Reporting financial performance and describing two new financial statements.

The balance sheet and The Companies Act 1985

1. Schedule 4 to The Companies Act has a choice of two formats for the company balance sheet. One is the horizontal form but the common one is the vertical form (Format 1).

   Below is the full Companies Act Format 1:

			£'000	£'000	£'000
A.	Called up share capital not paid				10
B.	Fixed assets				
I	Intangible assets				
	1.	Development costs	15		
	2.	Concessions, patents, licences, trade marks and similar rights and assets	25		
	3.	Goodwill	100		
	4.	Payments on account	10	150	
II	Tangible assets				
	1.	Land and buildings	680		
	2.	Plant and machinery	1,204		
	3.	Fixtures, fittings, tools and equipment	600		
	4.	Payments on account and assets in course of construction	50	2,534	
III	Investments				
	1.	Shares in group undertakings	40		
	2.	Loans to group undertakings	150		
	3.	Participating interests	650		
	4.	Loans to undertakings in which the company has a participating interest	100		
	5.	Other investments other than loans	40		
	6.	Other loans	50		
	7.	Own shares	100	1,130	3,814

C. Current assets

   I   Stocks

	1.	Raw materials and consumables	810	
	2.	Work in progress	430	
	3.	Finished goods and goods for resale	518	
	4.	Payments on account	34	1,792

   II   Debtors

1.	Trade debtors	739	
2.	Amounts owed by group undertakings	143	
3.	Amounts owed by undertakings in which the company has a participating interest	26	
4.	Other debtors	54	
5.	Called up share capital not paid	–	
6.	Prepayments and accrued income	137	1,099

   III   Investments

1.	Shares in group undertakings	103	
2.	Own shares	15	
3.	Other investments	340	458

   IV Cash at bank and in hand   136

                                       3,485

D. Prepayments and accrued income

E. Creditors: amounts falling due within one year

1.	Debenture loans	400	
2.	Bank loans and overdrafts	324	
3.	Payments received on account	61	
4.	Trade creditors	458	
5.	Bills of exchange payable	78	
6.	Amounts owed to group undertakings	49	
7.	Amounts owed to undertakings in which the company has a participating interest	84	
8.	Other creditors including taxation and social security	61	
9.	Accruals and deferred income	134	1,649

F. Net current assets (liabilities)   1,836

G. Total assets less current liabilities   5,660

H. Creditors: amounts falling due after more than one year

	1.	Debenture loans	1,000
	2.	Bank loans and overdrafts	260
	3.	Payments received on account	10
	4.	Trade creditors	104
	5.	Bills of exchange payable	38
	6.	Amounts owed to group undertakings	44
	7.	Amounts owed to undertakings in which the company has a participating interest	59
	8.	Other creditors including taxation and social security	624
	9.	Accruals and deferred income	17

2,156

I. Provisions for liabilities and charges

1.	Pensions and similar obligations	726
2.	Taxation, excluding deferred taxation	344
3.	Deferred taxation	100
4.	Other provisions	39

1,209

J. Accruals and deferred income — — 3,365

2,295

K. Capital and reserves

I Called up share capital 500
II Share premium account 260
III Revaluation reserve 500
IV Other reserves

1.	Capital redemption reserve	100
2.	Reserve for own shares	50
3.	Reserves provided for by the articles of association	110
4.	Other reserves	58

318

V Profit and loss account 717

£2,295

Notes:

(a) I have included figures to make it easier to follow.

(b) Some of the items are rarely found in practice.

(c) Greater detail can be shown, e.g. under B.II 1. Land and buildings could be shown separately.

(d) Headings where there are no amounts can be omitted, e.g. if there is no called up share capital not paid (C.II 5) then the words can be omitted.

(e) The actual letters (A etc), roman numerals (II etc) and arabic numbers (1, 2 etc) are nearly always omitted.

(f) In respect of each item, the corresponding amount for the previous year should also be shown.

(g) Called up share capital not paid can appear at A or C.II 5.

(h) Prepayments and accrued income can appear at D or C.II 6. C.II 6 is preferred.

(i) Accruals and deferred income can appear at J or at either E9 or H9. E9 or H9 are preferred.

2. Most of the words will be familiar to you. Some will be new. References to group undertakings and participating interests are to groups. Group accounting is an advanced subject and is not dealt with in this book. Similarly we will not deal with own shares. There are many references to called up share capital not paid. Some companies issue shares for payment by instalments. Sometimes the final instalment is indefinitely delayed and this gives the company a chance to call on funds from shareholders if they should need to by calling up the final instalment. Naturally investors do not like partly paid shares and they are rare.

3. Intangible assets are assets which have real value but no physical substance. You will see examples in B I. These only appear on balance sheets when they had an identifiable cost. For example, XY PLC might buy a trade mark from another company. The cost could then appear on XY's balance sheet. However, it is common to remove it from the balance sheet by charging it to profit and loss account. Most companies have intangible assets, often of enormous value, but they do not usually appear on the balance sheet.

4. E8 is a separate heading for outstanding VAT, PAYE, national insurance and other taxes.

5. Provisions require some explanation. Some company balance sheets contain a class of LIABILITY called *provisions*. These are defined in the Companies Act as:

'A Provision is any amount retained as reasonably necessary for the purpose of providing for any liability or loss which is either likely to be incurred, or certain to be incurred but uncertain as to amount or as to the date on which it will arise.'

Got it?

Provisions are:

(a) Amounts retained – this is a very confusing term. Think of retained meaning 'is a liability'.

(b) Where there is doubt about whether the liability exists at all.

(c) Where it is certain that a liability does exist but that amount or the date of payment are uncertain.

Examples of provisions are:

An employee of A Ltd damaged some property of B, a customer. The matter is subject to a court action sometime in the future. There is a probability that A Ltd will have to pay damages (thus a liability exists), but the amount and date of payment are uncertain. B Ltd guarantees its products for 12 months from the date of sale by retailers. At any balance sheet date there is a liability to put right faulty products arising out of the guarantee. The amount of this liability and the date of payment are uncertain. A best estimate has to be made to quantify the liability. Company C has contracted to pay pensions to some employees in respect of past service. The amount payable depends on the length of life of the pensioners. This is unknown but estimates based on statistical evidence can be made.

6. Thus provisions are liabilities which are uncertain as to:

     existence *or* amount *or* date of payment.

You will have realised that the word provision also occurs in the phrase 'provision for depreciation'. A depreciation provision is within the definition of a provision as it is 'an amount retained as reasonably necessary for the purpose of providing for any loss which is certain to be incurred but uncertain as to amount (cost less estimated residual value) or as to the date on which it will arise (date of disposal)'.

7. *Retention* in these circumstances is not easy to grasp. Suppose X Ltd starts in business with £1,000 of capital and trades profitably for one year so that its balance sheet shows:

Liabilities:	£	Assets:	£
Share capital	1,000	Fixed assets at cost	3,000
Profit and loss account	4,500	Current assets	8,000
Current liabilities	5,500		
	11,000		11,000

The company now has net assets of £4,500 more than the net assets provided by the shareholders. Thus the company can pay a dividend of £4,500. However, no depreciation has been charged. If it had (say at 20%) then profit would have been £3,900 only. Thus the dividend could be £3,900 only. It can be said that the depreciation reduces the legal maximum of dividend and so forces the company to *retain* resources in the business.

The Companies Act and the profit and loss account

8. There are four formats given in the Companies Act 1985 for the profit and loss account. Of these 1 and 3, and 2 and 4 are the same but in vertical and horizontal form respectively. As the vertical form is the common usage in the UK, we will ignore formats 3 and 4. In this chapter we will concentrate on Format 1 as it is the commonest form.

Profit and loss account

9. Format 1 is:
   1. Turnover
   2. Cost of sales
   3. Gross profit or loss
   4. Distribution costs
   5. Administration expenses
   6. Other operating income

7. Income from shares in group undertakings
8. Income from participating interests
9. Income from other fixed asset investments
10. Other interest receivable and similar income
11. Amounts written off investments
12. Interest payable and similar charges
13. Tax on profit or loss on ordinary activities
14. Profit or loss on ordinary activities after taxation
15. Extraordinary income
16. Extraordinary charges
17. Extraordinary profit or loss
18. Tax on extraordinary profit or loss
19. Other taxes not shown under the above items
20. Profit or loss for the financial year.

This is not unlike the profit and loss accounts you have prepared for internal use but does have some special features and also lacks some items you would expect. There is no space for dividends. As a result the format is followed, but is usually amended to conform with real needs.

10. To see how it works out in practice we will look at an example:

Mahonia Ltd
Profit and loss account for the year ending 30 June 19x4

		£'000
Turnover		1,760
Cost of sales		1,226
Gross profit		534
Distribution costs	241	
Administrative expenses	63	
		304
Profit on ordinary activities before interest		230
Interest payable		26
Profit on ordinary activities before tax		204
Tax on profit on ordinary activities		68
Profit on ordinary activities after tax		136
Dividends		94
Retained profit for the year		42

Notes:

(a) Some lines have been omitted altogether. These either relate to groups (which we ignore as it is an advanced subject) – lines 7,8 – or are relatively rare – lines 6,9,10, 11, 19. Lines 15, 16, 17,18 have almost ceased to be used since the coming of FRS 3 (see below).

(b) Ordinary costs, expenses and overheads appear in lines 2, 4 and 5. Unfortunately, the Format does not state how costs should be allocated between these three categories. In particular, the practice is to include rather more in cost of sales than we would in profit and loss accounts for internal use.

A common division is:

Cost of sales:	Opening stocks and work in progress
	Direct materials and expenses
	Direct labour
	Fixed and variable production overheads including depreciation
	Research and development costs
	Less: closing stocks and work in progress
Distribution costs:	Sales salaries and commissions
	Advertising
	Warehousing costs of finished goods
	Travelling and entertaining
	Carriage out including depreciation of vehicles
	Overhead costs of sales outlets
	Discounts allowed
Administrative expenses:	Salary costs of administrative personnel (e.g. accounting function, directors and general management)
	Overhead costs of administration buildings
	Professional fees
	Bad debts

This division is clearly appropriate for a manufacturing company but can be adapted for trading companies and service providing companies. Essentially the cost of sales is the cost of making or buying-in the product whether it be a good or a service.

There can be considerable variation in this analysis in practice.

11. In addition to the relatively few lines of the format, the Act requires a large number of *notes attached to and forming part of the profit and loss account*. A set of notes which complies with the requirements are:

Notes attached to and forming part of the profit and loss account

(a) Accounting policies:

Fixtures and fittings are depreciated on the fixed instalment method over a period of 10 years.

Motor vehicles are depreciated on the reducing balance method at a rate of 25% a year.

(b) Interest – is that paid on the 13% debenture loan 1989/92.

(c) Profit – is stated after charging the following items:

Auditors' remuneration £13,000

Depreciation of fixed assets £20,000

Directors' emoluments £100,000

of which the chairman received £36,000 and the range of directors' emoluments and the number of directors within each range was:

£15,001 – £20,000 – 2
£30,001 – £35,000 – 1

(d) Tax payable is corporation tax on the profits of the year at 35% less marginal relief.

(e) The average number of employees during the year was 16. Their remuneration was:

Wages and salaries – £95,000
Social security costs – £9,000

I do not intend to review the detailed requirements of the Act as they are very voluminous but the above will give you a flavour of the requirements and details can be found in the Act or more advanced texts.

Reporting financial performance

12. As we have seen above, the Companies Act has numerous requirements on the format and content of company accounts. In addition company accounts are required to conform to the accounting standards. There are now 20 Statements of Standard Accounting Practice (SSAPs) still in force. Some are discussed in this book especially SSAP 12 Accounting for Depreciation and SSAP 9 Stocks and Work in Progress. There are also the newer Financial Reporting Standards (FRSs) of which there are now eight.

13. The FRS which we will discuss in this section is FRS 3 – Reporting Financial Performance. It has important effects on the Profit and Loss Account and introduces two new Financial Statements:

(a) Statement of total recognised gains and losses.
(b) Reconciliation of movements in shareholders' funds.

Profit and loss accounts under FRS 3

14. Here is an example of a profit and loss account according to the requirements of FRS 3:

Bigtime Plc
Profit and Loss Account
For the year ending 31 December 19x5

	Continuing operations	Acquisitions	Discontinued operations	Total	
	£million	£million	£million	£million	
Turnover	325	55	71	451	3
Cost of sales	230	31	55	316	4
Gross profit	95	24	16	135	
Net operating expenses	31	15	22	68	5
Operating profit	64	9	(6)	67	6

...continued

	Continuing operations £million	Acquisitions £million	Discontinued operations £million	Total £million	
Profit on sale of properties		36		36	7
Loss on disposal of discontinued operation			(12)	(12)	8
Profit on ordinary activities before interest	90	9	(18)	91	9
Interest payable				(12)	
Profit on ordinary activities before taxation				79	10
Tax on profit on ordinary activities				(22)	
Profit on ordinary activities after tax				57	11
Minority interests				(6)	12
Profit before extraordinary items				51	13
Extraordinary items				–	
Profit for the financial year				51	14
Dividends				20	
Retained profit for the financial year				31	
Earnings per share				32p	15

Notes:

Line 1. The figures are presented over four columns. The first two are concerned with operations that took place this year and will also continue next year. The third column is concerned with the results of that part of the company which was discontinued during the year. The final column is the total of the first three columns. What is meant by operations which are continuing, discontinuing and acquisitions will be discussed later in this chapter.

Line 2. This indicates that column 1 is for operations which have been in operation at least since the previous year and column 2 is for operations which were acquired during the year.

Line 3. This is the total sales or turnover in the year divided up into the three columns with the total in the fourth.

Line 4. This is the cost of sales. What is included in cost of sales is discussed in paragraph 10 of this chapter.

Line 5. These are distribution costs, administration expenses and some other items.

Line 6. This is the profit which flows from the normal operations of the company and excludes some special or unusual items.

Line 7. This is a gain which occurred because of some one-off sale of properties. Companies regularly sell and replace fixed assets. Usually there is some gain or loss on sale because depreciation is an approximate process as we have discussed in the chapter on depreciation and fixed assets. Such small adjustments should be included in lines 4 or 5. Line 7 is for more unusual items or where the gains or losses are material.

Line 8. When a distinct and separate part of the company's operations is discontinued or sold, then there is usually a gain or loss on disposal as it is unlikely that the undertaking, disposed of, will be realised for exactly its book value.

Line 9. You will remember, from paragraph 9, that the Companies Act requires interest to be shown as a separate item. FRS3 requires profits on ordinary activities before interest to be highlighted, as it is in this line. Interest is then shown.

Line 10. The theory is that the profit before interest should be shown as this figure can be compared between companies that may have quite different financing arrangements. We will discuss this more in the chapters on interpretation. This line shows the profit after deducting interest but highlights the profit before taxation.

Line 11. This line shows the profit after deduction of taxation payable on it. Readers can now see the effect on profit of taxation. Taxation on companies is generally Corporation Tax but other taxes may be involved especially where there are overseas operations. This area is well beyond the scope of a foundation work on accounting!

Line 12. Most PLCs are not single companies but *groups*. Bigtime PLC is the holding company and it is in this company that the shareholders own shares. However, Bigtime owns a number of *subsidiary companies* and our profit and loss account is, in fact, a grouping together of all the profit and loss accounts of Bigtime and its subsidiary companies. Some of the subsidiary companies have some outside shareholders and the procedure is to include all the profit of all the companies in lines 11 and above. Some part of the profit of subsidiaries with minority shareholders belongs to those shareholders and line 12 takes it out. The whole subject of Group or Consolidated Accounts is one for more advanced texts.

Line 13. Extraordinary items are defined as 'material items possessing a high degree of abnormality which arise from events or transactions that fall outside the ordinary activities of the reporting entity and which are expected not to recur.' FRS3 considers these to be so rare that it gives no examples and puts no amount for it in the illustrative example. I have included the item to show you where it would be put, if there was an extraordinary item.

Line 15. Earnings per share is calculated on the profit attributable to equity shareholders, after accounting for minority interests, extraordinary items and preference dividends. As there are no preference dividends here, the relevant profit is line 14. It is divided by the number of shares in issue. There can be considerable complications with this but they are for advanced studies in accounting.

Continuing and discontinued operations and acquisitions

15. Public companies are not static enterprises doing the same thing year after year. They tend to sell or close subsidiary companies or close down activities that are no longer profitable. Also they tend to buy subsidiaries by buying from each other or

by acquiring whole PLCs or private companies in takeover bids. For example, Grand Metropolitan, the food and drinks group, completed a 500 million dollar sale of Alpo, its US petfood business, to Nestle; and Partco bought a company called Downey Autoparts. You can read of these things in the city pages of every daily paper.

Readers of accounts like to compare profits from year to year and to make forecasts of profits in future years. They do this for many reasons including the making of investment decisions. Clearly the profits of year 1 cannot be reasonably compared with the profits of year 2 if year 1 profit included the results of a major business which was sold in year 1 and year 2 profit includes the profit of a major subsidiary acquired in year 2. The need for profit statements to distinguish between continuing, discontinuing and newly acquired operations is obvious. However it was not a requirement until FRS 3 came into force in 1993.

What is meant by discontinuance and acquisition is not precise but is discussed at length in FRS 3.

Broadly the terms are:

(a) *Discontinuance* These occur when sale or termination is in the period or before the earlier of three months after the commencement of the subsequent period and the date when the financial statements are approved (this mostly means three months as few accounts are approved until at least three months after the year end). To be regarded as a discontinuance:

  (i) The sale or termination must have a material effect on the nature and focus of the reporting entity's operations.

  (ii) The sale or termination must represent a material reduction in the company's operating facilities resulting from either its withdrawal from a particular market (whether class of business or geographical) or from a material reduction in turnover in its continuing markets.

  (ii) If it is a termination, the former activities must have ceased permanently.

  (iv) It is essential that the assets, liabilities, results of operations, and activities of an operation must be clearly distinguishable physically, operationally and for financial reporting purposes. You will see that the sale of a subsidiary company probably fulfils this condition. The closing down of operations in say Australia will probably do so also but the discontinuance of one among a range of products may be more problematical.

(b) Acquisitions are simply operations of the reporting entity that are acquired in the period. They may be whole companies, whole groups or individual businesses.

Interpretation

16. In the case of Bigtime, what can readers learn from looking at the profit and loss account? We see that the company had an operation which was unprofitable and which actually lost £6 million in the financial year. However it has now been disposed of (albeit at a loss on book value of £12 million) and will no longer cause losses to Bigtime. At the same time the company acquired an operation which

contributed £9 million to profits in the first year of ownership. What all this means for future profits is unknown but things do seem to be promising.

Details of the acquisitions and disposal of operations are usually given elsewhere in the Report and Accounts – in the notes or Directors' report. Note that acquisitions and disposals can be of whole companies or of divisions or geographical markets.

Exceptional items

17. In the example you have reviewed above, there are two items which are special. They are:

   (a) Profits or losses on sale or termination of an operation.

   (b) Profits or losses on the disposal of fixed assets.

   They are required by FRS 3 to be shown separately. There is also a third category, not included in the example – costs of a fundamental reorganisation or restructuring having a material effect on the nature and focus of the reporting entity's operation.

   There are some other items which are dealt with in FRS 3. These are called exceptional items. These are defined as:

   'Material items which derive from events and transactions that fall within the *ordinary* activities of the reporting entity and which individually or, if of a similar type, in aggregate need to be *disclosed* by virtue of their size or incidence if the financial statements are to give a true and fair view.'

   Examples culled from a small survey of recently published accounts include costs of withdrawal of a drug by a pharmaceutical company, closure and disposal of some stores in a DIY chain, abortive acquisition costs, release of pension provision no longer required, costs of withdrawing from property development.

   These need to be disclosed. How this is done varies from company to company. However they should be attributed to continuing and discontinued operations as appropriate. One way of showing them is to restructure lines 3 to 6 by expanding them to more columns. Another way is to disclose them in notes attached to, and forming part of, the profit and loss account.

Statement of total recognised gains and losses

18. An example of one of these financial statements is:

Bigtime PLC
Statement of total recognised gains and losses
for the year ending 31 December 19x5

	£million	Notes
Profit for the financial year	51	1
Unrealised surplus on revaluation of properties	21	2
Currency adjustments on investments	(6)	3
Total recognised gains and losses relating to the year	66	4

Notes:

1. This is line 14 taken from the profit and loss account – check paragraph 1.

2. Not all gains and losses go into the profit and loss account. A good and common example is the unrealised surplus arising out of a revaluation of land and buildings as in our illustration.

3. Another example is the gain or loss on translation of foreign currency assets. This seems to appear in a great number of company accounts.

4. The thinking behind this statement is that the profit and loss account is supposed to record all gains and losses. However some gains and losses (as the two here) do not go into the profit and loss account. Consequently there is a need for a short statement to gather together all gains and losses.

   Many companies will have no gains or losses other than those going through the profit and loss account. In such cases it is enough to make a statement to that effect immediately below the profit and loss account and not provide a statement of total recognised gains and losses.

Reconciliation of movements in shareholders' funds

19. An example of one of these financial statements:

Bigtime PLC
Reconciliation of movements in shareholders' funds
for the year ending 31 December 19x5

Total recognised gains and losses for the year		66	1
Dividends		(20)	2
New share capital issued:			
Rights issue	23		3
Scrip dividend alternative	2	25	4
Goodwill purchased		(11)	5
Net increase in shareholders' funds		60	6
Opening shareholders' funds		187	7
Closing shareholders' funds		247	8

Notes:

1. You will see this figure comes from the statement of total recognised gains and losses.

2. You will also see that this figure comes from the profit and loss account.

3. This is the proceeds of an issue of shares with pro rata rights to subscribe given to all shareholders. The £23 million is the actual net proceeds (new shares at nominal value + share premium – expenses of issue).

4. Many public companies now give their shareholders a choice between a cash dividend and additional shares. In this case the total dividend was £20 million with £2 million being taken as shares and £18 million as cash.

5. When a company is purchased and becomes a subsidiary the fair value of the actual net assets (fixed and current assets etc) is incorporated in the accounts.

However the amount paid for the acquisition is usually more than the fair value of the actual net assets. The difference is goodwill and is written off straight to reserves. Thus, suppose £50 was paid for an acquisition then shareholders' funds are reduced by £50 being cash or other consideration leaving the company. Net assets acquired were valued at £39 and these are now owned so the shareholders' funds rise by £39. The difference is £11 goodwill and is a net reduction of shareholders' funds. Of course the goodwill is a real, though intangible, asset but it is not recognised on the balance sheet.

6. This is the total so far – check it!

7. and 8. are self – explanatory

The objective of this statement is to bring together all increases and reductions of shareholders' funds which occurred in the year. Other examples of changes you might see include redemption of preference shares and reinstatement of goodwill in respect of businesses sold, previously written off to reserves.

Other matters

20. This is a foundation text so I have not covered some aspects of the profit and loss account and the other two statements. These aspects include taxation, reconciliation of historical cost profits and losses, other methods of calculating earnings per share, prior year adjustments, provisions for losses on operations to be discontinued, segmental analysis and comparative figures (= corresponding figures of the previous period). Life is not simple and the possible complications which can arise in preparing published accounts seem almost limitless!

Summary

❒ The Companies Act requires companies to prepare their balance sheets in one of two formats. Format 1 is the common one.

❒ Provisions are liabilities with doubts as to payability, amount or timing of payment. They are also estimates of uncertain reductions in value, e.g. depreciation and doubtful debts.

❒ The Companies Act 1985 Schedule 4 requires the profit and loss accounts of companies to be in one of four forms. The common one is Format 1.

❒ The Format requires some rejigging to be usable and it contains some lines which are for use in large companies which are groups. It also contains some lines which are not used because of the virtual removal of the concept of extraordinary items by FRS 3.

❒ Since the Format is used by companies of all types – manufacturing, trading and service providing – the three expense headings are used. However there is some variation between companies as regards into which heading particular expense categories are put.

❒ The Companies Act has a large number of detailed requirements which lead to pages of notes attached to and forming part of the profit and loss account.

❏ FRS 3 – Reporting Financial Performance – adds to the format requirements of company profit and loss accounts.

❏ Among the requirements is for separate disclosure of the results of continuing and discontinued operations and acquisitions.

❏ Companies are also required to produce a statement of total recognised gains and losses and a reconciliation of movements in shareholders' funds.

Points to note

❏ An actual company balance sheet is not as long as the example. This is partly because many items can be omitted as not relevant to the particular company. However the main reason is that the real balance sheet is a summary and the details appear in pages of notes attached to and forming part of the accounts. The Companies Act has some 40 pages of detailed requirements as to disclosure of balance sheet items and this means that notes are usually very lengthy in order to give the required disclosures.

❏ The best way to become familiar with the format and also the detailed requirements is to read through lots of actual published profit and loss accounts. They are interesting in themselves and it is fascinating to try to find information which is very important but which is given little prominence.

❏ Actual profit and loss accounts conform to the Companies Act requirements but also to the Accounting Standards. Many of the features you will find in actual profit and loss accounts are because of the Accounting Standards rather than the Companies Act.

❏ In preparing company profit and loss accounts, the requirements of the Companies Act and all relevant Accounting Standards must be met. Accounting Standards means SSAPs and FRSs, including FRS 3.

❏ In practice it is not always easy to determine whether a disposal or termination comes under the FRS 3 definition and it can be even more difficult to extract the figures for the Accounts.

❏ The separate disclosures required by FRS 3 and shown in lines 7 and 8 are sometimes treated as exceptional items and entered above line 6.

Self-testing questions

1. Give the main headings in Format 1.
2. Define provision and list some examples.
3. What are partly paid shares?
4. Why do intangible assets appear on balance sheets only in certain circumstances?
5. What is meant by 'retained'?
6. Why is the company balance sheet usually quite a short document?
7. How many formats can a company choose from for its profit and loss account?
8. Write out Format 1.
9. In which expense category might the following appear: Discounts allowed, directors' salaries, stationery, water rates?

10. Why is the profit and loss account relatively short despite the large requirements of the Companies Act for detailed information?

11. What statutory or other provisions determine the form and content of the profit and loss account?

12. What new financial statements were introduced by FRS 3?

13. What divisions of the results are required by FRS 3?

14. Where, on a profit and loss account, should ordinary adjustments to depreciation arising out of sales appear?

15. Define 'extraordinary items'.

16. Why is the distinction between continuing, discontinued and acquired operations desirable?

17. What particular discontinued operations should appear as such in a particular profit and loss account?

18. What three categories of exceptional items should appear below the operating profit?

19. Define exceptional items.

20. State some items which might appear in a statement of total recognised gains and losses.

21. Give some examples of items appearing in a reconciliation of movements in shareholders' funds.

Exercises

1. From the following data relating to two companies Samantha Ltd and Damian Ltd, prepare balance sheets. The relevant year is 19x2.

	Samantha	Damian
Tangible fixed assets	12,567	1,030
Goodwill, patents and trade marks	500	320
Stocks	6,390	124
Trade creditors	3,870	67
Debtors	6,800	87
9% Bonds payable 19x7	1,000	
8% Convertible loan 19x4/19x6		250
Corporation tax on 19x2 profits	540	307
Taxation and social security due	967	86
Bank overdraft	260	
Cash at bank		55
Final dividend proposed – ordinary	690	120
– preference	70	
Issued ordinary share capital (20p shares)	2,300	700
Share premium	1,678	
Revaluation reserve	239	
Profit and loss account at 31.12.x2	?	86
7% Preference shares of £1 each	1,000	
Capital redemption reserve	500	

Note that convertible loans are just loans with an option attached. The lender can convert the loan into ordinary shares on dates stated in the loan deed and at specified rates of conversion. Convertibles are quite common.

2. The trial balances of Ams Ltd and Trad Ltd as at 31.12.x8 are:

(Ams Ltd makes pottery articles – at the year end there were no stocks of raw materials or work in progress).

(Trad Ltd is an importer of brassware which it packages – there were no stocks of packaging material).

(All figures in £'000)

	Ams Ltd		Trad Ltd	
	£	£	£	£
Land at cost	240		160	
Buildings at cost	650		315	
Buildings depreciation		180		68
Plant at cost	175		28	
Plant depreciation		131		10
Stock	54		75	
Debtors and creditors	62	47	76	50
Purchases and sales	350	895	280	680
Production overheads	81		31	
Direct labour	57		43	
Discounts	6	10	4	3
Warehousing costs			70	
Warehousing labour			62	
Interim dividend	20		10	
Advertising	38		12	
Cost of sales office	15		13	
Salesmen's remuneration	39		26	
Delivery van costs	28		14	
Administration costs	44		20	
Legal charges	5			
Bad debts	12		14	
Research and development			21	
Bank		12	87	
Share capital – Ords 20p		100		80
Share capital – Pref £1 – 10%		50		100
Share premium		80		65
Capital redemption reserve				120
Profit and loss account		171		105
15% debentures		200		80
	1,876	1,876	1,361	1,361

For Ams Ltd:

(a) Depreciation is Buildings 2% on cost: Plant 25% reducing balance.

(b) A doubtful debt provision of 3% of debtors is to be set up.

(c) Auditor's remuneration of £15,000 is to be provided for.

(d) Interest on the debentures is to be provided for from the date of issue on 1.7.x8.

(e) The delivery van costs include licences for the year ending 31.3.x9 of £8,000.

(f) A bonus issue of one ordinary share for every four held is to be put through at 31.12.x8.

(g) The dividend on the preference shares is to be provided.

(h) An ordinary dividend of 10p on the ordinary share capital is proposed. The bonus shares do not rank for this dividend.

(i) Closing stocks were £62,000.

(j) Corporation tax of £52,000 is to be provided on the profits of the year.

Required:

(a) Prepare a profit and loss account in Format 1 and a balance sheet as at 31.12.x8.

(b) 'Why cannot we put money aside in a general reserve like other companies?' asks the production director. Answer his question.

For Trad Ltd:

(a) On 28.12.x8, new plant costing £36,000 was delivered and began to be used. This transaction has not yet been put through the books.

(b) Depreciation is: Buildings 4% on cost: Plant 15% straight line on all plant in use at the year end.

(c) Stock at end is £69,000.

(d) An additional bad debt is to be recognised £3,000.

(e) Warehousing costs include rates for the half year to 31.3.x9 £8,000.

(f) The interim dividend includes the half year dividend on the preference shares to 30.6.x8.

(g) A rights issue of 1 for 5 on the ordinary shares was effected in December 19x8. The price was 55p per share and the monies were held in a special bank account. Costs of £2,000 are to be charged against the share premium account. None of this appears in the trial balance but should now be incorporated in the accounts.

(h) Corporation tax is to be provided at £12,000.

(i) The interest on the debentures for the half year ending 30.6.x8 has been paid and included in the administration costs. The remaining half year should be provided.

(j) The company is being sued by another company for a breach of copyright. The outcome is uncertain but a prudent provision for damages and costs is £10,000.

(k) A final dividend on the ordinary share capital of 7.5p per share is proposed together with the remaining half year's preference dividend.

(l) A transfer of £10,000 to preference share redemption reserve is to be made and also a transfer to plant replacement reserve of the same amount.

Required:

(a) A profit and loss account for the year in Format 1 together with a balance sheet as at the year end.

(b) The sales director remarks that having made the transfers in (1) above the company will have the cash available to redeem the preference shares and to buy more plant. Explain why this is not so.

3. (a) From the following figures of Huge PLC for the year ending 31 December 19x8, prepare a profit and loss account, statement of total recognised gains and losses and reconciliation of movements in shareholders' funds:

Turnover (c)	456	Taxation	18
Cost of sales (c)	287	Minority interests	5
Distribution costs (c)	36	Dividends (cash)	12
Admin expenses (c) (ex. next item)	23	Dividends (scrip)	3
Bad debt (collapse of major customer) (c)	46	Number of shares in issue	120 million
Restructuring costs – major subsidiary	51	Unrealised surplus on	
Profit on disposal of discontinued operations	76	revaluation of property	102
Turnover (a)	223	Currency translation	
Cost of sales (a)	180	difference	(24)
Distribution costs (a)	21	Goodwill written off	8
Admin costs (a)	29	Opening shareholders'	
Interest	27	funds	249
Turnover (d)	88		
Cost of sales (d)	42		
Distribution costs (d)	12		
Admin costs (d)	9		

Note: (a) = acquired, (c) = continuing, (d) = discontinued.

All figures (except number of shares) are in £ million.

(b) Discuss the results and the possible future of the company. Why do you think the disposal was made? Comment on the results of the acquisition. Why might a loss be recorded in the first year?

Assignment

❑ *From the following figures of Great PLC for the year ending 31 December 19x7, prepare a profit and loss account, statement of total recognised gains and losses and reconciliation of movements in shareholders' funds:*

Turnover (c)	*769*	*Taxation*	*13*
Cost of sales (c)	*453*	*Minority interests*	*9*
Distribution costs (c)	*121*	*Dividends (cash)*	*22*
Admin expenses (c) (ex. next item)	*67*	*Dividends (scrip)*	*4*
Losses on leases where tenants have defaulted	*10*	*Number of shares in issue*	*230 million*
Reorganisation costs – major subsidiary	*22*	*Unrealised surplus on*	
Loss on disposal of discontinued operations	*49*	*revaluation of property*	*52*

Turnover (a)	109	Currency translation	
Cost of sales (a)	51	difference (gain)	12
Distribution costs (a)	11	Goodwill written off	22
Admin costs (a)	15	Opening shareholders	
Interest	39	funds	249
Turnover (d)	37	Costs of debenture issue	12
Cost of sales (d)	20	Proceeds of rights issue	120
Distribution costs (d)	15		
Admin costs (d)	7		

Note: (a) = acquired, (c) = continuing, (d) = discontinued.

All figures (except number of shares) are in £ million.

Discuss the results and the implications for the future.

32 Cash flow statements and company finance

The balance sheet of an enterprise shows the assets and liabilities at a particular moment in time. From an inspection of balance sheets of the same enterprise one year apart, it is possible to discover:

(a) Changes in individual assets and liabilities.

(b) Changes in total assets.

(c) Changes in total liabilities.

A partial explanation for the changes is the profit and loss account which explains:

(a) Profit earned in the period.

(b) Appropriations of profit in the period, e.g. drawings in a sole trader or partnership; taxation and dividends in a company.

For many years companies were required to produce a Statement of Source and Application of Funds (often called a funds flow statement) to explain working capital changes as it was required by SSAP 10. SSAP 10 did not specify the format of the statement although an example was given. As a result various forms were found in practice and confusion reigned. In general the funds flow statement was not understood by non-accountants and only with difficulty by accountants.

The first Financial Reporting Standard (FRS 1) produced by the new Accounting Standards Board was a replacement for the funds flow statement called the Cash Flow Statement. It remains to be seen whether this statement will be better understood and therefore be more useful to users of accounts. Your author thinks it will be.

The cash flow statement

1. The object of the statement is to show cash flows. It is possible for a company to be profitable and yet to run out of cash. For example an expanding company may make profits and yet cash problems arise because of:

   (a) Increases in turnover involve increases in debtors and stocks so that cash does not come in as fast as increased turnover is generated.

   (b) Expansion involves capital expenditure so that cash is needed to buy fixed assets.

   Unless these cash shortages are addressed and money is raised by new capital or borrowings, the company may find itself unable to pay its creditors. In effect, as well as making profits, the directors must manage their cash resources.

   The cash flow statement summarises the cash flows in and out during a year and consequently is an indication of how the company is faring in relation to cash and how well the directors are managing cash.

   FRS 1 does not require all companies to produce a cash flow statement. Exemptions are given to:

   (a) Small companies as defined in the Companies Act.

(b) Wholly owned subsidiaries where the parent company publishes consolidated accounts including the subsidiaries concerned.

The easiest way of understanding these statements is to follow the production of one from the data in a profit and loss account and balance sheet and this we will do. We will then see what lessons can be drawn from it.

Cash flow statements

2. Here are the balance sheets of Cashflow Ltd as at two dates a year apart and also the summary profit and loss account for the year ending 31 December 19x2:

Cashflow Ltd
Balance Sheet as 31 December (all figures in £'000)

	19x1	19x2
Fixed assets		
Cost	2,560	2,720
Less Depreciation	1,435	1,710
	1,125	1,010
Current assets		
Stocks	976	1,378
Debtors	1,450	1,769
	2,426	3,147
Creditors – amounts falling due within one year		
Creditors	830	860
Overdraft	234	117
Taxation	88	123
Dividends	40	47
	1,192	1,147
Net current assets	1,234	2,000
Total assets less current liabilities	2,359	3,010
Creditors – amounts falling due after more than one year		
16% Debentures	400	600
Net assets	1,959	2,410
Capital and Reserves		
Share capital (£1 shares)	600	700
Share premium	350	500
profit and loss account	1,009	1,210
	1,959	2,410

Profit and Loss Account for the year ending 31 December 19x2

	£	£
Turnover		6,462
Cost of sales		4,040
Gross profit		2,422
Overheads (including depreciation)		1,920
Operating profit		502
Interest		101
Net profit before taxation		401
Taxation		123
Profit after tax		278
Dividends		
Interim	30	
Final	47	77
Retained profit		201

Studying these accounts you may see:

(a) The company has made a profit, will need to pay corporation tax, has paid an interim dividend and intends to pay a final dividend.

(b) Fixed assets at cost have increased so some new fixed assets have been acquired.

(c) Stocks and debtors have both increased.

(d) Creditors have increased only slightly and the overdraft has come down

(e) The company has borrowed some more money by issuing some more debentures.

(f) The company has raised some money by issuing some new shares.

The cash flow statement is now given with supporting notes which are a part of the statement:

Cashflow Ltd
Cash flow statement for the year ended 31 December 19x2

a.	Cash flow from operating activities		243
b.	Returns on investments and servicing of finance		
c.	Interest paid		(101)
d.	Taxation		(88)
e.	Capital expenditure and financial investment		
f.	Purchase of tangible fixed assets	(360)	
g.	Sale of tangible assets	43	(317)
h.	Equity dividends paid		(70)
	Cash outflow before financing		(333)
	Financing:		
i.	Issue of ordinary share capital	250	
j.	Issue of debenture loan	200	450
k.	Increase of cash in the period		117

Reconciliation of net cash flow to movement in net debt

Increase in cash in the period	117
Cash inflow from increase in debt	(200)
Change in net debt	(83)

Analysis of changes in net debt

	At 1 Jan 19x2	Cash flows	At 31 Dec 19x2
Overdraft	(234)	117	(117)
Debt due after one year	(400)	(200)	(600)
	(634)	(83)	(717)

Note to cash flow statements

Reconciliation of operating profit to net cash inflow from operating activities

Operating profit	502
Depreciation charges	415
Loss on sale of tangible fixed assets	17
Increase in stocks	(402)
Increase in debtors	(319)
Increase in creditors	30
Net cash inflow from operating activities	243

Not included as a note to the cash flow statement but necessary for you to see what has happened is a reconciliation of fixed assets:

		Cost	Depreciation	Book Value
r.	at 1 January 19x2	2,560	1,435	1,125
s.	Sold in year	200	140	60
		2,360	1,295	1,065
t.	Addition in year	360		360
u.	Depreciation in year		415	(415)
v.	at 31 December 19x2	2,720	1,710	1,010

The items sold fetched £43,000 so the loss on sale was £60,000 less £43,000 = £17,000.

Line r shows the position at the beginning of the year. The company had fixed assets which had originally cost £2,560,000 and which had been depreciated by £1,435,000.

Line s removes from line r the fixed assets which were sold in the year.

Line t adds the fixed assets which were bought in the year.

Line u adds the depreciation for the year (which appears as an expense in the profit and loss account). Note that this is depreciation on both the old and the newly acquired fixed assets.

Line v shows the fixed assets held at the end of the year and the total or accumulated depreciation on them.

Now we will explore how the statement is constructed and then we will consider the story that it tells.

(a) Operating profitably usually produces a positive cash flow measured here at £243,000. This is obtained from the profit and loss account but first some adjustments have to be made as the profit and loss account measures value flows not cash flows. The adjustments required are in the note above. Depreciation is not a cash flow but is in the profit and loss account so it has to be added back. Similarly with the loss on sale where the actual cash flow is shown separately in line (g). Intuitively you will realise that cash flow from sales is less than sales if debtors have increased as they have. Similarly increase in stocks must involve a reduction in cash resources and an increase in creditors means an increase in cash resources.

(b) This company has no income from investments as it has no investments but these will appear in many statements.

(c) Interest paid is on the debentures and the bank overdraft.

(d) The tax paid in the year is the tax on the previous year's profits as corporation tax is paid nine months after the year end.

(e) These are the acquisition of fixed assets but can also be the acquisition of subsidiary companies in groups.

(f) During the year £360,000 was spent on fixed assets.

(g) Some assets were sold and fetched £43,000.

(h) Dividends paid are the final dividend from last year (£40,000) + the interim of this year (£30,000). This year's final dividend will be paid in the year ending 31 December 19x3.

(i) 100,000 new ordinary shares of £1 each nominal were sold for £2.50 each and as a result the company raised £250,000 and share capital increased by £100,000 and share premium by £150,000. New issues of ordinary shares for cash are normally issued to existing shareholders in proportion to their holdings and are called rights issues.

(j) A further issue of debentures raised £200,000.

(k) The final line shows that the company had an overall increase in cash of £117,000 in the year.

The following two statements are not easy to follow. Look first at the analysis of changes in net debt. Net debt shows how much the company owes at the year ends. If you look again at the balance sheet you will see that at each of the two year ends, there were two items of debt the overdraft and the debentures. This statement shows how they have changed in the year and you will see that the two year end positions are as in the balance sheet.

The Reconciliation of net cash flow to movement in net debt reconciles the main cash flow statement to the changes in net debt.

So what does this cash flow statement tell us?

(a) The company made a profit of £502,000 but after adjusting for depreciation and loss on sale of fixed assets the positive cash flow from trading was (£502,000 + £415,000 + £17,000) – no less than £934,000.

(b) An increase in stocks of £402,000 and of debtors £319,000 was partly financed by an increase in creditors of £ 30,000. The net effect of these three things was an absorption of cash of £691,000 and so the net contribution of operations to cash was only £243,000.

(c) Finance was also obtained from shareholders £250,000 and by long-term borrowings at £200,000.

(d) Total cash inflows are thus £243,000 + £250,000 + £200,000 = £693,000.

(e) Outgoings of cash were:

	£
on interest	101,000
on dividends	70,000
on tax	88,000

and on fixed assets £360,000, partly financed by sales of old fixed assets £43,000.

(f) Total outgoings are therefore £576,000

(g) Income less outgoings is £693,000 less £576,000 = £117,000. As a result the bank overdraft has come down by this amount.

3. The things to watch for are:

(a) The major financing experience of companies is that most cash comes in from operations and most goes out on new fixed assets. Observe the extent that this is so.

(b) Frequently the positive cash flow from operations is diminished by absorptions from increases in stock and debtors only partly financed by increases in creditors.

(c) Interest is a large absorber of cash and the effect of high interest rates has become a cliché in analysing the ills of business.

(d) Dividends do not usually absorb major amounts of cash.

(e) Tax payments are also not usually great absorbers.

(f) New financing in the form of rights issues or borrowings are sometimes found. If the borrowings are relatively large then see if the company has reached dangerous levels of gearing.

(g) The net effect on cash and cash equivalent can be seen.

(h) Many groups buy or sell subsidiaries and the effect of this on cash flow can be traced. Sometimes the effect is large borrowings or rights issues and sometimes there is no effect on cash as the consideration is new shares or loan stock.

(i) Some companies show net cash flow from operations as I have in line (a) but some companies will give more detail as:
    (i)   Cash received from customers.
    (ii) Cash payments to suppliers.
    (iii) Cash paid to or on behalf of employees.
    (iv) Other cash payments.

Preparing cash flow statements

4. An approach to preparing a cash flow statement from a profit and loss account and the balance sheets at the beginning and end of it might be:

   (a) Prepare a fixed asset reconciliation as in my example. This will give you:
       (i) payments to acquire fixed assets.
       (ii) Receipts from sales of fixed assets.

       These are required for the investing activities part of the statement.
       (i) Depreciation.
       (ii) Loss/profit on sales of fixed assets.

       These are required for Note 1 for the statement.

   (b) Complete Note 1 of the statement.

   (c) Complete the statement proper by entering:
       (i) Interest paid and received and dividends paid.
       (ii) Corporation Tax paid.
       (iii) Investing activities from (a) above.
       (iv) Issues and redemptions of share capital and loans.

   (d) Sum the statement. This will give you the increase in cash and cash equivalents.

   (e) Check (d) by preparing Note 2: the analysis of changes in cash and cash equivalents during the year.

Sources of finance

5. Individual people can supply finance to companies by investing in new issues of shares and debentures. Many people have shares in companies. Fewer, perhaps, have debentures. Listed companies can issue loans evidenced by debentures to the public generally and each investor will then have part of the loan. While many individuals invest in companies, most company investment is by institutions. These include pension funds, insurance companies, venture capital companies, investment trust companies and unit trusts. These institutions generally invest in quoted shares and debentures so that they can both buy and sell easily.

6. There are some institutions which lend specific or fluctuating amounts to companies. Notable among these are the banks who lend both on overdraft and for specific periods. Other institutions include building societies, leasing companies, hire purchase companies and factoring companies. Government agencies also lend to companies and many make grants for specific purposes.

Instruments

7. Companies can issue a range of instruments:

   (a) **Shares.** These can be ordinary or preference or even more exotic. Most, however, are ordinary. Private companies normally raise their capital from private investors, primarily members of one family. Shareholdings are normally permanent except when the whole company is sold or when shareholders die. In the latter case, shares usually descend to family members.

Public companies can raise their capital from the public generally, although a majority of the shares in a public company are usually held by institutions. One of the attractions of being a public company with a listing on the stock exchange is that new capital can be raised from shareholders by a rights issue. This can apply to private companies but generally the shareholders (mostly family) do not have the funds for new issues.

(b) **Debentures**. We have discussed these in Chapter 25. Generally private companies borrow from institutions especially banks. Listed companies can borrow from the public generally (but including institutions) by issuing loans to the public.

(c) **Hybrid and sophisticated instruments**. There are many different types of instruments dreamed up by finance houses and merchant banks. These are not for a foundation text.

Specific asset finance

8. A very general suggestion is that fixed assets should be financed by long-term finance – share capital and retained profits. Correspondingly, working capital should be financed by short-term finance including trade credit and bank overdrafts. There is no general rule and indeed no specific relationship between assets and company finance. Building societies get along very well by having very long term assets (loans on mortgage) and very short-term finance (investors' accounts). We will review some assets and how they might be financed:

(a) **Land and buildings**. These are often financed by mortgages granted by institutions such as building societies and insurance companies. Property represents a large investment by a company and an alternative is to lease or rent properties. In this way the financing of the premises occupied by a company is effectively carried out by a landlord.

(b) **Other fixed assets.** Some fixed assets – e.g. ships and aircraft – can be financed like real property. Others can be financed specifically by leasing or hire purchase.

(c) **Debtors**. A way of financing debtors is through factoring. Essentially this is a loan by the factoring company which fluctuates according to the amount of the loan.

(d) **Stocks.** Stocks are often financed by overdrafts. However a modern approach is to make the supplier provide the finance. This can be done specifically by a technique called *just in time*. The supplies are stocked by the supplier and delivered just in time to be used by the company. It can also be done by simply taking a very long time to pay the supplier.

9. You will have appreciated from the cash flow statements that companies need to obtain money from investors in order to finance their activities. People have savings which they need to invest. They can invest directly in companies or they can invest indirectly by buying life assurance and endowments and enter into pension schemes. Life assurance companies and pension schemes invest much of their investors' money in companies. In addition investors can invest in investment media like unit trusts. Much investment is in shares in companies which are owned

by others (they are in a sense second hand!) and the Stock Exchange exists to enable these sales and purchases to take place. When an investor buys a share on the stock exchange from another investor money changes hands but none of it reaches the companies concerned.

Summary

❑ The funds flow statement has now been superseded.

❑ Enterprises need to make profits. They also need to manage cash resources so as not to find themselves unable to pay debts as they fall due.

❑ FRS 1 cash flow statements requires all companies other than small companies and subsidiary companies (there are some other exemptions) to prepare a cash flow statement each year to accompany the profit and loss account and balance sheet.

❑ Points to watch for in a cash flow statement include:
  (i) The difference between profit and cash flow from operations.
  (ii) The outflows from interest, dividends and taxation.
  (iii) The relationship between investing activities and operating cash flows.
  (iv) The extent of new finance.
  (v) Whether the net effect over the year is positive or negative.

❑ Companies can receive finance from a wide range of sources from private investors to large institutions. Private companies have a more restricted range of opportunities.

❑ A range of instruments can be issued from shares to debentures.

❑ Some forms of finance are designed for specific assets including mortgages, leasing, hire purchase and factoring.

Points to note

❑ Students should learn the format.

❑ Take care to pick out payments in the year for dividends and tax.

❑ Make sure you have correctly summarised the movements in fixed assets – this is where students go wrong.

❑ Distinguish bonus issues (where there is no cash flow) from rights issues (where there is cash flow).

❑ Receipts for rights issues may be found from increases in share capital + increases in share premium.

❑ The cash flow statement as envisaged in FRS 1 has a mixture of bracketed and unbracketed figures, e.g.:

Interest received	2,400
Interest paid	(1,540)

Make sure you put brackets where they are wanted and omit then when they are not. This is important when doing the additions.

❒ The net cash flow from the statement should be the same as the net cash flow from Note 2. In examinations do not look for any difference as:

(i) This costs time.

(ii) You will probably not find the difference.

(iii) If you do you may make perhaps one mark while losing 10 because you did not do something else!

❒ Share capital and retained earnings (= the shareholders interest in a company) are described as *equity* and borrowings are described as *debt*.

❒ There is no real connection between specific types of finance and specific assets. Essentially a company raises the necessary finance in the most appropriate way for it and invests the money in the desired assets. It so happens that some institutions sell their financing schemes for specific types of asset and companies benefit from this.

❒ A company needs to have adequate working capital. How much this is depends on many factors. However, given an acceptable level of stock, debtors and bank overdraft, the working capital must be sufficient to enable creditors to be right. What is right is a combination of not paying too quickly but not taking so long that the creditors enforce payment by legal action. Suppliers must remain happy but not too happy!

❒ All forms of finance have a cost. The cost of equity is the dividend. The cost of debt is interest. An apparently free form of finance is creditors – taking a long time to pay. This is both damaging to suppliers and can be dangerous. Large companies tend to be slow payers.

Self-testing questions

1. Why can companies be profitable and yet go bust for want of cash?
2. Which enterprises are exempt from the requirements of FRS 1?
3. Write out a pro forma cash flow statement with Notes 1 and 2 and a fixed asset movement summary.
4. What points of interest may emerge from a review of a cash flow statement?
5. How can you check the correct completion of a cash flow statement (at least some aspects!)?
6. List some investing institutions.
7. List some instruments acknowledging finance by companies.
8. List some assets and how they may be financed.
9. Distinguish debt from equity.
10. What are the costs of finance?

Exercises

1. Here are the balance sheets of Weerdflow Ltd as at two dates a year apart and also the summary profit and loss account for the year ending 31 December 19x2:

Weerdflow Ltd
Balance Sheet as 31 December

	19x1 £'000	19x2 £'000
Fixed assets		
Cost	2,380	3,140
Less Depreciation	1,862	730
	518	2,410
Current assets		
Stocks	980	1,230
Debtors	635	910
	1,615	2,140
Creditors – amounts falling due within one year		
Creditors	750	1,560
Overdraft	257	620
Taxation	146	325
Dividends	200	160
	1,353	2,665
Net current assets	262	(525)
Total assets less current liabilities	780	1,885
Creditors: amounts falling due after more than one year		
12% Debentures	100	300
Net assets	680	1,585
Capital and reserves		
Share capital (£1 shares)	100	170
Share premium	180	330
Profit and loss account	400	1,085
	680	1,585

Profit and Loss Account for the year ending 31 December 19x2

Turnover	8,500
Cost of sales	6,150
Gross profit	2,350
Overheads (including depreciation)	1,000
Operating profit	1,350
Interest	100
Net profit before taxation	1,250

...continued

Taxation		325
Profit after tax		925
Dividends		
Interim	80	
Final	160	240
Retained profit		685

Note that in the year fixed assets (Cost £2,100,000, written down value £350,000) were sold for £280,000.

Required:

(a) Prepare a cash flow statement.

(b) Visit or write to a range of institutions and found out how they can finance companies. Include banks, venture capital companies, leasing companies, HP companies and factoring companies.

(c) Obtain the annual reports and accounts of some listed companies and explore their financing.

Assignment

❏ The books of Shawm PLC, musical instrument suppliers, at the ends of the years 19x5 and 19x6 included the following figures:

	31 December 19x5		31 December 19x6	
Fixtures at cost	240,000		280,000	
Depreciation of fixtures		142,000		
Sales		673,720		821,000
Purchases	505,200		540,710	
Opening stock	87,400			
Closing stock	121,000		130,100	
Distribution costs	61,800		70,400	
Admin expenses	52,300		48,000	
Interest	5,000		10,600	
10% debenture		50,000		80,000
Interim dividend	6,000		6,000	
Trade debtors	201,000		280,400	
Trade creditors		82,000		96,900
Accruals		2,800		4,300
Prepayments	4,200		5,100	
Land at cost	40,000		109,000	
Buildings at cost	93,000		158,400	
Buildings depreciation		44,640		
Cash at bank	6,100			
Bank overdraft				14,710
Ordinary shares of 50p each		10,000		12,000
Profit and loss a/c		291,240		
Share premium				60,000
Capital redemption reserve		5,600		5,600

Notes:

(a) Depreciation policy on the fixtures is 25% reducing balance and on the buildings 4% on cost.

(b) Corporation tax is estimated at £13,800 on the 19x5 profits and £32,000 on the 19x6 profits.

(c) The directors recommend a final dividend of 30p a share for 19x5 and 30p a share also for 19x6.

(d) The directors resolve to make a provision for doubtful debts of 1.5% of debtors at the end of 19x6.

Required:

(a) Prepare profit and loss accounts (Format 1), balance sheets, cash flow statements, statements of total recognised gains and losses, and reconciliation of movements in shareholders' funds for 19x5 and 19x6. (Cash flow statement 19x6 only.)

(b) Write a commentary on what the company has achieved over the two years. Discuss particularly, capital expenditure, financing and dividend policy.

(c) Suppose the company had sold a subsidiary business in 19x6 and in the same year had purchased another. Suppose also that the company had spent £30,000 on resurrecting a branch in 19x6.

How would these events affect the financial statements?

❐ Obtain the annual report and accounts of a major public company (ask friends or relatives to write to the secretary of a major public company or many college libraries have collections of them). Write a report on the profits earned. You should include comments on continuing, discontinued and acquired operations, the layout and presentation and the contents of the three financial statements. Photocopies of extracts from the report should be included in an appendix.

33 Regulatory framework of accounting

Introduction

This chapter considers the regulation of accounting in the UK.

The regulators

1. Double entry bookkeeping developed by experimentation in Renaissance Italy. It was not invented. It was not a requirement of the law. It just grew because business people needed it. In the nineteenth century, the balance sheet and, later, the profit and loss account were also developed because the business and investment communities needed them. Again, there was no legal or other requirement for the form and content of financial statements, just a need which accountants met by experimenting and discovering new methods. In very recent years the funds flow statement was developed and has now been replaced by the cash flow statement. Also new are the statement of total recognised gains and losses and the Reconciliation of movements in shareholders' funds.

2. In the nineteenth century, the need for a balance sheet and profit and loss account to be prepared for shareholders of large companies was recognised and a legal requirement for these financial statements was laid down in a succession of nineteenth century Companies Acts. The law required financial statements but did not lay down the form or content.

3. In the twentieth century, a series of Companies Acts began to specify the *content* of financial statements and finally the 1981 Companies Act also specified the *form* of financial statements. Statutory regulation of accounting continues and major changes occurred in the Companies Act 1989. Statutory regulation occurs in legislation other than The Companies Acts – the Building Societies Acts, Charities Act and many others.

4. In recent years, there has been a great deal of regulation of accounting in the following areas:
   (a) The form of financial statements.
   (b) The content of financial statements.
   (c) The extent of disclosure of financial data.
   (d) The accounting principles to be followed.

5. The regulation has come from primarily:
   (a) The Companies Acts.
   (b) The professional accounting bodies in the form of Statements of Standard Accounting Practice (SSAPs).
   (c) The new Financial Reporting Council.
   (d) The Financial Reporting Standards.
   and secondarily:

(e) The Stock Exchange.

(f) International accounting standards.

(g) The European Union.

The need for regulation

6. The need for some form of financial statements summarising the performance and position of an enterprise has been covered in Chapter 1 of this manual. In summary this need is to enable actual and potential owners, managers, creditors, tax authorities, employers and other contact groups to make informed judgements on the past performance and actual position of an enterprise and to take decisions based on those judgements.

7. However, there is a tendency in those reporting (e.g. managers to owners, directors to shareholders) to:

(a) Present financial statements in a form which they (and not the recipients) find convenient.

(b) Give only the minimum information which will be acceptable, or rather less than that.

(c) Fail to disclose data they do not wish known (e.g. their own remuneration).

(d) Use a variety of accounting principles without disclosing which have been used.

8. As a consequence, various regulatory bodies began to dictate the form, content, extent of disclosure and principles to be used of accounts. This process is fairly well advanced now but will continue for many years.

Regulation by the State – the Companies Acts

9. Since the middle of the nineteenth century there has been a steady development in the regulation of accounting by companies in the form of successive Companies Acts. The most recent was very extensive changes in the Companies Act 1981.

10. This Act is now codified with several others in the Companies Act 1985 as modified by the Companies Act 1989.

11. The Companies Acts' accounting requirements cover the following ground:

(a) Accounting records to be kept.

(b) Statutory books to be kept.

(c) Annual accounts to be produced.

(d) The use of required formats.

(e) The use of specified accounting principles.

(f) An overriding requirement for the accounts to give a *true and fair view*.

(g) The giving of particular detailed information about each item in the accounts.

The requirement (f) is a very difficult idea which is generally discussed in auditing texts. Briefly, true means accounts must be simply true. For example, if the balance sheet shows Land at Cost £2 million, that must be a true statement. The reality may be more complicated. Should legal charges be included, for example? Fair is altogether harder. Does straight line depreciation fairly spread the cost of an asset over the years of its useful life or would reducing balance method do the job more fairly?

12. The *financial statements* required are:
    (a) A profit and loss account for each accounting reference period.
    (b) A balance sheet as at the date to which any profit and loss accounting is made up.
    (c) Notes attached to and forming part of the financial statements.
    (d) Where a company does not trade for profit, an income and expenditure account.

    Note that a cash flow statement is not required under the Companies Act.

13. The *form* of the financial statements is also prescribed:
    (a) The balance sheet must be in one of two formats (i.e. vertical or horizontal) shown in schedule 4 of CA 1985.
    (b) The profit and loss account should follow one of the four formats (two vertical and two similar horizontal) shown in schedule 4 CA 1985.
    (c) Corresponding amounts for the previous year shall also be shown for all items.
    (d) Set off is not permitted (e.g. bank accounts in credit against overdrafts).
    (e) Departure from a Format is only permitted if preservation of the true and fair view requires it.
    (f) Once selected, a Format should be used for all subsequent years.

Regulation by quasi-statutory bodies and self-regulation

The Financial Reporting Council

14. In 1991 the Government set up a quasi-statutory body – the Financial Reporting Council – to encourage good reporting standards.

15. It has several subsidiaries:
    (a) The Accounting Standards Board
    The Board replaces the old Accounting Standards Committee and is now the prime issuer of accounting standards. It issues Financial Reporting Standards (FRSs).

    Before issuing a new standard the Board issues Financial Reporting Exposure Drafts (FREDs) for discussion.

    (b) The Financial Reporting Review Panel (FRRP)
    This body reviews departures from Accounting Standards and Companies Act requirements found in actual published accounts and, if necessary, can seek an order from the Court to remedy them.

    (c) Urgent Issues Task Force (UITF)
    This body makes rulings on areas where an accounting standard or Companies Act provision exists but where unsatisfactory or conflicting interpretations have developed or seem likely to develop. A surprising number of matters have been subject to UITF pronouncements, most of them very technical.

Statements of standard accounting practice

16. Until 1991, the principal body which developed required accounting practices was the Accounting Standards Committee which produced Statements of Standard Accounting Practice (SSAPs) which were then approved by the professional bodies and became binding on professional accountants.

17. In 1991, this system ceased and was replaced by the Financial Reporting Council and its subsidiaries. We will consider now the SSAPs which are still in force. Some of the SSAPs are highly technical. Some, however, are relevant to students at Foundation level and the provisions of these have been incorporated into this manual.

SSAPs issued

18. At the time of writing, the following SSAPs are in issue:
    1. Accounting for associated companies.
    2. Disclosure of accounting policies.
    3. Earnings per share.
    4. The accounting treatment of government grants.
    5. Accounting for value added tax.
    8. The treatment of taxation under the imputation system in the accounts of companies.
    9. Stocks and long-term contracts
    12. Accounting for depreciation.
    13. Accounting for research and development.
    15. Accounting for deferred taxation.
    17. Accounting for post balance sheet events.
    18. Accounting for contingencies.
    19. Accounting for investment properties.
    20. Foreign currency translation.
    21. Accounting for leases and hire purchase contracts.
    22. Accounting for goodwill.
    24. Accounting for pension costs.
    25. Segmental reporting

Financial Reporting Standards

19. The production of SSAPs ceased when the Accounting Standards Committee was replaced by a subsidiary of the Financial Reporting Council – the Accounting Standards Board. The ASB issues Financial Reporting Standards (FRSs). Current FRSs are:

    FRS 1 Cash flow statements
    FRS 2 Accounting for subsidiary undertakings
    FRS 3 Reporting financial performance
    FRS 4 Capital instruments
    FRS 5 Reporting the substance of transactions

FRS 6   Acquisitions and mergers

FRS 7   Fair values in acquisition accounting

FRS 8   Related party disclosures

Some of these have replaced SSAPs (e.g. FRS 2 and FRS 6). Probably all the existing SSAPs will eventually be replaced by FRSs.

We have dealt with FRS 1 and FRS 3 in the second chapter on Companies. The other FRSs are not relevant to a foundation text in accounting.

Statements of Recommended Practice (SORPs)

20. Some industries need accounting standards for their particular purposes and they can produce Statements of Recommended Practice (SORPs). The ASB has a role in approving these. Its policy is to recognise producers of SORPs instead of the SORPs themselves.

International accounting standards

21. In addition to the SSAPs which apply in the UK, there are also International Accounting Standards which are promulgated by the International Accounting Standards Committee. These IASs have explored much the same ground as the SSAPs (e.g. stocks, depreciation etc) and come to much the same conclusions. In general, compliance with an SSAP will automatically achieve compliance with the corresponding IAS.

The European Community

22. The UK and the Republic of Ireland are both members of the European Union (EU). One of the management institutions of the EU is the *Commission*. The Commission's duties include the harmonisation of company law throughout the EU and to that end it has issued a number of *Directives*. Each member country is obliged to incorporate the Directives into its own company law. However, there are many optional clauses and while substantial harmonisation in the areas dealt with has been achieved, there are still substantial differences. The principal Directive of interest is the Fourth, that on company accounting. The Companies Act 1981 (now the Companies Act 1985) was the Act which incorporated the Fourth Directive and introduced the Formats and many other features to English law. The Seventh Directive was incorporated by the Companies Act 1989.

Over the next few years many aspects of company law including accounting requirements will be the subject of Directives and eventually incorporated into English law. It is also worth noting that the Accounting Standards are also influenced by EU Directives.

The Stock Exchange

23. The Stock Exchange has issued some accounting rules which listed (= quoted) companies must follow. These are fewer than the requirements of the Accounting Standards and the Companies Act and they need not be considered at this level.

Some regulations

24. We have seen some regulations in the chapters on company accounting. Other regulations have been reviewed in the areas of stock and depreciation (SSAP 9 and SSAP 12). As you progress in accounting beyond the foundation level, you will meet ever more detailed regulations, both in statutory form and in the form of accounting standards. We need not consider many of these in this foundation text.

Accounting principles

25. The Companies Act requires the following principles to be adopted:
    (a) The company shall be presumed to be carrying on business as a *going concern*.
    (b) Accounting policies shall be applied *consistently* from one financial year to the next.
    (c) The amount of any item shall be determined on a *prudent* basis.
    (d) All income and charges relating to the financial year to which the accounts relate shall be taken into account without regard to the date of receipt or payment – the *accruals* convention.
    (e) In determining the aggregate amount of any item, the amount of each individual asset or liability that falls to be taken into account shall be determined separately.

    For example, the concept of lower of cost and net realisable value must be applied to individual items of stock and not to stock as a whole.
    (f) These rules can be departed from if:
        (i) There are good reasons for doing so.
        (ii) The reasons and effects are explained in the notes.

An example of departure may be because the company is not a going concern.

Thus the Act prescribes that accounts must conform to the going concern convention, the prudence convention, the consistency convention, and the accruals convention.

The required prudence convention specifies:
    (a) Only profits realised at the balance sheet date shall be included in the profit and loss account. This is really the realisation convention.
    (b) All liabilities and losses which have arisen or are likely to arise in respect of the financial year to which the accounts relate or a previous financial year shall be taken into account, including those which only become apparent between the balance sheet date and the date on which the Accounts are signed by the Board of Directors.

This last statement is a very clear exposition of the prudence convention.

Item (e) is a requirement which has no particular name in accounting literature. Shall we call it the individuality convention?

SSAP 2 – disclosure of accounting policies

26. SSAP 2 was issued in 1971. It is not a statutory pronouncement but the law has recognised accounting standards as best practice and so it has, at least, statutory

recognition. Like all the SSAPs, it was approved by the accounting bodies and is mandatory on all qualified accountants.

The standard distinguishes three ideas:

(a) Fundamental accounting principles.

(b) Accounting bases.

(c) Accounting policies.

27. **Fundamental accounting principles** are defined as the broad basic assumptions which underlie the periodic financial accounts of business enterprises. In this manual we have referred to them as the accounting conventions. SSAP 2 mentions only four:

(a) The 'going concern' concept: the enterprise will continue in operational existence for the foreseeable future. This means in particular that the profit and loss account and balance sheet assume no intention or necessity to liquidate or curtail significantly the scale of operation.

(b) The 'accruals' concept: revenue and costs are accrued (that is, recognised as they are earned or incurred, not as money is received or paid), matched with one another so far as their relationship can be established or justifiably assumed, and dealt with in the profit and loss account of the period to which they relate; provided that where the accruals concept is inconsistent with the 'prudence' concept (paragraph (d) below), the latter prevails. Revenue and profits dealt with in the profit and loss account are matched with associated costs and expenses by including in the same account the costs incurred in earning them (so far as these are material and identifiable).

(c) The 'consistency' concept: there is consistency of accounting treatment of like items within each accounting period and from one period to the next.

(d) The concept of 'prudence': revenue and profits are not anticipated, but are recognised by inclusion in the profit and loss account only when realised in the form either of cash or of other assets the ultimate cash realisation of which can be assessed with reasonable certainty; provision is made for all known liabilities (expenses and losses) whether the amount of these is known with certainty or is a best estimate in the light of the information available. Note that 'accruals' in SSAP 2 covers both the accruals convention and the matching convention discussed in this manual.

28. SSAP 2 makes the point that since the four fundamental accounting principles underlie all financial statements, there is no need to state them specifically in each set of accounts. However, if accounts are prepared under any other, different principles, the facts should be explained.

You may care to contrast these with the Companies Acts list.

29. **Accounting bases** are the methods which have been developed for expressing or applying the fundamental accounting concepts to specific financial transactions and items. There is often more than one recognised accounting basis for dealing with particular items. For example:

(a) Depreciation — straight line
 — reducing balance

		–	sum of digits
(b)	Stock valuation	–	FIFO
		–	weighted average cost

30. **Accounting policies** are the specific accounting bases judged by business enterprises to be most appropriate to their circumstances and adopted by them for the purpose of preparing their financial accounts. A business has a choice of accounting basis in, for example, stock valuation. It may choose FIFO or AVCO. The actual basis chosen is called its accounting policy. For example, if it selects FIFO, FIFO is its accounting *policy*.

31. **Disclosure.** SSAP 2 requires that the accounting policies followed for dealing with items which are judged material or critical in determining profit or loss for the year and in stating the financial position should be *disclosed* by way of note to the accounts. The explanations should be clear, fair and as brief as possible.

32. **Examples of disclosure** of accounting policies, taken from recent published accounts:

   (a) '**Depreciation of Tangible Fixed Assets**

   Depreciation is provided by the group in order to write down to estimated residual value (if any), the cost or valuation of fixed assets over their estimated lives by equal annual instalments, mainly on the following bases:

Freehold and long leasehold buildings	Over estimated useful life (24-100 years)
Short leaseholds	Over remaining period of lease
Fixtures and fittings	Over 10 years
Vehicles and equipment	Over 5 years

   Depreciation arising on the revaluation surplus of properties is charged to profit and loss account and then transferred to the revaluation reserve.'

   (b) '**Property Development**

   In the case of certain property development projects the interest on the capital borrowed to finance the project is, where separately identifiable and to the extent that it accrues during the period of development, capitalised as part of the cost of the asset.'

   (c) '**Credit Sales**

   Profit is taken on goods sold on credit when the sale is effected, except that a deferral is made in respect of the 12 month extended credit sale which are not subject to interest. The service charge on other credit sales is taken to trading profit as it accrues.'

   (d) '**Copyrights**.

   Copyrights are included in the balance sheet at a nominal amount. Acquisitions are written off in the year of purchase.'

   (e) '**Research and development**

   Expenditure on research and development is written off in the year in which it is incurred.'

   (f) '**Restoration**. Provision is made at current prices for the cost of restoring land from which minerals have been extracted.'

Other SSAPs

33. Some of the SSAPs refer to relatively advanced matters. Some are of interest at foundation level. Among the latter are:

34. **SSAP 13 – Accounting for research and development**. Many companies (e.g. companies in pharmaceuticals, chemicals, electronics, aerospace) engage in expenditure on research and development. The rules are:

   (a) The cost of fixed assets acquired or constructed in order to provide facilities for R. and D. activities over a number of accounting periods should be capitalised and written of over their useful lives through the profit and loss account.

   (b) Expenditure on pure and applied research should be written off in the year of expenditure through the profit and loss account.

   (c) Development expenditure should be written off in the year of expenditure except in the following circumstances:

   (i) There is a clearly defined project.

   (ii) The related expenditure is separately identifiable.

   (iii) The outcome of such a project has been assessed with reasonable certainty as to its technical feasibility and its ultimate commercial viability considered in the light of factors such as likely market conditions (including competing products), public opinion, consumer and environmental legislation.

   (iv) The aggregate of the deferred development costs, any further development costs, and related production, selling and administration costs is reasonably expected to be exceeded by related future sales or other revenues.

   (v) Adequate resources exist or are reasonably expected to be available, to enable the project to be completed and to provide any consequential increases in working capital.

   In these circumstances, development expenditure may be deferred to the extent that its recovery can reasonably be regarded as assured. If one such project is deferred then all should be. Amortisation to profit and loss account should be systematic, begin with the first commercial production or use, and be allocated to successive periods by reference to sales or use. There should be reviews of each project and in any that seem doubtful or unviable, deferred expenditure written off immediately.

   (d) The accounting policy adopted towards research and development and all relevant figures should be disclosed.

35. The rules on deferring R. and D. are very conservative and, as a consequence, very little R. and D. expenditure is actually deferred. One effect of this is that companies that do R. and D. show lower profits than companies that do not. And yet, on balance, one would expect that companies doing R. and D. would have a better future than those that do not. Hopefully, investors will be able to evaluate company performance and future prospects by reference to all the facts disclosed and not simply to profits. It is worth noting that investors and industry generally in the UK are often accused of 'short-termism'.

SSAP 17 – accounting for post balance sheet events

36. This SSAP looks at events that occur after the balance sheet date. It distinguishes adjusting events from non-adjusting events. Adjusting events are those that provide additional evidence of conditions existing at the balance sheet date. Examples include the collectibility of debts, the saleability of stocks, and the amount payable in connection with uncertain liabilities. Non-adjusting events are those post balance sheet events which concern conditions which did not exist at the balance sheet date. These include losses caused by events after the balance sheet date such as fires, strikes, nationalisation, changes in foreign exchange rates.

    The SSAP requires that adjusting events change the financial statements and non-adjusting events do not. This is good common sense. If, however, a major loss occurs after the balance sheet date, then the loss will not affect the financial statements but should be disclosed so that investors know about it. An example might be a company with substantial assets in a foreign country which undergoes a revolution after the balance sheet date and the assets are lost to the company.

SSAP 18 – accounting for contingencies

37. A contingency is a condition existing at the balance sheet date, where the outcome will be confirmed only on the occurrence or non-occurrence of one or more uncertain future events. A contingent gain or loss is a gain or loss dependent on a contingency. Examples are legal actions, guarantees to third parties and speculations on the price of commodities.

    The SSAP requires that:
    (a) Contingent gains should not be accrued (= incorporated in the actual financial statements) and should be disclosed only if it is probable that the gain will be realised.
    (b) A material contingent loss should be accrued if it is **probable** that a future event will confirm a loss which can be estimated with reasonable accuracy at the date the financial statements are prepared.
    (c) A material contingent loss, which is not accrued, should be disclosed, except where the possibility of loss is **remote**.

    You will see that these requirements make sense but again are very conservative – ignore gains but count losses!

SSAP 22 – accounting for goodwill

38. Goodwill is defined as the difference between the value of a business as a whole and the aggregate of the fair values of its separable net assets. Fair values are a contentious issue and we will not consider the matter here. The SSAP requires that no amount should be included in a balance sheet for non-purchased goodwill. Purchased goodwill should not be carried in a balance sheet as a permanent item. Generally purchased goodwill should be eliminated from the accounts immediately on acquisition against reserves. It is possible to capitalise purchased goodwill and amortise it on a systematic basis to the profit and loss account, but the following apply:

(a) It should not be revalued and, if there is a permanent diminution of value, should be written off immediately.

(b) The useful economic life should be estimated at the time of acquisition and no account should be taken of future expenditure or events.

(c) The economic life chosen may be shortened but not increased.

The accounting policies adopted for goodwill should be disclosed.

The rules on accounting for goodwill are also very conservative. Normally a company may spend say £2 million on an acquisition and this will include some goodwill, say £1.2 million. The effect is that the net assets of the acquiring company are reduced by £1.2 million if the goodwill is written off straight away as it usually is. Capitalisation and amortisation are not usually adopted as this will lead to a reduction of profits (by the amount of the amortisation) for some years to come.

SSAP 21 accounting for leases and hire purchase contracts

39. This SSAP deals with the consequences of the *substance over form* convention in accounting. The idea is that some transactions have a legal form which is different from the underlying economic reality. In such cases the real economic substance of the transaction is accounted for rather than the legal form. A good example is the hire purchase contract. The legal form is that the ownership of the asset is retained by the finance company until the final instalment has been paid. The substance of the contract is that the asset belongs to the user who borrows and repays the debt with interest. Accounting for HP is explained in the chapter which includes HP contracts and is in accord with this SSAP.

40. Leases can be of two types:

(a) Operating leases. These are of the type where an assets is leased for a time – like hiring a car for a week.

(b) Finance leases. These are in, legal form, simply like operating leases – the hirer or lessee uses the asset and pays hiring charges. However, finance leases are those lease contracts where:

(i) The contract transfers substantially all the risks and rewards of ownership of the asset to the lessee.

(ii) This should be presumed if, at the inception of the lease, the present value of the minimum lease payments including any initial payment, amounts to substantially all (normally 90% or more) of the fair value of the leased asset. Present value and fair value are technical terms which I will not explain here.

Operating leases should be accounted for by simply charging the rental payments to profit and loss account. Finance leases should be accounted for by treating the transaction as the purchase of the asset with the aid of a loan. The rental payments are seen as repayments of capital and payments of interest.

Summary

❒ Bookkeeping and accounting developed in a totally unregulated way until this century.

❏ Regulation is now carried out by:
  (i)   The law in the form of the Companies Act and other Acts and regulations.
  (ii) The Financial Reporting Council.
  (iii) The Stock Exchange.
  (iv) The International Accounting Standards Committee.
  (v)   The EU.

❏ The need for regulation arises out of:
  (i)   Diversity of accounting practices.
  (ii) Tendencies not to bother with good accounting records.
  (iii) Diversity of form.
  (iv) Tendencies to secrecy.
  (v)   Tendencies to put information in the most favourable light.
  (vi) Tendencies to overstate/understate profits.

Regulation is in the following areas:

(i) Companies Act:
  –   accounting records to be kept
  –   accounting statements to be produced
  –   format of accounts
  –   information to be disclosed
  –   accounting principles to be followed
  –   requirement for a true and fair view
  –   requirements (including time limits) for filing accounts for public inspection with the registrar of companies and submission to shareholders.

(ii) SSAPs and FRSs:
  –   accounting statements to be produced (cash flow statements and some others)
  –   information to be disclosed
  –   accounting principles to follow
  –   detailed methods for measuring profit and capital.

❏ The Companies Act requires the accounting principles of going concern, consistency, prudence, accruals and individuality.

❏ SSAP 2 describes four fundamental accounting principles – going concern, accruals, consistency and prudence. It also distinguishes accounting bases (methods like depreciation and stock valuation) from accounting policies which are the actual bases adopted by an enterprise.

❏ SSAP 2 requires disclosure of accounting policies.

❏ Many SSAPs and FRSs cover advanced matters.

❏ SSAP 13 makes it difficult to carry forward, as an asset on the balance sheet, any Research and Development expenditure.

❐ SSAP 17 distinguishes post balance sheet events as adjusting (events casting light on balance sheet values) or non-adjusting.

❐ SSAP 18 is very conservative and prudent on incorporating and disclosing contingent gains and losses.

❐ SSAP 22 dislikes showing even purchased goodwill on the balance sheet and prohibits non-purchased goodwill from appearing at all.

❐ SSAP 21 prefers substance to form in HP and leasing contracts.

Points to note

❐ It is important to note several ideas:

(i) The prime influence in the *form* of accounts comes from the EC Directives which are incorporated in UK Company Law. The required formats in the Companies Act 1985 are of European origin and in many ways unsuitable for use in the UK.

(ii) The prime influence on the content and extent of disclosure comes from the Stock Exchange and the Government who are concerned to ensure investors receive adequate information. This desire upon the part of the Government to see fair play in financial markets can be seen in the extensive accounting requirement of the Companies Act 1985 together with tight audit requirements.

(iii) The prime influence on the accounting principles to be adopted comes from the accounting bodies and now the FRC. They have been influenced by a number of scandals (e.g. GEC AEI in the 1960s) and by a growing sophistication amongst institutional (e.g. pension funds, insurance companies, unit trusts) investors that has enabled fund managers to become aware that no comparison can be made of the results of two companies if different principles are used in measuring the results.

❐ The UK company law has for many years required company financial statements to give a 'true and fair view' of the results and state of affairs (profit and loss account and balance sheet). What exactly a true and fair view is, is very difficult to assess and depends upon the circumstances. This difficult concept is usually discussed in auditing texts.

❐ Regulation in the US has been much more extensive than in the UK and continental Europe. The reasons for this may include (a) a higher regard for business and hence accounting, (b) more extensive business education with earlier recognition of the faults in traditional accounting, (c) the tendency for US investors who lose money on Stock Exchange deals to sue the auditors of the companies they invested in. Often the cause of action arose from doubt as to the appropriate accounting principles to be used. As with most things, US ideas tend to find their way across the Atlantic in due course.

❐ Before an FRS is published and approved, an exposure draft (FRED) is published. This is a proposed FRS and comments and suggestions are asked for from interested parties. The final FRS takes into account these comments and suggestions. Exposure drafts, unlike FRSs, are not mandatory on accountants, but they usually set out current best practice.

❏ When I was a student, finding out how to account for a transaction meant looking through textbooks or trying to compare the transaction with similar but different transactions or seeing what other companies did. Now the method is to consult the regulations whether Companies Act, other Acts of Parliament, SSAPs, SORPs or FRSs.

❏ Note the overriding requirement that all accounts should show a true and fair view even if this means contravening regulations. However any such departure must be patently justifiable and be fully disclosed.

❏ An axiom of good accounting practice is disclosure. If the accounting policy and facts and figures about a transaction are fully disclosed then readers can understand the matter however it is accounted for.

❏ Where regulation is silent, and despite all the SSAPs, FRSs, SORPs etc it often is, then it is possible sometimes to consult the idea of Generally Accepted Accounting Principles as a guide.

❏ More advanced studies in accounting have tended to become a study of the regulations.

Self-testing questions

1. How did accounting and bookkeeping come about?
2. Accounting regulation applies in what areas?
3. Where has accounting regulation come from?
4. Why is accounting regulation necessary?
5. List the general Companies Act 1985 accounting regulations.
6. What financial statements are required by the Companies Act?
7. What forms must financial statements take?
8. What are corresponding figures?
9. What replaced the Accounting Standards Committee?
10. What are the functions of the ASB, the FRRP, the UITF?
11. List the SSAPs still in force.
12. List the FRSs in force.
13. What are SORPs and how does the ASB regulate them?
14. List and explain the accounting principles required by The Companies Act.
15. Distinguish and define fundamental accounting principles, accounting bases and accounting policies.
16. Explain SSAP 13 and distinguish the accounting treatment of fixed assets, research and development.
17. Explain SSAP 17 and distinguish adjusting events from non-adjusting events.
18. Explain contingencies and distinguish contingent losses and contingent gains.
19. Explain SSAP 22 and distinguish purchased from non-purchased goodwill.
20. Explain SSAP 21 and distinguish HP, operating leases and finance leases.

Exercises

1. Suppose you are on the Board of a public company. The company has had a bad year. What attitudes might the Board take towards the form of, content of, disclosures in, accounting principles used in and the laying and delivering of the annual accounts?

2. The price of limited liability is disclosure. Discuss.

3. The accounts of a medium sized public company have been prepared, but before they can be published certain notes must be drafted to explain the calculations of some of the figures in the accounts, and to show that the accounts conform to best accounting practice. As an accounting technician, you are a member of the team engaged in writing these notes, with special responsibility for the note on Accounting Policies.

   Required:

   (a) Write a memorandum on The Companies Act requirements on accounting principles.

   (b) Give FOUR examples of matter for which different accounting bases may be recognised, including a brief explanation of how each one may have a material effect on the reported results and financial position of the business.

   (c) Find some published reports and accounts and comment on the statement of accounting policies therein.

4. Examine the accounting policies sections of some actual published accounts and consider them from the point of view of accounting principles and the regulations.

Assignment

❐ *It is February 19x5 and Gilbert is worried that the company he runs – Dicey PLC- has had a bad year in 19x4 and the loss shown by the profit and loss account will attract a take-over from another company or pressure from the institutional shareholders to remove him from his post as chief executive. He takes an interest in the way in which the profit is measured and tries to find ways of improving the measure of profit. He considers the following areas:*

   (a) Depreciation is straight line throughout and the Board has just approved the incorporation in the 19x4 accounts of a revaluation upwards of the company's freehold factory and branch offices.

   (b) The company completely redecorates all its properties every four years. The year 19x4 was one of them and the cost has been very high. Gilbert considers that the four yearly nature of the redecoration distorts profits and thinks the cost could be amortised over four years.

   (c) The Board decided just before the year end to close down the branch in Liverpool and the assets there have been valued at break up value which is lower than the former book values. Gilbert thinks that as the close down will not take place until April 19x5, the 19x4 balance sheet could have the former book values.

   (d) The company has placed a contract with Bootle University engineering department for the development of a new widget. The contract began in 19x3 and the widget has reached the prototype stage. Before putting it into production, much work remains to be done and environmental and safety approvals will have to be sought. Gilbert thinks that the costs so far can be capitalised.

(e) The company signed an agreement in 19x4 for the purchase of 1,000 tons of Hedonite in January 19x5 for use in the production of a product. In January, a cheaper substitute material was found and on delivery of the Hedonite it was immediately sold at a good profit. Since the contract for the purchase was signed in 19x4, Gilbert thinks the gain could appear in the 19x4 profit and loss account.

(f) At the beginning of 19x4, the company purchased a business, paying a substantial amount for goodwill. At the time, Gilbert was horrified at the thought of this meaning a reduction of net assets and the goodwill was capitalised and is being amortised over five years including 19x4.

(g) Being short of cash, the company acquired at the beginning of 19x4 some executive cars on hire purchase despite the high APR. The interest has been calculated using the APR. Gilbert thinks this is too complicated and suggest charging the interest to profit and loss account over the years on a simple time apportionment basis.

Required:

Comment on Gilbert's ideas.

34 The accounting conventions

The accounting conventions have been discussed or mentioned at many points in this manual. This section brings the subject together and reviews all the accounting conventions and discusses their justifications, drawbacks and consequences.

The business entity convention

1. The business is seen as an entity separate from its owner(s) or proprietor(s).

   (a) The justification for this convention is that the proprietor and other interested parties (e.g. lenders, tax man) are concerned to know the profit earned by and the capital employed in the business (or each business if the proprietor has several).

   (b) The drawbacks of this convention are:

      (i) It is artificial – the assets and liabilities are in law those of the proprietor not of some artificial entity 'the business'.

      (ii) The accounts do not make clear to creditors what actual assets are available to meet their claims or what other liabilities must be met out of the assets.

   (c) The consequences of the convention include:

      (i) Assets and liabilities are arbitrarily included in a balance sheet on a subjective view of what assets and liabilities are properly those of the business. Some assets, e.g. motor cars, are both business and private assets.

      (ii) The capital of the business is seen as a liability of the business to its proprietor.

      (iii) Drawings and losses are regarded as a reduction of this liability.

      (iv) Profits and capital introduced are regarded as an increase in this liability.

The money measurement convention

2. Transactions are recorded in money terms. Financial statements are drawn up with revenues, expenses, assets and liabilities being expressed in money terms.

   (a) The justification for this convention is that financial statements are intended to summarise the events of the financial year and the position of the business at the end of the year. To do this effectively, a common unit of measurement must be used and that common unit of *measurement* is money.

   (b) The drawbacks to this convention are that:

      (i) Transactions, events and facts that cannot be recorded in money terms are ignored. For example, relevant facts about a business such as the quantity of orders on hand, the existence of satisfied customers or competent management are not included in financial statements.

      (ii) Financial statements are drawn up from the entries in the books. The entries in the books are made from data concerning individual transactions. This *transaction* based approach to accounting means that facts about the business which are not derived from transactions are not recorded in the accounting system. For example, purchased goodwill is included in the system since it is derived from a transaction (the purchase), but goodwill acquired from successful trading is ignored.

(iii) Money, as a unit of measurement, is unstable. Price levels change with inflation (or rarely, deflation). Historical cost accounting implies wrongly that the currency has stable value. Clearly, measurement of, say, distance using a unit (say the kilometre) whose value fluctuated with time, would be quite unacceptable.

(c) The consequences of this convention include:

(i) Exclusion of non-transaction based facts.

(ii) Exclusion of relevant data which are not measurable in money terms.

(iii) Assumption that it is reasonable to show, for example, fixed assets at written down value £x when x is composed of costs at different times.

(iv) Focusing attention on the financial aspects of the business when other aspects may be of equal or greater importance.

The historical cost convention

3. Assets and expenses are entered into the books at their actual cost to the business.

(a) The justification for this convention is that historical cost is *objective* and *verifiable*. Any alternative convention (e.g. showing assets at realisable value) would be subjective and thus lead to a wide variation in measurement. The cost convention provides a universal, consistent and simple method of recording assets and expenses. An argument used in favour of unamortised cost as the value of fixed assets is that the value required is the value in use represented by its cost and not the value on resale represented by what some hypothetical buyer might value it at.

(b) The drawbacks of this convention are:

(i) Items having no cost are left out of account.

(ii) In times of changing price levels, serious distortion occurs when, for example, depreciation based upon the historical costs of earlier years is set against revenues at current prices.

(iii) The actual information required by managers, investors, etc may be current values of assets and values based upon historical costs may be irrelevant for their purposes.

(c) The consequences of the convention include:

(i) Assets are valued at cost or cost derived figures (e.g. unamortised cost for fixed assets).

(ii) Revenues at current prices are matched with historical costs.

(iii) Items which had no cost are ignored.

(iv) Unrealised gains are ignored.

(v) Relevant information (e.g. the real value of capital employed in the business) is not given.

The going concern convention

4. The going concern convention assumes that the enterprise will continue in operational existence for the foreseeable future. The balance sheet and profit and loss account are drawn up on the assumption that there is no *intention* or *necessity* to liquidate or *curtail* significantly the scale of operation.

   (a) The justification for this convention is simply that it is true. If it were not so, then liquidation values would need to be substituted for the historical cost based figures.

   (b) The drawbacks to this convention are that:

      (i) It may mislead – some firms do cease trading shortly after publication of accounts drawn up on the going concern basis.

      (ii) Information is not given on the consequences of abandoning the convention. The consequences of such abandonment may be important information to an unsecured lender.

      (iii) Alternative courses of action cannot be evaluated. For example, the use of historical cost based values may indicate a satisfactory return on capital employed whereas knowledge of potential realisable prices for fixed assets may suggest that the business should be wound up and the sums realised invested elsewhere.

   (c) The consequences of this convention include:

      (i) Fixed assets are valued at unamortised costs.

      (ii) Current assets are valued at lower of cost and net realisable value in the normal course of business.

      (iii) Liabilities that will arise only in the event of liquidation (e.g. redundancy pay), are ignored.

      (iv) In company accounts, shareholders' funds are divided between payable and non-payable liabilities.

      (v) Information about the consequences of liquidation is not given.

Periodicity

5. This convention requires that a balance sheet and profit and loss account should be produced at regular intervals. Most businesses produce annual accounts and the Companies Acts require annual accounts for companies. Public companies produce half yearly interim accounts and many businesses produce monthly or quarterly accounts for internal purposes.

   (a) The justification for this convention is that ongoing information about the business is required at regular intervals for all sorts of purposes – performance evaluation, tax computations etc.

   (b) The drawbacks of the convention are:

      (i) It is assumed that business transactions can be identified with particular periods. In practice, many transactions (e.g. buying a fixed asset), have consequences for many periods.

    (ii) Periodic income determination leads to comparisons of the results of successive periods. As the pattern of business activity changes over time, this comparison may be misleading.

    (iii) A range of conventions have had to be developed (matching, realisation, prudence) to relate transactions to specific time periods. Differing accounting bases (e.g. depreciation methods) can cause difficulty in comparing different businesses.

    (iv) In very short period accounting (e.g. half yearly or shorter), seasonal variations can mislead.

(c) The consequences of the periodicity convention are:

    (i) Much effort is required to prepare the periodic accounts.

    (ii) Arbitrary allocation and apportionment methods are required.

    (iii) Some commentators consider that it has led to a degree of short-termism. Annual profits become more important than the long-term view.

The realisation convention

6.   This convention requires that the profit on any given transaction is included in the accounts of the period when the profit is *realised*. Realisation means when a transaction (e.g. a sale) has occurred which gives legal rights to the receipt of money.

(a) The justifications for this convention include:

    (i) The *critical event* principle. The trader as a businessman is in business to *sell* things. It is suggested that buying goods and collecting debts are relatively easy. The hard bit is selling the goods and consequently it is at that point that the profit is earned.

    (ii) The *certainty* principle. When goods are bought, the profit that will be made is not certain. It is not certain that the goods will be sold and a profit made. When the goods are sold, there is certainty that a profit has been made and how much the profit is.

    (iii) The *asset transfer principle*. On the sale the goods cease to be the property of the trader and become the property of his customer. The trader ceases to have goods; instead he has a debt due to him. The value of the debt is the sum due.

(b) The drawbacks to this convention include:

    (i) Unrealised or holding gains are ignored. For example, an asset may have increased in value while it has been held by the business but no recognition of this increase is made until the asset is sold.

    (ii) Distortions can occur when the trading cycle is long. For example, the profit on long-term contracts accrues over the period of the contract and does not occur suddenly on the completion of the contract. In practice, the realisation convention is modified in the case of long-term contracts.

    (iii) The convention is unnecessarily cautious in waiting until a sale before a profit can be recognised.

(c) The consequences of the convention include:

    (i) Fixed and current assets are valued at cost or cost derived amounts.

    (ii) Holding gains and unrealised gains are ignored.

The matching convention

7. The matching convention requires that in an accounting period, costs are matched with related income. Where costs have been incurred and there is no related income in the period or in future periods with which the costs can be matched, they are treated as an expense of the accounting period.

   (a) The justification for this convention arises out of the periodicity convention. The profits of the period are revenues from transactions less all associated costs. Which revenues should be included is determined using the realisation convention. Any costs not associable with the future revenue are written off as they are incurred.

   (b) The drawbacks to this convention include:

      (i) The difficulty of determining which costs are associated with particular revenues. The whole business of depreciation and total absorption cost finished goods and work-in-progress valuation are features of the matching convention.

      (ii) The use of different matching methods (e.g. depreciation methods) by different accountants leads to the results of enterprises not being comparable one with another.

   (c) The consequences of the matching convention include:

      (i) Valuations of stock and work-in-progress on a balance sheet which include time related costs (e.g. rent) for expired periods.

      (ii) The inclusion on a balance sheet of assets with no tangible value, e.g. development costs.

      (iii) The inclusion of estimated liabilities where provisions are necessary to match costs with revenues.

The accruals convention

8. The accruals convention is also a consequence of the periodicity convention. Revenues and costs are recognised and included in the profit and loss account as they are accrued (earned or incurred), not as they are paid or received.

   (a) The justification for this convention is that receipts and payments are to a degree random as to timing, whereas the earning of a revenue or the consumption of a resource can be accurately related to specific time periods.

   (b) The drawbacks to this convention include:

      (i) The work required to apportion expenses to time periods.

      (ii) Financial statements become more complex (than say cash flow accounting), with a consequent loss of intelligibility to the layman.

   (c) The consequences of the convention include:

      (i) The inclusion of prepayments and accruals in a balance sheet. The meaning of these words is not apparent to the layman.

The convention of conservatism or prudence

9. This convention requires that:

(a) Revenue and profits are not anticipated but are recognised by inclusion in the profit and loss account only when realised in the form of cash or other assets (e.g. a debt) the ultimate cash realisation of which can be assessed with reasonable certainty.

(b) Provision is made for all known liabilities (expenses and losses) whether the amount is known with certainty or is a best estimate in the light of information available. As an example, Dick is in business to service cold stores equipment on a contract basis. By 31 December 19x5 the following irrevocable contracts had been signed:

A. £5,000 a year for 19x6, 19x7 and 19x8. Expected costs to Dick are in the region of £3,000 a year.

B. £6,000 a year for 19x6 and 19x7. Expected costs to Dick are £7,000 for 19x6 and £7,400 in 19x7.

The prudence convention requires that in the 19x5 accounts:

(i) The profit on contract A should be ignored. It will fall into 19x6 and 19x7.

(ii) The loss on contract B (£2,400) should be included.

(c) The justification for this convention is that accountants are cautious people. The natural optimism of businessmen needs to be countered by the pessimism of the accountants. It is felt that where doubt exists, it is better to err on the safe side.

(d) The drawbacks to this convention include:

(i) It is unnecessarily pessimistic.

(ii) The tendency to understate asset values tends to lower the appropriate prices for shares on the stock exchange.

(e) The consequences of this convention are that:

(i) Profits are not anticipated.

(ii) Holding gains are ignored.

(iii) Potential losses (even future losses) are fully reflected in the accounts.

Consistency convention

10. This convention requires that there is consistency of accounting treatment of like items within each accounting period and from one period to the next. For example, the straight line method of depreciation, once chosen for vehicles, should be used for *all* vehicles and for all periods.

The justification for this convention seems self evident if comparability over time is to be achieved. However, its extension to all businesses seem desirable, but has not been achieved.

Other conventions

11. There are some other ideas which some writers consider to be conventions. These include:

(a) **Materiality**

Accounting is concerned with the measurement of profit and capital and the presentation of the results to interested parties. In essence it is a summarising process. Too much detail in the annual accounts and the view is obscured. Insignificant items are merged with others and are not shown separately. The problem is making a decision as to what is material and what is not material. For example, bad debts always occur to Smith PLC. However, each year the total of bad debts is small relative to other items in the accounts and the total is included in cost of sales and not shown separately. However, in 19x5 a particularly large bad debt caused a downward jump in profits after several years of increases. To explain the downward jump the bad debt has to be disclosed separately. In practice, decisions on whether items are material enough to affect the view given by the accounts and hence to require disclosure, are very difficult. Some accountants and auditors use percentages (e.g. 5%) of net profit or net assets as a measure of materiality but there are no easy approaches.

(b) **Dual aspect**

The double entry system requires all transactions to have two entries, one on the debit of an account and one on the credit of the same or a different account. This enables balance to be maintained in the accounting equation – capital = assets – liabilities. The detailed application of this convention ensures that balance sheets always balance but does not ensure that the balance sheet is correct in other ways.

(c) **Substance over form**

Some transactions have a legal *form* which is different from the underlying commercial reality or substance. In such cases, for accounting purposes, *the substance is preferred to the form*. In this chapter we have seen this in the treatment of leases and hire purchase contracts.

Another example is **Goods sold subject to reservation of title** ('Romalpa' transactions). The legal form of these transactions is that goods are sold with the agreement that ownership of the goods does not pass from the vendor to the buyer until payment is made. The substance of the transactions is that they are normal credit sales with the reservation of title clause in the contract for sale being of importance only if the buyer becomes insolvent. They are normally accounted for using the substance approach.

Summary

❐ Financial statements measure and demonstrate profit, capital and other ideas. They are drawn up using a number of accounting conventions.

Conventions include:

(i) Business entity.

(ii) Money measurement.

(iii) Historical cost.

(iv) Going concern.

(v) Accruals.

(vi) Conservatism or prudence.

(vii) Consistency.

(viii) Materiality.

(ix)   Periodicity or continuity.

(x)   Realisation.

(xi)   Matching.

(xii) Dual aspect.

(xiii) Substance over form.

Points to note

❐ The entity convention is implicit in company accounting where the idea of a separate business is the legal reality.

❐ Separate businesses imply separate double entry systems. Remember that in questions which concern the take-over of one business by another, or an amalgamation of businesses, that you view the matter from the right perspective. Focus on one entity at a time.

❐ Money has been the accountant's method of measurement from time immemorial. However, its problems in times of inflation have led the accounting bodies to seek alternative systems of accounting. I have not dealt with accounting for the changing purchasing power of money in this manual as firstly, it is a fairly difficult and advanced business and secondly, inflation is now very small and accountants seem to have lost interest. Over the years a number of methods have been mooted. These include Current Purchasing Power (CPP) and Current Cost Accounting (CCA). The latter was the method advocated in SSAP 16 which is now withdrawn. In practice some companies still present their accounts using CCA but also present them in the conventional way. The problem with these systems is that they are complex and hard to understand. Investors seem to lack confidence in them. Some moving away from conventional accounting regularly occurs as assets are revalued upwards. However even this practice is less relevant as property values have stagnated.

❐ The historical cost basis of producing financial statements arose out of the system of double entry bookkeeping, since in a double entry system, assets and expenses are recorded at their cost. It naturally followed that when periodic financial statements were developed, the available data from the double entry system should be used. Accounting is sometimes said to be transaction driven.

❐ The going concern convention has given rise to some discussion in recent years with the closure of large numbers of industrial plants in the UK. It should be noted that while most of an enterprise can be a going concern, a part can be measured using liquidation values.

❐ Most of the problems of accounting measurement arise out of the periodicity convention. The difficulty is deciding what revenues and expenses should relate to any particular year. In addition, the labour involved in apportioning expenditure and building up stocks and work-in-progress costs is considerable. In future, with computers able to summarise data on stocks, debtors and creditors at any time, more frequent financial statements will be produced.

❐ The realisation convention, which prevents unrealised gains being taken into account, can distort the view given by accounts. The practice of revaluing properties is an exception to the convention and is widespread.

❐ The prudence convention in the past led to the true position being viewed as 'at least as good' as that shown. This is in some way comforting, but not to a shareholder who has sold his shares at a price which is a fraction of that which he could have obtained if the true position had been known.

❐ Where the prudence convention conflicts with other conventions, the prudence convention should prevail.

❐ You may have noticed that many of these conventions seem to overlap. They do, and some writers consider that, for example, the accruals convention encompasses what I have called the separate conventions of realisation, matching, accruals and historical cost. Clearly there is an overlap between matching and accruals and between realisation and accruals.

Example of financial statements showing use of accounting conventions

Business entity	**Nasturtium Ltd**		
Periodicity	**Trading and Profit and Loss Account for the year ending 31 December 19x2**		
Money measurement			£
Realisation	Sales		400,000
Matching	*Less:* Cost of goods sold		250,000
	Gross profit		150,000
Accruals	Wages	61,000	
	Rent and rates	13,500	
	Sundry overheads	31,900	
Prudence	Provision for loss on future contracts	4,700	
Materiality	Uninsured loss of stock by fire	6,800	
	Depreciation	6,910	124,810
	Net profit		25,190
	Balance sheet as at 31 December 19x2		
Historical cost	Fixed assets at cost		52,500
	Less Depreciation		21,000
			31,500
	Current assets		
Prudence	Stock	28,000	
	Debtors	61,000	
	Prepayments	1,900	
		90,900	

... continued

	Creditors: amounts falling due within one year		
Going concern	Creditors	36,000	
Substance over form	HP commitment	2,000	
	Overdraft	26,480	
		64,480	
	Net current assets		26,420
	Total assets less current liabilities		57,920
Going concern	Creditors: amounts falling due after more than one year		10,000
			47,920
	Capital and reserves		
	Called up share capital		2,000
	Share premium account		6,000
	Profit and loss account		39,920
			47,920

Self-testing questions

1. What is the business entity convention and what is its justification, drawbacks and consequences?
2. What is the money measurement convention? List its drawbacks and consequences.
3. What is the historical cost convention? What is its justification? List its drawbacks and consequences.
4. Define the going concern convention. What is its justification? List its drawbacks and consequences.
5. What is the justification for the periodicity convention? What are its drawbacks and consequences?
6. What is the realisation convention? State the justifications for this convention. What are its drawbacks?
7. What is the matching convention? What are its drawbacks and consequences?
8. Define the accruals convention and list its drawbacks and consequences.
9. Define the prudence convention. List its drawbacks and consequences.
10. What is the consistency convention?
11. What is the relevance of materiality to accounting?
12. Give two examples of 'substance over form'.

Exercise

☐ Watkin is in business as a manufacturer of fishing tackle. He is consulting his daughter who is a certified accountancy level 1 student about certain items which puzzle him in connection with his accounts which are in preparation. These are:

(a) I garage my car at a house down the road as I have no room at my own house. This costs me £15 a week. I use the car about 30% for getting to work, 30% on business and 40% for private motoring.

(b) Due to breakdowns in some machinery which has now been replaced, I have been unable to manufacture as many goods this year as last year. However, my order book is now three times what it was at the end of last year and stands at six months' work.

(c) A supplier told me that he was considering cutting off credit to me as my business liabilities are large in comparison with my business assets.

(d) My bank manager tells me my return on capital has been very good but my capital employed includes the property at cost less depreciation which I bought in 1960 for £10,000.

(e) In the last year's accounts there was no figure shown for potential redundancy pay which I know now amounts to over £13,000.

(f) I have some special fishing rods which I have had in stock at cost for many years at £100. I am negotiating now to sell these to a Japanese business acquaintance for £1,500. How will these appear in the accounts?

(g) I would like my accounts prepared more frequently than once a year as the way things are I like to see how I am going month by month.

(h) I have sent 100 rods to an agent in Germany on a sale or return basis. I think he has sold some but I have not yet had any information from him.

(i) I know I had two cheques of £100 each from Harry for part of the factory I let off to him for the second half of the year and which he still rents. However, that covers four months only and in the draft accounts the accountant has put £300 as rent received. Is this right?

(j) I have agreed to buy 50 special rods from a supplier in France at 360 francs each. This was a very high price and now I will get only 8 francs to the pound. I only bought them to please an old customer and I have contracted to sell them to him at £35 and I have carriage of £100 in total on them.

(k) I depreciate my machinery on a straight line basis and this seems to put part of my machinery into a nil value on the balance sheet. Could I change to some other method of depreciation?

(l) Last year's accounts did not seem to include the petty cash in hand of £15 or the loan to my secretary of £70.

(m) The business is buying a van on hire purchase. The agreement says that the van belongs to Carp Van Finance PLC until I have paid the last instalment.

(n) I have 2,000 metres of glass fibre tubing in my yard which will not be mine until I have paid GFT Limited, the suppliers, because it says so on their invoice.

Required:

Explain these matters to Watkin in terms of the accounting conventions and how they will be treated in the accounts. Comment on the usefulness of the accounts in the light of these matters.

Assignments

❐ *Some commentators aver that there is such a thing as creative accounting and some have even written books about it. Directors stick to the minimum disclosure requirements and often fail to disclose relevant facts. In the past, financial statements showed very little but at least the position shown was at least as good as that shown. Many companies show profits in their accounts and go bust a few weeks or months later. Modern reports and accounts are so complex and the language is so arcane that even accountants cannot understand them.*

Required:

Comment on these statements, referring where appropriate to regulation and the accounting conventions.

❐ *The Multinational Mega Group PLC has subsidiaries worldwide and is in a wide variety of industries from oil exploration, pharmaceuticals, agriculture, tourism and health care to aerospace. The annual report and accounts tells me it made a profit of exactly £2,643,782,000 to the nearest thousand. On second thoughts that seems to be only one line of the profit and loss account.*

Required:

Comment on these thoughts.

Appendix A: Answers to selected exercises

Chapter 1

Exercise 2

It means that Rich left assets (business, stocks and shares, building society deposits, house, furniture, paintings etc valued at £x less any liabilities (e.g. unpaid telephone bill) £y so that the net amount came to £2,624,000. His executors will have to pay a lot of Inheritance tax on this!

Exercise 5

(a) Several words come to mind: importers, traders, manufacturers (in a small way), retailers, wholesalers.

(b) Partnership.

(c) Imported goods need to be paid for before delivery, goods bought in UK will need payment perhaps two or three months after delivery, some items will be in stock before sales, sales to wholesalers will be on credit and receipt of cash may be two to four months after sales, sales to public will not be on credit.

(d) Invoices, credit notes, statements of account, delivery notes, advice notes, cheques (or other bank payments systems), import documentation is more complex.

Exercise 10

(a) Actual and potential: shareholders, directors, bank, suppliers, customers, employees, institutions such as Stock Exchange and local authority planning deptartments, public, pressure groups.

Chapter 2

Exercise 1

Dr side: Discount allowed £34.21 Cash total £1,500.52

Cr side: Discount received £2.34 Cash total £767.81 Balance £2,375.71

Chapter 3

Exercise 1

Mark up 85.7%, Gross profit: £3,000, gross Profit margin 46%.

Exercise 3

(a) (i) Yes unless it was not bought for resale – it might be for personal use of a director.

    (ii) No.

    (iii) No.

    (iv) No.

    (v) No.

    (vi) Yes but see argument in (i) above.

Exercise 12

(a) Alfred Gross profit £21,640, Net profit £10,560

Alfred Gross profit £21,640, Net profit £10,240

(b) Mark up 95.5%, Gross profit margin 48.8%. Some businesses are high mark-up (e.g. jewellery, furniture, expensive clothing) and some are low mark-up (e.g. supermarkets). I leave you to argue about the reasons.

Chapter 4

Exercise 1

(a) Fixed assets £66,900, Current assets £30,656, current Liabilities £15,190, capital £82,366.

Connections: consider stock and debtors.

Exercise 2

No: The following were none of these: the contract (had no cost), the caravan (not business), the life policy (not business), the fur coat (not business).

Fixed assets: scales, the estate car.

Current assets: tinned goods.

Current liabilities: overdue rent, due to wholesalers.

Exercise 10

(a) Add to fixed assets and to capital .

(b) Add to stock and to creditors.

(c) Add to prepayments and deduct from bank .

(d) Deduct from stock (£210) and add £300 to Bank and £90 to Capital.

(e) Deduct from bank and add to cash in hand.

(f) Add £3,000 to bank and to loan.

(g) Deduct from cash in hand and capital.

(h) Add to capital and to bank.

(i) Add £105 to debtors and £20 to capital and deduct £85 from stock.

(j) Add to fixed assets and deduct from stock.

Chapter 5

Exercise 1

Item 1	(a)	(b)	(c)	
Cost	8,000	8,000	8,000	
Year 1	1,560	4,176	2,600	Profit and loss account
End of year 1	6,460	3,824	5,400	Balance sheet
Year 2	1,560	1,996	2,080	
End of year 2	4,880	1,828	3,320	and so on
Rate used	£7,800/5	52.2%	$5/15 \times £7,800$	

Exercise 3a

(a) No Depreciation.

(b) Cost is £73,500. Write off over 18 years or 30 years? Tricky!

(c) Cost is £4,340 – amortise over six years.

(d) Adopt same policy as other plant (consistency convention). Policy might be straight line, reducing balance or other. In first year may apportion from purchase date, first use date or take whole year or perhaps half year.

(e) £2,000 No Depreciation, £60,000 × 30/600 = £3,000.

Chapter 6

Exercise 5

(a) Dr Balances: Jones £961.15, Williams £519.15, Evans £2,408.32, Purchases £1,316.29. Cr Balances: Fraser £882.90, McLeod £2,700.32, Scott £576.63, Bank overdraft £3,319.72, Customs & Excise £74.00, Sales £1,739.06.

(b) Financial statements: Profit and loss account – sales and purchases

(c) Balance sheet: Debtors £3,888.62, Creditors £4,159.85, Customs £74, Bank £3,319.72

Exercise 7

Total of Dr side £2,765. Cr side has profit and loss account £1,525 and Stock c/d £1,240. The £1,240 is b/d on the Debit of the new period.

Exercise 9

Total of Dr side is £123,072 and this is the transfer to profit and loss account. Balance b/d in new period is £11,119 on the Cr side.

Chapter 7

Exercise 1

Balances will be at end of year:	Asset at cost	Provision	Profit and Loss Account
19x5	£2,346	£469.2	£469.2
19x6	£6,486	£1,766.4	£1,297.2
19x7	£6,486	£3,063.6	£1,297.2
19x8	£6,486	£4,360.8	£1,297.2
19x9	£6,486	£5,658	£1,297.2
19x0	£6,486	£6,486	£828

Exercise 3

19x7 Asset at end of year £4,386, Annual depreciation £877.20, Provision a/c £1,803.6, Disposal loss on sale £760

19x8 Asset at end of year £4,386, Annual depreciation £877.20, Provision a/c £2,680.8

Chapter 8

Exercise 1

King – Trial balance totals £380,566, Gross profit £104,131 Net profit £14,739, Fixed assets £59,894, Current assets £81,131, Current liabilities £50,140, Long-term liabilities £30,000, Capital £60,885.

Chapter 10

Exercise 1

Imprest made up with £83.56. Column totals are: Total £57.94, Travel £6.27, Sundries £10.15, Stationery £6.22, Motor £15.10, Post £8.20, Account £12.00. Corresponding debits are on appropriate expense accounts except the £12.00 which is to the account of Walters Ltd in the purchase ledger. Balance at end is £42.06.

Chapter 11

Exercise 1a

Edward: Debtors control a/c – Dr side £122,388, Cr side £97,330, Balance £25,058.

Creditors control a/c – Dr side £125,459, Cr side £139,762, Balance £14,303.

Exercise 3

Brenda: Correct control a/c balance – £15,031 + £487 – £100 = £15,418.

Correct list – £15,277 + £231 – £90 = £15,418.

Chapter 12

Exercise 1

. Informational: add to cash book – £2,438 – £100 + £1,000 = £3,338

Timing: adjust bank statement balance – £2,546 +£1,566 – £234 – £540 = £3,338

Chapter 13

Exercise 1

Chaos (customers not picked up etc), inefficiency (late arrivals etc), drivers disobeying orders or, if no orders, doing their own thing, cash takings not recorded and not received at head office, payments made for goods and services not received.

Chapter 14

Exercise 3

Dr Bad debts a/c £3,624, Cr Provision for doubtful debts £1,108. Profit and loss account – Bad debts £3,624, Provision £1,108. Balance sheet – Debtors £156,582.

Exercise 6

Invoice is £480 + VAT £84 = £564.

Jane: 19x6 Sales £480, Due to Customs £84 and Debtors £564. 19x7 Discount allowed £14.40.

Paul: 19x6 Purchases £480, Due from Customs £84 and Creditors £564. 19x7: Discount received £14.40.

Exercise 10

Dr Motor vehicles £7,000 and Motor expenses £107. Profit and loss account for 19x5 – HP interest $((12+11)/78 \times £600)$ £176.92. Balance sheet – HP commitment $(£6,000 + £600 - 2 \times £550)$ £5,500, HP interest in advance £423.08. Profit and loss account for 19x6: HP interest £423.08.

Chapter 16

Exercise 1

(a) £6,400 +£500 + £405 + £600 = £7,905 (NB – ignore settlement discount)

(b) £1,200 or £1,280 – £128 – £40 = £1,112 – select £1,112 as lower.

Balances:

(a) FIFO: 90 x £18 = £1,620.

(b) LIFO 50 × £12 + 40 × £18 = £1,320.

(c) AVCO 90 × £17.11 = £1,540.

Chapter 17

Exercise 1

(a) £50.00 + £28.00 + £9.60 = £87.60 per batch or £0.0876 per tin.

(b) Materials and components + production overheads.

(c) Regular overtime premiums should be included in overheads and recovered from all production.

(d) £87.60 × 1.5 = £131.40 – this is a direct cost of this batch.

Chapter 19

Exercise 1

Terri: Prime cost £661. Total manufacturing cost £1,494, Work in progress adjustment - £5, Cost of sales £1,571, Operating profit £149, Net loss after interest -£68.

Chapter 20

Exercise 1

	Turnover	Cost	Profit	Debtors	Provision
A:	£650	£450	£200	£250	–
B:	£300	£305	(£5)	£70	£14

Chapter 21

Exercise 1

(a) Letting profit £31,202, Sales profit £21,798

(b) Many costs are fixed and would not be saved. Some alternative use may be found of the vacated facilities. Some customers might not use a department if the other closed down.

(c) Problems are: apportionment of unspecified costs, treatment of let caravans sold, buildings depreciation.

Chapter 22

Exercise 1

Hugh: Capital £55,900

Exercise 2

Alan: Debtors £9,801

Exercise 4

Winnie: Sales £253,866, Purchases £179,904, COGS £177,706, Gross profit $3/7 \times £177,706$ = £76,160.

Chapter 23

Exercise 1

Gross profit on bar – £1,035, Net loss on bar – £87, Surplus £943, Prize fund – £1,732, Accumulated fund 19x6 £2,017, 1907 £2,960, Current assets £3,423.

Chapter 24

Exercise 5

	Gaynor	Amanda	Samantha	Total
(a) Profit shares	£5,736	£6,786	£2,118	£14,640
(b) Current accounts	£3,336	£4,486	£118	£7,940
Capital accounts	£8,000	£5,000	£5,000	£18,000
(d) Profit shares	£920	£1,970	(£290)	£2,600

(This assumes that no abatement occurs in interest, commission and salary – agreement needs to make this clear.

(e) No effect in first year but interest on capital will be different in future.

Exercise 8

B: Balance of Realisation a/c £2,868 – split equally. Payments to partners John £16,786 and Mary £12,964.

Exercise 10

Write up goodwill – £25,000 equally. Write down goodwill £30,000 as 3:2. Balance of capitals: Alec £17,500 Ben £22,500

Exercise 12

	Louise	Manuel	Nathan
Capitals	£7,100	£21,200 (Loan)	(£2,000)
Appropriation	£15,671	£2,955 (Interest)	£9,774
Current accounts	£9,741	£5,674	
Capitals	£7,100	£18,200 (Loan)	(£2,000)

Net assets will be £38,445

Chapter 25

Exercise 2

Benefits of limited liability both to limit liability to third parties and to avoid the effects of misconduct by one's partner.

Exercise 7a

Garmston Ltd: Profit and loss account: Profit before interest – £61,080, Bonus – £6,108, Profit after interest – £48,072, Final dividend – £25,000, Retained profit – £8,872.

Balance sheet: Fixed assets – £12,760, Current assets – £242,300, Current liabilities – £144,608, Net assets – £60,452, Retained profits – £10,452.

Exercise 9

Final balance sheet: Ordinary capital £120,000, Prefs £20,000, Share premium £32,000, Capital redemption reserve £20,000, Profit and loss account £160,000, Property revaluation reserve £30,000, Debenture premium £2,000, Debentures £40,000, Total £424,000. Net assets £424,000.

Chapter 26

Exercise 3

	-3	-4	-5	
(a) Debtors/sales	89.6	106.5	121.7	days
Creditors/purchases	94.9	121.7	151.8	days
Current ratio	1.17	1.43	1.36	
Acid test	0.75	0.75	0.76	
Stock turn	64.4	129	126	days

(b) Stock increasing at a faster rate than turnover. Difficulty in collecting debts (and/or policy to grant longer credit to raise turnover). Creditors are harder to pay despite increase in overdraft. Classic case of overtrading!

Exercise 6

	Abel	Ben	Cain	Darren
Return	24-15=9	26-15=11	12	18-15=3
Capital	96	35	126+24=150	9
ROCE	9%	31%	8%	33%

Remember that a higher risk requires a higher return.

Chapter 27

Exercise 1

Boring: Debt/(Equity + Debt) × 100 or 100/1,400 × 100 = 7%. Interest/Profit before interest × 100 = 16/356 × 100 = 4.5%. May be calculated as 356/16 = 22 times.

Exercise 5

Proton: Eps – 6p, PE – 10, Dividend yield – 5%, Dividend cover – twice.

No! 60p is the price at which a small number of buyers and sellers will trade. To attract a higher number of sellers, a higher price has to be offered.

Chapter 28

Exercise 1

(a) Sparks: Profit £53,300 – (£28,590 + £5,483 + £2,080 + £6,300) + £3,000 (WIP) = £13,847. Balance sheet: Assets £27,120, liabilities £13,051, Capital £11,821.

(a) Problems: Drawings in excess of profits, too high WIP, high staff costs (fees too low?), rising overdraft.

Chapter 29

Exercise 2

Profit: at 400,000 pairs: Labour method £40,000, Capital method £30,000, at 600,000 pairs: Labour method £80,000, Capital method £100,000.

Shows effect of economy of scale (more contributions but same fixed costs). Problem of risk. Condition (i) better to use labour, condition (ii) better to use capital.

Chapter 30

Exercise 2

Forecast profit and loss account:

Admin	39,600	Sales – credit		161,000
Selling	10,000	– cash		133,000
Depreciation	10,000			294,000
Advertising	11,000	Opening stock	42,000	
Directors	22,000	Purchases	178,850	
Net profit	18,350	Closing stock	37,800	183,050
Total	110,950	Gross profit		110,950

Chapter 31

Exercise 1

Samantha: Fixed assets £13,067, Current assets £13,190, Current liabilities £6,397, Long-term liabilities £1,000, Capital and reserves £18,860, Profit and loss account £13,143.

Exercise 2a

Ams: profit and loss account: Turnover £895, Gross profit £391, Admin £78, Distribution £114, Interest £15, Profit before tax £132, Dividends £75, Retained £57.

Balance sheet: Fixed assets £730, Current assets 3124, Current liabilities £196, Long-term liabilities £200, Ordinary capital 125, Profit and loss account £203, Capital and reserves £458.

Appendix B: Case studies

Case study I: The Elms Retirement Home

Jane Ash owns and manages a retirement home for elderly people in Sheinton. She has been in business for several years with some success but feels that the business is not as profitable as it should be. To find out what improvements may be possible she has begun to subscribe to the Interfirm comparison scheme of the Rutland Retirement Residences Register. We will begin with the trial balance extracted from her books at the year end 31 December 19x6:

Wages	30,200	Share capital	115,000
Director's salary	10,400	Profit and loss a/c	3,915
Heat and light	6,550	Depreciation buildings	20,700
Food	12,760	Depreciation furniture	15,400
Telephone	732	Depreciation vehicles	13,290
Repairs	6,200	Loan at 12%	50,000
Motor expenses	2,190	Bank overdraft	20,600
Bank interest	2,800	Creditors	3,298
Loan interest	6,000	Fees	105,000
Advertising	3,340		
Rates	4,290		
Water	1,190		
Garden maintenance	3,800		
Cleaning	2,220		
Debtors	1,680		
Stocks of food	940		
Premises at cost	180,200		
Furniture etc at cost	51,300		
Vehicles at cost	20,411		

Notes:

(a) Depreciation is: Buildings straight line over 30 years (on buildings cost £130,200), Furniture etc straight line over 15 years, vehicles 25% reducing balance.

(b) Accruals: Accountant's fee £1,600, Electricity £432.

(c) Prepayments: Motor expenses £280, Rates £720.

(d) The loan (from Cressage Assurance PLC) is being repaid by instalments over the next 10 years.

(e) The shares are owned 80% by Jane and 20% by her mother. No dividends have been paid.

(f) Stock of food at 31 December 19x6 was valued at £1,245.

(g) The home has room for 12 residents and average occupancy was 92%. Average turnover was 28%, defined as the number of new residents a year compared with maximum capacity.

Required:

(a) Prepare financial statements for 19x6.

The RRRR produced a set of statistics based on the average returns of all subscribers. These showed the following:

Wages	24.1	Advertising	1.6
Heat and light	5.7	Rates and water	5.1
Food	10.3	Garden	2.2
Telephone	0.8	Cleaning	2.4
Repairs	4.2	Depreciation – buildings	2.2
Motor expenses	2.3	Depreciation – other	6.2
Interest	3.1	Proprietorial remuneration	21.6

All figures are percentages of gross fees received.

In addition, the average occupancy was 94.3% and turnover 16%.

(b) Write a report to Jane commenting on the performance of the Elms in comparison with the figures produced by RRRR and suggesting ways in which Jane may improve her profitability.

(c) Comment on the problems of standardising accounting measurement revealed by this case.

Case study II

The second case study is an extended exercise in bookkeeping containing sections on:

(i)   Books of prime entry.

(ii) Sectional balancing.

(iii) Closing entries.

(iv) Final accounts preparation.

David commenced in business as a wholesaler of lawnmowers on 1 January 19x4. His first month's transactions were:

			£
Jan 2	Purchases on credit:	Barbara	800
		Jane	1,524
	Rental invoice from Edna, quarter to 31.3.x4		500
	Rates invoice from Haytown Council quarter to 31.3.x4		360
	Cheque from David's private account paid into bank		6,000
Jan 3	Purchases on credit:	Jane	380
	Credit note from Barbara		36
	Insurance invoice from Paula – year to 31.12.x4		168
	Paid Edna by cheque		500
Jan 4	Invoice from Dawn for motor van		3,000
	(price included licence y/e 31.12.x4 – £85		
	and insurance y/e 31.12.x4 – £240)		
	Sales invoice – George		730
Jan 5	Cheque from Jessica – Loan at 12% pa		2,000
	Purchases on credit – Barbara		1,210
	Paid Paul by cheque		168
Jan 8	Sales invoice – Philip		826
	Cheque for cash:	Wages	102
		Drawings	100
		Petty cash	20
	Paid Dawn by cheque		3,000
	Petty cash payments:	Petrol	5
		Sundries	11
Jan 9	Purchases on credit:	Louise	360
Jan 15	Cheque for cash:	Wages	104
		Drawings	100
		Petty cash	25
	Sales invoice – Nigel		1,043
Jan 17	Paid Barbara by cheque		764
	Nigel paid (after discount of £26)		1,017
	Petty cash payment:	Petrol	7
		Sundries	18
Jun 18	Paid Jane		1,524

Jan 19	Paid Louise (after discount of £18)		342
Jan 20	Purchases on credit – Louise		180
	Sales invoice – Jeff		682
Jan 22	Cheque for cash:	Wages	101
		Drawings	100
		Petty cash	30
	Sales invoice – George		2,430
Jan 23	Purchases on credit – Nora		2,450
Jan 24	Petty cash payments:	Petrol	6
		Sundries	6
		Drawings	8
Jan 24	Sales invoice – Miles		960
Jan 25	Paid Nora £2,450 less 2% discount		
Jan 26	Sales invoice – Philip		2,812
Jan 27	Purchases on credit – Barbara		1,611
Jan 28	Miles paid £960 less $2\frac{1}{2}$ % discount		
	Purchases on credit – Jane		180
Jan 29	Cheque for cash:	Wages	103
		Drawings	110
		Petty cash to make up to float of £40	
	Credit note from Jane		141
Jan 30	Invoice for petrol from Matilda		168
	Sales invoice – George		136

Required:

(a) Enter all transactions into appropriate books of prime entry.

(b) Enter all transactions into double entry accounts. You should use three separate ledgers:
  (i) Sales ledger.
  (ii) Suppliers ledger.
  (iii) General ledger.

(c) Balance off accounts where necessary and prepare a trial balance.

(d) Prepare sales ledger and suppliers ledger control accounts.

(e) Prepare a trading and profit and loss account for the month of January and a balance sheet at 31 January, taking into account:
  (i) Stock at 31 January consisted of:
    16 'A' type mowers which had cost £30 each
    14 'B' type mowers which had cost £43 each
    50 'C' type mowers which had cost £21 each
    6 'D' type mowers which had cost £14 each

(ii) PAYE and national insurance owing at 31.1.x4 was £207.

(iii) Depreciation policy is 30% reducing balance.

(f) Enter the transfers to trading and profit and loss account in the general ledger accounts.

(g) Compute the gross and net profit to sales percentages.

(h) Compute the return on capital employed assuming that David's labour is worth £7,200 a year.

Case study III

The following case study gives practice in:

(i) Drawing up a partnership agreement.

(ii) Preparation of partnership accounts.

(iii) Resolving the problems of partnerships when a partner retires or dies.

Parts (a) and (c) are suitable for role playing with roles for each of the three partners.

(a) Oliver, Phyllis and Quintin intend to set up in business as builders merchants. Details of the partners and the business are:

Oliver: is a wealthy accountant. He is intending to invest £20,000 in the business but to work part time only (eight hours a week) mainly in the accounting, systems andcommercial areas.

Phyllis: is currently unemployed, having been made redundant from a bankrupt builders merchant firm. She can invest some £2,000 in the business and intends to work full time on the administration, purchasing, stock control and delivering to customers activities.

Quintin: is a representative for a firm of building material manufacturers. He intends to invest about £5,000 in the business and work part time (about ten hours a week). His main activity will be selling, as he intensive connections in the trade.

The business: The business will be conducted from leased premises. A lease for 20 years on a new property has been obtained at a market rent of £4,000 a year. It is envisaged that profits should be around £25,000 a year.

Required:

(a) Draw up a list of matters that should be included in the partnership agreement.

(b) Draw up appropriate specific clauses on the subjects of:
    – profit/loss sharing
    – whether or not to maintain separate partners' capital and current accounts.

(c) At the end of the first year, the trial balance of the partnership was:

	£			£
Fixtures at cost	10,900	Capitals	O	20,000
Vehicles at cost	16,380		P	2,000
Drawings O	3,100		Q	5,000
P	8,700	Sales		241,720
Q	4,630	Creditors		38,609
Purchases	204,135	Bank		9,450
Rent	3,000			
Other overheads	25,838			
Debtors	40,096			
	316,779			316,779

Stock was valued at cost at £23,600.

Other overheads included rates in advance of £248 but did not include accruals of £1,200.

The fixtures are expected to have a life of ten years with no salvage value.

The vehicles are expected to have a life of four years with a residual value of £4,000.

Required:

Trading and profit and loss and appropriation account for the first year of the partnership and balance sheet as at the end of the year.

(c) As at the end of year one, Quintin is promoted in his job to another part of the country and wishes to withdraw from the partnership.

Required:

Detail suitable arrangements for the withdrawal of Quintin. The following points may be borne in mind:

(a) The lease has become worth £5,000.

(b) The customers introduced by Quintin are likely to continue to buy from the business but a representative will be required. The representative will cost £15,000 a year and will spend one third of his time on existing customers and two thirds on developing new business.

(c) Bank overdraft facilities of £20,000 have been agreed but future working capital requirements will pre-empt about £15,000 of that.

Case study IV

The next case study gives practice in:

(i) Preparing accounts in columnar form to demonstrate the performance of departments or branches.

(ii) Calculating and evaluating performance and liquidity ratios.

(iii) Critically assessing the information contained in accounts but hidden except to the
perceptive observer.

(iv) Using accounts to make decisions.

Part (e) is suitable for role playing with parts for Jonas and each of the branch
managers.

Jonas owns a business manufacturing light fittings. Sales are handled by three
branches, in Manchester, Birmingham and Exeter. Each branch has been open for 10
years and each branch manager has been in office since the opening. Each branch is
autonomous as to bookkeeping, selling prices, the incurring of overheads and working
capital control.

For 19x5, the trial balances of the three branches showed:

	Manchester	Birmingham	Exeter
	£'000	£'000	£'000
Sales	1,040	1,530	764
Purchases (from Jonas at fixed prices)	744	1,170	475
Stocks 1.1.x5	256	260	203
Debtors	264	127	223
Creditors	62	97	40
Bank	9	1	6
Fixed assets at cost	164	134	102
Depreciation to 1.1.x5	131	46	50
Wages	114	118	115
Rent	18	44	30
Rates	9	36	13
Repairs	49	3	6
Advertising	36	48	11
Discounts allowed	2	68	–
Other overheads	30	33	31
Head office a/c 1.1.x5	490	392	405
Remittances to head office in 19x5			
Less purchases made	46	23	44
At 31.12.x5:			
Stocks were	270	301	189
Overhead accruals	4	–	7
Rent prepayment	2	–	–
Rates prepayment	–	8	–

Depreciation policy is 25% reducing balance for all branches.

Required:

(a) Prepare trial balances in two column form for each branch as at 31 December 19x5.

(b) Prepare trading and profit and loss accounts and balance sheets for each branch for 19x5.

(c) Compile a schedule showing performances and liquidity ratios for each branch.

(d) List what you can deduce from the accounts and your schedule about:

    (i) Jonas' requirements on supplying goods to his branches.

    (ii) Each branch manager's management strategies and performance.

(e) Jonas is now seeking to open a branch in London. It is his intention to ask one of the existing three branch managers to manage the new branch. Which one of the three should be appointed?

Case study V

This case study gives practice in:

(i)   Preparing accounting statements for managerial purposes.

(ii) Considering appropriate accounting policies and the effect on profit of different policies.

(iii) Drawing up financial statements for publication.

(iv) Discussing the nature of partnerships and how they differ from private limited companies.

N Ltd was formed to manufacture and market trailers and commenced business on 1 January 19x5.

The following information is available on the activities of the company in the year 19x5.

(a) On 1.1.x5 the company took over the assets of O, P and Co, being:

		£
Plant and machinery		116,000
Stocks	Raw material	36,240
	Work in progress	24,382
	Finished goods	102,485
Prepayment of rent		2,000

The consideration for the takeover was £350,000 satisfied by the issue of 200,000 ordinary shares of £1 each to the partners of O, P and Co, and £150,000, 15% debentures 19x0/-2 secured by a floating charge on all assets of the company.

(b) The trial balance (excluding item (a) above) at 31 December 19x5 showed:

	£
Sales	2,620,000
Purchases – raw materials	384,000
Purchases – finished goods	471,000
Direct labour	620,500
Carriage inwards	52,000
Royalties payable on production of trailers	6,000
Additional plant	204,620
Rent	40,000
Rates	36,000
Insurances	59,000
General overheads	446,000
Indirect labour	384,905
Proceeds of sale of machine	4,000
Bank overdraft	373,395
Bank interest	10,300
Debtors	493,250
Creditors	106,180
Directors remuneration	96,000
Proceeds of issue – share capital	200,000

471

(c) Of the expenses, the following analysis can be made (percentages).

	Production %	Distribution %	Selling %	Administration %
Depreciation	80	–	10	10
Rent	90	5	2	3
Rates	90	5	2	3
Insurance	70	5	10	15
General	60	10	10	20
Indirect labour	60	10	20	10
Directors' remuneration	30	15	20	35

(d) At the year end:

		£
Stocks	– raw materials	51,820
	– work in progress (excluding h and j)	62,709
	– finished goods	181,100
Accruals	– rent	8,000
	– rates	5,300
Prepayments – insurance		1,200

(e) The item Proceeds of issue – share capital, relates to the sale of 100,000 ordinary shares of £1 each at £1.50 each and 50,000 15% preference shares at par to Q.

(f) The plant and machinery taken over has an estimated further life of five years with a salvage value of 10% of its taken over value. The new plant is also expected to last seven years and have a salvage value of £30,000. The item sold was included in the taken over plant at £15,000.

(g) During the year there was a burglary when stock costing £90,100 was stolen. It has not been recovered and the loss is not insured.

(h) The company constructed three very large trailers early in the year for use as transporters to carry the company's products to customers. The cost of manufacture included materials £30,000 and direct labour £27,000.

(i) Directors' remuneration was:

	£
O (Chairman)	25,000
P	36,000
Q	14,000
R	13,000
S	8,000

(j) In February 19x5, a contract was signed for Z Ltd, for the manufacture of a special giant trailer. The contract price was agreed at £200,000 with completion in March 19x7. At 31.12.x5; work done to date had cost £86,000, the estimated costs to completion were £93,000 and £60,000 had been received on account and had been included in sales.

(k) Of the debtors £16,000 are considered definitely bad and £34,000 are doubtful.

(l) The company has commissioned a computerised budgeting system at a cost of £155,000 included in general overheads. This has been used in the business and four copies have been sold to other companies at £20,000 each. Firm orders for three more have been received and other sales are in prospect.

(m) The company proposed to pay the preference dividend and an ordinary dividend of 10p a share.

(n) Ignore taxation.

Required:

(a) Prepare two column trial balance incorporating item (a).

(b) Prepare manufacturing, trading and profit and loss account for the year 19x5 for internal purposes. You should devise suitable accounting policies. The directors are particularly anxious to maximise the measure of profit.

(c) Prepare a balance sheet as at 31.12.x5 in Format 1.

(d) Prepare a profit and loss account in Format 1 suitable for publication and complying (as far as the data is available) with the minimum requirements of the Companies Acts.

(e) Draw up a 'statement of accounting policies'.

(f) The company is in effect a partnership between O and P who were in business together before joining with Q in N Ltd. O and P work full time in the business, but Q only attends the weekly board meetings. R and S are employee directors with no shareholdings. Q is dissatisfied with the fees paid to him and the company's trading policy which is to expand by importing trailers from Italy.

Write a report, advising Q on possible remedies for his dissatisfaction and contrasting the rights of O, P and Q in the company.

Case study VI: The Boggis Disease Association

The Boggis Disease Association has a branch in Sheinton. The branch members raise money. Primarily the money raised goes to the Association which uses the money to relieve suffering from this debilitating disease and for research. Some money is retained for the relief of local sufferers and their families.

A fund raising book fair and a grand draw is planned for the near future. The budgets showed:

Book fair	£	Grand draw	£
Hire of hall	50	Printing tickets	145
Printing leaflets	80	Licences	50
Advertising	100	Prizes	100
Sundry expenses	50	Sundry expenses	30
Takings	500	Takings	900

After these two events, figures were collected and these were:

Book fair: Actual costs were hire of hall £65, printing £80, advertising £140, sundry expenses £22. The takings were £620 plus £120 profit on refreshments. It took an average of 10 hours each for eight members to collect 3,600 books. 1,420 books remained unsold. Twelve members gave an average of four hours each to the actual fair. At the fair, six new members were recruited. At the end of the day, members commented on how much they had enjoyed the day and the company.

Grand draw: Actual costs were printing £180, licences (which last a whole year) £50, prizes £160, sundry expense £42. The takings were £830. Members gave prizes valued at £410. It was not feasible to collect data on the time spent by members on selling the tickets. After the event, members commented on how hard it was to sell tickets. No new members were recruited or new sufferers identified by the draw.

Required:

(a) Prepare financial statements showing the results of the events.

(b) Comment on the outcomes in comparison with the budgets.

(c) Discuss the problems of accounting measurement in charities based on this case.

Appendix C: Six assignments

Assignment covering up to Chapter 6

Pendil Widget Wholesale company commenced business on January 1 19x1. The first month's activities can be summarised as:

Sales			Purchases		
Date	Name	Amount	Date	Name	Amount
4	Jones	120	2	Louth	250
5	Brown	88	5	Uckington	432
8	Robinson	234	9	Sundorne	500
10	Hughes	100	13	Hobart	800
14	Graeme	128			
17	Lilac	543	Cheques	Drawn	
19	Dawes	241	7	Wages	100
24	White	67	9	Rent	120
28	James	456	14	Louth	250
			15	Wages	120
			18	Hobart	800
Cheque	Receipts		20	Sundorne	200
1	Pendil – capital	2,000	21	Motor van	1,200
18	Jones	120	22	Wages	120
26	Robinson	100	29	Wages	125
29	Hughes	100	31	Drawings	150
Sales	Returns		Purchase	Returns	
27	White	7	7	Uckington	38
30	James	26	20	Uckington	15
Cash	Receipts		Cash	Payments	
15	Cash Sales	137	23	Van repair	92
20	Cash Sales	140	28	Paid into bank	100

Notes that cash receipts are retained as cash. Some payments are made from these monies in cash and some paid into the bank.

Required

(a) Enter all these transactions in books of prime entry and double entry accounts.

(b) Bring down the balances at January 31 19x1.

(c) Prepare a trading and profit and loss account for the month and a balance sheet as at 31 January. Note that stock was valued at 31 January at £597 at cost. The vehicle should last for two years, have no salvage value and be depreciated on the straight line basis. The rent is for the three months ending 31 March 19x1.

The exercise can be carried out ignoring VAT or assuming that the following are all inclusive of VAT at standard rate (17.5%): sales, purchases, sales returns, purchase returns, cash sales and the van repair.

The exercise can be carried out manually or using an accounting package such as Sage.

Assignment covering up to Chapter 17

Morris owns and runs a car hire business in Spelterbridge. His clients are local companies who hire cars from him on credit and are supposed to pay their accounts monthly. He purchases parts and other motoring costs from other local businesses. He owns his premises and has five staff who are paid monthly. At the end of May 19x5, he balances his books, pays his staff and his suppliers and sends out statements to his customers. The following data are relevant to these tasks:

Staff	Hours	Hourly rate	Monthly free pay
Edgar	168	£6.30	300
John	94	£5.60	460
Diana	182	£5.70	300
Erica	134	£4.30	nil
Brenda	108	£6.70	300

Sales	Owing 1 May	Sales	Cheques
Adam	£2,020.00	£1,340.00	£2,020.00
Bede	£800.00	£2,650.00	
Ceres	nil	£850.00	
Daffern	£653.00	£3,100.00	£400.00
Egham	£249.00	£2,156.00	£249.00

Purchases	Owing 1 May	Purchases	Cheques
Finn	1234	1200	1234
German	78	46	78
Hurrian	298	182	
Inglis	458	680	254

Petty cash	Payments	Balances 1 May	
Tea and coffee	96	Petty cash	86
Tips	64	VAT owing	1532
Travelling	139	Cash at bank	467

Bank statement

Date	Details	Dr	Cr	Balance	
May 1	Balance			747	C
May 2	103	280		467	C
May 4	Sundries		400	867	C
May 5	104	264		603	C
May 7	105	1234		631	D
May 10	Sundries		249	382	D
May 14	Charges	57		439	D
May 19	BACS Adam		2020	1581	C
May 23	106	78		1503	C
May 29	BACS Dividend		100	1603	C
May 30	107	254		1349	C
May 30	Balance			1349	C

Note that the sales and purchases all include VAT at 17.5%.

Required:

(a) Calculate the wages payable for the month to each employee. Each employee is entitled to an overtime rate of time and one half for all hours in a month over 160. The PAYE on each employee should be calculated by deducting the free pay for the month from the gross pay and applying a rate of 20%. Assume national insurance contributions are: employees 8% and employer 9%.

(b) Prepare a wage slip for Edgar.

(c) Calculate and list the sales ledger balances at 31 May and prepare a sales ledger control account for the month.

(d) For Adam the sales of £1,340.00 were four invoices and one credit note as:

Date	Document	Number	Amount
May 3	Invoice	268	198.00
May 10	Invoice	285	870.00
May 15	Credit note	13	104.00
May 23	Invoice	301	320.00
May 28	Invoice	315	56.00

Prepare a Statement of Account for May showing all transactions.

(e) Balance the purchase ledger accounts and prepare a list of balances at the end of May. Prepare a purchase ledger control account for May.

(f) The purchases from Finn in May were:

Date	Number	Amount
May 15	A647	670.00
May 23	A876	530.00

Prepare a remittance advice for the payment of Finn's account which will take place on 14 June.

(g) The imprest for petty cash is £350. Calculate the cheque to be drawn from the bank for cash to make up the imprest at the beginning of May. This cheque was drawn on 5 May. Show the petty cash book for May and bring down the balance at the end of the month. State the amount to be drawn at the beginning of June to restore the imprest.

(h) One of the petty cash payments in may was to Brenda. this was on 19 May and was for £10.20 in reimbursement for a train journey to fetch a car back from a client. Design a suitable petty cash voucher using this payment as an illustration. What documents should accompany the voucher when Brenda presents it to Pendil?

(j) Write up the cash book for May. Include cheques for net wages and for the payment of PAYE and national insurance. Both these cheques were drawn on 31 May. Assume there were no other cheques drawn or bank lodgements other than those indicated by the data above.

(k) Tick over your cash book to the bank statement. Make such amendments to the cash book as you think necessary. Calculate and bring down the balance on the cash book. Reconcile this balance with that shown by the bank statement and prepare a reconciliation statement.

(l) Prepare the VAT account.

Assignment covering up to Chapter 16

Harriet's trial balance at 31 December 19x8 showed a debit total of £305,862.23 and a credit total of £307,544.03 and a suspense account was opened for the difference. While search was made for errors the profit and loss account was extracted and showed a profit of £34,692.46.

The errors found were:

(a) The purchases account was under added by £100.

(b) A debit to interest account £1,023 was in fact interest of £347 and the balance off the loan.

(c) A payment of salaries of £690 had been posted to wages as £960.

(d) A receipt from Hughes, a customer, of £481 had not been posted to Hughes' account.

(e) The VAT on the petty cash book credit side totalling £21.76 for April had not been posted to the VAT account.

(f) Depreciation on the fixtures (value at 31.12.x8: Cost £5,456 and net book value £2345.00) had been calculated on cost at 25% instead of on the correct reducing balance method.

(g) The bank statement balance £2,365.98 had been included in the trial balance instead of the cash book balance of £2,871.02.

(h) The stock had included an item valued at cost £247.00. This item could in fact only be sold in January 19x9 at £100 less 10% sales commission.

(j) The debtors included a debt due from Hollis £800 which is definitely bad.

(k) The trial balance included on the credit side a deposit paid to Jim's garage £900. This is actually the deposit on a new car bought in December 19x8. The amount payable is £7,000 less the deposit + interest of £1,180. The agreement allows for 24 monthly instalments of £303.33.

Show that the trial balance now balances and calculate the correct profit.

Assignment covering up to Chapter 23

Problem Consultancy Ltd is a company incorporated on 1 January 19x4 to provide consultancy services to the Health Service and similar organisations. The company is non-profit-making and is supported by fees charged to its customers and by an annual grant from a charitable trust.

The trial balance at 31 December 19x4 showed

Account title	Debit balances	Credit balances
Cash at Bank	2,800	
Sales		208,439
Grant from charitable trust		100,000
Salaries	167,200	
Motor cars	80,200	
Motor expenses	12,453	
Rent	6,000	
Rates	5,200	
Insurances	4,311	
Heat and lighting	3,890	
Printing, stationery and advertising	4,508	
Share capital		100,000
Equipment	16,400	
Furniture	23,600	
Computer	6,200	
Debtors	94,550	
Creditors		2,566
Petty cash book balance	243	
VAT account		12,460
PAYE and national insurance		6,189
Sundry expenses	1,329	

(a) The cash at bank balance has been reconciled to the bank statement and the reconciliation shows that one of the debtors (The Pendil Hospital Trust) paid by BACS £6,200 on 29 December 19x4 and that £440 was paid out by direct debit to the Association of Consultants on 31 December 19x4 as the subscription for 19x5.

(b) Salaries do not include a special 19x4 bonus to certain staff which amounts to £2,400 and will be paid early in 19x5.

(c) The management has not yet determined depreciation policy. However it is felt that:

(i) The vehicles would last four years and have salvage values of 20% of original cost.

(ii) The equipment would last five years and have no salvage value.

(iii) The furniture would last 10 years and have no salvage value.

(iv) The computer would last for three years and have a salvage value of 10% of its original cost.

(d) Motor expenses include road fund licences of £1,200 which are for the 12 months ending 31 May 19x5.

(e) The rent does not include a payment of £4,000 made in January 19x5 for the half year ending 31 March 19x5.

(f) The stock of stationery was inventoried on 31 December 19x4 and found to be £1,100 at cost.

(g) The debtors were reviewed and it was felt that two debtors totalling £800 would not be collectible and that a credit note would have to be given to the Barsetshire Health Trust for £2,400 plus VAT.

(h) The petty cash was counted and the actual cash on hand amounted to £203. It appeared that nobody was to blame for the deficit and that procedures should be tightened up.

(i) During the year, an employee was dismissed and has lodged a claim for unfair dismissal. The company denies liability but feels that a provision of £1,000 would be prudent.

(j) The trial balance does not balance and an investigation revealed the following errors:

(i) An invoice to Ratlinghope Health Trust for £2,300 was correctly entered in the sales daybook but entered in the sales ledger account as £3,200.

(ii) An invoice for £856 was entered into the account of Rodington Trust instead of to Reaside Trust.

(iii) An invoice for electricity (£186 net of VAT) was entered into the printing, stationery and advertising account.

(iv) The VAT included in transactions which were entered in the purchase daybook for October 19x4 (£720) was entered on the credit side of the VAT account.

(v) A cheque paid to an employee (£230) to correct an error in salary payment was entered in the cash book correctly but the double entry was not completed.

Required:

(a) Complete the trial balance and show that it now balances.

(b) Devise and state appropriate depreciation policies and show the fixed asset and depreciation accounts for 19x4 and 19x5.

(c) Prepare an income and expenditure account for 19x4 and a balance sheet as at 31 December 19x4.

Assignment covering up to Chapter 30

Taliesin Ltd has a wholesale linen business in Arleston. The financial statements for 19x8 (all figures in £'000) showed:

Profit and Loss Account

Sales	2389
Cost of sales	1465
Gross profit	924
Wages	254
Other overheads	196
Depreciation	84
Operating profit	390
Overdraft interest	75
Net profit before tax	315
Taxation	85
Net profit after tax	230
Dividends	150
Retained	80

Balance Sheet

	Cost	Depr	NBV
Land	200	–	200
Buildings	253	120	133
Equipment, vehicles etc	481	243	238
	934	363	571
Stock			244
Debtors			398
			642
Creditors			366
Overdraft			490
Taxation			85
Dividends			70
		1011	(369)
			202
Share capital 20p shares			50
Profit and loss account			152
			202

Notes:

(a) Stocks at the beginning and the end of the year were the same.

(b) The Board is considering the preparation of forecast accounts for next year. Their thoughts turn on:

(i)   Sales up 10%.

(ii)   Stocks increased to three months purchases.

(iii)   Debtors collection period as 19x6.

(iv)   Wages down 20% but redundancy payment of £20,000.

(v)   Other overheads up 5% (but see below).

(vi)   Depreciation policy: Buildings: over 50 years Equipment etc 15% reducing balance.

(vii)   Overdraft interest about £60,000.

(vii)   Taxation 20% of net profit.

(ix)   Dividends the same as 19x6.

(x)   Gross profit ratio 40%.

(c) The Board intends to buy a vehicle. It estimates this will cost £18,000 to buy, will last four years and then be sold for £2,000; will cost £10,000 a year to run but save £16,000 of the projected overheads.

Prepare forecast a profit and loss account and balance sheet for 19x9.

Assignment covering the whole book

Harbridge PLC has the following plans at the end of 19x5:

(a) Close Branch C as it is unprofitable.

(b) Sell in the United States.

(c) Raise £10 million to finance new investment in a factory in Presteigne.

You have been retained to consider these plans and write a report on them. Facts you find are:

(a) Department C is one of 12 in the factory. It makes only widget type G2. Currently the costs of the department are:

  (i) Direct costs £186,000.

  (ii) Specific Departmental overheads £120,000.

  (iii) Share of general factory overheads £80,000.

  (iv) Share of general group costs £45,000.

(b) If manufacture of Widget G2 (average sales 100,000 at £4 each) ceased the widgets would have to be imported at a price of £3 each.

(c) Sales in the US would be at a very low price being marginal cost + 20%.

(d) The balance sheet of the company shows (in £million):

  (i) Fixed assets £11.4.

  (ii) Current assets £16.1.

  (iii) Current liabilities £14.4 (including overdrafts of £6.1).

  (iv) Debentures repayable in eight years £5.9.

  (v) Share capital £4.0 (in £1 shares).

  (vi) Reserves £3.2.

The company's shares are quoted at £3 each after a recent rise.

Appendix D: Glossary

Absorption the sharing out of the costs of a cost centre among the products which use the cost centre.

Accounting standards authoritative statements of how particular types of transaction and other events should be reflected in financial statements. Formerly these were SSAPs but are now called FRSs – Financial Reporting Standards.

Accounting Standards Board a quasi-statutory body which issues accounting standards in the UK.

Accruals (that which has accrued, accumulated, grown) expenses which have been consumed or enjoyed but which have not been paid for at the accounting date.

Activity based costing a relatively new system of product costing which collects costs according to cost drivers.

Allocation the charging of discrete, identifiable items of cost to cost centres or cost units. A cost is allocated when the cost is unique to a particular cost centre.

Amortisation an equivalent word to depreciation: commonly used for writing off, as an expense to profit and loss account, of the capital cost of acquiring leasehold property.

Attributable profit that part of the total profit currently estimated to arise over the duration of a contract which fairly reflects the profit attributable to that part of the work performed by the accounting date.

Benefits in kind goods or services provided by a company to directors and others in addition to cash remuneration. The best known are the provision of free use of a motor car. The value of benefits in kind are usually taxable.

Bond a formal written document that provides evidence of long-term indebtedness. Bond has mainly American usage; the British equivalent is debenture.

Break-even the level of activity at which neither a loss or a profit is made. Often shown in a break-even chart.

Budget a formal quantitative expression of management expectations generated for any area that management deems critical. Examples are the sales budget, purchases budget, cash budget and capital expenditure budget.

Capital expenditure expenditure that provides long-term benefits. Most capital expenditure is on fixed assets.

Carrying value the value of an asset as recorded in the books of account. It may be undepreciated cost or based on some other valuation method.

Competitive tendering a system whereby costs are minimised by requiring all inputs to be put out to a tender to a variety of suppliers and the cheapest selected.

Consideration, in accounting usage, the amount to be paid for the acquisition of a business. The consideration may be in cash or other assets or securities.

Continuous inventory the process of recording the amount of stock of each category on a continuous basis so that the amount of stock held of any category can be instantly discovered without recourse to a physical inspection in the warehouse.

Contra (against) a bookkeeping entry by which a liability to a supplier is reduced by (is set against) a sum due by the supplier who is also a customer.

Contribution the difference between the sales price of a product and its associated variable costs.

Cost centre a location, function or item of equipment in respect of which costs may be ascertained and related to cost units.

Cost convention the accounting convention whereby goods, resources and services are recorded at cost. Cost is defined as the exchange or transaction price

Cost driver an activity which generates cost.

Credit control a generic term for all those measures and procedures instituted by a firm that trades on credit to ensure that customers pay their accounts. Procedures include evaluation of a customer's credit worthiness and comprehensive collection procedures.

Debenture a document which creates or acknowledges a debt. Commonly used for the debt itself. Debenture deeds issued by companies usually contain details of the loan and have clauses concerning payment of interest, repayment of capital, security etc.

Direct costs those costs comprising direct materials, direct labour and direct expenses which can be directly identified with specific jobs, products or services.

Disclosure the procedure whereby some fact, figure or explanation is given in financial statements or in a note attached to them. The alternative is to lose the fact or figure in a composite item.

Discounted cash flow (DCF) a method of capital investment appraisal where future cash flows (in and out) are discounted back to the present time. The sum of these is called the net present value.

Dividend a distribution of its earnings to its shareholders by a company. A distribution of part of the sum due to creditors in bankruptcy or liquidation.

Drawings cash or goods withdrawn from a business by a proprietor for his own use.

Earnings another word for profit, used particularly for company profits.

Equity the ordinary shares or risk capital of an enterprise. Also a system of law and a trade union for actors.

Exceptional items material items which derive from events or transactions that fall within the ordinary activities of the reporting entity and which need to be disclosed by virtue of their size or incidence if the financial statements are to give a true and fair view.

Exposure draft a document issued on a specific accounting topic by the Accounting Standards Board for discussion. After representations, discussions and amendments it may become an accounting standard.

Extraordinary items material items possessing a high degree of abnormality which arise from events and transactions that fall outside the ordinary activities of the reporting entity and which are expected not to recur. They are exceedingly rare.

Floating charge an arrangement whereby a lender to a company has a floating charge over the assets generally of the company. Gives the lender priority of repayment from the proceeds of sale of the assets in the event of insolvency. Banks frequently take a floating charge when lending.

Futures contracts for the sale and purchase of commodities at an agreed price and for delivery and settlement at an agreed future date. Trading in futures, often by professional speculators, tends to stabilise prices.

Group a set of interrelated companies usually consisting of a holding company and its subsidiary and sub-subsidiary companies.

Insolvency the state of being unable to pay debts as they fall due. Also used to describe the activities of practitioners in the fields of bankruptcy, receivership and liquidation.

Intangible assets assets which have long-term value but which have no physical existence. Examples are goodwill, copyright, patents and trademarks.

Inventory a detailed list of articles of any kind. Used by accountants as another word for stock.

Leasehold land rented from the owner of the freehold. Leases can be for any period. Leases with less than 50 years to run are called short leases and other leases are called long leases. It is possible to buy a leasehold interest in the property and when this has occurred the cost appears on the balance sheet. It is then amortized (depreciated) over the period of the lease.

Liquidation the procedure whereby a company is wound up, its assets realised and the proceeds distributed to the persons entitled.

Listed companies companies whose shares are quoted on a recognised stock exchange.

Marginal cost the additional cost incurred by the production of one extra unit.

Market value the amount that an asset would realise if sold on a completely open market. Market values are influenced by whether the asset would be sold by forced sale or in the normal course of business and by whether the value takes into account existing use or possible alternative uses.

Negotiable instruments a document of title that can be freely negotiated (transferred) by delivery or delivery with endorsement. Examples are bills of exchange and promissory notes.

Opportunity cost the cost of a foregone alternative.

Outsourcing the procedure where functions (e.g. accounting, computing etc) are performed by outside companies for a fee instead of in-house.

Par value an amount specified in the memorandum of association for each share and imprinted on the face of each share certificate. It is the figure which appears on the balance sheet for share capital. As a value it has no significance.

Premium an amount paid in excess of par or nominal value. Premiums can arise on issues and redemptions of shares and debentures.

Prime cost the total of direct costs.

Pro rata in proportion to.

Quoted company a company whose shares are listed on the Stock Exchange, the Unlisted Securities Market or the new Alternative Investment Market.

Receivership the appointment of receiver to take over an asset which is the subject of a charge given to a lender. A receiver can be appointed by a court, or by the lender when the terms of the loan deed allow.

Reporting the process whereby a company or other institution informs interested parties (e.g. shareholders) of the results and position of the company by means of financial statements.

Returns profits or gains flowing from the ownership of assets (e.g. return on capital employed); damaged, undelivered or unwanted goods sent back to vendor; a document or report required to be submitted to some authority (e.g. the annual return of a company).

Secured liabilities obligations where the probability of payment is enhanced by the creditor taking a charge over an asset (a fixed charge) or assets generally (a floating charge).

Securities financial assets such as shares, debentures and loan stocks.

SORP statements of recommended practice, a statement of accounting practice in a particular industry produced by some Industry body which is itself approved by the Accounting Standards Board.

SSAP statement of standard accounting practice. These are mandatory in preparing financial statements.

Standard cost periodically predetermined costs calculated from management's estimates of expected levels of costs and of operations and operational efficiency and the related expenditure. Standard costs can be compared with actual costs and the variances analysed.

Total absorption cost a system of costing where all costs (or just production costs) are ascribed to products. Thus the total absorption cost of a product includes its direct cost and a fair share of both fixed and variable overhead costs.

Turnover another term for the total sales in a period.

Unsecured creditors those creditors who do not have the benefit of a charge over any asset.

Write-off to write something off is to debit it to profit and loss account. If something has continuing value (e.g. a fixed asset) then the whole cost is not written off but only a part of the cost (by the depreciation process).

Written down value the cost of an asset less accumulated depreciation. Also known as net book value and carrying value.

Index